'A terrific read'

Constance Craig Smith, *Daily Mail*

'A vivid and detailed account of her rise to sporting greatness and her struggles to attain equal treatment for women in a shockingly discriminatory sport . . . *All In* describes a life comprising one epic struggle after another, both on and off court'

Fiona Sturges, *Guardian*

'Compelling . . . *All In* is a brave and moving book, a must-read for tennis fans and a vivid slice of social history . . . its achievement is to sound like Billie Jean herself'

Melanie Reid, *The Times*

'[King] writes candidly about a career that led the way for women's sports as we know them . . . thoughtful, soul-searching'

Tim Adams, *Observer*

'Extraordinary . . . a compelling portrait of modern America'

Rebecca Myers, *Sunday Times*

'A cracking read'

Norma Clarke, *Literary Review*

'This is the story of a remarkable sporting career, but also of the cultural mores that King has done so much to shift'

The Times, Sports Books of the Year

'King's determination to ensure fair recognition, and later fair reward, for her talent and effort would place her at the heart of campaigns for equality both on and off court . . . a blistering autobiography'

Nicholas Wroe, *Guardian*, Sports Books of the Year

'*All In* is the story of a true champion, one with an indomitable spirit'

Martin Chilton, *Independent*, Best Books of the Year

'This is a fascinating, energizing, inspirational book from a woman who continues to set the standard for making a positive difference in the world'

Clare Balding

'She's a wonderful voice of reason and experience. Hers is a wonderful story'

Judy Murray

'She changed how women athletes and women everywhere view themselves and she has given everyone, regardless of gender or sexual orientation, a chance to compete both on the court and in life'

Barack Obama

'Powerfully honest and unapologetic . . . a story about the personal strength, immense growth and undeniable greatness of one woman who fearlessly stood up to a culture trying to break her down'

Serena Williams

'Truly inspirational'

Women's Tennis Association

'Billie Jean King's strength, energy and personality shine on every page of this gripping autobiography that will inspire tennis and non-tennis fans alike'

Business Insider

'True to its title, *All In* is bracingly candid . . . Ms King does nothing by half-measures – so much the better for readers, sport and the many women she encouraged and empowered'

Economist

'Thrilling . . . King is full of incredible stories . . . *All In* is both a moving memoir and a piece of social history – a record of a life, a sport and a world transformed'

Katherine Cowles, *New Statesman*

'King not only helped change the paradigm for women's tennis players but also the marketplace for female athletes, and she played a significant role in the women's movement'

New Yorker

'It's easy work to be a former champion, easier still to be a legend – after all, the job requirements are nothing beyond showing up. But it's not easy to be an activist, and it's certainly not easy to commit your life to pushing the world closer to how you want it to be. *All In* reads as a manifesto, like *Letters to a Young Poet* with a heavy dash of bell hooks . . . Her book is a powerful rallying cry, in a life full of them, for how she hopes we play the game after she's gone'

Caitlin Thompson, *The New York Times*

'In the pantheon of tennis greats, Billie Jean King stands alone'

O, the Oprah Magazine

'*All In* tells King's story in full, while serving up insights on leadership, business, activism, sports, politics, marriage equality, parenting, sexuality and love'

Stylist

'King describes the challenges she faced and the issues she continues to fight for in urgent and vivid terms, coalescing into a powerful self-portrait of an inspiring athlete and activist'

Time

'Tennis legend Billie Jean King transformed the game . . . A recipient of the Presidential Medal of Freedom in 2009, Ms King says she's "still going full blast" to promote equality and inclusion in sports and beyond'

Emily Bobrow, *Wall Street Journal*

'King is not a former tennis champion on a late-life victory tour. She is a woman who approaches each day with an open heart and clear intention'

Washington Post

All In

AN AUTOBIOGRAPHY

Billie Jean King

with Johnette Howard and Maryanne Vollers

PENGUIN BOOKS

UK | USA | Canada | Ireland | Australia
India | New Zealand | South Africa

Penguin Books is part of the Penguin Random House group of companies
whose addresses can be found at global.penguinrandomhouse.com.

First published in the United States of America by Alfred A. Knopf 2021
First published in Great Britain by Viking 2021
Published in Penguin Books 2022

001

Printed and bound in Great Britain by Clays Ltd, Elcograf S.p.A.

The authorized representative in the EEA is Penguin Random House Ireland,
Morrison Chambers, 32 Nassau Street, Dublin D02 YH68

A CIP catalogue record for this book is available from the British Library

ISBN: 978–0–241–98846–6

www.greenpenguin.co.uk

Penguin Random House is committed to a
sustainable future for our business, our readers
and our planet. This book is made from Forest
Stewardship Council® certified paper.

To Ilana, my love, my partner,
to the moon and back

To my parents,
for their love, laughter, and the values that they instilled
in me that continue to shape my life every day

To my brother, R.J.,
whom I love, for a lifetime of support
and unconditionally loving me back

To everyone who continues to fight for
equity, inclusion, and freedom

Fight for the things that you care about, but do it in a way that will lead others to join you.

—RUTH BADER GINSBURG

All In

Preface

WHEN I WAS a girl I'd sit in my elementary school classroom in Long Beach, California, staring at the big pull-down map of the world, and daydream about the places I'd go. *England, Europe, Asia, South America, Africa!* Even then, I felt that borders had no hold on me. They connected me. I can't remember a time when I didn't have a restlessness, an ambition, and an urgency. As much as I loved my family and hometown, I always knew that my life would somehow take me beyond their embrace.

I was born in the wartime 1940s, reared in the buttoned-down 1950s, and came of age during the Cold War and rebellions of the 1960s. My father was a firefighter, and my mother was a homemaker who sometimes sold Tupperware and Avon products to help us get by. They were both determined to give my younger brother, Randy, and me a loving existence that was more stable than their broken families had been. But unrest was all around us. My early life played out against the backdrop of the civil rights movement, the women's movement, the Cold War, assassinations, and antiwar protests of the 1960s; the LGBTQ+ rights movement would come later.

When I began playing youth tennis in the 1950s, college sports scholarships didn't exist for girls. The only women's pro sport was the Ladies Professional Golf Association, which was founded in 1950 by thirteen players but was still working to build purses and gain traction. The modern women's sports movement as we know it essentially started the day nine of us players and a sharp businesswoman named Gladys Heldman, the publisher of *World Tennis* magazine, broke away in 1970 to create the first women's pro tennis circuit, ignoring the sneers from a male-run tennis establishment that told us no one would pay to see us play, and then repeatedly threatened us with suspensions when it looked as if folks might.

I didn't start out with grievances against the world, but the world certainly seemed to have grievances against girls and women like me: There was the principal who wouldn't sign a permission slip to excuse me for a week-long tennis tournament until my mom went to the school office and said, "My daughter is a straight-A student. What could possibly be the problem?"; the elementary school teacher who sent a note to my parents explaining that she was marking me down a grade because "Billie Jean occasionally takes advantage of her superior ability" during recess playground games; the local tennis official at my first tennis tournament, Perry T. Jones, who turned heads by yanking me out of a group photograph when I was eleven years old because I was wearing white shorts, not a white skirt or white tennis dress.

Pursuing your goals as a girl or woman then often meant being pricked and dogged by slights like that. It made no sense to me. Why would anyone set arbitrary limits on another human being? Why were we being treated as "unreasonable" for asking reasonable questions? Why were we constantly told, *Can't do this. Don't do that. Temper your ambition, lower your voice, stay in your place, act less competent than you are. Do as you're told*? Why weren't a female's striving and individual differences seen as life enriching, a source of pride, rather than a problem?

If I felt that way, I wondered how the people of color around me felt. When I was young I'd seen photos of how the Little Rock Nine students had to walk past an angry white mob to desegregate their Arkansas school in 1957, and how six-year-old Ruby Nell Bridges still had to be escorted daily by four federal marshals to attend classes at her previously all-white New Orleans school three years later. I knew the stories of how Althea Gibson and Jackie Robinson broke the color barriers in their respective sports, tennis and baseball.

The all-white country clubs that hosted tennis tournaments I began playing in were noticeably different from Long Beach's Polytechnic High, the racially mixed school I attended. Poly was integrated in 1934, nine years before I was born. But my high school didn't offer varsity sports for girls; free tennis instruction in the public parks was my only option.

As time passed, the incidents kept piling up. There was the sight of the top-ranked teenage boys getting free meals at the lunch counter at the Los Angeles Tennis Club while my mother and I sat outside on benches behind the courts, eating the brown-bag lunches we brought. We weren't comped, even though I was a top junior player, too. There was the future adviser who introduced himself to me after I won a match at age fifteen and said, "You're going to be No. 1 someday, Billie Jean"—a thrilling first—only to have him tell me later, as casually as if he were appraising my backhand, "You'll be good because you're ugly."

After I married Larry King and rose to No. 1 in the world, I still faced constant questions about whether playing tennis was "worth it," and when I was going to retire and have children.

"Do you ask Rod Laver the same questions?" I'd respond, referring to one of the great male players of my era.

Even if you're not a born activist, life can damn sure make you one.

The older I got, the more I aspired to. There wasn't just unrest in the world around us. There was a storm gathering inside me.

TO THIS DAY my 1973 "Battle of the Sexes" match against Bobby Riggs remains cast in the public imagination as the defining moment for me where everything coalesced and some fuse was lit. But in truth, that drive had been smoldering in me since I was a child. What the Riggs match and its fevered buildup proved was that millions of others felt locked in the same tug-of-war over gender roles and equal opportunities. I wanted to show that women deserve equality, and we can perform under pressure and entertain just as well as men. I think the outcome, and the discussions the match provoked, advanced our fight. A crowd of 30,472, then a record for tennis, came to the Houston Astrodome for the match that September night. An estimated 90 million more watched the event worldwide on TV, a record for a sporting event.

Along the way, it has always amazed me when people saw me as a separatist. I'm an egalitarian, and I always have been. I've always pushed for everything to be equal, everyone pulling together, though I know how hard that is to achieve.

What's become clear to me is that people and leaders of every generation have to argue and re-argue the details and meanings of eras for themselves. Coretta Scott King put it perfectly when she wrote, "Struggle is a never-ending process. Freedom is never really won. You earn it and win it in every generation."

Today the work of the Southern Christian Leadership Conference and the NAACP is carried on by groups such as Black Lives Matter. The feminist arguments advanced by NOW helped inform the #MeToo movement and TIME'S UP. The 1969 Stonewall uprising led to ACT UP, which eventually led to LGBTQ+ rights and then marriage equality, gains that once seemed unfathomable. It wasn't so long ago that women were fighting to get a few precious slots at medical schools and law schools. Now women run for president and sit on the Supreme Court and are celebrated with handles like "Notorious RBG." (May she rest in power.)

Two of the unchanging, overarching lessons of my life are that people's existence is rarely improved by sitting still in the face of injustice, and that the human spirit should never be underestimated. The human spirit can't be caged.

What starts as a spark of ambition can not only lift you personally, it can change the world. The personal is political. A murmur rising from one soul can become a roar expressed by many. An act of defiance—insisting on basic human dignity, equal pay for equal work, a front seat on the bus—can ignite a movement that alters history. It may even sweep you into the company of presidents and queens, heroes and groundbreakers and contrarians who refuse to accept the status quo, especially when it renders them inferior or seems designed to erase them completely.

My life is proof of all that.

When I was outed as gay in 1981, corporate sponsors deserted me overnight. Today I laugh and think, "Wait—I get *paid* now to be a lesbian?"

But I'm getting ahead of myself . . .

Early on, what was most apparent to me was that the world I wanted didn't exist yet. It would be up to my generation to create it. We were born on the cusp of the Baby Boom and walked a tightrope between shedding the old and shaping the new. For me, the timing turned out to be a profound blessing—and a burden that nearly broke me by age fifty, to a degree that few people know. Sometimes my biggest opponent was me.

Along the way, people often thought I was angry. They were wrong. More than anything, I was determined.

I won my share of fights.

But let me tell you how I truly became free.

Chapter 1

I CAN STILL REMEMBER exactly what it looked, felt, and sounded like on that September afternoon in 1954 when my life changed forever. The sky overhead was bright as a bluebird's wing. The Southern California sun felt warm on my skin, and I could smell the spicy bark of the eucalyptus trees that surrounded the public tennis courts at Houghton Park in Long Beach. A handful of boys and girls were lining up for their drills as I arrived with my friend Susan Williams for my very first session with a coach named Clyde Walker. It wasn't long before the *thwock-thwock-thwock* of the balls being struck on our court blended into the noise rising from the adjoining court, too.

Susan had introduced me to the sport a few weeks earlier by asking me a simple question as we sat in our fifth-grade classroom: "Do you want to play tennis?"

"What's tennis?" I replied.

I listened intently as Susan explained that in tennis you could run, jump, and hit a ball—three things I loved about basketball and softball, two of the team sports I played. Susan invited me to play at the Virginia Country Club, to which her family belonged. I was predictably awful, but Susan thought it was funny when I blasted a ball over the fence and shouted, "Home run!"—a first, I'm guessing, at the venerable VCC.

On the way home my mind was racing. That night I asked my father, "Daddy, which sport would be best for a girl? You know, in the long term."

My father put down his newspaper and thought for a while. "Well, there's swimming, golf, and"—I waited for it—"tennis."

Tennis! I had tried swimming, but I was the worst in my class at the YWCA. The great female star Babe Didrikson Zaharias played golf, but to me golf looked too slow. Tennis seemed just right. I liked the variety and mental challenge. I liked being able to hit the ball over and over. Tennis fascinated me from that first day I played with Susan, using a borrowed racket.

When I pestered my parents for my own racket, I wasn't discouraged a bit when they reminded me that money was tight, and that I'd have to buy it myself. I did odd jobs for neighbors, who smiled and indulged me when I told them my goal. I weeded flower beds, swept sidewalks. My mom advanced me $2, and I rode my bike to a local pharmacy, where I bought candy and then resold it to the other kids at a small markup.

I put every nickel and dime I earned into a Mason jar above the kitchen sink. After a few months I couldn't wait anymore and my parents took me to a sporting-goods shop. When my parents approached the salesman and said they'd like to see tennis rackets for their daughter, I mustered the courage to ask him what $8.29 could buy. He showed us a sweet little wood racket with a purple-and-white throat and a purple grip. I thought it was beautiful. I bought it and slept with it that night . . . and the next night . . . and many, many nights after that.

While I'll remain forever grateful to Susan for introducing me to tennis, it was Clyde Walker whose free instruction made the sport come alive for me. Once Clyde showed us how to hit a proper groundstroke, I loved the pure feeling of the racket strings connecting cleanly with the ball, absorbing its energy and hurling it back. I couldn't get enough of the thrill of making contact—how the transference of energy shoots through your fingers, your arm, your shoulder, and how your whole body is involved as you swing. I loved the drama of it all, too—chasing down each ball, the universe of possibilities that opened up as I drew my racket back, then that split-second pause where everything hangs in the balance as you're preparing to hit a return. There was something swashbuckling and instantly addictive about all of it. I loved the challenge and suspense of trying to hit a perfectly executed shot and the charge I got when the ball landed out of my opponent's reach. Then I couldn't wait to get the next ball and do it again.

By the end of that first afternoon with Clyde I knew I had discovered my sport. It was as if a window into my future had been flung open. I was only ten, but in the breathy way that ten-year-olds think, I was already certain it was my destiny, and I just had to tell somebody.

"Mom! Mom! I found out what I'm going to do with my life!" I said when she arrived to pick me up in our green DeSoto. "I want to be the No. 1 tennis player in the world!"

She smiled. This was not unlike the time a few years earlier when I stood in the kitchen as we were drying the dishes and told her, "Mom, I'm going to do something great with my life—I just know it! You watch."

This time—as then—my mother looked at me and said the absolutely best, most revolutionary thing she could have said to a girl like me in 1954: "Okay, dear."

I WAS GRATEFUL that my parents resisted setting limits on me, which is different from saying that my upbringing was always progressive. My mom and dad were strict and conservative in many ways, but they also told my brother and me we could be anything we wanted to be. When Randy, who is five years younger than me, announced at the dinner table one night that he also intended to be a pro athlete—a Major League Baseball player—both my parents covered their faces with their hands, then peered out through their fingers with a look that said, *Not you, too?* Mom was already driving me to tennis matches all over Long Beach and beyond. My dad later said we wore out three cars between Randy and me.

Randy ended up playing Major League Baseball for twelve years as a relief pitcher with the San Francisco Giants, Houston Astros, and Toronto Blue Jays. I went on to win thirty-nine singles, doubles titles, and mixed doubles titles at the four major or "Grand Slam" tournaments—the U.S. Open, Wimbledon, Roland-Garros (also known as the French Open), and the Australian Open—and accomplish a few other special things. I don't think there is just one factor that explains our athletic success. I think a combination of lucky genes, incredibly devoted parents, opportunity, and chance all played a role. We were fortunate to grow up in Southern California with its perfect weather for developing athletes year-round. Sports was the air we breathed.

The term "snowplow parent" hadn't been invented when we were kids, but it wouldn't have applied to my folks anyway. They supported us but never pushed us to be sports stars. They concentrated more on being life coaches. Even my ultra-competitive father, who was a terrific athlete, never cared if we won or lost our games. "Did you try your best and have fun?" he'd ask, same as my mother did.

My parents always treated Randy and me equally, which was unusual for many families then. But when I didn't share the same love of shopping or painting my fingernails that my mother did, I would notice the look on her face. She earned a cosmetology license the year she was engaged to Dad, and she was always so stylish in her pinched-waistline dresses and impeccable hair and makeup. I eventually learned that she had been a fast runner and terrific swimmer as a girl and used to body-surf in fifteen-foot-high ocean waves before she married my dad. On our swimming outings, Randy and I would thrash around, but she'd just float serenely, bobbing in the rolling waves like a cork. I'm sure I inherited some of her athletic talent, but she always played her abilities down. She had strong ideas about what was "ladylike." She was happier (and far less conflicted) when I told her I was eager to sign up for cotillion like the other girls.

Later, once I started to question my sexual orientation, it was hard for me to forget those kinds of messages, or the day my hot-tempered father was driving Randy, my mother, and me to a tournament when I was about thirteen. We passed two men walking together down the street, and it triggered Dad's memory. He told us a story about a man in the service who propositioned him. "I'd have clocked him if he hadn't backed off," my father said. I believed him.

The competing cues and emotions were hard for me to reconcile at times, but I also knew that people on both sides of my family had repeatedly demonstrated an independent streak. In the end, that was the temperament I gravitated toward, too. Both the Moffitts and the members of my mother's clan, the Jermans, came from mining and oil-geyser towns on the western frontier. They kept their heads down and worked, worked, worked. But they also bucked convention and seemed incapable of remaining quiet or complacent once they were fed up with something. They were passionate, gritty, action-oriented people.

I was named after my father, Willis Jefferson "Bill" Moffitt, a hardy Montana boy who grew up in Livingston, a railroad town on the banks of the Yellowstone River. When my dad was thirteen, his mother, Blanche, packed him and his two siblings into the family's Model A Ford and drove off from their home, leaving his father, William Durkee Moffitt Jr., behind with a hangover and a knot on his head. Blanche had cracked a window screen over W.D.'s skull for coming home violent and drunk one too many times. She pointed the car west and didn't stop until she reached the Pacific Ocean at Long Beach, where she knew nobody. I guess she thought that if she was going to start over it might as well be in the sunshine rather than in the shoulder-high drifts of Montana snow. She and W.D. never lived together again, but they never divorced, either. He sent Blanche a bit of money each month to help support them. Blanche enrolled their three children in Long Beach's first-rate public schools, where they thrived.

Dad went on to become a basketball standout at both Long Beach Polytechnic High and Long Beach City College, where he occasionally competed against Jackie Robinson, then a four-sport star at Pasadena Junior College. (My father had a cherished photo of them playing on the same court.) Dad was strong-jawed and handsome, and he loved dancing to big-band music in the seaside ballrooms. So did my mother, Mildred Rose Jerman, who everyone called Betty. She was seventeen years old and still in high school when they started dating. Later, she wore my father's miniature basketball trophy on a chain around her neck, even after it chipped her front tooth one day as she leaned down to take a sip from a water fountain.

After their third date she told her mother, Dot, she was going to marry him.

"Well, has he asked you?" Dot said.

"No, but he will," my mom replied.

Dot never seemed overly warm to me, but she was considerate and gentle. Blanche was different. My father's mother was a hard-edged woman who chainsmoked Chesterfields, drank black coffee all day, and was full of colorful sayings such as "If they don't watch it, I'll lay 'em out in lavender!" She was tough, but then she'd had some staggering disappointments in her life even before she abruptly packed up her children and left W.D.

She was born Hazel Campbell in 1897 in Lowell, Massachusetts, to a Scottish teenager who was living in a home for unwed mothers, and she was given up for adoption before she was three. Her new parents, Jefferson and Georgia Leighton, changed her name to Blanche and moved with her to Butte, a mining boomtown in central Montana. Her mother opened a candy shop there, and her father worked as a carpenter. Blanche became such a gifted pianist she was sent back east to train at the Boston Conservatory for two years. But she had to come home when Georgia died and her father stopped paying her tuition. Blanche took a job working at the railroad depot in town, and that's how she met W.D., who was a brakeman on the Northern Pacific line. They moved to Livingston after they married and rented a house just beyond the tracks, where they could hear the whistle and rumble of the steam locomotives passing by, or step outside and look down the street and see the Absaroka mountain range rising in the distance.

My father was born in Livingston in 1918, two years before his brother, Arthur, and two years after his sister, Gladys. Blanche used to say W.D. was a nice enough man when he was sober, but he was a nasty drunk. Sometimes he'd beat her in front of their kids, and one day my dad, then only twelve, finally had enough. As W.D. wound up to take yet another swing at Blanche, my father stepped between them and told W.D., "If you hit her again, I'll kill you." W.D. backed off.

Montana was a progressive state then, and I always wondered

how it impacted my father's egalitarian views about women. The state legislature approved a woman's unlimited right to vote in 1914, six years before the rest of the country. Two years after that, Montana's Jeannette Rankin was the first woman elected to the U.S. Congress. The state still had a Wild West feel, and women were already working on ranches and in other fields usually reserved for men when America entered World War I in 1917. After that, they filled even more jobs that Montana's departed men used to do.

My father grew to be just under six feet tall and powerful as an ox. After finishing his associate degree at Long Beach City College he was offered a basketball scholarship to Whittier College. He lost his scholarship when he had to skip his first semester because of acute appendicitis. It was 1940, and the country was still digging out of the Great Depression. He went to work full-time running the produce section in a grocery store and never returned to college. By then, his brother was working in a coat hanger factory to help Blanche keep their family afloat, and Gladys was trying to work her way through nursing school. It was a wonder Dad had the money to take my mom dancing when they were courting.

Mom and Dad always said they had only $3 between them when they were married on May 17, 1941. My father landed a job with the Long Beach police force, but he said the work tested his faith in humanity. He often felt bad for the troubled souls he encountered, not knowing what hardships they faced. When America entered World War II after the attack on Pearl Harbor, my father and his brother enlisted in the Navy. I have a photo I love that shows them with big smiles on their faces, looking so handsome in their sailor whites. Mom, who was only twenty, found out she was pregnant with me ten days before my dad shipped out. They hadn't planned on a baby so soon, and she was anxious and scared.

Dad was stationed in Norfolk, Virginia, when I was born on November 22, 1943. He sent a handwritten card that read "For my little daughter who I haven't seen, but will be holding in my arms soon, I send all a father's love, for always and always."

For a strong-willed and opinionated man, Dad could be a real softie. Throughout his life he never stopped getting teary-eyed at the playing of our national anthem. Rather than rejoin the police when his Navy years were done, he took a job with the Long Beach fire department and stayed there for thirty-five years. At one point, Mom wanted him to study for the officer's test, which would mean a bigger paycheck, but Dad liked the action. He was an engineer, driving the trucks and maintaining the pumps. Sometimes he'd take me to the fire station when I was young and hold me in one arm as we slid down the brass pole. He'd let me play with Old Sam, the house cat who would slide down the pole too when he heard the alarm sound. There was an Associated Press photo to prove it.

Dad insisted that we all kiss each other good night and say "I love you" before we went to bed, for the same reason my mother named me after him when he was away during the war: My father's work was dangerous, and there was no certainty he would return home. One of my dad's scarier nights on the job involved the injury of a coworker and the death of two others during the massive Signal Hill oil refinery fire that rocked Long Beach in 1958. The blaze left ash and droplets of oil falling from the sky and took three days to put out. You could see flames shooting out of the hilltop plant from our home.

Later in life my dad liked to talk about the good things he remembered about his firefighter days and Montana childhood. He returned to his home state again and again to fish the rivers and breathe the crisp mountain air. But the memories of his unstable upbringing never left him. Mom was the same regarding hers. He and she were a perfect match in that way, too.

MY MOTHER'S FATHER, Roscoe "Rocky" Jerman, was born in northern Pennsylvania, but his family moved to the dusty oil-drilling town of Taft, California, in the late 1800s. There is a sepia-toned photograph of Rocky at age nineteen, the tallest among a group of oil workers standing on the massive rotary platform of a drilling rig. For a while he tried bare-knuckle prizefighting, but his main line of work was oil leasing, well drilling, and wildcat speculating. His life was a series of booms and busts.

I'm not sure my mother knew the details of how Rocky met my grandmother, Dot, or even who Dot's parents were. My grandmother's death certificate listed her parents' names as "unknown." I have no idea how she got to California or who fathered Dot's first child, whom she named Doris after herself. Dot and Rocky were married and living in Taft when my mom was born on May 26, 1922. Three years later, Rocky and Dot moved to Long Beach and eventually split up, leaving Dot to fend for herself with her two children. Rocky remarried quickly and didn't want anything to do with them.

Dot eventually had at least six husbands, by my mom's count. (When my mother mentioned that to me once, I saw tears in her eyes and tried to console her by saying, "Don't worry, Mommy—it's not a record.") Mom told me about a night Dot had to sneak out the back window with her to escape an abusive man she married after Rocky. But beyond that, my mother rarely talked about those chaotic years. Dot got a job at a commercial laundry operating a big steam press, and finally married a kindhearted man, a Navy veteran named James Kehoe, who treated my mom and her sister like his own children. He was the grandfather Randy and I knew and loved.

Looking back now, I can see that both my parents carried a generational sense of loss and yearning. They were generous with affection and constantly urged Randy and me to be observant and respectful of other people. But talking about intimate or painful feelings was never their style. They were married for sixty-five years and determined to leave the dysfunction and instability of their childhoods behind. They told us so. The best way they knew how to accomplish that was by imposing a rigor and a discipline on themselves that was passed on to us. If you wanted something, you worked and waited for it—case closed. Integrity was paramount. They refused to complain or dwell on the past; the past was something you couldn't fix. All that mattered was here and now. Quitting or making excuses was also not allowed. If the subject of a divorce involving someone we knew came up, they'd hastily assure Randy and me that it would never happen to them because, well . . . it just wouldn't. "We're going to be together forever," my mother would say. "Family is the most important thing."

My parents were both loving, devoted, complicated people. Especially my dad. Most of the time he was funny and charming, the kindest, most patient guy in the world. He was known as one of the coolest heads in the fire department under duress. When there was a family crisis, Dad was always the first one called. As a rule, the bigger the problem, the better he was. But he was unpredictable. You never knew when something would set him off or provoke a rage. It could be hitting his thumb with a hammer, or me making a noise in the hall when he was asleep after pulling another twenty-four-hour shift. Dad would get a look in his eyes that you didn't want to see, because you knew he was ready to blow.

My father was never violent with us, but he could be scary. Once when I was a little girl he lifted me in the air and began screaming in my face, chiding me for something I had done. He didn't seem aware of how long he was squeezing my arms until my mom began yelling, "Bill! Bill!" and I was saying, "Daddy, Daddy, put me down!" We ended up laughing after he blinked, caught himself, and lowered me to the floor. I was like Dad in that respect: fast to blow up, quick to move on. My mother, on the other hand, would fall quiet and grow distant when she was uncomfortable or disapproved of something, shutting down discussions altogether. To me, the silence felt somehow worse.

I can see now that I learned to compartmentalize my own feelings from an early age. I was a highly inquisitive, energetic kid who would probably be labeled hyperactive or hypervigilant today. I asked a million questions. I was always analyzing things. I became acutely sensitive and extremely attuned to reading the feelings of everyone around me, hoping to prevent trouble or just make sure everyone was okay. When my dad was asleep I felt safe because he was home. But when he was up and agitated I was on high alert, eager to calm things down. I became good at knowing how to get my dad in a good mood, when to nudge back, what buttons to press.

Those impulses spilled into things outside my family, too. If I was picking sides for one of our neighborhood games I'd make sure some of the worst players were not chosen last, just to make them feel included. I figured everyone wants to belong. If Randy or I saw someone getting picked on at school or on our block, we became the anti-bullying squad. Other kids noticed. I was surprised, for example, when they elected me president of the school glee club though I was the worst singer in the group. I think it was because I was already learning to lead.

Long after my parents retired and moved to Arizona, my mother finally told me a little more of her personal history, but never all of it. She just smiled a little cryptically and said something that, for better and worse, became a deeply embedded coping mechanism of my own: "Every family has its secrets, Billie Jean."

Chapter 2

MOM MOVED BACK in with Grandma and Grandpa Kehoe to await my birth after Dad left for the Navy. Later, when the Douglas Aircraft Company sent Boy Scouts door to door to recruit housewives for four-hour factory shifts as part of the war effort, my mother signed on. She became one of the legendary "Rosie the Riveters" at the plant, which churned out C-47 transports and B-17 bombers. Today there's a park in Long Beach to honor the women. By the time I was learning to talk those war-era women workers were getting laid off across the country to make way for the returning soldiers and sailors. It was as if everyone was expected to snap back to the old standards. The pressure to conform was strong.

African Americans who had fought against facism overseas were often subjected to the same Jim Crow segregation practices in the military that they experienced in civilian life in the States. Women were supposed to return to their housework and raise kids. Aspiring to anything beyond the sanctioned female careers—nurse, secretary, teacher—was treated like a quixotic quest or, worse, an act of self-indulgence that might prevent male breadwinners from supporting their families. (Before 1974, an adult woman couldn't get a credit card in her own name unless her father, husband, or employer signed for it. In some states, women still couldn't serve on juries.)

During the war, many folks tasted an independence they hadn't known before. Something had to give, and eventually a lot did. Just not right away.

My mother, strong and resourceful as she was, seemed completely sold on the prevailing idea that a woman's path to fulfillment was marriage and children. I loved to spend time with her, and I could always count on her to stick up for me when it was important. But she had a traditional view of my place in the world, too. One day when I was playing a spirited touch-football game in the front yard with the neighborhood boys, she ordered me into the living room. I had no idea what I had done.

"Billie Jean, you have to be a lady at all times," she said.

"But Mom, what does that mean—'be a lady'?"

"You *know*," she said, looking a little exasperated. And that was it. No more football for me.

My parents took advantage of the GI Bill to buy a tidy little one-story tract home on West 36th Street in the Wrigley Heights section of Long Beach. Every other house in the neighborhood was more or less the same, built from the same two or three basic sets of blueprints. My father proudly put his stamp on our place over the years, paneling some rooms, adding a garage, building a den with a fireplace. He planted rosebushes everywhere because my mother loved them so. Our swatch of lawn was immaculate.

By the age of four I was pestering my parents for a sibling. When I found out that my mother was pregnant, I seriously thought they were having a baby just for me. The day Randy was brought home from the hospital I kissed his pudgy cheeks and drank in his milky sweet, baby-powder smell. I couldn't get enough of him. I thought, *Finally, I have someone to share everything with!* Now our household looked like something out of *The Donna Reed Show,* the classic 1950s TV program, complete with a working dad, a stay-at-home mom, two kids, and an adorable black-and-white spaniel named Bootsie, who my mother and grandfather had let me pick out at the dog shelter.

Randy and I were as close as could be as kids. It was Randy who gave me my family nickname, "Sis." We walked to school together, played catch. When I began winning tennis tournaments he'd eagerly wait for me to get home and arrange my newest trophies on the shelf, then do a recount for me. The first time I took a tennis trip to the Midwest we cried our eyes out at the train station. After he declared his dream to be a pro athlete too, we'd practice signing our autographs in big florid strokes. We also liked to mimic our father's colorful language—"Bust your bahoola!" we'd boom, bumping shoulders and dissolving into laughter—not always realizing until we were chided that some of Dad's other expressions were too salty to repeat.

Before the 405 freeway came through Long Beach, our working-class neighborhood of Wrigley Heights literally sat on the wrong side of the railroad tracks that divided the city in two. Active oil derricks dotted the streets around us. Some remain to this day. Randy and I would ride our bikes to a trestle just a few blocks away and emerge on the other side in upscale Los Cerritos, where many of our schoolmates lived. We'd roll by the stately brick estates with manicured lawns and realize there was more out there in life than in the world we came from.

As the elder child, I had a head start on Randy when it came to our lifelong bond with Dad over sports. Dad would read the baseball box scores to me daily. By kindergarten I had already asked him for my own bat, which he made for me from a piece of scrap wood. I'd constantly pester him to watch me tear from my friend Molly's tree just down the block to a tree in front of our house, a distance of about sixty yards. "Time me, Daddy! Time me!" I'd plead. Randy, then still waddling in diapers, would sometimes try to run with me. I vividly remember the gratitude I felt when Dad told the neighborhood boys there would be no more games on our front lawn unless they stopped refusing to let me play too.

I loved to rebound for Dad when he shot at our garage basketball hoop, and I could see why he was recruited after his Navy tour to play for St. Louis in the Basketball Association of America, one of the precursors to the NBA. Dad turned down that opportunity in order to raise our family. He could still make one hundred free throws in a row. I'd count each of his made baskets out loud as I passed the ball back to him, my excitement rising as his streak grew.

It was the postwar baby boom, and our neighborhood was crawling with children. I was always physically mature for my age and well coordinated. Once I held my own in softball games, my father's coworkers always wanted me to play shortstop or third base on their teams at their fire department picnics. There, I learned an important lesson that applied later in life, in other contexts: Men and boys will accept you more easily when you excel at something they value.

When my parents took Randy and me to Los Angeles to watch our first Pacific Coast League baseball game between the L.A. Angels and the Hollywood Stars when I was nine I expected it to be a thrilling day—until I looked down on the field and it dawned on me for the first time that all the pro players were men. Before that day I had heard about the American Dream and thought it applied unconditionally to me. I believed that I could go as far in anything as my abilities would take me. I was a girl who loved to play ball and compete. I was as good at it as any boy my age, and while I had a growing sense that that somehow made me different, I disliked being called a tomboy or unladylike. I wasn't trying to be a boy—I *liked* being a girl. Now I had smacked into a wall; it was the first time I realized that no matter how good I was, my life would be limited because I was female.

"What's wrong, Sis?" my mom asked me on the car ride home.

I just kept staring out the backseat window, too upset to talk.

AS A FIREFIGHTER, Dad often worked twenty-four hours on and twenty-four hours off. When he came home from overnight duty at the firehouse he would start the coffee and make breakfast for Mom so she could sleep in a little. He'd do chores around the house without her asking. I still have some of the love notes my father never stopped writing to my mom over the years in his beautiful longhand script, calling her "Darling" and thanking her for being such a wonderful wife and mother. Mom was a terrific homemaker, and she loved hooking rugs, sewing many of the clothes I wore, baking special things for us. She was shy, but if she felt something was important to her children, she could get animated. Before my matches, she'd sometimes write me little notes of encouragement, reminding me about tactical points to keep in mind, then exhorting me, "Go get 'em, Tiger."

My parents rarely went out for a night on the town and drank alcohol only on special occasions, when my mom might nurse a

Grasshopper and my dad might sip on Scotch. They loved to listen to my dad's records—jazz and big-band music were the soundtrack of my childhood. They loved Ella Fitzgerald—especially her scat singing on *Ella in Berlin*—Louis Armstrong, Tommy Dorsey, Glenn Miller, Count Basie, Shirley Bassey, and the jazz trombonist Jack Teagarden. Sometimes my parents would roll up the living room rug at the pleading of Randy and me and entertain us by dancing a little together. My mom would even show off a bit. That was their idea of stepping out.

Some of Dad's other habits, like our 8:30 a.m. Saturday bedroom inspections and the chores Randy and I had to do before we could go off to play, seemed a carryover from his Navy days. Suppertime was also sacred at the Moffitt house. We were expected to be at the kitchen table ready to say grace by 5:30 sharp. I can remember many a time when I'd be running and yelling at Randy over my shoulder, "C'mon! You know how Daddy is when we're late!" We'd often talk at the dinner table about current events, maybe how the Dodgers were doing, then it was homework time. We went to bed early, though I often used that private time to indulge my love of reading—history, biographies, any kind of nonfiction fascinated me.

My mother was always frugal because she had to make things work in the household on my father's salary. We weren't among the first folks on our block to have a TV set, because my parents simply didn't have the money. One of my first experiences watching television was a visit to our neighbors when I was nine to watch the 1953 coronation of Britain's Queen Elizabeth II. It was my first taste of the terrific pomp and ceremony that the Brits bring to so many things, including Wimbledon. I would be fortunate to be part of that in the years to come.

One of the greatest things my mom ever did for me was sit me down when I was ten and show me our family budget. I had no idea that every time I flipped on the light switch it cost something, or that every trip in the car cost money for gas. She wanted me to understand that if she or my dad didn't want to buy us something they weren't being uncaring—it was because we couldn't afford it. We always had enough to eat, but we typically lived on tuna casseroles, meat loaf, canned veggies, and the occasional Sunday roast; we had margarine instead of butter. I can't remember dining in a restaurant until I was eleven years old. Even then, Mom and Dad wouldn't let us order a milkshake *and* fries with our burgers; we had to choose one or the other because of the cost. Even at home, it wasn't uncommon for my father to remark, "Boy, you kids really eat a lot," or for my mother to shoot us a disapproving look when we reached for another portion. To this day, going to a restaurant and having everyone order whatever they want secretly thrills me.

For Randy and me, the scrutiny created a conflicted relationship with food that has lasted our entire lives. If I got a little money as a kid, I'd go to the store and buy Three Musketeers bars as a treat. It was soothing to have the freedom to eat what I wanted. Once I began traveling for tennis as a teen without my parents, I started binging on ice cream and other treats and my weight began to roller-coaster. It has remained a struggle throughout my life.

My parents' rules and views could be a challenge as I got older. They remained an inhibiting voice in my head long after I reached adulthood and left home. But I never questioned my parents' love and devotion, and I yearned throughout my life to repay them in kind. I constantly strove never to disappoint them. I knew they wanted only the best for us.

Even as a girl, I could see how my parents' values helped me navigate what life and tennis threw at me. They taught me delayed gratification at a very young age, and so I not only knew how to work and wait for what I wanted, but I had the faith and confidence that I could make my goals come true. I knew what it felt like to be challenged, unwelcome, or penalized for being different and how to push on anyway. I had empathy for people, but I was no pushover. I could stick up for myself. All of those traits helped me when I turned my ambition toward tennis.

From my first hitting session with Susan Williams, I knew that a country club membership was not available to a blue-collar girl like me. But that hurdle seemed less important by the time Susan and I met Clyde Walker in the summer of 1954. We sought him out because our softball coach, Val Halloran, who later coached us to the Long Beach city championship, told us there was "this nice man" giving free tennis instruction at Houghton Park. I soon learned that Southern California was a hotbed for tennis, and that public-park kids like us were fueling it. Before long, I was following Clyde each day to the other public parks in Long Beach where he taught during the week: Mondays at Silverado, Tuesdays at Houghton Park, Wednesdays at Somerset, Thursdays at Ramona, and Fridays at Recreation Park.

"You again?" Clyde would say, laughing when he saw me coming. But he always had a soft spot for me.

I was still among the tallest kids in my elementary school class photos then. Clyde asked me early on, "How old are you anyway? Fourteen?" I said, "No, sir. I turn eleven in November." He seemed happily surprised. I could tell he was thinking, *Whoa, we've got a live one here.*

Clyde was a kind man, then in his late sixties, with thinning hair and a bulbous nose. He reminded me of Jimmy Durante, the gravel-voiced comedian. Clyde liked to jingle the change in his pockets, which always drove me crazy. But he loved us, and we loved him. His belief was important to me.

It wasn't long before Clyde mentioned entering Susan and me in a tournament. One day soon after that I asked him, "Clyde, can you make me a champion?"

He said, "No, Billie Jean. But with hard work, you can."

INSPIRED BY CLYDE'S WORDS, I flung myself into working on my game. Whole lives are woven from thinner threads of hope than the assurance he gave me. I spent every spare moment hitting balls at home against the wooden fence that ran along the small slab of driveway in front of our garage. I don't know how our long-suffering neighbors coped with the noise the ball made before that beat-up fence finally gave way and fell down—or how they felt after Dad replaced it with a cinderblock wall and my thumps in the night resumed. He put up a spotlight so I could keep hitting after dark. *One more ball, one more ball,* I'd tell myself.

When I quickly wore out my first racket, Clyde took me to a barrel of used ones at Houghton Park and pulled out a Spalding Pancho Gonzalez signature model. I loved that one too. Pancho was an early hero of mine. I cleaned the black-and-white frame every night. I painted the strings with clear nail polish, hoping it would help them last. I wrapped adhesive tape around the top of the racket's wood frame to protect it from scuffing against the cement courts we played on.

The initial competition Clyde entered us in was a novice event at Long Beach City College over the 1954 Christmas holidays. I lost my match to Susan, 6–0, 6–0, but the lopsided score only motivated me more. Susan was a brilliant student and exceedingly gracious, but I think we initially became fast friends because she was a born all-around jock, same as me. She was the best tennis player in our Long Beach age group at the time, but, just the same, I didn't like failing to win even a game from her. My first goal was to become better than she was, and I told my parents so.

As important as the extra effort I poured into my game was, my life might have turned out very differently without Clyde's dedication and vision to complement my parents' support. I was very lucky. He came to California from Tyler, Texas, where he had coached at some country clubs before he was hired by the Long Beach Parks and Recreation Department. At first, nobody in our city government supported his sizable aspirations for the junior tennis program. But Clyde convinced them. A decade before I showed up, he was already taking his pitch for a five-year plan and fund-raising to the local newspapers. "Who will be our Moses?" he asked, noting how tennis was a terrific lifetime sport for kids, how it could build civic pride, how Long Beach lagged behind surrounding Southern California towns in producing tennis standouts.

Clyde eventually teamed up with the Long Beach Tennis Patrons and Century Club, two community groups that shared his dream of making the city an incubator for future champions. They provided financial support that helped promising players like me travel to tournaments and stay in the game. At the time, even the $2 entry fees were tough for my folks to cover.

It helped, too, that Clyde had a magic touch with kids. He was patient, easygoing and nonjudgmental, which was fortunate for me because I knew absolutely nothing when I first turned up. Even following tennis's scoring system for games and sets was a challenge for me at first: *15, 30, 40?* "Shouldn't it be 45, not 40?" I asked Clyde. *"Love" means "zero"? Since when? Says who?*

Clyde believed in finding ways for a child to succeed right away, which was also smart. He put us through drills that were more like games and kept us engaged the full ninety minutes. He stood behind newcomers like me and guided us through each stroke as we dropped the ball and swung through it. "This is a forehand . . . This is a backhand," he'd say, as if he was letting us in on a magical secret. He believed in teaching the fundamentals first, starting with our groundstrokes. Unlike many of today's coaches, it was a long time before Clyde finally let us hit (or "rally") with each other. But I had an attacking game even then—I just didn't know it was an actual style. It just fit my go-go-go personality.

As soon as we began a point I'd rush the net. Then I'd hear his voice:

"Billie Jean, please back up to the baseline."

"But Clyde, I like it up here! It's me! It's more fun hitting the balls in the air."

"I know, I know—that's what we call a *volley*," he said as I marched back to the backcourt. There was so much to learn.

JERRY CROMWELL LIVED near Susan and me, and he was the only other kid who followed Clyde to the various courts five days a week after school. After Susan moved away because her father, a Shell Oil executive, was transferred to Denver, Jerry was my best friend. He was still small and a year behind me at Los Cerritos Elementary, but he'd been playing tennis longer and he was already good by age nine.

Clyde told us that ever since he started coaching he had been looking for a kid with a passion to play. In Jerry and me, he now had two. He said that Jerry and I were the first ones out of the hundreds, maybe thousands, that he had coached who loved tennis more than anything in the world, burned to be the best, and were willing to put in the work. That, of course, only made us double down even more. Jerry still jokes about how I somehow whipcracked and cajoled him into walking the three miles to school together one year to build our leg endurance for tennis.

After Clyde's group sessions, Jerry and I would routinely stay on the court hitting. Clyde would often linger and coach us on more advanced strokes: half-volleys, volleys, overheads. He had us do crosscourt and down-the-line drills running back and forth across the baseline. Then, when it was too dark to continue, we'd pile into Clyde's '48 Chevy and he would take us home on the rare days when one of our parents couldn't pick us up. Some nights Clyde would take us to his house first and his wife, Louise, would give us snacks or avocados picked fresh from their tree. Jerry grew to be six feet two and played some terrific tennis for the University of Southern California and various U.S. national teams. He could've turned pro. He was that good.

Like my father, Clyde rarely put limits on me. He started all junior players with underhand serves. But I could pound overheads very soon. As soon as Clyde taught me a proper serve, I began to add different spins. Then one day I watched Clyde teaching Jerry the American twist, a glorified topspin serve with a little side hop. It's called a kick serve today.

"Clyde, can you teach me that too?" I asked.

"Girls don't do the American twist," Clyde said. The conventional thinking then was the stroke was too hard on a young girl's body because she would have to throw the ball up behind her. Though I couldn't articulate it this way at the time, I saw this as yet another cue to me as a girl to temper my ambition. It ranked right up there with similar thinking at the time that girls and women were so physically delicate we couldn't play full-court basketball, run the longer races at the Olympics, or do a zillion other things because it might hurt our reproductive organs. We were actually told this.

Clyde relented when I asked, "Can I at least try the American twist?" I got it on the first try, and he was thrilled. After that, I was allowed to serve the same as any guy.

OF COURSE, me being me—which is to say, an unconventional girl with robust enthusiasm—my drive could sometimes create . . . complications. I've always said God gave me extra energy. I felt like there were never enough hours in the day for tennis and everything else I wanted to do, especially since Mom and Dad insisted that I remain well rounded.

I had always been a very good student before I started tennis, but now they warned me that they wouldn't let me play if I fell below a B in any major subject. That happened once when I got a C in high school chemistry. I convinced Dad to let me play again after four weeks, which felt like a lifetime to me. Before that, we had a knock-down, drag-out stalemate after my fifth-grade teacher called home one day and, to Dad's astonishment, said that I was in danger of failing reading.

"But how can that be?" he said. "I have to tell her to turn off the light every night because she's reading in bed."

I put in the effort. My problem was that I was suffering from social anxiety and a fear of public speaking, something that still gnaws at me. I'm much more uncomfortable giving public presentations than I ever let on. As a child, it was more acute. I hated being called on in class because I would have to speak. On that particular day, my teacher had called on me to give my oral book report assignment and I froze. She concluded that I was unprepared.

When I got home, Dad was waiting for me. He made some stern attempts to convince me, "You have to go back to school and get through your oral report." My mom backed him up. When neither of them would budge, the conversation escalated into me trilling loudly in my ten-year-old voice, "But I *can't* do it, Daddy! I *can't*! You might as well punish me now!" Calmly he repeated, "Sis, you have to do it." I stormed to my room and flung myself on my bed, where I sobbed and thrashed and wailed extravagantly for what seemed like hours.

Mom eventually came to check on me. Then my dad tried a different tack. He asked me gently, "Tell me about the book you're reading now." It was about Peter Stuyvesant and early New York. "Why don't you practice giving a report on it with me," Dad suggested. And so, between my sniffles, that's what we did. I made some notes. Before I went to bed my mom helped me give nose drops to my Raggedy Ann doll because I said Raggedy had been upset too. Somehow, I made it through my oral presentation the next day, knees knocking, and I passed reading.

About a year later, when I was eleven, my love of tennis became an issue again. I had obsessively begged my parents for a piano since kindergarten after listening to Grandma Moffitt coax beautiful songs out of the spinet she kept in her living room. It took my parents until I was in fifth grade to save enough money to buy a used one. That also happened to be the year I started working with Clyde and found tennis. It didn't go over too well when I sat at our piano just ten or eleven months after we got it and told my mom I thought I should stop music lessons because they were interfering with my sport.

Oh, boy.

She began pacing back and forth and let me have it. "We saved all those years, Billie Jean, and you wanted a piano—you got it." *Pace, pace, pace.* "Now you are going to finish what you start." *Stern look.* "You're not quitting until I am satisfied that you can read music and play it well. Got it?" *Hands on hips.* "That's just the way it works around here!"

She was magnificent. My dad could never be that strict with me. After another year of lessons, maybe two, I was able to play "The Dream of Olwen" by Charles Williams straight from the sheet music at a recital. Afterward, I looked up at Mom expectantly, and she kept her word. But I will never forget what she said to me then: "You're good enough to stop now, but I wish you would play forever."

Today, a Clavinova piano similar in size to the spinet we had sits in the New York City apartment I share with my partner, Ilana Kloss. I still have the sheet music to "The Dream of Olwen," and every now and then when I try to play it again, I always think about my mom.

MY FAMILY WORSHIPPED at the First Church of the Brethren in Long Beach, which sat just a short walk from our home in Wrigley Heights. As if I didn't have enough sports-minded thoughts already, the minister there was the Rev. Bob Richards, an Olympic pole vaulter who had won a bronze medal in 1948 and gold medals at the 1952 and 1956 Summer Games. He was the first athlete to appear on the front of the Wheaties cereal box, and he later worked as a television spokesman for the brand. He also became a popular motivational speaker. The newspapers nicknamed him "the Vaulting Vicar," but we knew him as a spellbinding orator and dedicated athlete who would do his workouts on the field next to our church.

For an aspiring athlete like me who wanted to be the best, it just didn't get any better. I would walk with Randy on Sundays to hear Rev. Richards's homily even if my parents had to skip a service. You can still find some of his recordings on YouTube. His stem-winding sermons were so inspirational I'd feel shot out of a cannon when he was through. Most of the time, it seemed as if he was speaking directly to me.

Rev. Richards was an enormous influence in my life. He called sports "the language of self-reliance" and stressed how rigorous self-analysis was vital to recognize your weaknesses and work on them. Like Clyde and my father, he preached that champions in life and sports aren't so much born, they're made. He often used himself as an example. "You will never meet a more mediocre man than the one standing in front of you," Richards boomed one day, his cadence rising, the emotion building as he went. "I am five feet ten, 185 pounds. Average brain, average voice. Average!

"And yet—"

Richards often added cliffhanger pauses like that, and I would be absolutely rapt by the time he continued—"And yet, you don't *give in* to your weaknesses! *Nooo!* You *take* what you've got and turn it into power. Run till your legs are strong! Climb rope and your arms will get strong! The difference between a champion and the rest of us is just *that little bit more* that a champion puts out. Why, I think of the great Rocky Marciano in boxing. He had weak arms. But he went to the local pool and he worked on those upper arms. He became heavyweight champion of the world!"

His point was: It's up to you. So get going.

The Brethren sprang from the same theological roots as Mennonites. They believe that Jesus directed them to live simple lives of peaceful action glorifying God and spreading His word through good works. That sounded good to me. In our church we were told you weren't judged by how often you worshipped but by how you acted. Were you kind? Were you good? Did you live a life of service?

Rev. Richards also preached tolerance, which was an important validation for a girl like me who was already bumping up against conventional thinking. He told parables about his own career. After a Russian athlete congratulated him with a hug for winning gold at the 1952 Helsinki Olympics, Richards was sharply criticized in the U.S. for accepting the show of fellowship since the Cold War was on. He disagreed. He told us that he saw it as a moment of grace. He made a point at our services to emphasize that everyone was welcome. Some of our church members were conscientious objectors to military service, and they sat side by side with veterans who had served.

Being part of that atmosphere at such an impressionable age captured my mind and my heart. Sometime between sixth and seventh grade, I asked to be baptized. No one suggested that I do it. The Brethren believe in free will, and that your choices are between you and God alone. So one Sunday in front of my parents and the congregation, Rev. Richards opened a curtain behind the altar to reveal a large baptism tank with a front panel framed by two sets of stairs. After I declared that I had accepted Jesus Christ as my personal savior, Richards stepped into the tank. I wore a white sheet wrapped around my bathing suit and descended the stairs on the other side, prepared to be symbolically reborn. He dunked me three times as he baptized me in the name of the Father, the Son, and the Holy Spirit. I came up gasping when it was all over.

I read the Bible every night through junior high and high school, and I often led prayer meetings before Sunday school class. I didn't smoke or drink, and I carried a Bible with me on the tennis circuit for years. It gave me comfort as I tried to adjust to life on the road and sleeping in a string of unfamiliar homes and beds. For a while, I seriously considered becoming a missionary. (When I told Chrissie Evert that, her eyes widened and she said, *"Me too!"*)

It wasn't until I got a bit older that I began to question some of the scriptural interpretations we were taught, especially regarding women. I also learned that years after Rev. Richards left Long Beach to lead a different congregation he veered toward extremist right-wing politics—an about-face that still stuns me. He even mounted a quixotic campaign in the 1984 U.S. presidential election for a reincarnation of the old Populist Party, which now espoused white-nationalist views. It's difficult for me to reconcile such activities with the man I once knew.

Back then, Richards showed me how a champion could inspire others. His assertion that you could change people's hearts and minds through sports became a bedrock, animating belief of mine too. He gave me confidence that I could transcend the contrary messages I kept getting about whether sports was any place for a girl. He was another person telling me faith and hard work could get me through.

I never lost trust in some of the basic tenets I learned then, like the emphasis on kindness and living a life of service filled with good acts. Even now, when I face political adversaries or folks with different philosophical or religious beliefs, my background helps me have a dialogue. It's amazing—even transformative—what you can learn and accomplish when you genuinely listen to people and engage them with respect, rather than judge them because they're different from you.

I BEGAN TO GET a better sense of the Southern California tennis landscape as I played more tournaments. In the spring of 1955, Jerry Cromwell, Susan Williams, and I were among five of Clyde Walker's players from Long Beach who were chosen to compete in the Southern California championships at the prestigious Los Angeles

Tennis Club. I was excited to know I was leaving the novice ranks and entering my first sanctioned tournament. I'd also earn my first junior ranking.

Somehow, my mother and I were given the wrong date for the start of the thirteen-and-under bracket. We arrived a day late, but Joe Bixler, the Wilson sporting goods company rep who was checking in the players that day, was sympathetic and willing to let me make up the first round. My opponent, Marilyn Hester, was generous enough to agree. That meant I'd have to play two matches in one day if I won the first, but I didn't care. I was thrilled to be playing on the same courts where I knew many famous players had competed, and I became more excited when Joe handed me two brand-new balls for my match. I had never played with fluffy new balls. I held them up to my nose and breathed in that new-tennis-ball smell. I rolled them around in my palms and felt the scruffy texture on my skin.

I defeated Marilyn in straight sets, but that's all I recall. I guess that seems odd, since it was my first sanctioned match, but it actually became a career-long pattern of mine. I rarely lingered on victories. My next opponent was Ann Zavitovsky, a big, strong girl with more experience than me. I remember that match more clearly because she had to teach me that balls that land on the lines are in. She beat me after I extended her to 6–all in the third set and I wound up with so many blisters on my feet I could hardly walk. I had never played more than two sets.

All of that paled in comparison, though, to something else that happened that day. When my mother and I arrived that morning at the Los Angeles Tennis Club, we were told all the junior players were lining up to take a photo on the front steps. I was happily taking my place with the others when a pear-shaped man with a penguin's waddle approached. In front of everyone he said, "You! Little girl! Out! You can't be in the picture wearing shorts. You need a skirt or dress."

That was my first (but hardly last) run-in with Perry T. Jones, president of the Southern California Tennis Association, whose headquarters was at the Los Angeles Tennis Club. Though the club only required players to wear white, he made his own additional rules. Everyone called Jones "the Czar" because he commanded his kingdom like a tyrant. He had rigid ideas about how players should look, talk, and act. Over the years I found some of his stances infuriating and others hysterically funny. Once Susan Williams and I won an award as high schoolers, and, at the banquet, the Czar presented each of us with a new racket and . . . a baby doll. Seriously?

On that first day I met Jones, I was only aware that my poor mother, who had made me those beautiful shorts, was mortified. She was so upset she bought a new bolt of white fabric and began sewing me a new dress that night, using a coffee cup to trace out the scalloped edges of the hem. It never occurred to me to be humiliated by Jones's rebuke. I was upset for my mom—and then I got angry. I had already played plenty of other sports wearing shorts. I had already played plenty of other sports and never had an adult act like this. So why was tennis so unwelcoming?

"Don't worry, Mom," I told her. "I'll show him someday."

It only made me want to win more.

I spent that summer and the ensuing ones playing as many matches as I could. But I had to learn to balance my drive with my temper. I guess I came by it honestly. Dad always taught Randy and me that winning wasn't the most important thing, but boy, did he hate losing. He was ejected from some of his night league basketball games for fighting. Mom and I would be watching from the stands while his teammates dragged him off the court, still screaming and making a fuss. We'd turn to each other with an embarrassed look that said *Oh, my God!* And yet, while we could have done without the spectacle, I loved my dad's intensity and I'd defend him. "Mom! He's just competitive! He can't help himself!" I'd say.

My dad knew better, though. When I began playing tennis I sometimes threw my racket on the ground if I got frustrated. Once I made the mistake of doing it in front of Dad at a tournament. He was quiet but boiling the entire drive home. As soon as we were out of the car he marched me into the garage.

"Billie Jean, give me your racket. You obviously don't care about it," he said, firing up his power saw.

"No, Daddy! *No!*" I cried. "I promise I won't throw it again!" It was my only racket. He took it from me anyway, and my eyes widened when he held the wooden neck of it an inch away from the whirring blade. Again I yelped, *"Please, Daddy! Don't!"* After a long pause spent looking at me, he switched off the saw and handed my racket back. Then he warned me, "I'm taking you off the court if you have an outburst like that again." I meant it with all my heart when I promised him I never would. (Not that it lasted. Forever is a very long time.)

By the summer of 1956, just before I entered eighth grade, I was starting to win a lot of matches and happy to begin getting some notice in the *Long Beach Press Telegram*. The writers were calling me a "local whiz" and "the Long Beach tennis wonder." Still, I had never seen my name on the front page of the sports section until, one day, there it was—a headline that screamed, "Moffett Eliminated." What! They misspelled my last name, and under the same headline, there was a brief account of my 6–0, 6–0 quarterfinal loss at the National Junior Public Parks tournament.

"What is *wrong* with these people?" I snapped, throwing the paper down on the kitchen floor.

Then I noticed my dad and mom watching me.

For the next ten or fifteen minutes, Dad patiently led me through why I had to let it go. He explained, "Yesterday is not important. You should learn from history, but you can't change it. It's done." He told me how important it was to live in the moment, because that's how athletes succeed. Then he made a rule: From that day on, I could not read my press clippings—and I didn't for the rest of my career. I still have to be forced to read anything about myself.

When my parents died some sixty years later I found boxes and boxes of magazine and newspaper articles about Randy and me that they had saved for us. I had no idea.

After that embarrassing loss, I was still practicing as hard as ever. But I was missing shots that I should've made and I didn't know why. The answer became clear months later when my eighth-grade science teacher showed us a slide show in class and I couldn't read the captions.

When my parents took me to the optometrist we learned I was

shockingly nearsighted. Luckily, my vision was easily corrected to 20/10. With glasses, I now had the eyes of a fighter pilot. My tennis improved immediately, although I could be in trouble if it rained or the lenses fogged up during a match. I was even more concerned when people told me there had been only one major tennis champion by then, male or female, who wore glasses: Jaroslav Drobny of Czechoslovakia, the 1954 Wimbledon champion.

I decided that was another thing I'd have to change.

TENNIS DOESN'T REALLY have an off-season in Southern California, because the hard courts and perfect weather make it possible to play year-round. There was a tennis event in a different city just about every weekend. For my parents, that meant the expenses piled up for gasoline, meals, and entry fees for tournaments, which was a strain for us back then.

The good news was that the Long Beach Tennis Patrons pulled together to support the most promising young players. I'll never forget the patrons' names because, like the many people who helped me over the years, they were heroes to me: Al Bray, Gene Buwick, Charles Felker, Ted Matthews. Along with the Century Club, another all-volunteer civic group that pitched in, the Patrons helped young players with fees and travel expenses. I'm not sure how many of us would've managed without their aid.

Just as important was the individual attention we received, the doors that were opened for us as junior players, and the connections we made. An example: As juniors, Jerry and I weren't allowed on the courts without an adult player at the grandly named Lakewood Country Club, which was actually a county-owned public park in Long Beach. Al Bray, who was the best adult male player in Long Beach, and Gene Buwick, who was number two, usually invited us to practice with them at Lakewood on Saturday mornings.

Jerry and I soaked up a lot of tennis lore while at Lakewood. I was always an avid student of tennis history. I had read about the nineteenth-century origins of the sport, and Wimbledon's stature as the most important tournament in the world. I knew about the worldwide coverage of the 1926 "Match of the Century" in Cannes between the French icon Suzanne Lenglen, who once went seven years without a loss, and twenty-year-old Helen Wills, a three-time U.S. champion who crossed the Atlantic by ocean liner because she was so determined to play Lenglen. I memorized the score: Lenglen won, 6–3, 8–6. I devoured Doris Hart's autobiography after she swept the Wimbledon singles, doubles, and mixed-doubles titles and rose to No. 1 in 1951. I read about the teenage sensation Maureen "Little Mo" Connolly, a five-foot-five powerhouse from San Diego whose career was ended prematurely in 1954 by a horrific leg injury that she suffered when a cement truck sideswiped a horse she was riding on the side of a road.

At Lakewood and the other venues we began to play, Jerry and I encountered people with firsthand stories about stars like Jack Kramer, Don Budge, Pancho Segura, Tony Trabert, Ken Rosewall, and L.A's self-taught Richard "Pancho" Gonzalez, a son of Mexican immigrants. Gonzalez became one of the greatest players of any era.

Lakewood was also the first place where I heard about Bobby Riggs. Even then, everyone seemed to have a Riggs story. He was the son of a Los Angeles minister, and an early protégé of Perry T. Jones before he fell out of favor with the Czar for hustling players into betting on their matches. (I guess that was Bobby's idea of passing around the collection plate.) He stood only five feet seven but he had a colorful personality, terrific racket skills, and a great strategic mind. He was just twenty-one when he won the triple crown at Wimbledon in 1939, sweeping the singles, doubles, and mixed doubles. But then, like so many great players, his career was interrupted by World War II. He served in the Navy and spent time in Guam before touring after the war as a barnstorming "contract" pro, which meant forgoing the traditional amateur tournaments for a series of paid events staged by a promoter.

By the 1950s, many of the great male stars had left the amateur ranks to do the same. Only a few women, most notably Lenglen, Pauline Betz, and Gussie Moran, were invited to tour as pros by then. I knew the decision disqualified them from playing Wimbledon and the other three majors, which still invited only amateurs. Even then,

I questioned what was so special about winning those Grand Slam titles if most or all of the best men's and women's players weren't in the tournament. In our house, pro sports meant being the best.

I found myself questioning a lot of other things as well. Later that summer, I attended the Pacific Southwest Championships for the first time. The event was held every September right after the U.S. National Championships (now the U.S. Open), so most of the top players made it their next stop. That particular year, the news was still full of stories about the Supreme Court's issuing a clarification, in May 1955, that "separate but equal" schools and other public facilities were not only unconstitutional but must be desegregated "with all deliberate speed." I remember asking my parents about some images of segregationists I'd seen in the newspaper, and they remarked that it wasn't right for anyone to prevent children from getting an education or going to school together. So discrimination was on my mind as I sat watching the Pacific Southwest matches. It was my first time back to the Los Angeles Tennis Club since Perry T. Jones pulled me from the photograph for wearing shorts. My father's former college opponent, Jackie Robinson, had been with the Brooklyn Dodgers for eight years by then, and I was used to the idea that athletes came in all colors. But as I looked down on the grandstand court from my seat high in the bleachers, I was struck by how white everything was. Everybody played in white shoes, white socks, white clothes. Even the balls were white. Everybody had white skin. Where was everybody else?

At that moment, I had an epiphany that I'm sure had something to do with the incidents in the news, the hurdles I was already experiencing, and the messages I was hearing from Rev. Richards on Sundays: I told myself that day that I would spend my life fighting for equal rights and opportunities for everyone, so no one felt scorned or left out. I believed our church's teaching that I was put on this earth to do good with my life. Now I had a better idea what my calling could be: I could bring people together through tennis. If I was good enough and fortunate enough to be No. 1 in the world, tennis would be my platform.

WHEN I LOOK back now, I'm amazed at the personal contact I had with so many accomplished players and people who helped me. Those experiences helped make me the human being and player I became. Remember, there was no tennis to watch regularly on TV when I was developing my game, no hopping on the internet to call up YouTube videos of how a top player hit her forehand or serve. Southern California was a mecca for champions, and I was lucky enough to meet some of them and watch others from the stands. On that same first trip of mine to the Pacific Southwest tournament, I asked everyone, "Who should I see?" They directed me to a faraway side court. That's the first time I saw Rod Laver, then only seventeen and a rising Australian star. Many people now think he was the greatest male player ever. Serendipitous things like that happened often.

Another high point of my summer was being a ball girl with Susan Williams for a Recreation Park exhibition match between the three-time U.S. Nationals champion Doris Hart and the top-ten player Beverly Baker Fleitz. When they invited us to play doubles with them afterward, all I could think—besides *Oh my God, I'm playing doubles with Doris Hart!*—was what superbly skilled athletes they were. Trading shots with them gave me a greater sense of how precise their strokes and ball placement were, how efficiently they moved around the court.

Later, getting to practice with Darlene Hard, a budding star on the women's circuit, drove home even more how talented the top players were. Darlene was twenty-one years old when we met but already a veteran of Wimbledon as well as a doubles titlist at the French Championships (Roland-Garros). She was a lively California girl who was studying pre-med at Pomona College. She and her mother, Ruth, knew Clyde Walker from competing on the local scene, and Darlene sometimes helped him with his clinics. One day, Clyde asked her to hit with me. Playing one-on-one with Darlene, who wound up in the International Tennis Hall of Fame, changed my outlook because I got my first extended taste of what it meant to play at a high level. The pace and depth of her shots were a revelation.

Amazingly, Darlene not only agreed to play with me a couple more times, she also offered to drive the forty miles from Pomona and pick me up at my house to do it, even though it could take her as long as an hour and a half one way in bad traffic. I would be jumping out of my skin as I waited to hear her coming down 36th Street in her red Chevy convertible. It had a twin-pipe hot rod muffler that announced when she was near.

Sometimes Darlene would join me for a meal with my family after we practiced. It was my chance to barrage her with questions about all the things I longed to know: *What's it like to play a major? Is Wimbledon as great as they say? Tell me about some of the places you've been!* Darlene filled me in on Althea Gibson, whom she anticipated she might compete against at Wimbledon. (Sure enough, Althea defeated her in the 1957 final.) When I saw Darlene again over the next few years, her predictive powers remained sharp. She was always raving about a smooth young Brazilian player named Maria Bueno, who later became No. 1. She also mentioned a tall, rawboned Australian teenager named Margaret Smith, who was later better known by her married name, Court, and would become one of my fiercest rivals. When Darlene announced, "Margaret is really the one to watch," it broke my heart a little. I wondered if she would ever tell me I was good enough to make it on the tour. She never did. Inside, I felt that familiar restlessness churning in me again.

Being around Darlene and other champions enriched my life. It also made me want to be better than any of them.

Chapter 3

JUST A FEW MONTHS after I met Darlene, I finally saw what it looked like to be the absolute best in the world. I was sitting in the bleachers at the Los Angeles Tennis Club when Althea Gibson strode out in the sunlight for a match at the Pacific Southwest Championships. She was transfixing even before she swung her racket. Althea stood five feet eleven and was a lithe 140 pounds. Her coffee-colored skin looked beautiful cast against her brilliant white tennis outfit. Her arms and legs were impossibly long and lean, and she moved like a gazelle. She wore a faint frown of utter concentration as she bounced the ball at the baseline, preparing to serve. When she rocked back, floated her toss high in the air, and brought her racket through in one smooth, explosive motion, the ball shot off her racket with a crack.

I had just seen what I wanted to be. And if you can see it, you can be it.

I watched Althea closely that day, tracking every move. For a while I would zero in on just her hands, then her footwork. I noticed how incredibly efficient her movements were, and how still her head remained as she connected with the ball. Althea played an aggressive serve-and-volley game, my preferred style. I studied when she approached the net, how intimidating her long wingspan was when she chose to attack, how she executed shots and plucked volleys out of the air as if guided to where the ball would be by some awesome sense of premonition.

Could I ever be that good? I knew I was going to have to work awfully hard to try to get there. It helped me that Althea's backstory was proof that anything could be done—a fact that stayed with me as much as her game.

Althea was born in Silver, South Carolina, to Daniel and Annie Bell Gibson, who were sharecroppers on a cotton farm before they moved to Harlem when Althea was a child. I can only imagine what a culture shock it must've been for them to relocate from an area of open spaces to a small apartment on a crowded, noisy stretch of 143rd Street near Lenox Avenue. By chance, the area was a designated Police Athletic League zone and sealed off from traffic during the day so people in the neighborhood could play organized sports. That's where Althea learned paddle tennis, and by twelve she had become the New York City women's champion.

Some neighbors saw Althea's obvious talent and chipped in for her to learn tennis at the Black-owned Cosmopolitan Tennis Club in the Sugar Hill section of Harlem. Soon she was winning junior events organized by the all-Black American Tennis Association, the amateur tennis equivalent of the Negro leagues in baseball. She quickly found an important patron and mentor in Dr. Walter Johnson, the same Virginia physician who was active in the ATA and would later help Arthur Ashe. Johnson sponsored Althea's advanced training.

In 1950, Althea became the first African American to compete in the previously all-white U.S. National Championships at Forest Hills. She was our sport's Jackie Robinson. She broke the color barrier in tennis three years after Robinson integrated Major League Baseball with the Brooklyn Dodgers. At the 1956 French Championships, she was the first African American to win a Grand Slam title. In the summer of 1957, when she beat Darlene Hard for her first Wimbledon singles title—"At last, at last!" Althea said as Queen Elizabeth II handed her the Venus Rosewater Dish that goes to the winner—she swept the doubles and mixed doubles too.

When I saw Althea walk out at the Los Angeles Tennis Club just a few months after that, she was thirty years old and at the peak of her tennis career. But I had a strange sensation as I watched the all-white crowd cheering for her. Three years had passed since the Supreme Court had decided its landmark *Brown v. Board of Education of Topeka* ruling that declared separate but equal public facilities were unconstitutional. Now a group of African American students who became known as the Little Rock Nine were trying to attend class at Little Rock Central High School, and the state of Arkansas refused to enforce the law. So President Dwight Eisenhower sent in troops to desegregate the school.

I couldn't stop thinking about a picture I had seen of one Black girl in particular, a fifteen-year-old named Elizabeth Eckford, who was impeccably dressed for her first day of school in a starched white blouse, crisp gingham skirt, and eyeglasses. Eckford was walking all by herself, with her schoolbooks clutched in her arms, and she was being followed and menaced by a clutch of angry white people who hissed and spat at her. Eckford kept her head up and showed no expression, but she must have been terrified. Could I have managed that?

As I watched Althea in her own perfectly pressed shirt and skirt, playing here in front of a different white crowd, I wondered, *What lonely road did she have to walk to get to this place?*

As a white person I obviously have not had to deal with the challenges that my sisters and brothers of color have faced. But when I was a thirteen-year-old girl, Althea inspired me. I knew if she had gone through what she had gone through and changed the world by her example, then maybe I had a chance too.

A year later when Althea published her memoir, I bought a copy and read it at least ten times. I slept with her book in my bed, next to my tennis sweater and racket. Even the title spoke to me: *I Always Wanted to Be Somebody*.

THE SAME WEEK I watched Althea, Jerry Cromwell and I won the junior singles titles in our respective fifteen-and-under age categories at the tournament. As a result, we were both given honorary memberships to the Los Angeles Tennis Club where I had just seen Althea play.

Having regular access to the place known as "the cradle of tennis" in Southern California did more than open a new level of competition for me. My family and I were exposed for the first time to a world of money and privilege we couldn't have imagined or accessed without tennis. When I was a child attending Los Cerritos Elementary, I didn't know that the more affluent parents were trying to get my neighborhood redlined out of the school. But my parents sure knew. They didn't tell Randy and me until years later that they were among those who attended meetings to defeat the effort.

The Los Angeles Tennis Club was located on a few acres of prime real estate in the swanky Hancock Park section of L.A., which is south of Hollywood and just around the corner from Paramount Studios. Before World War II, Clark Gable and Carole Lombard had a courtside box there. On any given day, Errol Flynn and Bette Davis might be around too, playing a friendly match. The club looked like a colonial Spanish palace with its white stucco walls, pillared entryway, and red tile roof. You walked through an arched front door and the first room you entered was a lounge filled with upholstered chairs and game tables for the members.

When my mother and I arrived it was still common to find Lucille Ball there playing backgammon. She was always nice and said hello to us, which thrilled my mom. Ozzie Nelson, then the dad on the hit television show *The Adventures of Ozzie and Harriet,* was often at the club with his handsome son, Ricky, an excellent junior player who all the girls had a crush on. Ricky eventually gave up tennis to be a pop star.

Another regular was Jack Webb, the star of the *Dragnet* TV show. One day he asked Mom, "What project are you working on?"—he genuinely thought she was an actress—and my mother was floored. "Oh. No . . . I mean . . . Oh dear, no—my daughter is a junior tennis player," my mother stammered. I always thought she was as gorgeous as any movie star, with her high cheekbones, perfectly coiffed hair, and dazzling blue eyes. I wasn't surprised Jack Webb did too.

As fun as those moments were, the bigger attraction of the club for me was the amateur and pro tennis stars we bumped into. On any given day I might see Louise Brough or Pancho Gonzalez practicing on the stadium court. You learn from the players who come before you, and I was lucky to be able to study some of the best. Unfortunately, the men weren't much interested in helping girls. Jack

Kramer and Pancho would fall over themselves to volunteer pointers to my contemporary, Dennis Ralston, the latest local boy star. But neither legend cast even a sideways glance my way. I used to crouch behind the seats to eavesdrop on what they were telling Dennis.

The boys got everything, and the girls got crumbs. After I had been at the club awhile, I had a few dates with a young amateur player named Dave Reed, and the subject of expenses matter-of-factly came up. He said, "Oh, we get financial help from the [Southern California Tennis] association"—Perry T. Jones's group. That was news to me. It burned me to hear that, and to know Dennis was signing for his free meals at the club lunch counter and Perry T. Jones was taking care of his expenses but not mine. I was a top junior too. I used to pass by that lunch counter and tell myself, *Billie, it's not always going to be this way*.

When I pulled back and assessed my game at this point, it took faith at times for me to stick with the serve-and-volleying style I preferred. Baseline players become proficient earlier because there are fewer shots and decisions to master and less risk baked into their games. At that age, the pattern is basically serve, return (or *return/ return/return*), repeat. We used to call the baseline players "pushers." At this point, they still usually beat me.

The losing killed me, but Clyde assured me it would be worth it in the long run, and he was right. I learned to take satisfaction from improving on things I was working on in matches, and not necessarily what the scoreboard said. To be a successful attacking player, I knew I had to have a strong second serve, the reflexes to snag my opponent's passing-shot attempts down either side of the court, and the soft hands to pick off volleys as I was charging the net. In time, my shot choices did become clearer. My judgment improved. I controlled more points by making the player across the net feel pressure from me.

In the spring of 1958, I went to the Dudley Cup in Santa Monica, which was a big event at the time. I was fourteen, and I had to overcome both a formidable player named Carole Caldwell and a brief relapse into my public-speaking phobia to win the title. After I pulled ahead in the second set and saw the winner's prize sitting courtside I realized if I won I'd have to say a few words to the crowd. Then I lost a few points I shouldn't have. *That's enough of that!* I chided myself. *You HAVE to do this. If you want to be the best you have to find your voice. No getting around it.* (If you've ever wondered why tennis players talk to themselves, the answer is simple: There's no one else out there to commiserate with.)

Making that leap was a breakthrough for me. But there were still a few things standing in my way of becoming No. 1. One of them remained Perry T. Jones. As head of the Southern California Tennis Association he had the power to decide which tournaments you could enter and how much money—if any—the association would contribute to cover your expenses. Most of us were afraid of running into the Czar by chance because we were worried he'd cite us for some petty dress code violation or other trumped-up infraction. If somebody spotted him coming, word raced around the courts and we'd scatter like pigeons.

I was now No. 2 in the Southern California Tennis Association's rankings for fifteen-and-under girls behind Kathy Chabot, whom I had never beat. Still, I figured my standing would earn me a trip east that summer to play in the national championships in Middletown, Ohio. They always sent the top two players from our section. When the Czar summoned me to his office at the Los Angeles Tennis Club to talk about it, I could hardly breathe. At first he regarded me the way an emperor might eye a serf who had just breached the castle moat. Then he got to the point: "I don't intend to send you to Middletown unless you defeat Kathy Chabot in the Southern California Championships."

"But what about Kathy? If I beat her, can she still go?"

"Of course," he said.

I was happy that Kathy was guaranteed a spot. But the Czar was being unfair to me. He was breaking precedent, yet I knew there was no arguing with him. I became so determined to make sure I won my place at nationals I started training like a maniac. I rose at 5 a.m. to do calisthenics and jump rope like a prizefighter. I hit balls in our driveway for an hour and a half before school, telling myself there was no way Kathy was going to beat me. I practiced again after school. Even when I wasn't physically practicing I was visualizing the match, picturing myself doing everything right. As I was washing dishes I'd daydream about seeing my second serves go in. In bed at night I'd imagine myself chasing down each ball, making every shot. Then I'd get up at the crack of dawn and start again.

And I did not lose that match. The Southern California Championships, like all my showdowns with Kathy, was a battle. But my game and my mind had turned a corner. I was relentless, determined, and steadier than I'd ever been. I won 6–3, 6–3.

Now Perry T. Jones grudgingly gave me permission to go to the nationals at Middletown. But he refused to cover my expenses. Later, when he found out that the Long Beach Tennis Patrons had stepped in to fill that void, he moved the goalposts yet again and added a new condition. "You'll need a chaperone," he told me.

Mom and Dad couldn't afford airline tickets. The only way I could get to Ohio was by train with my mother. We didn't have enough money for a sleeper cabin, and it took us three days one way. Mom suffered from motion sickness the entire trip and held an empty See's candy box under her chin when she felt like she might throw up. But she was a good sport.

I, on the other hand, absolutely loved the ride. I adored looking out the window and watching the scenery blur by, noticing how the land turned from desert to prairie to lush fields of wheat and corn. I loved the *clickety-clack* sound of the train wheels and how the swaying motion of the cars rocked me to sleep at night. It felt like a great adventure. It was bliss for a child who yearned to do great things and fantasized about going places.

When I got to Ohio everything was unfamiliar, starting with the gray Har-Tru clay courts, which are made of crushed stone. The only courts I had ever played on were concrete. Now it felt like I had marbles underfoot as I ran. It was hard to start and stop. To avoid overrunning the ball on clay once you finally do get going, you have to slide into shots, something I didn't yet know how to do. The bounces are also different, and the ball hung in the air more, which favored the pushers.

For the rest of my life, Har-Tru would be my worst surface (far worse than European red clay, which I actually ended up liking). I hadn't dropped a set in more than a month when I got to the nationals, but I lost decisively in the quarterfinals. Kathy Chabot and I got to the doubles finals but lost. She had trouble sliding too.

After the tournament, some of the girls went on from Ohio to Philadelphia and New Jersey to spend the rest of the summer on the grass court circuit. I couldn't go, and I was terribly sad as I watched their cars pull away from the hotel. When my mother saw me shoving away some tears she said, "Oh, honey, I'm so sorry we can't afford to send you with them."

"It's okay, Mom," I said. "Next year I'm going. Even if I have to hitchhike."

BY THE TIME I entered Long Beach Polytechnic High School as a tenth grader my tennis successes were starting to mount. My ranking was good enough to get me on the Wilson Sporting Goods list to receive two free rackets a year. I thought I had hit the big time. My parents and our extended family had attended Poly, and finally getting there myself in 1958 seemed like another rite of passage.

I felt a thrill every time I walked in Poly's front door past the sign that read "Home of SCHOLARS AND CHAMPIONS" and the Art Deco metal letters beneath that that ran the length of the entrance and read, "ENTER TO LEARN GO FORTH TO SERVE." I felt more grown-up walking across the sprawling campus with its large grassy courtyard in the middle. With more than three thousand students, Poly was bigger than some community colleges. The long interior hallways echoed with noise and spirited chatter. For the first time, I was in classes with kids of all different colors and backgrounds: Black, Brown, Asian, Native American. I loved it.

Poly was famous for its winning football, baseball, basketball, and track teams. But the closest a girl could get to a varsity sport was cheerleading. So while Randy could daydream about playing big-league baseball—the Dodgers had announced their move to Los Angeles the year before—more hard realities were leaking into my dreams. I still saw myself competing on Centre Court at Wimbledon. And yet, at that time it was impossible for a girl to imagine a long-term future as a tennis champion or a pro athlete, except on the fledgling LPGA Tour.

My internal conflict showed in a detailed composition I wrote for my sophomore English class that I began by imagining my life three years in the future, when I'd be eighteen:

> Here I am in New York City at 5 p.m. leaving by plane for Wimbledon, England. I still can't believe it. In one week I will be participating in what is considered to be the Tennis Championship of the World.

I described arriving at my London housing with an English family, how I delayed my morning practice on the grass courts until the city's famous fog had cleared. I seeded myself eighth and wrote expansive passages about every match I played until I lost in the quarterfinals to Darlene Hard, 10–8 in the third. I wrote a brief epilogue that included Ramsey Earnhart, a real-life heartthrob in California tennis who I had put onboard my imaginary flight to England with me. Now it was 1988:

> Here I am at home twenty-seven years later, sitting with my four wonderful children (at times they're wonderful). After the summer of '61 I entered Pomona College in California, spending five years and graduating with a master's degree. I married Ramsey Earnhart—remember that boy I met on the way to the plane that day? Even though I never did achieve my ambition in tennis, I'm so glad I went ahead and received a higher education than high school instead of turning out to be a tennis bum.

The conventional ending showed just how much I had started internalizing the standard script for middle-class white women of my generation. The boilerplate goal for a girl in my era on the cusp of adulthood was a college education at best and modest achievement, as long as it didn't interfere with marriage and children. Women were supposed to trade in their dreams for their husband's ambitions. It was my mother's stated dream for me too.

I still wanted to believe that I could lead a life without limits. But as I got older and looked around, it increasingly seemed like the world was telling me something else.

I'M OFTEN ASKED when I first questioned my sexuality, and I can only say it was a gradual awakening that didn't start until college. I know many people who say they knew they were gay in elementary school, but when I was growing up I had no idea. For the longest time I felt different. But I didn't know why. I didn't have the words.

People self-identify now when it comes to sexuality and gender, and I think it's a fantastic, positive development. Who you are is about how you feel inside. But it's hard to convey to many people today how different the world was for LGBTQ+ people then. Hardly anyone talked openly about gays and lesbians. It was literally dangerous to be gay, and almost unheard of to be out. Homosexuality was still criminalized in many states. The American Psychiatric Association, the largest organization of its kind in the world, listed homosexuality as a mental disorder until 1973 and didn't completely remove "sexual orientation disturbance" until 1987. Ignorance and fear, slurs and prejudices, acts of violence abounded.

I had crushes on plenty of boys beginning in grade school, and I loved that my parents were matter-of-fact about what goes on with our bodies. Mom gave me the birds-and-the-bees talk when I was in fifth grade. When she got to the part about how babies are conceived I said, "Ewwww. That's not fun, is it?" and she burst out laughing.

Beyond that, I can summarize the standard message girls received about sex in those days in three words: *Don't. Get. Pregnant.* Remember, in the 1950s there was no birth control pill. The Supreme Court's *Roe v. Wade* decision affirming a woman's right to get a legal abortion wasn't handed down until 1973. Unwed girls and women who got pregnant endured serious shaming. They were often told they "had" to get married or they disappeared from school, sometimes never to return.

Those kinds of messages—and other tensions over gender roles—crept into our family once Randy and I were seriously into sports. Our parents took side jobs because they barely had enough money to pay the bills. I sensed how Dad felt he had to live up to a standard of manhood that could be every bit as inhibiting as the rules women faced. He was uncomfortable that he couldn't provide enough with his firefighter's salary. His schedule allowed him to moonlight at a plastics factory. Mom sometimes sold Avon or Tupperware. She later took a job as a receptionist and a bookkeeper at a local blood lab. Before long, she was running the place and it was turning a profit, which she and the owner considered a triumph. But my father was occasionally insecure that Mom was working outside the home. They used to have long, intense discussions about work, sometimes even arguments. But the magic was that they talked it through.

"Your mother should've married someone with money," he'd tell me.

"Daddy, she wouldn't trade you for anything in the world," I'd reply.

Our exhausted parents became tired and cranky so often that Randy and I finally sat them down for a talk one night. We begged them to quit their side jobs. We said it wasn't worth it. When we offered to quit our sports instead, their eyes started to water. "You're not on earth to take care of us—we wanted you," my mother said.

Luckily, my tennis successes were continuing to pile up, which earned me some financial help from local tennis patrons. My father did quit his second job eventually. By January of my sophomore year I was No. 2 in my section of the state. By summer vacation I had kept my vow and earned my way onto the East Coast grass court circuit—and I didn't have to hitchhike to get there.

I was also chosen to tour with my first national select team, the 1959 U.S. Junior Wightman Cup squad, which was a huge honor. The cup was founded in 1923 by Hazel Hotchkiss Wightman, a great pre–World War I champion from California. Women's teams and girls' teams from Britain and the United States competed in five singles and two doubles matches. The cup went to whichever country's team won four matches first.

Southern Californian public-park players dominated our roster. The six of us who were on that junior team—Kathy Chabot, Pam Davis, Karen Hantze, Barbara Browning, Carole Caldwell, and me—remained friends for life. Few of us realized how good we were until we started competing back east that July. I took my first-ever plane ride to get there on a four-propeller Constellation that droned along at just over three hundred miles an hour. It took us eleven hours to fly from Los Angeles to Philadelphia, our starting point for the grass court circuit.

The tour was my first full immersion in the old-school East Coast tennis establishment. My world expanded in ways I couldn't have predicted. The Long Beach Tennis Patrons, the Century Club, and a few other local sponsors paid for me to tour, giving me just enough funds to get by. In the amateur tennis tradition, we saved money by staying as player-guests most of the time in the homes of tennis fans and wealthy supporters who were unfailingly welcoming, generous, and kind.

The Los Angeles Tennis Club and the show-biz swells there had always seemed swanky to me. But what I experienced on the East Coast, playing at venerated country clubs, experiencing day-to-day life with old-money host families who sometimes lived on sprawling estates, was a different kind of rich. Our team was on the move every week. It was quite an education.

Carole and I were chosen to room together, starting in Philadelphia. Our hosts were the Freunds, who lived in the upscale neighborhood of Chestnut Hill. Compared to California, everything in Philly seemed old and historic to me, from the Revolutionary War–era monuments to the cobblestone streets to the aged twin beds that Carole and I were assigned in the Freunds' top-floor bedroom. The mattresses sagged so much in the middle that my bum nearly touched the floor. Philadelphia was also where I discovered Bassetts Ice Cream, a delicious local specialty I couldn't stop eating.

Staying in private homes was a great way to meet people and learn how to get along with all types. I had to learn more of the social graces that were part of the tennis circuit culture, such as socializing during mixers at the elite private clubs that hosted our events. There was a pattern to these conversations. I'd be holding a glass of water in my hand, chatting with club members who were drinking highballs. One of the older men or women would inevitably lean over toward fifteen-year-old me and say, "So, tell me young lady, what are you *really* going to do with your life? Or are you going to be a tennis bum?"

I am doing what I want with my life, was what I wanted to say. Instead, I'd smile politely and say nothing, or assure them that I planned to attend college and marry because I knew that's what they wanted to hear.

When we arrived in South Orange, New Jersey, our next stop after Philly, I got to play the newly crowned Wimbledon singles champion, nineteen-year-old Maria Bueno of Brazil, on a sticky summer afternoon. She barely beat me, 6–4, 6–4, in a gritty match.

As I was packing my rackets, I was still replaying some points in my head and feeling a bit low about shots I'd missed. A man with black-rimmed glasses and a big, friendly smile came over and introduced himself. "Hi. I'm Frank Brennan," he said. "Don't let this get you down. You're going to be No. 1."

Nobody had ever said anything like that to me before. I was so taken aback I just stared at him.

Frank told me that he was a tennis coach who always checked out new players at the tournament. In the coming years, this generous, helpful man would become an influential mentor and contributor to my game. That first day, he had noticed that I was still playing with nylon strings and said he'd get me some Pakistani-made natural gut strings. Gut is more expensive but strongly preferred by top players for the better spin and control it helps create. He also explained that he was a self-taught player who worked for the U.S. Post Office and ran his own tennis camp on the weekends.

Soon after our first encounter, Frank invited me to his home in Fairlawn, New Jersey, for dinner with his family. I was accustomed to orderly dinners at my home, but mealtime with the Brennans was an Irish American free-for-all. He and his wife Lillian had nine kids—soon to be ten—and the "Amen" at the end of grace was like a starting pistol. Silverware flashed. Crumbs flew. There were so many Brennans they attended church in shifts.

The Brennan family would become like an extension of my own. I began staying with them on my trips back east, and Frank started coaching me. Clyde Walker was still my coach in Long Beach, and to his credit he never minded when someone else wanted to help. Frank was the first coach who traveled with me to some of my events. Eventually, he quit his post office job and ran an indoor/outdoor tennis facility that he built with a business partner, and I'd return there with other top players to hold clinics. His chats with me about strategy helped sharpen my game significantly. But he could also be blunt. He was the man who made the searing offhanded remark to me that "You'll be good because you're ugly" after predicting I could be No. 1. We were seated at the dinner table when he said it, and Lillian and a few of their kids told him, "That's horrible!"

Men routinely took the liberty of sharply remarking on women's appearances then. I think what Frank was trying to say, in his clumsy way, was that because I was pudgy and wore thick glasses I wouldn't have to deal with boys wanting to date me. It was untrue even then, but that didn't lessen the sting. I got past the remark after I got to know Frank better. And anyway, I had more towns to see and bigger battles to fight.

I WAS A HAPPY VAGABOND that summer. In addition to Philadelphia and South Orange, the eastern grass court circuit took us to events in Haverford, Pennsylvania, Wilmington, Delaware, then back to the Philly area for the U.S. National Lawn Tennis Association girls' eighteen-and-under championships, then on to the U.S. National Championships at Forest Hills. We had so much fun being on our own and traveling together. I was the youngest of the group, yet I somehow became everyone's confidante. Minor spats, boyfriend trouble, tennis dreams—I knew all, revealed nothing.

We spent one week at the Delaware estate of Willie and Margaret Osborne du Pont. She was a veteran member of our Wightman Cup team who was still winning matches into her forties, and she taught Carole and me how to use utensils properly at a formal dinner table. Willie, born in England, was a tiny, eccentric man who dressed in old-fashioned britches and puffed on a Sherlock Holmes–style pipe. He was one of the richest men in America, but he liked to smoke his own hams in an outbuilding on his enormous estate and rise at the crack of dawn to personally check on his thoroughbred racehorses. He would give me tours of the grounds in his old Chevy with a stick shift. One night I was startled to see him fall asleep at dinner midsentence. "Oh, that happens all the time," Margaret told us with a wave of her hand, carrying on as if nothing were amiss.

We stayed another week at the Oyster Bay, New York, estate of Rosalind P. Walter, the Squibb pharmaceutical heiress. The Broadway songwriters Redd Evans and John Jacob Loeb wrote the popular "Rosie the Riveter" song for Rosalind after she went to work at an aircraft plant in Connecticut during the war effort.

At one point that summer, the U.S. Lawn Tennis Association invited the great Maureen Connolly and England's Mary Hardwick to Philadelphia for a series of clinics with the junior girls. I had never met either woman, but I had been reading about them for years. I was beyond excited when I got to hit one-on-one with Maureen one day. As she walked ahead of me to the court I could see the deep scar on her right calf where the muscle had been gashed in her career-ending horseback-riding accident at nineteen. What made the timing of her injury more tragic was that she had swept the four Grand Slam singles titles in 1953, the year before she was hurt. She had tried desperately to make a comeback and failed. But her strokes were still exquisitely clean, crisp, and consistent when we practiced.

When Maureen invited me to dinner that night, I was ecstatic. As soon as we took our seats in the restaurant I started pelting her with questions. She was high-spirited, and I remember how her eyes flashed as she spoke. I wanted to know everything about her life, how she made it to No. 1, what she could tell me about how I could get better. At least she waited for dessert to deliver the blow. I was devastated when she said, "I don't think you have what it takes to be a champion. You're too self-centered, too undisciplined, and too egotistical to make it to the top."

I think I just went blank at that point. I sat there motionless. What made my unexpected dressing down all the more painful and surprising was that I'd heard that Maureen was usually such a kind person. I swallowed hard, but I didn't cry. I may have even thanked her for her observations on my dazed walk out the door. I got up the next morning and tried to play it off as if nothing had happened, but her words haunted me. I pulled out of it mostly by reminding myself that she didn't really know me. I told myself nobody could stop me but me.

A few years later, a friend of Maureen's approached me at Forest Hills with a story that he wanted to share. He told me he had been standing with Maureen at an event that same summer of 1959, discussing which of the girls might become great players. Maureen pointed at me and told him to watch for me, and only me. I looked at the man in disbelief. I had heard tales about how Maureen's coach, Eleanor "Teach" Tennant, goaded her players into better performance. Had Maureen been using the same reverse psychology on me? Maybe she thought praise would go to my head. She may have sensed my independent streak and figured, correctly, that I would react by trying to show her how wrong she was about me. But I'll never know for sure.

We never spoke about that conversation or, for that matter, about Maureen's quote in *World Tennis* magazine a few months after I met her saying that I could stand to lose twenty pounds, my groundstrokes needed improvement, and I took too many shortcuts. Maureen was correct about the first two—I could barely fit into my tennis dress after all the Bassetts Ice Cream and other goodies I ate on that first trip away from home, and the continental grip we were taught in California had disadvantages that affected our strokes. But shortcuts? I never took a tennis shortcut in my life.

I saw Maureen occasionally when I played the tour full-time. She was always friendly. She spent most of her time by then in Texas with her two children and her husband, Norman Brinker, the founder of restaurant chains including Steak & Ale, who was also credited with popularizing the salad bar. I think Maureen and I could have been good friends if we'd gotten to know each other, but she died of ovarian cancer in 1969. She was only thirty-four.

OUR SOUTHERN CALIFORNIA Junior Wightman Cup team marked our return to Philadelphia by rolling to the National Junior Girls Intersectionals title at the Germantown Cricket Club. We went undefeated in the twenty one matches we played that week, a record that still stands. Our next and last stop of the summer was New York City to play the U.S. National Championships at the West Side Tennis Club in Forest Hills. This was my first visit to one of the four majors, so it was a very big deal. I think we were all amazed, even occasionally overwhelmed, by the huge skyscrapers, the crowds thronging the Manhattan sidewalks, the taxis, the horns, the bustle and noise.

Our team was staying at the Roosevelt Hotel in Midtown. There were six of us sardined into one room with no air conditioning. At least the hotel was conveniently located just a few blocks from the subway we took to Queens. Once we disembarked there, I loved walking through the Tudor-style section of Forest Hills to get to the club. I knew that Alfred Hitchcock had filmed some of the scenes there for *Strangers on a Train,* one of my favorite movies, so being there myself now felt somehow familiar.

The clubhouse at the West Side Tennis Club had a stucco exterior, gabled roofs, and half-timber beams. The dark-paneled interior walls were lined with photos of past champions, and I studied them all. I loved sitting on the terrace overlooking the courts, sipping orange juice or a soda and watching the sun set behind the beautiful horseshoe-shaped main stadium. At the time there was also a fifteen-foot-high billboard of the tournament draws, and a person on a ladder would fill in the results as matches were played.

I was paired in the first round with one of the strongest girls,

Justina Bricka, a cagey sixteen-year-old lefthander from Missouri. I remember being up a set and ahead 5–4 in the second; I even had her at match point, 30–40. I lost anyway. Eliminated on day one.

Summer was over, and our Wightman Cup gang was breaking up. It was time to go back to school. We had all grown so close, parting felt bittersweet.

I flew from New York's Idlewild Airport (now JFK) back to Los Angeles nonstop. The flight was on a jet this time and took only five and a half hours, not eleven. As I peered out the window as the plane banked away from the airport I felt years older—even more sophisticated—than when I had left home.

As special as my first summer circuit trip was, my parents and I rarely talked with each other all those weeks because long-distance calls were so expensive. I was excited to land in sunny Los Angeles and scan the crowd in the arrivals hall for Mom and Dad. But somehow, we walked right past each other. When I turned around to see if I'd missed them, I finally heard my mother say, "Billie Jean . . . is that you?" El Chubbo had gained so much weight that my parents didn't recognize their own daughter. My mother wasn't thrilled, but neither she nor Dad said anything. During the drive south to Long Beach, I told them about how great our junior girls did, about my first look at Manhattan and Forest Hills, about the magnificent homes we stayed in elsewhere. But Mom and Dad, God bless them, really only wanted to know one thing: "Are you still loving tennis and having fun?"

I was loving it, all right. More than ever.

Chapter 4

M Y SUMMER RESULTS WERE strong enough to convince me to enter the main draw of the Pacific Southwest Championships that were held at the Los Angeles Tennis Club a month after I returned home, in addition to playing again in the junior division. I was fifteen, and moving up to the women's competition was a milestone moment. I advanced to the third round before I lost to twenty-year-old Ann Haydon in a brutally tough match. She barely held on 7–5 in the third. People noticed. When I came off the court, a Long Beach real estate investor named Harold Guiver jogged up to congratulate me and said, "I love the way you play, Billie Jean. I want to send you to Wimbledon. You're really good."

Harold was a terrific club player who stood only five feet four but he used to outwit nearly all his opponents, even Pancho Gonzalez when they were teenagers and playing for quarters on the public courts of Los Angeles. Harold was also a brilliant businessman and a world-class contract bridge player. He cared deeply about kids. I had no doubt he could raise the money to pay my expenses for a shot at Wimbledon. My dream of all dreams.

"Thanks, Mr. Guiver, but I'm not good enough yet."

He looked shocked and said, "Wait—you don't want to go?"

"Oh, I want to go terribly," I assured him. "But I haven't earned it. I don't deserve it yet."

He smiled and nodded. "When you're ready, we'll do it," he promised. "And I'll get some other Long Beach people to help you."

How many kids do you think would turn down that kind of offer?

But I had absorbed my parents' ethics. Also, I had seen Althea play by now and I had practiced with Darlene Hard and I didn't think I was ready for Wimbledon. I knew I was still developing my game.

As if to prove it, I lost the Pacific Southwest junior title that week to Karen Hantze, my Junior Wightman Cup teammate from San Diego. I had only beaten Karen once before, and I really thought I could do it this time. I even dominated her in the first set. But it was another match that slipped away from me. She won, 2–6, 9–7, 9–7. I couldn't finish her off. I was stuck. Then I had a wonderful piece of luck.

When I was younger, everyone—including Clyde Walker—compared me to the great Alice Marble because she was very aggressive and she had a terrific volley. I researched her and read that between 1936 and 1940 Alice had won eighteen Grand Slam titles—five in singles, six in women's doubles, and seven in mixed doubles. So I was very aware of who Alice was when Joe Bixler, the same big-hearted Wilson rep who had interceded for me at my first tournament after I arrived late, approached me one day at the Los Angeles Tennis Club. Joe told me Alice had seen me play in the Pacific Southwest women's draw and thought I showed great promise. "I've talked to her," Joe added, "and she'll teach you, if you want."

If I want? I couldn't believe it. I asked Clyde if it was okay to work with Alice—I didn't want him to feel I was deserting him—and he gave me his blessing immediately. "Are you kidding?" he said. "You get to learn from a former No. 1 player in the world like Alice Marble? I've taught you as much as I can, Billie Jean. It's time for you to learn from a champion."

Alice lived alone in a yellow-and-white bungalow in the working-class town of Tarzana out in the San Fernando Valley. Her living room was filled with memorabilia from her days as a triple-crown winner at Wimbledon, a five-time Grand Slam singles champion, and the top-ranked player in the world. During the week, Alice worked as a receptionist at a doctor's office. On weekends she gave tennis instruction on a neighbor's court. When I started training with her, she was forty-six years old with one functioning lung and a pack-a-day cigarette habit. Yet nothing dampened her fire.

Every Saturday morning when I didn't have a tournament my mom or dad drove me the forty-three miles from Long Beach to Tarzana. I would work all afternoon with Alice and stay overnight in her spare room. We worked all day Sunday until one of my parents picked me up and we made the long drive back.

The first time Alice put me through a drill we stood across from each other in the front court and she pounded balls at me over the net. Some of the blasts could have knocked me flat. Her rationale for it was not unlike a similar drill that Jimmy Connors's mother, Gloria, a former player herself, put Jimmy through as a boy, slamming balls at him while exhorting, "Get your tiger juices flowing, Jimmy! Tiger juices! If your own mother will do this to you, imagine what those other players will do!"

Alice was a tough woman. It became clear pretty quickly that she thought I was too soft. She could be encouraging but intense at the same time, and her demanding approach was just what I needed. I was in awe of her. The framed photographs on her walls were a reflection of her rich and varied life: diving for a volley at Forest Hills; posing between Clark Gable and Cesar Romero; dancing at the Wimbledon Ball with her mixed-doubles partner Bobby Riggs after each of them had swept all three titles at the 1939 championships. She pulled off the same sweep at the U.S. Nationals.

A promoter paid Alice $50,000 to turn pro after those triumphs. She toured for a year with Don Budge, Bill Tilden, and Mary Hardwick, dominating Mary 72–3 in their head-to-head series. She helped entertain troops during the war. My father saw Alice play an exhibition in Norfolk, Virginia, and remembered how impressive she was.

I spent hours sitting on Alice's overstuffed living room chair with her cat curling around my ankles as I thumbed through her scrapbooks. Sometimes she'd play the guitar and sing to me in the evenings in English and Spanish. Often, she would tell me stories.

Alice grew up in a blue-collar family in San Francisco and loved sports, particularly baseball, which her two older brothers played. The San Francisco Seals, a minor league team, adopted Alice as its mascot when she was thirteen, and she entertained fans by shagging fly balls during pre-game warmups. She sometimes played catch with the Seals' up-and-coming star Joe DiMaggio, who was also from San Francisco. DiMaggio later told a reporter, "She had a pretty good throwing arm."

When Alice's brother gave her a tennis racket at fifteen she learned to serve and volley on the public courts of Golden Gate Park because she realized she couldn't play baseball for a living. During the peak of her career between the two world wars she played the kind of attacking, power tennis that had been the exclusive domain of male stars like Don Budge. She stood five feet seven, often preferred to play in shorts rather than a skirt, and had the strongest serve anyone had ever seen by a woman. She charged the net and hit deep, penetrating drives that kept her opponents pinned in the backcourt. The press adored her independent streak and blond good looks as well as her game.

It didn't hurt that large swaths of Alice's life seemed lifted from a Hollywood movie. In 1934, when she was twenty-one, Alice collapsed during a match in Paris and was diagnosed with tuberculosis and pleurisy. She was told she would never compete again. As she fought her way back, Alice pursued a sideline career as a professional singer and made her debut at the Waldorf Astoria in New York in 1937, the same year she won a doubles title at the U.S. Championships.

Alice told me and anyone else who would listen that she had secretly worked with Army intelligence during World War II. She wrote in her memoir, *Courting Danger,* published just before her death in 1990, that she was shot in the back while escaping a Nazi double agent during a mission in Switzerland. Her friends in the tennis world were skeptical. But who's to say it didn't happen?

Alice was a civil rights activist as well as an early feminist. She talked about a day when women and girls wouldn't be censured for loving sports. As a writer for DC Comics, she oversaw the "Wonder Women of History" series about real-life role models such as Florence Nightingale, Susan B. Anthony, and Marie Curie.

One of her proudest accomplishments was helping Althea Gibson break the color barrier in tennis. By the end of the 1940s, Althea was the top woman in the all-Black American Tennis Association, but she still couldn't compete at the U.S. Lawn Tennis Association tournaments because she was African American. Alice wrote a famous editorial in the July 1950 issue of *American Lawn Tennis* magazine that made a case for integrating amateur tennis. "If tennis is a game for ladies and gentlemen," she wrote, "it's also time we acted a little more like gentlepeople and less like sanctimonious hypocrites . . . If Althea Gibson represents a challenge to the present crop of women players, it's only fair that they should meet the challenge on the courts." Alice added that if Althea was barred from the upcoming U.S. Championships at Forest Hills there would be "an ineradicable mark against a game to which I have devoted most of my life, and I would be bitterly ashamed."

The USLTA relented. There is a photo of Alice walking next to Althea down a gravel path at Forest Hills as Althea arrived to play one of her historic first matches. Althea and Alice are beaming and there are throngs of people jammed along the chain link fence, some of them applauding.

To me, Alice's public support of Althea remains every bit as important as Pee Wee Reese famously throwing an arm around his Brooklyn Dodgers teammate Jackie Robinson on the field as a sign of support while racists were making Jackie's life miserable. The civil rights fight was just coming to sports, and Alice was ahead of the curve. Without her intervention, who knows when or if Althea would've commenced collecting her six major singles titles or the Grand Slam doubles crowns she won with Britain's Angela Buxton, who also encountered discrimination on the circuit—including from Perry T. Jones. In 2019, Angela said Jones prevented her from continuing in a tournament at the Los Angeles Tennis Club after someone saw her competing and told him, "Don't you know she's a Jew?"

It was Angela who asked Althea to play doubles together in 1956, five years after Althea broke the color barrier at the majors. "No one has ever asked me before—of course I will," Althea told her. When a statue honoring Althea was installed on the U.S. Open grounds sixty-three years later, Angela journeyed to New York from her home in England, though she was not well, to honor her late friend.

For all of Alice's triumphs in tennis, her personal life was touched by tragedy. One night I asked her, "Alice, have you ever been in love?"

"Yes, with Joe," she said as she lit another cigarette, and then took a long pull. "He got killed in the war."

That's all she told me. I later read that Alice said she had married a handsome American fighter pilot named Joe Crowley. He was shot down over Germany ten days after she was in a car wreck and had a miscarriage with their first child back in the States. In her grief, Alice swallowed a handful of pills in a near-successful suicide attempt.

Her best friend, the actress Carole Lombard, also died in a plane crash. In 1946 Alice's right lung became so infected that most of it had to be removed. Alice missed two years of competition because of her compromised health, and whatever savings she had was mostly gone. That's why she was working as a receptionist and moonlighting as a tennis instructor when I met her.

Alice made an indelible mark on my life and my game. When we started working together in the fall of 1959 I was ranked nineteenth in the women's national rankings. After our four months together I had leapt to No. 4. Alice taught me things you can only learn from someone who's been the best in the world. She was the first of them who really explained the art and intricacies of tennis to me.

One day during a session she walked me from the baseline almost halfway to the net and pointed down, saying, "This is the service line, right?"

"Yes, ma'am."

She swept her racket back and forth in front of us and said, "This is the midcourt?"

Again, I said yes.

"Billie Jean, this is where most matches are won or lost. It's the players who miss these—the easy ones, the gimmes—that lose."

I already knew there were offensive, defensive, and neutral shots in tennis. But Alice strengthened my focus on where the ball landed, its speed and its spin, and then making smart, split-second decisions. I was losing too many matches after I got a significant lead.

It was Alice who first zeroed in on teaching me a different level of concentration, intensity, new ways to think. She never gave away points—she demanded that each point be played like match point, full out. She improved my forehand technique, showing me that I was hitting the ball too close to my body.

Another day she casually told me, "Your backhand volley is much better than mine." I was sixteen and the immortal Alice Marble was telling me this? I felt my face redden and I said, "Oh, no, Alice. It can't be." She said, "I am telling you, your backhand volley is excellent." Moments like that can work magic on a player's self-confidence. I was determined to use my backhand volley more and it became one of my signature shots.

Alice's independence, self-possession, and star quality also taught me a lot about how a champion behaved in the world. She always dressed well and looked sharp. She saw no conflict between being gracious and strongly asserting her opinions. When someone was helpful or hospitable, she wrote them a personal thank-you note, which became a habit of mine, too. After we finished our regular sessions on the court that was owned by her friend Mickey Goldsen, a famous music publisher as well as a tennis fan, we would always take time to hit with Mickey or his kids as a way of showing gratitude. Alice was teaching me how to build and nurture relationships. She believed that the little things matter and that they add up.

It's too bad I blew our relationship in the end.

Alice was not well, and she slept with a big green oxygen tank next to her bed. I could hear her hacking and coughing in her room when I stayed overnight. Every time Alice would fit one of her cigarettes into her little white plastic holder I wanted to stop her and beg her not to smoke. I could tell the cigarettes were making Alice sicker, and I worried about her. Every time Alice coughed it reminded me of my father's sister, Gladys, who died at thirty-six after a long and painful fight with cancer.

All of that was somewhere in the back of my mind one Friday evening when the phone rang in our kitchen and I ran to pick it up. It was Alice. She sounded awful. "Billie Jean, I'm sick in bed with pneumonia," she said. I could hear her rattling and gasping over the line. I didn't know what to say, and I blurted, "Well, I guess that means I won't be coming tomorrow."

"You selfish little brat," she snapped. She said I was rude and thoughtless and that I didn't care about anything but myself and tennis. Then she hung up on me.

I dropped the phone and ran into my bedroom. I was already crying as I flopped facedown on the bed. My mother was right behind me, saying, "Sis! What happened? What's wrong?"

Mom called Alice immediately to apologize after I explained. Normally, my parents would have made me make the call, but I was too upset to talk, too afraid of making another mistake. Looking back now, I wish I had gotten on the phone and told Alice myself that I didn't mean to sound so selfish, and that I was so sorry she was sick. Maybe that would have changed her mind. But I'll never know. Alice told my mom I should find a different coach. We never worked together again.

Alice lived another thirty years. She later said that because of our weekends together she discovered that she really liked coaching. She quit the doctor's office job and started training players full-time and organizing tournaments. When I won my first Wimbledon singles title in 1966, Alice wrote me a lovely, touching note. I wrote to her, too, and when I saw her at tournaments we were always cordial. But the abrupt end of our working relationship remains a regret. I was still young, but I was getting the sense that it didn't just take a village to raise a tennis champion. The higher altitudes of tennis could be a brass-knuckles place.

Chapter 5

I WENT FROM an A student in tenth grade to Cs and Ds in eleventh grade, even in subjects I enjoyed like biology and Spanish. I was getting a world-class tennis education, but my head was no longer in school. Along with playing tennis in my senior year, which began in 1960, I was dating a boy named Barry, my first deep love. He was an eighteen-year-old from Pacific Grove who was on his way to the University of California at Berkeley, where he played on the tennis team. I had dated other boys but I can't explain the chemistry between us because beyond tennis, we weren't alike at all. I was freckled and pale. He had dark hair and olive skin. He was studious. I was obsessed with tennis. He was Jewish. I wasn't.

I was serious enough about Barry, who was a year older, to wonder if I should apply to a college in the Bay Area too. But my grades had dropped off so much that the better universities like Berkeley were probably out of reach for me. Barry and I were also spending nearly all our time apart. The inevitable finally happened. A "Dear Billie" letter arrived. I found it on our piano, just like the other letters he used to send me.

I don't know how much our breakup had to do with religion. The funny thing is, Barry and I both ended up in life relationships with nice Jewish girls.

I debated throughout the 1960 presidential campaign with my conservative father. His dislike of Catholics, including John F. Kennedy, traced back to his biological grandmother being forced to surrender his mom for adoption at the Catholic-run home for unwed mothers where she was living when Blanche was born. I think Richard Nixon was the first Republican that Dad, a staunch union man, ever voted for. He explained it by grousing that he wasn't about to vote for the son of an Irish Catholic bootlegger just because Kennedy was a Democrat.

I, on the other hand, was ready for the New Frontier that Kennedy spoke about on the way to winning the election. I argued with my father that Kennedy's faith shouldn't matter and reminded Dad that he'd always told me that freedom of religion was a protected right in America. Kennedy was forty-three years old, our most dashing and youngest president ever elected, and I loved his inaugural address, in which he declared that "the torch has passed to a new generation of Americans." I was inspired by his talk of ushering in a new progressive era, and the ways he challenged every individual to funnel energy into lifting the nation and the world.

Idealism was in the air, and I was feeling it, too, until a disturbing incident that I've never discussed anywhere else, except in therapy. I was invited to take a road trip through Nevada and Arizona with two of my favorite female teachers and their families. They were traveling in separate cars to visit an out-of-state friend. I think I was invited along to babysit the small children that both couples had. I won't use the teachers' names here to protect the privacy of their children. Let's just call them Mrs. Smith and Mrs. Jones.

I rode the outbound leg of the trip with Mr. and Mrs. Smith and their son, who was maybe three or four at the time. Things got strange soon after we arrived at our destination. I was settling into a guest bedroom in their friends' house when Mr. Smith perfunctorily knocked on my door and let himself in. I was sitting on my bed reading, and I was startled. He pulled up a chair to sit close to me by the bed.

"You've been around a lot, haven't you?" he began.

"I don't know what you mean," I said.

"You know. You play tennis all over the place. You must have been with a lot of guys."

"What are you talking about—I've never slept with *anybody*!" I said truthfully. I couldn't believe this was happening, and I was frightened. Why was he here? Why was he acting so inappropriately and so unconcerned that his wife and son were in the next room? I asked Mr. Smith to leave, and he reluctantly did. When I heard the door click, I jammed the chair frame underneath the doorknob, just to be safe.

Today a sixteen-year-old girl might handle that situation differently. She might use her cell phone to reach someone she trusted for help or call an Uber and get the hell out of there. But I didn't see an easy way out. I felt like I couldn't tell his wife or friends because I didn't know if they would believe me. It would be my word against his.

I kept my distance from the Smiths the rest of that week. When it came time to drive back to Long Beach, I told my other teacher, "I really want to spend more time with you and Mr. Jones. Can I ride with you?" When Mrs. Smith interjected, "Oh no, we live closer. We'll take her," I was immediately anxious but again felt I had no choice.

At one point during the long drive back to Long Beach I was stretched out in the rear area of the Smiths' station wagon and dozing not far from their little boy, who was fast asleep. We were driving across the pitch-black California desert when I heard Mr. Smith announcing, "I'm tired." Then Mrs. Smith said, "Oh honey, why don't you lie down in the back and let me drive?"

We pulled over, and soon Mr. Smith was lying next to me. I turned away, but when the car started moving again I felt his hands on my back—then his right hand slid over my shoulder and down the front of my blouse. "Stop it!" I said in a hushed voice, yet as defiantly as I could. He ignored me as I shoved his hand away, and he tried again. My heart was beating out of my chest. "No!" I said over my shoulder, twisting farther away. The little boy was still slumbering next to us, and Mrs. Smith just kept driving. How did she not hear me? Mr. Smith refused to stop, so I turned back toward him now to confront him. Again I said, "Stop it!" Unfazed, he touched my breasts with one hand as he moved his other hand to grope between my legs.

That's when I gritted my teeth and punched him so hard in the chest it stunned him. He stared at me, and I kept my left fist clenched as I told him in a cold, hushed voice, "If you touch me again I will tell my dad. And he will kill you. I mean it. He will *kill* you."

That stopped him. He pulled away.

The second the Smiths' car stopped in front of my house I threw open the door and ran up the front steps with my bag. I took a deep breath to steady myself before going inside to see my parents and I gave them a big hug and acted as if nothing had happened. I wasn't kidding when I said my father would've tried to kill Mr. Smith for assaulting me. I didn't want my father to end up in prison, so I told no one.

Six decades later, the memory was revived by the torrent of similar or worse abuse stories that the #MeToo and TIME'S UP movements brought bubbling up. As we've learned, too, from the widespread abuses of boys by clergy members, the fear of speaking up about abuse is an all-too-common scenario, especially when there's a power imbalance involved. For a while after my episode, I flinched whenever I ran into older men in certain situations, or if I saw a man who resembled the one who assaulted me. I sometimes would sit in our living room looking at my father and thinking, *He has no idea what happened*. In time, I pushed the incident out of my mind.

My ability to suppress such unpleasant experiences rather than deal with them caused me a lot of angst later in life, when I habitually ignored, buried, or hid what was really going on. Of all the values my parents instilled in us, the most important was integrity. You didn't lie. You didn't cheat. You stood up for what is right. But I couldn't be true to myself or anyone else about some things, especially when the truth seemed explosive. That's a hard and lonely place to be. I would come to know it well. I was mastering what my mother meant when she told me, "Everyone has their secrets, Billie Jean."

IN THE SPRING of my senior year the USLTA ranked me No. 4 in the United States in both singles and doubles. When Harold Guiver, the businessman who had wanted to send me to Wimbledon the previous summer, made the offer again, I said yes. I felt I had put in the work and reaped enough results, thanks to Alice Marble, to earn a ticket to the center of the tennis universe. I will always be grateful for a favor that Perry T. Jones did for me that year as well, because I might not have done it for myself. He called me into his office at the Los Angeles Tennis Club one day and told me that Wimbledon had changed its rules and would no longer allow players to compete in both the juniors and the main draw, so I had to choose one.

"What do you think I should do?" I said.

The Czar said, "I think you should play the Wimbledon main draw."

Though the two-week tournament is located in the village of Wimbledon, technically it is hosted by the All England Lawn Tennis & Croquet Club. The club formally refers to the Wimbledon fortnight as simply "the Championships," as if the event resides on a plane of its own. Which it does. Wimbledon's history stretches back to 1877 for men; women joined play in 1884. I had been reading about the place and the origins of tennis in Victorian England since I was a little girl. To be No. 1, you had to win Wimbledon.

My roundtrip airfare to London and other expenses would cost $2,000, about as much as a new Volkswagen Beetle. Harold personally pledged some seed money and started a fund-raising drive to come up with the rest. He approached the Long Beach Tennis Patrons, the Century Club, local mom-and-pop businesses in Long Beach, even friends of friends. So many people chipped in. I didn't think things could get any better until Karen Hantze, my recent Junior Wightman Cup teammate, approached me one day at the Los Angeles Tennis Club and asked me to play doubles with her at Wimbledon. *I'm living a dream,* I told myself.

As much as I enjoyed the self-reliance and independent thinking that singles require, I've always loved doubles more. I like the variables, the strategy, the camaraderie and collaboration involved. Most of all, I love being on teams. Being able to share victories or ride out setbacks together was a welcome change from always going it alone as a singles player.

Karen and I had to sort out an early technicality about our partnership. Both of us typically played the left side of the doubles court, which is supposedly the dominant player's side. We flipped a coin to decide who stayed there. I lost. It turned out to be perhaps my luckiest coin toss ever. Having to learn to play on the right side, too, made me a much more versatile player. Ken Rosewall, one of the great Australian champions, once told me the most important point of every game was the first point, because it's how you establish momentum. Since every new game starts with a serve to the right court, there was more pressure on me to execute my service return there. I loved the added responsibility.

Karen and I got a nice sendoff when we left home in early June to play a couple of the British warmup tournaments before Wimbledon. We posed for newspaper photographers at Los Angeles International Airport, two California teenagers heading abroad wearing our ready-for-England coats and self-conscious smiles. We held up our rackets like the pros do so the Wilson logo was visible for the cameras, even though nobody was paying us to do it.

A day later I caught my first glimpse of England through the early-morning haze as our plane neared Heathrow Airport. The fields and foliage down below were so intensely green it seemed surreal. As we descended, the panorama of sparkling lakes and red-roofed houses came into sharper focus, and soon I could see the hedgerows and cars driving on the wrong side of the road. My knees were bouncing in place even before we landed. When I stepped off the plane my lungs filled with the cool, damp air. I had been here so many times in my mind it felt like déjà vu. I was anxious, but in a good way. Like the feeling you get when you're falling in love.

Mary Hardwick, the retired British tennis player, picked us up at Heathrow. She drove Karen and me to Bailey's, a once-elegant Victorian hotel near the Gloucester Road tube station in London. The next morning, Karen and I traveled to suburban Beckenham for the Kent Grass Court Championships, a Wimbledon tune-up. We stayed with an elderly woman in a dank, poorly heated house near a cricket ground. Karen and I shared an enormous upstairs room with two beds. We were each given five blankets and a hot-water bottle.

That night Karen and I lay awake in the dark, still buzzing because of the eight-hour time difference from Los Angeles. We tried to stay warm and talk over a downpour that sounded like metal ball bearings clattering on the roof. From across the room Karen said, "Hey Billie Jean, isn't it your high school graduation tonight? Would you rather be here or there?"

"Are you kidding me?" I said with a laugh. I had missed my senior prom and countless other things for tennis. Look where I was instead! "This is a privilege," I told Karen. "There's nowhere else in the world I'd rather be."

The tournaments leading up to Wimbledon are a much bigger deal in England and Europe than they are in the United States. I couldn't believe that the crowds and reporters from newspapers all over the world came hoping to get an early handle on who might win the championships. One of my favorite writers was Gerald Williams from the *Daily Mail* of London. With his black Clark Kent glasses and proper manners, Gerry seemed more like a scholarly headmaster than the sportswriters I encountered back home. He was married to a Scottish tennis player, and his knowledge of tennis was extensive. He went on to become one of the great BBC tennis announcers.

Gerry developed a paternal fondness for Karen and me and showed us the ropes. He would sometimes give us a lift in his car when we needed a ride. As usual, I was full of questions: *Why does everyone eat strawberries and cream during the championships?* Answer: The dish was a popular treat among the rich when it was served at the first Wimbledon in 1877, and the summer's first strawberry harvest coincides with the tournament. *Who gets to sit in the Royal Box at Centre Court?* Friends and guests of Wimbledon, including the royal family.

"What's Centre Court like?" I asked Gerry one day.

"Ahhh, come along, Billie Jean," he said. "You have to have a look at the place before the tournament starts. There's nothing like it in the world."

My pulse quickened as Gerry steered his little car down the narrow suburban London streets, by the brick townhouses and through the roundabouts until we were rolling down Church Road and—there it was! I was finally here! We had arrived at the black wrought iron gates of the All England Club and my first look at the place couldn't have been more perfect. The lush grounds were empty and still. Everything inside was dark green and purple, including the hydrangeas in large planters and masses of petunias spilling out of hanging baskets everywhere I looked. I remember the smell of the just-clipped grass as we walked in and the misty plumes of water that the sprinklers threw off as we passed the empty outside courts.

We followed a paved walkway and finally, looming in front of us, I saw Centre Court for the first time, the ivy-covered showplace where the biggest matches are played. I had been dreaming of this place for so long, and it was even better than I had imagined. It stood five stories high. From the outside it seemed even more massive than I had expected, more like a twentieth-century colosseum than a tennis stadium. Once inside, we walked in one of the painted cinder-block corridors and then ascended the ramps that led to the upper grandstands. When we neared the top, Gerry said, "Close your eyes and don't peek until I tell you." I trusted Gerry as he led me up the last bit of stairs and said, "All right. You can look now."

Down below was the most beautiful tennis court ever created.

I'm not sure how long we lingered there—I just know I tried to drink in every detail. As I looked around I was struck by the perfect symmetry of the place. The grass was impeccably groomed and a rich shade of green. Centre Court is so sacred that nobody is permitted to play on it the other fifty weeks of the year, except on special occasions like the Olympics. The hand-operated scoreboard was blank, awaiting its next names, but the large clock showed the right time of day. The walls and seats and railings were painted the same dark green as the rest of the grounds. The feeling was serene.

The tiered stands at Centre Court held more than fourteen thousand people and yet, once we were inside, the space felt intimate. The acoustics were astonishing, too, as I would soon find out. Even when Centre Court is packed, the crowd falls utterly quiet before each serve is struck. But during and after each point players are confronted by a wall of sound after they win a great rally, shrieks of panic when a drop shot seems likely to parachute down just out of reach, and patronizing "aaahs" when a makeable shot is missed. Sometimes the crowd gasps at double faults or titters after some points like a jury shocked by some awful courtroom revelation.

Buildings tell you stories if you pause and listen. They hold energy and history. I felt all of that that first afternoon, and every time I played Centre Court or sat in the stands as a spectator. No wonder it's called the cathedral of our sport. I've sat there over the years and thought about the players who came before me, the unforgettable champions and qualifiers who played their hearts out but never made it to the top. I imagined the great players in their all-whites floating like dancers across the grass: Suzanne Lenglen, Helen Wills Moody, Alice Marble, Don Budge, Fred Perry, Little Mo Connolly, Althea Gibson—everybody who was anybody. I tried to imagine the weight and pressure they felt and the joy and relief of their victories. I swear I could sense all of it from my very first time at Centre Court, and I meant it that first day when I turned to Gerry and said, "Can we just stay here forever?"

Until Wimbledon was canceled because of the worldwide pandemic in 2020, I hadn't missed the tournament in sixty years.

KAREN HANTZE AND I moved to a London bed-and-breakfast once our Wimbledon fortnight had begun. We washed our clothes in a basin and hung them to dry in our tiny room. The loo was down the hall. Our landlady followed tennis closely and she was openly skeptical that two teenage Yanks like us would survive even the early rounds. She wasn't about to waste her time on us. For breakfast the first morning she gave us each a roll and a glass of milk and wished us good luck.

The draw for singles, doubles, and mixed-doubles competitions are always posted a few days before a tournament begins, which means you can trace your potential matchup in each round if you keep winning and moving through your bracket. I never checked the entire draw before play began because I preferred to take it one match at a time and not worry about the future. But Karen, who had played Wimbledon the year before, insisted on dragging me to the board when they posted the doubles draw. We were unseeded, but we knew that Maria Bueno and Darlene Hard, the best women's doubles team, were recovering from cases of jaundice they had picked up in France. Karen looked at the remaining names on the board and said, "Billie Jean, we can win this thing!" Then she said it again, just to be sure I got it.

I did get it, but my debut singles match was scheduled first. Yola Ramírez of Mexico, an experienced player who had just lost in the final at Roland-Garros, was the fifth seed and I couldn't believe it when we were assigned to Centre Court. In addition to managing my nerves, I now had to do a crash course on an important Wimbledon tradition: Ever since King George V became a patron of the All England Club in 1910, the female players have curtsied and the male players have bowed in unison if a royal was present in the box when they entered Centre Court. (The tradition ended in 2003, except if the Queen or the Prince of Wales is present.) Karen and I laughed as she helped me practice sweeping my right leg behind my left and doing a little dip without tumbling over.

Even by Wimbledon standards, the opening week was abnormally wet. The matches were backed up from rain delays. Yola and I didn't take the court until early evening on Wednesday, Day 3. First we made a short indoor walk from the locker room to a little holding room where some officials made us pause. The walls there were lined with photos of past champions, and I checked out a few of them. When the door flung open and we got the go-ahead to walk out, it was like being born into a bright new world. My first ground-level look at Centre Court exploded into view. I saw the scoreboard again, but this time it had *my* name on it. When I scanned the Centre Court stands, thousands of strangers were now in their seats, blinking back at me as I looked up at them.

Before I walked out to play, I bent over and pressed my palm against the impeccably mowed grass, then plucked a blade and rubbed it between my hands. The court felt shorn as smooth as suede. *I'm here at last,* I thought. The most famous tennis court in the world.

When the match started I told myself what I always did: *One ball at a time. One ball at a time.* It worked for a while. Yola barely beat me in the first set, 11–9. I blitzed her in the second, 6–1. Then, in what I felt was a stroke of bad luck for me, the light was too dim for us to continue. There were no stadium lights at Centre Court in those days, let alone a roof. I was frustrated as Karen and I went back to our B&B. I told her I thought I could have won the match if we had kept playing. Now, anything could happen, and a few novel things did.

It's hard to imagine this today, but Karen and I were totally on our own that entire month we were overseas—no parents, no coaches, no agents, no chaperones. We had been feasting on candy bars and Wimpy burgers, a London treat. I made some other really bad choices, too, like deciding to take Ex-Lax because I heard it might help me drop some of the extra weight I had gained. I tried it for the first time the night of my suspended match with Yola. I figured how much could some little chocolatey squares hurt me? Answer: I was up all night running down the hall to the loo. *Way to go, Billie Jean.* I was not in good shape the next morning. It didn't matter. Yola went after my forehand in the final set and won easily.

At least Karen and I were still alive in the doubles draw. We were loose and giggly. Karen was technically perfect and just beautiful to watch, but she was also more deliberate and reserved than me. Already, I was getting a reputation as a talker on court. If I didn't like a line call, I said so. But most of my noise was directed at me: *"C'mon Billie! Move! That shot was El Choko!"* Sometimes we had to avoid looking at each other to avoid cracking up.

I was shocked when we made it through to the finals, even though Karen had called it. We finally impressed our landlady, too. As Karen and I kept winning, she added orange juice, then eggs and bacon to our breakfast menu. By the time we reached the finals we were "her girls" and we were served whatever we wanted. We invited her to be our guest at the title match.

Our opponents were two Aussies, Jan Lehane and Margaret Smith. They had won the Australian Championships that year, so nobody gave Karen and me much of a chance against them. I saw for myself why Darlene Hard said Margaret would be the next big thing in women's tennis. She was a tall, powerful girl who stood five feet nine and moved exceptionally well. She was a spectacular athlete, too. But in a pattern that I saw even in that first match against her, Margaret was a front-runner. If she got a big lead, she was unstoppable. When the score was close or she trailed, she could have trouble, susceptible to nerves as she was.

Karen and I broke Margaret's serve in the second game of our match, and we never let up the pressure. We pulled off the upset, 6–3, 6–4. On match point I remember letting out a yell and throwing a ball in the air. Then I saw our landlady standing and clapping like crazy in our competitor's box. At eighteen and seventeen, Karen and I became the youngest doubles team to win a Wimbledon title. We still hold that distinction. She and I were each handed a Duchess of Kent Challenge Cup, the winners' trophy. Soon the wonderful Boston sportswriter Bud Collins approached to congratulate us.

Bud always called himself a hacker, but he was a good enough player to win the U.S. Indoor Mixed Doubles Championship with Janet Hopps that summer. He had coached tennis at Brandeis University (one of his charges there was a young student activist named Abbie Hoffman) before switching to sportswriting for the *Boston Herald,* and then *The Boston Globe.* He became one of the greatest chroniclers and raconteurs tennis has known and literally wrote the encyclopedia on modern tennis.

Bud was a passionate booster of the game, and he and I had a shared disdain for the stuffiness in the sport. As his retort to tennis whites, Bud began covering tournaments in the loudest, most flamboyantly patterned trousers he and his tailor could cook up. It was his trademark by the time he began working as a TV commentator, starting at WGBH in Boston. Eventually, he moved up to the major networks, including NBC, the first in America to broadcast Wimbledon live. Until 1979, NBC broadcast only the gentlemen's singles final, on tape delay.

Karen and I didn't know that our doubles win entitled us to attend the formal Wimbledon Ball until Bud told us. When we said we had too little money between us to afford celebratory Wimpy burgers, let alone buy gowns for the ball, he offered to take us to dinner that night at a little Italian restaurant in Knightsbridge, not far from Harrods department store. We had a great evening discussing tennis nonstop from the appetizers through dessert, and a lifelong friendship was born.

When Karen and I returned to our B&B, we threw our clothes into our carry-on bags to catch the next flight back to the States. Pan Am, the airline we booked, knew we had won the doubles title and they said they'd arrange for a limousine to pick us up and take us to Heathrow. At the airport, there was another man waiting for us at the curb to check us in and take our luggage. Once we were onboard the plane, our pilot made an announcement from the cockpit—"Ladies and gentlemen, we'd like to inform you there are two Wimbledon champions aboard our aircraft"—and some passengers applauded. Then the flight attendants fussed over us the whole way back.

I couldn't wait to tell Clyde Walker about all of it. I considered our Wimbledon title a gift to him, my parents, the sponsors who paid my way, the city of Long Beach, every last soul who had ever helped me. I had visited Clyde in the hospital before I left because he wasn't doing well. His last words to me were his usual reminder, "Just have fun."

Karen and I flew to Philadelphia after Wimbledon to begin the summer grass court season. I had been there for three days when I learned that Clyde had died of cancer. He was sixty-nine years old. His wife, Louise, told me the only thing that kept him going the last week of the tournament was waiting for our results each day. He passed away knowing that he finally had his first Wimbledon champion. He was so much a part of my life—my coach, my mentor, my dear friend who felt more like family—that I still often catch myself wondering, *What would Clyde think if he saw this?* I still talk to him almost every day.

Chapter 6

I HAD ONE remaining summer commitment before I returned home to start my freshman year of college. I was thrilled to be selected to play in the Wightman Cup again—but this time for the U.S. women's team, not the junior squad. The Wightman Cup was the closest thing in tennis then to being on a big-league team since there was no women's pro tour or Federation Cup yet. Nor had tennis been reinstated at the Olympics.

I loved how we were sharply outfitted for the Wightman Cup in tailored white jackets with a fancy American eagle crest sewn on the chest pocket. I earned my first per diem payment from the USLTA on that trip—$14 a day—along with my plane ticket to play in Chicago. To underscore that we were representing our country, our names weren't on the scoreboard during the matches at the Saddle and Cycle Club. What you saw instead when you looked up was just "U.S.A. v. Great Britain."

The British team was led by the veterans Angela Mortimer, who had just won the 1961 Wimbledon singles title; Christine Truman, the Wimbledon runner-up; and Ann Haydon, the reigning French champion. They were joined by an impressive newcomer, Deidre Catt. The press was calling it the strongest British team ever assembled.

Because our best players, Darlene Hard and Nancy Richey, were ailing, our Wightman Cup roster looked like we were sending out sacrificial lambs. We were the youngest U.S. squad ever. Our top three players were eighteen and under: Karen Hantze, Justina Bricka, and me. We also had forty-three-year-old Margaret

Osborne du Pont as a doubles player/coach, and twenty-one-year-old Gwyneth Thomas. But none of the pre-competition predictions mattered to us once play began. Soon we teenyboppers had pulled off the biggest upset in Wightman Cup history, sweeping the first four matches played.

My first Wimbledon doubles title a month earlier, and now this. I had never won a junior singles national title, let alone an international competition. It was the most fun I'd ever had on a tennis court. Then I flew home, and nobody outside my family seemed to notice how dramatically my life had changed. I was back to being Billie Jean Moffitt from 36th Street in Long Beach.

THESE DAYS COLLEGE COACHES would fall over themselves to recruit a player who had already won a Grand Slam doubles title at seventeen. But sports scholarships were almost nonexistent for women when I began college in the fall of 1961. The 1972 passage of Title IX, the federal law that mandated equal opportunities for men and women at federally funded institutions, was still eleven years away.

Luckily, California state colleges were still tuition free then. What a godsend. I chose to attend Los Angeles State College (now known as California State University, Los Angeles) because the men's tennis coach, Cameron "Scotty" Deeds, was from Long Beach. He had known my father since their college years. Scotty used to hang out with my parents at the seaside dance clubs like the Palladium and Balboa when my parents were dating, and they became lifelong friends.

My father didn't want me living away from home, which was kind of funny since I had already traveled the world for weeks by myself. He wanted to protect his only daughter and keep us living together as a family as long as possible, which I found sweet. I had squirreled away $310 by not spending all of my USLTA per diem money that summer, and I used it to buy a 1950 Ford sedan with a burgundy paint job and a stick shift on the column to commute to school. The car, my first, was eleven years old but having it was a thrill for me.

Scotty introduced me to L.A. State's terrific women's tennis coach, Dr. Joan Johnson, a pioneering figure. She had co-coached the school's men's team in 1955 and 1956 and founded the women's program in 1959 as well as the Southern California Women's Intercollegiate Tennis League that we competed in. When Connie Jaster, Carole Loop, Carole Caldwell, Sue Behlmar, and I were teammates, one publication ranked us the top college team in the world.

Joan and Scotty were remarkably ahead of their time about treating men and women players equally. Scotty recruited male players who won three straight NCAA Division II championships, beginning in 1963. They had all of us practice together from 2 to 5 every afternoon, and the approach helped everybody improve their games. The women learned how to handle the men's power and speed. The men benefited from having to concentrate on accuracy and consistency.

Years before I arrived at college, I knew that many boys and men hate to lose to a girl or woman. I used to regularly defeat the men at Lakewood Country Club. I knew it wasn't considered ladylike to be so assertive, and women were encouraged, even expected, to protect male egos. When we walked off the court at Lakewood and someone asked us, "Who won?" I would say, "He did," though it was often untrue. You wouldn't believe the grateful looks and words of thanks I got from my playing partners when no one was around. (Unbelievable as it sounds, the same conditioning to defer to men and be less capable than I was reared up in me against Bobby Riggs late in our Battle of the Sexes match. I became distracted thinking about how humiliating it would be for Bobby to lose to a woman, and I briefly felt sorry for him—but I got over it.)

Gary Johnson, who became a two-time singles national champion for L.A. State, practiced with me daily. We were pretty closely matched. There was no hiding it when I defeated him. One time he got so ticked off he sent his racket pinwheeling over the fence and into the swimming pool.

To help me cover my college expenses, I took a couple of part-time jobs—one as the playground director at an elementary school, the other as a women's locker room attendant at L.A. State, a minimum-wage job that paid $1.15 an hour for folding towels and handing out equipment. In addition to tennis practices and matches and work, I carried a full course load and made the forty-mile round trip to school each day.

I was deeply grateful for Scotty's help. But I knew that on the other side of town, a young tennis phenomenon named Arthur Ashe had a full ROTC scholarship at UCLA to play tennis while studying business administration. The golden boys of California tennis, Stan Smith and Dennis Ralston, both had full-ride tennis scholarships at the University of Southern California, and the next year, so would Jerry Cromwell.

When I got to college, I was still the unreconstructed straight arrow who carried a Bible on my tennis trips, the kid whose grade school teacher mailed a note home to her parents commending them for rearing a child who conscientiously turned in a dime she found lying on the floor. I loved spending hours picking the brains of professors and teaching assistants around campus, and I logged a lot of time in the library, indulging my love of reading. But much of that time was spent kicking around ideas and searching the stacks for topics that *I* wanted to read—not necessarily material related to my coursework. I devoured books on history and psychology. All the same, I was frequently on academic probation and often skipped classes, except for my course on the British Empire.

It's a paradox, I know. I value education. I've always had a huge appetite for learning that persists to this day. I've always loved drilling down to the details, meaning, and origin of things. In hindsight, I guess the best way I can explain that time is that I was one of those restless students who wasn't on a quest for a framed degree I could hang on the wall as much as for insights and information that dovetailed with what I hoped to do with my life, which was tennis. Tennis always seemed to dominate. My thoughts were consumed with how we were going to make tennis a pro sport, and how to ensure that women wouldn't be left out. If I came along in the sport today, I'd have skipped college and gone straight from high school to the pros. But back then, I was trying to figure out a path and a world that didn't exist yet for women, a world you couldn't find in any college course catalog or structured march to a degree. There was this gap between what I thought I was capable of and the world as it was. I saw that gulf clearly. I was less sure how to breach it.

What was revealing about that time is what *did* resonate with me. During my first year of college, for example, I became fascinated with the work of Maxwell Maltz, a plastic surgeon who wrote about the mind-body connection. A cornerstone of Maltz's work was his observation that superficial changes in a patient's outward appearance were meaningless if the interior way patients saw themselves was unchanged.

Maltz wanted to create a way to help patients improve their self-image. He came up with a process he called Psycho-Cybernetics, a system of ideas that he claimed could help people lead a more fulfilling life. Maltz believed we can literally condition our minds for success. One of the techniques he advocated was visualization—seeing yourself doing something correctly so you can master it. Boy, did that strike a chord with me. It's basically what I had been doing all along, especially as I studied Althea Gibson and the many great players who came through Los Angeles, or when I peppered Clyde Walker, Alice Marble, and Darlene Hard with questions. As I said earlier, I truly believed that if you can see something, you can be it. Maltz cited the science behind that. He explained how our nervous systems can't distinguish between real and imagined experiences, and how each of us has an inner mechanism we can program to achieve results automatically.

It made a lot of sense to me, and the idea is accepted practice today. You often see world-class athletes in sports like gymnastics, diving, and aerial skiing pause before they start and close their eyes to visualize their routines; sometimes they'll pantomime entire sequences of moves before they begin.

Even before I discovered Maltz I would often visualize how I should play my matches from three vantage points: my side of the court, my opponent's side of the court, and an aerial view. In my mind I'd imagine myself on the baseline hitting the ball, then switch to how the person receiving the ball might behave. I'd construct imaginary points, sometimes even entire games as if I were hovering over the court watching myself and my opponent react to each ball that was struck.

It was all very real to me, and I felt that my game improved because of it. If you can anticipate or dictate things in tennis, you're a step ahead of your opponent. You have a better chance of controlling points.

The longer I went to L.A. State, the more I became convinced that being No. 1 in the world was going to require full-time devotion to the sport. I felt that I wasn't practicing or competing enough anymore. We played a modest schedule each spring and then I'd put my racket away for weeks in the fall and winter, shaking off the cobwebs again when Wimbledon and the summer grass court season came back around. I was a part-time player now, and my uneven results showed it. When I ventured back out into tournament play at the close of my freshman year I lost a disheartening match to Karen Hantze in straight sets at the Southern California Championships in May 1962, which felt like a serious step backward. Afterward, I retreated to the parking lot and cried my eyes out in my car. I had played her deuce after deuce, advantage point after advantage point, but I was unable to finish her off. Now my gut ached, my head hurt and I was berating myself: *You could have had that match and you lost it! Why can't you finish? If you keep losing at this level, how are you ever going to be No. 1? So many people have put so much into you, and you're letting them down!*

I don't think I had ever felt such doubt or felt so sad and sorry for myself about a tennis match. But there were times I had come close. That's another paradox many people don't understand about athletes, especially the best ones. As great as winning is, the spike of elation comes and goes quickly. The prevailing emotion is often relief, not undiluted joy. But losing? Losing is forever. Results are literally carved in stone, written in ink, engraved on the silver chalices they hand out to champions. Losing eats at you.

Stefanie Graf once told me she used to pace the floors for days after she lost. Chrissie Evert told Bud she trashed her London hotel room and stayed in her bathrobe for three days eating junk food after her 1977 Wimbledon semifinal loss to Britain's Virginia

Wade. Something vital snapped in Bjorn Borg after John McEnroe defeated him at the 1981 U.S. Open and took away his No. 1 ranking. Borg, who was famously and meticulously driven, walked right out to the parking lot without showering, took a car to the airport, and boarded a flight. Three months later, he retired at the age of twenty-six. "When you're No. 2 or 3, you're nobody," Borg told the stunned McEnroe, who couldn't talk him into returning.

All tennis players who make it to the very top, including me, would probably tell you they hate losing more than they love winning—except maybe Roger Federer. You can certainly see the agony on Roger's face when he loses. He and Rafael Nadal have wept openly after some of their Grand Slam finals defeats. Then again, Roger cries unashamedly when he wins, too, so who knows? He's such a positive role model for boys, especially, who are afraid to show their emotions. He gets an immediate release as soon as the match is over, and then he moves on.

I wish I could have done that more. No one ever saw me sobbing in public after a match, even though I often felt like crying. But here's the deal: You have to realize in tennis everybody fails by the end of each tournament except one player. It's single-elimination, a zero-sum game. One bad day and you're a tomato can being kicked down the road, on to the next city. It can kill your spirit if you let it.

Champions adjust. Champions are masters at being resilient. To succeed, you have to find a way to reconcile everything—chasing goals, believing you will succeed but absorbing failure, and the loneliness of knowing that no one can help you on the court but you. You have to somehow use all of it as motivation, because when that aversion to losing and your drive to win goes—especially in a one-on-one sport like tennis—you're cooked. Matches not only test your skill but reveal who you are, how hard you're willing to work or fight. Chrissie's dad and coach, Jimmy Evert, used to say, "You're going to get out there and look at that big green rectangle and *decide*."

I probably tapped into that fear and loathing of losing more than the good times in my career. I was always scared to death I'd never make it to No. 1. Nothing was ever good enough to me. It's what drove me even after I started winning Grand Slam titles, when

I walked out to play Bobby Riggs, when I had to keep playing for financial security long after six surgeries left me with centipede-like scars curling around both knees.

I obviously had no way of knowing that any of that lay ahead for me as I put my car in gear and drove away after that loss to Karen Hantze in the spring of 1962. I did know that Wimbledon was only eight weeks away, and I told myself if I wanted to stay in the game—let alone ever be No. 1—I had to get a lot better, right away.

Playing again on the U.S. Wightman Cup team was an encouraging start. We beat the Brits four matches to three, on their home turf. Then it was time to return to the All England Club. I was still ranked third in the U.S. and went into my second Wimbledon unseeded again in singles. For my first match I drew Margaret Smith, by now the most formidable player in women's tennis and the No. 1 seed after winning the Australian, Italian, and Roland-Garros singles titles that year while I was handing out towels at L.A. State.

Months earlier, I had told my parents I had a strong premonition that Margaret and I would play each other in our opening match at Wimbledon. They just chuckled. Now, here we were. The press nicknamed her "the Aussie Amazon." Nobody gave me a chance.

MARGARET SEEMED TO have a wingspan that stretched from net post to net post. Rosie Casals would later nickname her "the Arm." As it turned out, it wasn't just Rosie's colorful imagination. When some university researchers in England measured Margaret for a study on athletes, they found that her arms were three inches longer than average for a woman her size.

Margaret's revolutionary trainer at the time was Stan Nicholls, who worked with Olympic athletes and Australia's Davis Cup team. Margaret was the first woman tennis player to lift weights and do full-body circuit training. She was a powerful player. She developed her legs and superb cardio fitness by running over sand hills back home. Her shots had sting. Her fitness and court coverage were terrific.

Margaret was a scrappy kid who played every sport in school but gravitated to tennis at an early age. Her father worked in a dairy factory in Albury, their hometown in New South Wales. Margaret started hitting tennis balls with a fence board and won her first tournament with a hand-me-down racket with a square-shaped frame that a kindly neighbor gave her. She became very good, very fast. Her first coach, Wal Rutter, brought her to the attention of former Aussie champion Frank Sedgman, who helped her receive better tennis instruction in Melbourne. A wealthy young businessman there named Bob Mitchell became Margaret's benefactor.

By the time we met at Wimbledon in 1962, Margaret was nineteen, just a year older than me, but she had already competed in nine Grand Slam tournaments, winning four of them. Nonetheless, parts of her game were still raw or predictable. The night before our match, which was actually a second rounder since Margaret and I had both drawn first-round byes, I spent time strategizing with my friend Carole Caldwell, who had handed Margaret a rare defeat earlier in the month at Manchester. We agreed that the best approach was to target Margaret's forehand since her backhand was steadier.

I also knew that Margaret was playing under extraordinary pressure. Australia had a rich tradition of men's tennis champions, but the country had never had a female Wimbledon singles titlist by the time Margaret came along. It was being trumpeted that this was the year.

There was also the inevitable talk of Margaret finishing a Grand Slam sweep of the four majors, since, with her wins at the Australian and Roland-Garros, she was halfway there. The press was fixated on her. The Brits were openly rooting for her. But her own tennis federation had not made it any easier on her. After Margaret declined to travel the circuit with the Australian team that year because she clashed with Nell Hopman, the team's coach, the Lawn Tennis Association of Australia refused to let Margaret train or even mix with the other Australian players. I later learned that on the morning of our match, the LTAA had sent Margaret a good-luck telegram, in an apparent attempt to break the ice. But by then the tension was already ratcheted up. Margaret had everything to lose, and both of us knew it.

When we walked out onto Centre Court, it was unusually full for a second-round match despite the cool and blustery weather. Margaret started strong and took the first set, 6–1. But I genuinely felt that I was still settling into my game and, anyway, I could see that Margaret was battling the wind. She was having trouble with her timing because of her long backswing. I pushed hard into her forehand and kept trusting my passing shots when she rushed the net. It finally began to pay off. I took the second set, 6–3. Now the Wimbledon fans, who always love an underdog, were cheering me on. I gave away four inches in height to Margaret but little else. This had become a dogfight.

Margaret came out possessed in the third set and took back control. She was leading 5–3 and serving to me at 30–15, two points from victory. But perhaps that was her problem: The end was in sight and she wanted it too much. When I snapped off a running backhand down the line to even that game at 30-all, the crowd shrieked and Margaret seemed to seize up. I couldn't tell you exactly what she was gripped by—anxiety, mental fatigue, shock?—but whatever it was, I could feel that something had happened. I stormed back to win that game—and the next one. I broke her serve again, and now I was serving for the match at 40–love. Triple match point.

Margaret saved one with an emphatic overhead smash. I wobbled and double-faulted to squander the next point. The crowd gasped. Two match points erased. Just one left. I ignored the murmuring now and spat a few choice words at myself under my breath. *Concentrate! You can do this!* On the next point, I followed my serve with a sharp backhand volley and then there was a split second where I heard nothing—Margaret had dumped the ball into the net, she and I looked at each other—and the fans, who were stunned for a split second as well, shot to their feet here and there and roared and roared.

I threw my racket high in the air, and I was told later that I did a bit of a hop, skip, and jump to the net. Honestly, I was numb, completely overcome. Margaret flung her racket to the side of the court and looked like a ghost as we shook hands. Still, she managed to say, "You played well. You deserved to win." Bless those Aussies, ever gracious in defeat.

Later that day in the Wimbledon tearoom I noticed that many of the Aussie officials looked as white as a sheet when they saw me. I was so naive, someone had to explain to me that it was because they had taken a financial bath with the London bookmakers by betting so heavily on Margaret to win. "You have no idea what you've done to some of these people," I was told.

The upset made me the first unseeded player in Wimbledon's eighty-six-year history of ladies' tennis to beat a No. 1 seed in her opening match. My father learned that I'd won when the Los Angeles radio station KNX called him at the firehouse to get his reaction. The next day, the newspapers reported that when Margaret came to the interview room afterward, her voice was a thin whisper as she looked out at the waiting reporters and said, "This feels like a courtroom."

As for me, I would never be the same. I had confirmed what I thought I was capable of doing.

Neither Margaret nor I knew it at the time, of course, but that Wimbledon singles showdown was the first of a thirty-four-match rivalry between us that would span thirteen years and some epic matches. We would be the top two players of our generation. But on that first day, I felt Margaret's pain so intensely I teared up when the photographers rushed the court to take pictures of her with her face buried in her towel. Then I stuck up for her when it was my turn in the interview room, telling reporters, "Australia expects too much from Margaret. Margaret is truly a great champion and as soon as the Australian lawn tennis association and the Australian public start taking pressure off her, she'll do better. She has a great future."

I advanced two more rounds at Wimbledon before Ann Haydon, a familiar Wightman Cup foe, beat me in straight sets in the quarterfinals. But my pal Karen Hantze Susman, who had recently married, went on to win her first and only Grand Slam singles title that fortnight. What a thrill. Then Karen and I won the doubles for the second year in a row.

When the USLTA and the U.S. State Department asked me to represent the United States later that summer at the Moscow International Tennis Tournament, there was no chance I was going to say no. As a girl whose patriotic father signed up to fight for America, I always relished the chance to represent my country. Also, Russia would be only the second foreign country I'd ever visited, at a time when few Westerners traveled behind the Iron Curtain. The invitation deepened my belief that there were opportunities to make a global impact through tennis.

At that moment, Cold War relations between the United States and the U.S.S.R. were unbelievably tense. An American U-2 spy plane had been shot down by the Soviets in 1960. In April 1961 the U.S. had backed a botched invasion at the Bay of Pigs by some Cuban exiles hoping to reverse Fidel Castro's Cuban revolution. Later that summer, East Germany built the Berlin Wall. By 1962, the Soviet Union was secretly sending missiles to Cuba, which would soon set off the Cuban Missile Crisis and yet another face-off with the U.S.

My parents didn't want me to travel to Moscow, but I couldn't wait to get there, even after our team was warned that our hotel rooms would probably be bugged. What I remember most, other than my first taste of caviar and seeing the famous brightly colored domes at St. Basil's Cathedral, was that everything was gray. The buildings, the cars, even the skies were unrelentingly dreary. The food was terrible, and there seemed to be little of it. It was August, but the temperature never rose above 55 degrees. Late in the week, our players' bus got stuck in traffic when two Soviet cosmonauts who had been circling the earth returned safely and were being paraded through Moscow as heroes. Thousands of fans waited two hours for us at the stadium until we arrived to play. Our last day, some of us asked if there were Sunday religious services we could attend, and we were told none were available in the atheist Soviet Union. That stuck with me.

On the flight home I couldn't stop thinking how fortunate I was to have been born in America. When our plane touched down at Idlewild, I literally got down on my knees and kissed the tarmac.

MY LAST STOP BEFORE returning to college was the U.S. Nationals at Forest Hills. The crowds seemed thinner. Bill McCormick, a syndicated sports columnist, took a swipe that week at the "stodgy" tennis authorities for not opening tournaments to pros as well as amateurs. He said that since Jack Kramer's professional promotions started siphoning off the top amateurs the "pristine pure division" of the sport had become "as colorless as skimmed milk."

The biggest excitement was around Australia's Rod Laver and their amateurs, led by Margaret Smith. Rod was slight and stood only five feet eight, but he could dominate anybody. He was a left-handed genius on the court, technically perfect, and—until Roger Federer came along—the best all-around tennis player I've ever seen. Laver had been a friendly, familiar face on the circuit for almost as long as I'd been competing. He won Forest Hills that year to become the first Australian to win a Grand Slam sweep, and the first male player to pull it off since Don Budge in 1938. Then, in another foreboding sign for amateur tennis, Laver turned pro in December.

I fell out of Forest Hills in the first round. I won my first set but had to retire after I became dizzy and fell behind 0–5 in the second against Victoria Palmer, a seventeen-year-old American who had beaten me the year before in the final of the junior nationals grass court championships in Philadelphia. She went all the way to the Forest Hills semis, her best Grand Slam finish ever. Her other claim to fame? Bud Collins and the fellow historian Ted Tinling christened Vicky tennis's first female grunter. She's had many imitators since.

Once back at L.A. State, I spent a lot of hours sitting alone again in the library, ignoring my textbooks as I reread Maltz and some others I discovered. At this point, I was a two-time Wimbledon doubles champion, a Wightman Cup winner, an athlete who had represented my country overseas and beaten or nearly beaten the top women in the world. And yet I was headed back to being a part-timer who didn't compete for weeks at a time and worked menial jobs to pay for my living expenses. Was this all there was?

I would sit at that library desk for hours rolling a tennis ball back and forth on the table, thinking about the future of my sport. How were we going to grow women's tennis into a major professional undertaking? What could I do? I was already beginning to sense that tennis players needed to unite to stand up to the USLTA and other officials who ran the local sections like personal fiefdoms. I was envisioning a day when tennis could be played with men and women competing together on equal footing rather than only practicing together the way we did at L.A. State.

Nothing about my sport had significantly improved—especially for women—since I'd had my epiphany at the Los Angeles Tennis Club seven years earlier. The clothes were still white, the balls and most of the players were white, and so were the spectators.

Althea quit amateur tennis in 1959 at the pinnacle of her career after having swept the singles titles at Wimbledon and Forest Hills in back-to-back years. As she memorably explained it, "You can't eat trophies." I would sometimes repeat her line later. Althea went on to break the color line in women's golf, too, and chase the small purses on the fledgling LPGA tour. To make a living, she even played tennis as the opening act at Harlem Globetrotters' games, a sight that was as painful to me as Jesse Owens racing a horse for money late in his career, or a broke Joe Louis—another African American icon—working as a casino greeter in Vegas.

The men who ran tennis back then thought you had to have attractive babes to draw fans to women's events, so they paired Althea for those 1959 Globetrotter exhibitions with Karol Fageros, a Floridian whose biggest claim to fame was wearing gold lamé underpants when she played the 1958 French Championships. That earned Karol a ban from Wimbledon a few weeks later until she promised to wear white panties instead. "I didn't think it would create such a sensation," Karol said, "but every time I hit a shot in Paris, flashbulbs went off." Photographers laid on their backs to take photos up her skirt. Though Karol was once ranked as high as No. 5 in the world, Althea beat her 114 of the 118 matches they played.

In short, the formula in tennis hadn't changed much from a decade earlier when Bobby Riggs was the last promoter who tried to launch a women's tour. Riggs's sexed-up matches between "Gorgeous" Gussie Moran and Pauline Betz didn't attract enough fans. They weren't competitive, either. Betz was a strawberry blonde who had once dated Spencer Tracy. She won five majors and was still a much stronger player than Gussie, who had scandalized Wimbledon herself by wearing Ted Tinling–designed lace panties ten years before Karol Fageros arrived. Gussie reprised her outfit on Riggs's tour and Pauline wore leopard-print shorts when they played. The laundry didn't matter. Fans yawned and stayed away.

If Jack Kramer, the top promoter of my day, had offered me a professional contract with a legitimate tour at any point in my amateur career, I would have signed in a heartbeat. But he never asked a single woman to tour. That's why 99.9 percent of us were amateurs when Althea or even I came along. To Kramer and the rest of the men in charge of tennis, we were invisible.

Chapter 7

AFTER I RETURNED for my sophomore year, Marcos Carriedo, my friend and mixed-doubles partner at L.A. State, kept telling me about this guy I had to meet, a freshman named Larry King with whom he played bridge in the school cafeteria. "You two are perfect for each other," Marcos said. "Larry doesn't drink or smoke either, and he's going to come out for the tennis team." I wasn't interested in blind dating, so I kept putting Marcos off. Then one day he and I ran into each other just as I was stepping out of the library elevator to leave and he was coming in.

"Billie Jean! Get back in! He's here! You've got to come meet Larry."

"Marcos, come on."

"I'm serious, Billie. You'll like him. He's a great guy."

"What is with you, Marcos? I'm busy. And I'm not interested."

"Get in," Marcos insisted as he held open the elevator door, tugging at my arm.

We went to the fourth floor, and as we were walking across the room I noticed a blond guy sitting at one of the library tables and reading a book with his feet propped up on the chair next to him. He had his shoes off and was wearing loud red socks. *Wow, if only that were him—he is gorgeous,* I thought. I was surprised when he looked up as Marcos and I approached and Marcos said, "Larry, this is Billie Jean, the girl I've been telling you about."

Well, hell-looooo, I thought, amused about my reluctance before. We shook hands and chatted a bit, but honestly, when I saw that face, that smile, that was it. Larry was seventeen, a year younger than I was. Other than how young and handsome he looked, I remember being struck by how sincere and friendly he was.

I don't remember exactly what we talked about that day, just that we hit it off right away and I wanted to know more about him. Larry was smart, and I love smart. He told me later that he did a double take at me, too, because he didn't expect me to look like I did, either. He had first heard about me over the summer when his father was reading the newspaper and remarked out loud, "Huh. A local girl won the doubles title at Wimbledon." When Larry looked at the article, the photo showed my face contorted as I lunged for a shot. Not the kind of picture you'd send in for your screen test.

After that first hello, Larry and I would see each other around campus—"It was hard work to always 'accidentally' bump into her," he joked later—and we began spending time together. We really were straight arrows, and we had an old-fashioned courtship. Larry often wrote me letters daily when I was traveling for tennis, and I tried to write back as best I could. Before we went out dancing for our first date, I took him to my house to meet my parents over dinner. Mom and Dad and Randy tried to act casually when we arrived, but Larry was the first boy I had ever brought home from college so they knew this must be significant.

As was often the case when Dad was involved, the conversation was memorable. As he fired up the outdoor grill, Larry tried to make small talk with him. He was admiring the beautiful roses my dad had planted for my mother and said, "What's the pH of the soil, Mr. Moffitt?"

"What?"

"Well, roses need acidic soil—"

"What the *hell* are you talking about?" Dad cut him off, looking up now from what he was doing.

I tried not to laugh. I said, "Daddy, it's not a big deal. Larry is a biochemistry major."

Things got awkward again once we sat down to eat. Dad had splurged for steaks for dinner. Larry loved steak but disliked char-broiled anything. Mom had made a salad, and Larry didn't eat salad, either. As the dinner conversation bumped and lurched along, Dad accidentally called Larry "Barry"—as in my ex-boyfriend. There was a long silence after that one. But honestly, Larry didn't care.

Later, when Larry wasn't around, Dad said, "What's with this guy with his 'Ps' and 'Hs'? What kind of dippity-do asks a guy that kind of question in his own backyard?"

It was almost as funny as the time Dad and I were watching Elvis on *The Ed Sullivan Show* and my father huffed, "He'll never make it."

Dad and Mom ended up liking Larry pretty quickly, even if Dad sometimes thought Larry was flaky. And Marcos was right: Larry and I were perfect for each other. He had a steady, easygoing charm. We used to spend hours sitting in the library at L.A. State talking about my dreams for tennis and his ideas for how to make them happen. We fell in love quickly and became inseparable even though we're very different people. I can be a hot-tempered perfectionist, but nothing seems to faze Larry. I was someone who gushed emotion; Larry constantly showed me he loved me but it was often hard for him to talk about what he was feeling inside. His upbringing had been as unsettled as mine was orderly.

Larry grew up in Eagle Rock, a Los Angeles suburb nestled between Glendale and Pasadena. His father, James, was a tool-and-die maker from Dayton, Ohio, who was stationed in Pasadena during World War II. He sent for his wife and two sons to join him in California when he was discharged. Larry was still just a very young boy when his mother passed away there after giving birth to his baby sister, Mary Ellen. When I met Larry fifteen years later, the loss was still difficult for him to talk about. "I was two. She died," is all he said.

Larry's family struggled after that. His dad married a woman with two daughters, and they had a son together. Their blended family now had eight mouths to feed and money was a problem. Larry's stepmother, Bunny, worked in a pottery factory and as a waitress. His dad started a cleaning business, and everyone was expected to pitch in. The older boys worked with their father washing windows and screens in houses and dormitories. There were hundreds of towels that also had to be washed, dried, and folded every night. But

Larry was fine with all of it. He rolled with just about anything that came at him.

"The way I look at it, you can't control what happens to you, but I think you can control how you react," he said. "So why not make the best of every day?"

The six King children often had to fend for themselves because their parents were so busy. Larry became used to spending hours and hours reading as a child. He'd often sit near his dad and read every section of the newspaper as James dropped the pages to the floor after reading them first. Once he was in school, studying always came easy to Larry. He excelled at math. He had a photographic memory. He was a strong conceptual thinker. Exams were never a problem for him. But by his own admission, Larry could get sidetracked pretty easily too. An example: Larry was in line for a full academic scholarship to the University of Southern California, but he missed the deadline to send in the paperwork.

A family friend helped Larry land a $50 academic grant to attend L.A. State instead. Until we met, Larry intended to stay only a year and then head to USC. Our lives could've missed crossing paths. Larry played for L.A. State's tennis team as a sophomore, and he was a good player. But he was always self-deprecating about his talent, telling people, "If you really analyze it, I was more of an equipment manager. I was a serve-and-volleyer without a serve."

Larry had a strong self-image, but his ego wasn't out of control, which I loved about him. He was an unthreatened man. He didn't begrudge other people's successes or act as if their achievements came at his expense. Larry's father came from a socially conscious Quaker background, and Larry always said he was deeply affected by that side of his dad. One summer, James drove their family to the Sierra mountains for an eagerly anticipated family reunion. As they neared the front gate of the campground where they intended to stay, James spotted a sign that read "Whites Only. No Colored Allowed" and he stopped the car.

"We're not going in there," James said, and he turned the car around. Some of the kids began to cry. Larry, who had been looking forward to the trip for months, was as upset as anyone to go home. But he never forgot that lesson, either. What it said to him was that everyone deserves to be treated like a human being, and you shouldn't just say it, you need to live it.

One day after we began dating, we were walking hand in hand past the tennis courts at L.A. State and I was grousing about something I thought was unfair. Larry stopped and turned to me and said, "You realize you're treated like a second-class citizen because you're a girl, right?"

"What do you mean?" I said.

"I'm the seventh man on a six man tennis team and I'm treated better than you are. You're the best athlete at this school. You should be getting special treatment, not me. And yet you get zero."

No other guy had ever spoken so bluntly to me about sexism, let alone added that he had a problem with it as well. I've always said it was Larry King who first made me a feminist, and it started that day.

The word *feminism* was just starting to creep into popular usage by the spring of 1963 when we had that talk. Betty Friedan's runaway best seller, *The Feminine Mystique,* had been published only a few months earlier, in February. Friedan's book is still considered one of the landmark opening salvos in the second wave of the women's liberation movement. (The first wave started in the mid-nineteenth century and moved from fighting for equal property rights for women and opposing domination of married women by their husbands to fighting for women's right to vote, which was granted when the Nineteenth Amendment to the Constitution was ratified in August 1920. While the law helped white women, nonwhite women were routinely discouraged or prevented from voting until the Civil Rights Act of 1964 outlawed discrimination on the basis of sex, race, color, religion, and national origin.)

In her book, Friedan challenged the prevailing notions that women achieved complete fulfillment through housework, marriage, child rearing, and subsuming their own sexual desires. She assailed the idea that "truly feminine" women had no "natural" desire for higher education, careers, independence, or a political voice. Rather, what Friedan's reporting showed was that many women were deeply dissatisfied, but they felt voiceless, powerless, and stuck. Her book sold more than a million copies in the first year alone.

That same year, the President's Commission on the Status of Women, which former First Lady Eleanor Roosevelt initially chaired, published its two-year study that described the tremendously unequal landscape for men and women in numerous areas of American life, particularly for women of color. Those findings hastened the 1963 passage of the Equal Pay Act, which made it illegal to pay women less than men for the same work. (We're still waiting for its full compliance.)

The civil rights movement was exploding across America as well. The summer of 1963 began with the horrible news of the assassination of the Mississippi-based civil rights leader Medgar Evers in his driveway a few weeks before I returned to Wimbledon; it ended on August 28 with the epic March on Washington, where the Rev. Dr. Martin Luther King Jr. gave his mesmerizing "I Have a Dream" speech that included so many unforgettable lines, including his resounding hope for a day when all children "will live in a nation where they will not be judged by the color of their skin, but by the content of their character."

I was in New York that day, about to start play at the U.S. Championships, but I dearly wished I could have been in Washington. I wanted a world that reflected the vision Dr. King described. I kept watching the news footage of his remarks to the hundreds of thousands of people gathered on the Mall, marveling at how the enormous crowd stretched backward from the Lincoln Memorial as far as the eye could see. Change and upheaval seemed to be happening everywhere I looked. And I was questioning a lot too. College became a time of drift and uncertainty for me.

When I got back to England in the summer of 1963 I again felt like I had to play my way back into tournament form and at times I took out my frustration on myself or anyone else within earshot. At Manchester, I blew an overhead and yelled out, "Good ol' Billie Jean! I thought you were going to let me down, and you sure did."

I felt a bit better when I got to the Federation Cup, a new women's team competition. We could finally say there was something progressive happening in women's tennis. The original Federation Cup boasted a sixteen-nation field, which was an exciting expansion of the two-nation format the Wightman Cup offered. When I saw the trophy after we arrived, I told my teammates and longtime friends Darlene Hard and Carole Caldwell, "You guys, we have to win this because it's history! Every time we look at the trophy, we'll be the first!" We did win the inaugural event by beating Australia in the final. I played Margaret Smith only in doubles, which Darlene and I won to clinch the title.

When Wimbledon began just days later, I continued to play well despite a frequent drizzle that kept blurring my vision through my glasses. But my on-court histrionics were starting to attract mixed reviews. A good portion of the press thought my tortured patter was funny or a fine show of spirit, and the writers started hanging nicknames on me such as "the peppy chatterbox" (ugh), the "effervescent Californian" (better), and "the myopic pepper pot" (now wait a minute . . .). But many of the players were not amused—including Margaret, who griped publicly about my emotional displays and "verbal retorts." She didn't care that we were on a collision path to play each other and her criticisms might motivate me more. I was again unseeded but I upset Maria Bueno in the quarterfinals and England's Ann Haydon Jones in the semifinals. Ann had married Pip Jones, a businessman and tennis official, the year before.

I was now in my first Wimbledon singles final, and Margaret was across the net and seeded No. 1, the same as the previous year. As for what happened next, well . . . I could blame the rain that delayed our match two days. But honestly, I think the real culprit—again—was that I wasn't a full-time player and I didn't have the emotional and physical stamina to maintain my edge. In a way, I had no business being in a Wimbledon final after having played only two tournaments since spring. But Margaret was sure ready. She beat me 6–3, 6–4.

It was one of those matches where I literally felt pinned in the backcourt as she kept pounding shots at me. This time Margaret didn't falter under the weight of becoming Australia's first female

Wimbledon titlist or the specter of losing to Little Miss Moffitt, the unknown from Long Beach who had cost her so much the previous year. Back then, my shocking victory was such big news that Margaret's father told the *Sydney Morning Telegraph* that he wanted Margaret to see a psychiatrist. Not very nice. When I couldn't duplicate that upset I became terribly frustrated.

When I went on to the U.S. Nationals and lost to England's Deidre Catt in the fourth round at Forest Hills, I was despondent. And far worse news kept coming.

In September four young Black girls were murdered in the bombing of the 16th Street Baptist Church in Birmingham, Alabama, during their Sunday school class. Their names were Denise McNair, who was eleven, and Carole Robertson, Addie Mae Collins, and Cynthia Wesley, who were all fourteen. The Ku Klux Klan was blamed.

In October I was driving to school in stop-and-go traffic on the 710 freeway and I saw a Greyhound bus in my rearview mirror coming up fast behind me. When I realized the bus was not going to stop I threw my car into neutral just before it slammed into me with a horrible bang—the start of a five-car chain reaction that sent my knees slamming into the dashboard and my neck whiplashing forward and back. Cars did not have mandatory seat belts in those days. My old Ford was crushed like a soda can. By some miracle, I wasn't hurt enough to be hospitalized. But my knees would cause me chronic problems that required surgery the rest of my life.

On November 22, 1963—my twentieth birthday—I had just left my geology class and was walking toward the tennis courts when I saw Larry urgently motioning for me to hurry up toward him. I broke into a jog, then started running when he kept it up. That's how I learned that President Kennedy had been shot. I remember crying with my teammates when the official word came that Kennedy was pronounced dead at a Dallas hospital. My birthday has never felt the same since.

Two days after that, I was sitting on the sofa and watching the live TV coverage of JFK's alleged assassin, Lee Harvey Oswald, being taken in police custody to the county jail when Jack Ruby leaped forward and shot Oswald with a .38 caliber revolver. It was disturbing and surreal to see in real time.

Tennis was not just dissatisfying then, it was starting to feel more unimportant than I could recall. Larry and I went to my parents' house for Christmas and my mom tried her best to make it as special as ever, but it wasn't a joyful time. New Year's Eve was the same; I just didn't feel like celebrating. By now, Larry and I were starting to talk about planning a future together, and I was all for it when he decided to switch from biochemistry to pursuing a law degree. That sounded terrific. He was exceptional at diagnosing and fixing problems. But when spring classes resumed at L.A. State, I didn't feel much like studying myself.

I began pulling out of my sadness when I went out one day and just started hitting the ball around. When I don't exercise for a while I always feel a craving for physical activity. It's hard for me to stay depressed on a tennis court. It took me about three months to get back into shape after the car accident, but by January I felt well enough to start playing matches again. The pure physical joy of whacking the ball can wipe your mind clean and make all your troubles go away. But only for a while.

My results at the 1964 summer majors—a semifinal loss to Margaret at Wimbledon and a quarterfinal loss at Forest Hills to Nancy Richey, both in straight sets—again triggered frustration. I actually wondered if I should quit. A good number of my tennis contemporaries were getting married by then, and a few were even starting to have kids. I was torn.

I was almost twenty-one, and I couldn't win a major singles title. Something had to change. And out of the blue, something remarkable did.

I HAPPENED TO BE standing in my parents' kitchen in Long Beach when the phone rang one day in September 1964. When I picked it up, I was surprised when a man with an Australian accent said, "Hello, would this be Billie Jean Moffitt?"

The voice on the other end introduced himself as Bob Mitchell and added, "You probably don't know who I am . . ."

"Are you kidding? Of course I do!" I said. He was the Melbourne businessman who financially supported Margaret and another Aussie star, Roy Emerson, who was the No. 1 male amateur in the world. Mitchell laughed and said, "That's right. And I'd like to help you, too."

When Mitchell said he wanted to pay my way to Australia to train with the great Australian coach Mervyn Rose, it was like the world stood still. I couldn't believe my ears. Merv was one of the best tennis coaches in the world at the time. He had been working with Margaret and many other great Australian players, and he was known as a man who could look at your game, take it down to the studs if need be, and rebuild it into something much better and tighter. Whatever he did, it usually worked.

It was the offer of a lifetime, and I told Bob that. I also said I would have to think about it and get back to him. What about Larry? What about school? I'd be gone for at least three months. Larry didn't hesitate.

"You've got to do it, Billie Jean!" he said.

"But what about us, Larry? I don't want to leave you. It's not fair to you."

"We'll be fine," he insisted. "I'll still be here. And you'll never get a chance like this again. You always said you want to be the best, right? Well then, go for it. Don't waste your talent."

"But I'd have to drop out of school."

Larry smiled and said, "I hate to tell you this, but you really don't belong in school right now. You're not that crazy about it anyway."

It wasn't a lie. As I thought about what to do, my mind started reeling back to those days I sat in my elementary school classroom staring at that big pulldown map of the world and dreamed about going places. I thought about how once I started to play tennis, I was determined to be No. 1 in the world. I said it to Alice Marble, I said it to Clyde Walker, I said it to myself too many times to count.

I thanked Larry. Then I called Bob Mitchell and told him I'd take his offer.

Three weeks before I was due to fly to Australia, Larry and I had lunch at a coffee shop in Long Beach. He reached in his pocket, slid a little box across the table that contained a quarter-carat diamond ring in a gold setting, and asked me if I would marry him. I looked at him, overwhelmed, and then I looked at my watch to freeze the moment: It was 2 p.m., October 4, 1964.

"Yes! Yes! Of course I'll marry you!" I exclaimed.

Larry told me much later that his father hadn't been able to pay him for the work he'd done all summer for the family cleaning business, so Larry took a second full-time job washing dishes in an Italian restaurant to make installment payments on my engagement ring. Larry wanted to do things right.

Chapter 8

WHAM! WHAM! BAM! Roy Emerson and Owen Davidson were pounding balls at me as fast as I could return them.

"C'mon, Billie!" Emmo shouted.

"Go, go, go!" Dave-O said.

I wanted to be a full-time player, and now I was getting my wish. This was how the Aussies practiced: two on one, a drill called Threes. Emerson was a twenty-seven-year-old powerhouse who had already won seven of his twelve Grand Slam singles titles. He would stand at the net and try to hit me with the ball as hard as he could. Davidson was my age, at least, a terrific lefthander who sent me around the court like a pinball. After five minutes I thought I was going to collapse—and that was just the first day.

I've always said the Australian men made me No. 1, and those sessions were an important part of it. At L.A. State, the women's and men's teams practiced together, and a few times I played doubles for our men's team in non-conference matches. But for the most part, our American men—especially our best players—never thought to include us when they hit together. I thought it was wild that I had to travel to the other side of the world to find top-level men who were open-minded about female accomplishment and didn't mind training with me.

I wish young players today would do more two-on-one drills. You can't beat it for all-around training. When the ball hits the ground—*boom*—another is immediately put in play. There's a real art to being on the "two" side of the net. Your job is to make the ball go just far enough away from the receiver that the receiver has to work hard to keep the point alive. It sharpens your concentration and teaches you how to control the ball rather than just trying to put away every shot. On the receiving side, the drill gives you an experience that's closest to a match situation. Your pulse rate keeps climbing as the minutes tick off. We did the drill until we cried "uncle." If you're fit enough to make it one against two for twenty minutes nonstop, full out, you build confidence that you can get through the toughest match. Then you rotate positions.

From the moment I arrived on Australian soil, I knew I'd made the right choice. There are plenty of oft-repeated sayings about how champions are made in the moments nobody sees, and it's true.

I WAS BASED IN Melbourne, a big, lively, sprawling city on the southeastern tip of Australia. The national tennis championships had always been held there, and the place was packed with tennis enthusiasts. Most of the big houses in Toorak, where Bob Mitchell lived, had courts out back. Toorak was considered the Beverly Hills of Melbourne.

Bob knew all of the finest players in Australia then, and they used his private court for training and practice. He even sent a handful of them to charm school and paid for elocution lessons so they would represent Australia well on the international circuit. When I arrived, Bob set me up with my own room in his house, provided my meals and transportation, and gave me unlimited access to his court. From the outset, I was neck deep in champions, hitting daily with the best of the best. In the Aussie "mate" (or friend) tradition, most of the guys seemed to have nicknames. Along with Emmo and Dave-O, I sometimes played with "Rocket" Rod Laver, Ken "Muscles" Rosewall, and John "Newk" Newcombe, as well as Australia's best women, Lesley Turner, Robyn Ebbern, and Margaret. Geoff Pollard also came by to play.

I was living a real-time version of that party question, "If you could have dinner with any three people in tennis history, who would you choose?" How would you like to have two of the best players ever, Margaret and Rod, hitting Threes with you? It didn't happen often, but it did happen. Everyone helped each other. And you can't tell me the synergy we had didn't have an impact. The eight of us retired with a combined 208 Grand Slam titles in singles, doubles, and mixed doubles. Think about that. What a privilege it was to parachute into such a rich and welcoming tennis culture.

I was invited to luncheons and barbeques with everyone from local tennis volunteers to the great Lew Hoad, the former No. 1 amateur and contract pro. A lot of old-timers still swear that Lew was the best tennis player they ever saw. He and his wife, Jen, were kind enough to invite me to drinks at the White City Tennis Club in Sydney to get acquainted. That kind of camaraderie was one of the great things about those glory days of Australian tennis. Everyone was part of a big family, training, traveling, and socializing together. It was so much fun.

During my first phone call with Bob Mitchell, I asked him the obvious questions that anyone would ask: Why did he want to do this for me? What did he want in return? He told me, "I think you deserve it. You don't have the opportunities some of these Australian girls like Margaret have to train or travel. And I heard you don't get much personal coaching." That was all true. But Mitchell had another reason for reaching out to me that I didn't know about when I said yes.

He, like the Lawn Tennis Association of Australia, thought Margaret was not appreciative enough of all that had been done for her. In addition to bankrolling her training and travel, Bob had gone the extra mile for Margaret to the point of commissioning a painting of her in 1962 for Australia's National Portrait Gallery. Bob's unspoken motivation for bringing me to Australia was his hope that I might teach Margaret some humility—preferably by kicking her ass. Frank Deford, the wonderful *Sports Illustrated* writer, noted the irony of that a few years later when he wrote that Margaret was responsible, in a roundabout way, for "creating the monster"—me—"that cost her complete domination of her era."

If Margaret had any misgivings about training alongside a rival such as me, she never let on. Our politics would grow increasingly far apart later in life when she repeatedly attacked the LGBTQ+ community—even kids—and I called her on it. But in 1964 she was, like all the Aussies I met, unfailingly gracious and hospitable. She was a quiet person by nature who kept to herself. But I did get to know her a little better during the four months I was in Australia. We actually had some things in common, from our blue collar roots to our deep religious faith to our love of our sport.

At about the same time I was following Clyde around Long Beach's public parks as a kid, Margaret and some neighborhood boys were sneaking through a hole in the fence at a private tennis club near her home to hit, using whatever discarded tennis balls they found. Margaret, the youngest of four children, grew up in a tiny rented house without much money or comforts. She left home to train in Melbourne with Frank Sedgman when she was fifteen. Tennis was her ticket out.

Margaret definitely had a tough streak in her, and she stood up for her rights when she felt mistreated. I had already witnessed that before our 1962 Wimbledon match during her standoff with the LTAA over the national team coach Nell Hopman. That took guts. Tennis was wildly popular and so much more respected in Australia than it was in America. The credit for that went to Harry Hopman, a champion player and coach for twenty-two Australian Davis Cup–winning teams, and to Nell, his first wife, who was an excellent player, coach, and promoter. Harry was well regarded, but Nell had a reputation as a cheapskate and a bully. Margaret, even at age nineteen, was having none of it.

Shortly after I arrived in Australia I was asked by a local reporter, "Why are you here?"

I said, "I quit college and came down here to work with Mervyn Rose to try to be No. 1 in the world."

It was the first time I had ever said that publicly, and I thought it was important. I didn't want to hide my ambitions anymore, which is what women were expected to do. The reality was that I had put my life with my fiancé and family on pause, quit college, trusted a complete stranger to keep his word, and traveled eight thousand miles to the other side of the world with no guarantees. It was a huge gamble, but I felt it was one worth taking, especially with my new coach, Merv Rose.

Merv had a reputation for being tough and quirky. He was a powerful lefthanded player who won the Roland-Garros and Australian singles championships and five major doubles titles. He also had a temper. Some folks would later call him the John McEnroe of his day. Merv was famous for breaking three rackets in a single match. Another time, it started raining during a final and he tossed off his sneakers and played in his socks and won. He had a great sense of humor, but he was all business when he was coaching. He was the first full-time coach I ever had. I adored the man.

Merv took one look at chubby me—I was carrying a soft 155 pounds on my five-foot-five frame when I arrived—and he said, "Okay, Billie Jean, let's see if you can do some road work." I knew the Australians were fitness fanatics, especially Emmo and Margaret, and if that's partly how they became the best, then I was willing to run my butt off too. You have to pay the price. Besides, I was getting teased about my weight on arrival, which was always a sensitive topic for me. Instead of even calling me a Sheila—Aussie slang for a woman—I was hearing, "Here comes Two-Ton Till." Not good. I dropped fourteen pounds by the time I left.

November is warm in Australia, but December is the real start of summertime in the Southern Hemisphere and the temperatures can be brutal, often topping 100 degrees. I sweated buckets running before breakfast to get in shape. In the afternoon I'd hit with Davidson, Emerson, or whoever else came by. In between I had a long private session with Merv starting at about 9 a.m. The other players and I were thrilled when it came time for tournaments because the matches felt so much easier than practice. Our drills made me so much stronger psychologically, emotionally, and physically.

The first thing Merv did was remake my serve by teaching me to shorten my backswing and toss the ball more forward, and higher. That gave me greater extension and more power. It also put me a step or half step into the court already on my follow-through, giving me a split second more time to react to my opponent's return. My serve became a better weapon.

Merv also set out to retool my feeble excuse for a forehand, the shot that opponents loved to attack, and a stroke that had defied everyone else's best attempts to fix. Like Alice, Merv told me I was hitting too close to my body. His solution was to shorten my backswing and make sure I kept the racket head in front of my wrist on the follow through for increased control and accuracy. Today we don't teach the forehand that way—the technique is more dynamic, the swing path is longer, and the racket speed is faster. But that's not what I was taught.

My new motion looked strange, and it felt even worse at first. I was unlearning habits I'd honed my entire life. But the result was a much better forehand.

Merv also wanted me to examine how I thought the game. He was a huge proponent of percentage tennis, which basically means hitting the shot that gives you the best chance to win the point with the least amount of risk. That was a bit hard for me to reconcile because I loved the aesthetic joys of the game, the satisfaction that comes with hitting a perfectly placed shot on the run or playing a beautifully constructed point, and the charge you feel when the crowd responds to your showmanship or dramatic shots. What Merv stressed is that every decision should be for a tactical advantage, period. He would tell me to watch other players closely and then quiz me afterward: Why did someone choose a particular shot? Why did it work or not work? His approach was so rigorous I sometimes got headaches from how hard I was concentrating.

I was working more than I had ever worked before, and a leap of faith was required because it didn't pay off right away. Between training sessions I was traveling all over Australia to compete. In Adelaide, I lost a three-set match to a little-known fourteen-year-old when I had thirty-five double faults with my new serve. More upsets followed. Mastering my new forehand took time too. The Federation Cup was going to be played in Melbourne at the end of January, followed by the Australian Nationals. The tennis world would be coming to us. I wondered if I was going to make a fool of myself when it did.

"Keep at it, Billie Jean," Merv kept repeating. "It might take months or even a year, but this is going to pay off."

"Why are you changing so many things? Why?" Lesley Turner said to me one day in the locker room after another dreadful loss. "You're already No. 4 in the world!"

I said, "Lesley, you are so sweet. And I hear you. I probably could stay top eight the rest of my career. But I want to be No. 1. I came here to become No. 1."

I spent my birthday and Christmas alone, and I was so happy when my dear friend Carole Caldwell, who was by then Carole Graebner, arrived to play the Federation Cup with me in January 1965. Larry and I tried to stay in touch by writing, and he was working some extra hours so we could afford a few long-distance calls. But it was hard being apart for so long. Having Carole in Australia was wonderful. She had married Clark Graebner, a top player who was later one of the protagonists in John McPhee's classic tennis book, *Levels of the Game*. For the Federation Cup we were a two-woman team, and I served as playing captain because the USLTA didn't send a third player. Australia won the cup, 2–1, by sweeping both singles matches from us. We played in suffocating humidity and sweltering temperatures that topped out at 107 degrees. It was amazing we didn't get heatstroke.

I made it to the final of the Australian Championships, but Margaret beat me in straight sets, again denying me my first Grand Slam singles title. And yet, as uncharacteristic as it was for me, I actually wasn't that devastated. I knew I was still adjusting my game and, having seen Margaret up close for four months now, I wasn't that surprised when she ended up running off a fifty-eight-match winning streak that year, or a 105–7 overall record. Everyone was starting to wonder if she was unstoppable.

When I flew home from Australia, I knew in my bones that I was better situated to compete than I'd ever been before. I was a full-time player now, fully committed, expertly trained, and fitter than ever. Larry and I were thrilled to be reunited, and we began planning our September wedding.

When I went back on the road that summer, Margaret and I kept missing each other. At Wimbledon, I won the doubles with Maria Bueno, who had asked me to play after Karen Hantze Susman took a break to have a baby. But Maria beat me in the semis of women's singles and won her second straight Wimbledon title. Margaret and I didn't meet again until the U.S. Nationals. Once again, it was a final.

When I walked on the court that day I knew Margaret was playing some of the best tennis of her life. But I was too. I was using that solid percentage game I had learned in Australia, and it was working. I thought I had her at 5–3 in the first set—until Margaret caught fire and swiped it. I was ahead 5–3 in the second set, too. To my shock, I didn't win another game. Final score: 8–6, 7–5. *What had just happened?*

At first I was devastated and angry at myself. I left the grounds and took a long walk with Frank Brennan on Continental Avenue in Queens, and I told him, "I'm so upset I can't breathe." It was my fourth consecutive loss to Margaret in a Grand Slam. I wasn't making mistakes that day so much as she kept playing better. She poured it on.

As I dissected the match with Frank, I realized something that would change my life, something Margaret seemingly already understood: The difference between a champion and the rest of the field is having the ability to lift your game when you're under the greatest pressure. I had played conservatively against Margaret when I should have been in her face, going for my shots, playing to win. It's something Roger Federer expressed similarly after he began lashing winner after winner in the fifth set to beat his longtime nemesis, Rafael Nadal, in their epic 2017 Australian Open final. Federer said, "I just kept telling myself, 'Victory goes to the brave.'" I played it too safe against Margaret that day. That's why I lost. Now I was convinced that I'd unlocked what created the gap between us—and how I could erase it. I knew I could beat her.

As I finished my walk with Frank, I said, "I'm going to win Wimbledon next year."

LIKE SO MANY OTHER things in our life, the wedding date that Larry and I landed on was governed by tennis. We chose a Friday evening, September 17, 1965, so our tennis friends could attend between the end of U.S. Nationals and the start of the Pacific Southwest Championships. Many of them were in our wedding party. Sue Behlmar and Marcos Carriedo, our L.A. State teammates, served as attendants along with my brother, Randy, and Larry's siblings, Mary Ellen and Gary. Carole Graebner was a beautiful matron of honor. My dear friend Jerry Cromwell was there too.

We had the ceremony at the First Church of the Brethren, just four blocks from my childhood home. It was an old-fashioned wedding. I borrowed my cousin Donna Lee's wedding dress because we were the same size and I figured, why buy a new one? I took my vows in a veil and her beautiful gown of white Chantilly lace. The train was trimmed with pearls and sequins. We splurged for a bouquet of white roses for me. Larry wore a black bow tie, black pants, and a crisp white dinner jacket. We looked just like the little couple they put on top of wedding cakes.

My dad was teary-eyed as he walked me down the aisle. Mom looked radiant. Larry's stepmom and his father were beaming. Everyone waved goodbye as we drove off to our honeymoon. Though Larry and I used to spend hours making out while we were dating, we didn't have sex until our wedding night. Being a virgin until marriage wasn't that uncommon in those days. He was twenty, I was twenty-one, and it was a far more naive time. We spent the weekend at a lodge in the mountains.

When I look back at those wedding photos, I'm struck by how fair and slender Larry was, how young we both looked, and how happy we were. We were so much in love. I thought we'd be together the rest of our lives, have two to four kids, the whole nine yards.

NOBODY CAN REALLY tell you how married life should be. You figure it out as you go. Larry had one year left at L.A. State, and I decided to go back to school as well that fall. We moved into a small one-bedroom apartment in Alhambra, a suburb near campus. We had $300 between us, a bed, and a few other pieces of furniture. Larry and I loved children and agreed we wanted to have them someday—just not yet. We thought we should wait until he had his law career going and I stopped playing competitive tennis. This was a fairly unusual choice then; a lot of our friends were already on their second child.

Beyond that, I was determined to be a conventional "good" wife. I told myself my life wasn't about just me now, and I wanted to be there for Larry much like my mom had been for my dad. I hardly played tennis that fall and winter. Larry had a full course load and he was working the night shift at the Seal Right ice cream carton factory, a job he got after he asked my father for permission to marry me and Dad said, "Well, how are you going to support her, Larry?"

I took a job as a coach in Pasadena for a junior tennis community program for $32 a day. I would take Larry a homemade lunch and sit with him at 2 a.m. while he ate. When Larry came home in the morning the apartment would be clean, the laundry folded. We'd sleep a few hours and head off to school. Some days I'd stroll by the window of one of his classrooms just because I thought he was so handsome, and I'd think, *Oh no!* when I'd see him nodding off because he was so tired.

Scotty Deeds, our tennis coach, helped us earn a little more extra money by getting us jobs keeping statistics for L.A. State's basketball team and passing out hot dogs and Cokes in the press box during football games. Still, Larry and I were barely squeaking by. Our idea of a big outing became sharing a twenty-five-cent ice cream sundae in the student union. Eventually, I had one of those moments like Scarlett O'Hara has in *Gone With the Wind* where she vows she'll never go hungry again. One night I told Larry, "I can't keep living like this!" I was serious.

By December, Larry had received a response from the Boalt School of Law at the University of California at Berkeley, his first choice, one of the top law programs in the country. Initially, he was unsure whether he should apply there. His terrific LSAT score ranked in the top quarter of the top 1 percent nationally, but working full-time had adversely affected his grades. I urged him to try for Berkeley anyway, telling him, "C'mon Larry, what's the worst that can happen?"—a remark that sounded brave until the envelope arrived and we were too scared to open it right away. We finally mustered the courage to quit staring at it and sat down on the bed to read the letter together. We were shaking as Larry unfolded it and he said, "Oh, my God . . ."

When I looked, I saw that it read "Welcome. And congratulations . . ."

"*Yes!*" I yelled.

At about the same time, we learned that I would end the year ranked No. 1 in the United States for the first time in the USLTA rankings. That was a thrill, too. We agreed that Larry would finish his spring credits and graduate in June, but I would stop classes again and resume being a full-time player. As it turned out, I would never return to college. It was the first big thing in my life I didn't finish, and falling just short of completing my degree still bothers me. But I was all in.

I got a big taste of tennis's insider politics almost immediately. When the USLTA board convened in February for what was usually a rubber-stamp approval of the year-end rankings, I was forced to share the 1965 top spot with Nancy Richey, who had been bumped down to No. 2. It was the first time the ranking committee had been overruled in eighty-one years. The backroom effort was led by Stan Malless, a USLTA big shot who ran the Midwest section. A few people told me, "Stan was mad at you and he was emphatic" because I had skipped his National Clay Court Championships that year. He joined Al Bumann, president of the Texas association, in lobbying for Nancy. Nancy's father, George, was a well-connected teaching pro in Texas. He was so competitive he forbade Nancy and her brother, Cliff, who was also a top player, from speaking to opponents on tour, a habit they loosened only when they got older.

I was furious about the ranking machinations and told reporters so. And while the USLTA was undercutting me, the South African promoter Owen Williams had reached out to me and said he was willing to pay me $1,100 in expense money plus round-trip airfare to travel to Johannesburg for the prestigious South African Tennis Championships in March 1966. That was more money than I had ever seen at that point, and light years beyond the $14 to $28 per diem the USLTA paid us. The foreign players used to laugh because the USLTA paid *them* more to compete at our U.S. Nationals than it paid us. I was starting to think that just about everything about amateur tennis was rotten.

Agreeing to play in South Africa at that moment in history required a bit of soul searching. The fight to isolate South Africa because of its apartheid system wasn't nearly as pitched as it became, but there was a simmering debate by early 1966 about whether visiting or staying away from South Africa was the best strategy.

Nelson Mandela had been sentenced to life in prison twenty months earlier. The International Olympic Committee had voted to ban South Africa from the Summer Olympics after prodding from activists in Britain and Europe. But in America, the push for the wide-ranging cultural, economic, and sports boycotts that South Africa eventually suffered wasn't widespread yet. Most of the world's top tennis players still went to South Africa then, if invited. Even Arthur Ashe, the only prominent African American player on tour, kept petitioning to play there because he felt he could make a bigger statement by showing up. It would be another decade before Arthur changed his mind about supporting the boycotts in the mid-1970s.

I had no idea what I'd find if I traveled there. I did know that when I looked around we were neck deep in our own horrible struggles over segregation and racism in the United States, and that conflict was global. I thought a lot about how I had traveled to play in Moscow at a time when Cold War tensions between the U.S. and the Soviet Union were high, though not everyone agreed with that trip. Our government's philosophy then was that it made more sense to engage people. Ultimately, I decided to go to South Africa.

I eagerly looked out the window as my plane began its descent to land at the airport on the outskirts of Johannesburg, but there wasn't a lush African forest or an exotic herd of animals to be seen. All I could make out below were red dirt fields, open-pit mines, and the hardscrabble eastern townships where nonwhites were forced to live. Once I got closer to the city and the tournament's permanent home at the Ellis Park sports complex, I was happy to see some familiar faces. The event was a long way for an American to travel, but it was a major stop on the Southern Hemisphere circuit and it felt like old times when I renewed acquaintances with so many of the Australians I'd trained with the previous year, including Owen Davidson, Roy Emerson, and Margaret. Margaret and I hadn't played since my galling loss to her in the U.S. Nationals final.

All told, Margaret had beaten me nine straight times over four years, and I hadn't pried away even one set from her. When we played in the final this time, our match took only fifty-five minutes and I routed her, 6–3, 6–2. The painful insights I had gained at Forest Hills about what made Margaret a dominant champion—that ability of hers to lift her game on command, her knack for sensing when those moments arrived in a match—had now worked for *me*. And I told myself if the recipe worked against Margaret, the best in the world, it should work against anybody.

When I went looking for that extra gear that I wanted, I found it that day. I wasn't handcuffed by doubt or my fear of losing, as I was in our previous meeting. I was lifted by my determination to do whatever it took to win. I seized my chances, went for my shots despite the pressure. I adjusted better to the 5,700-foot altitude by shortening my backswing on my forehand and relying a lot on my kick serve while Margaret struggled to keep the ball in play. It's easy to send the ball flying to the fence in the thin air if you take the ball late. She seemed rattled. I never let up.

I was twenty-two, but I felt as if my career was really just beginning. The spell was broken. Now, anything seemed possible. Margaret had a 9–1 advantage in our head-to-head encounters before I won that Johannesburg match. I played her dead even the remainder of our careers.

Chapter 9

I'D LOVE TO SAY it was all smooth sailing after my win in Johannesburg, but I picked up a hard-to-diagnose illness on that trip and fell knee-crawling sick. I wasn't allowed to leave the country for a week and my doubles partner, Rosie Casals, refused to leave without me because she was so worried about my health. Once we did start the two-day journey back home, I decided to forgo wearing the girdle I'd worn on the trip there for the same silly reason anyone wore a girdle then: I wanted the slim-fitting pencil skirt I was traveling in to fit better. I wanted to look presentable when I met my host family. It's a wonder I didn't cause myself an embolism.

It's funny how a single win can sometimes work alchemy. After I beat Margaret in Johannesburg, I continued to stack up victories for months even though I was still fighting whatever bug I had contracted. I had a significant role in our U.S. team's Federation Cup win over Germany in Turin, Italy, in May. It was the first time the USLTA had allowed me to compete on red clay in a team competition although I had been begging them for years. I felt some pressure once play began, and cherished it when my teammates Carole Graebner, Julie Heldman, and I won the title, and I beat Françoise Dürr and Ann Jones on the way to the final.

I would've liked to linger in Europe after that to play more tournaments and sock away some desperately needed savings for Larry and me. Some of the European promoters, like the South Africans, were much more generous with expense money than the Americans. But the USLTA wanted me playing back in the States, where I was starting to be a crowd draw. Since the controversy over the No. 1 ranking with Nancy Richey earlier that year, I thought I had to follow orders—or else. That's how it was in amateur tennis then.

I returned for tournaments in La Jolla, California, and Tulsa before heading back to England for Wimbledon. Logging that many miles wasn't the optimal way to prepare, but I was determined to overcome it. By now I had collected four Grand Slam doubles titles and I was still looking for my first singles crown in fourteen visits to a major.

I was seeded fourth for Wimbledon behind Margaret, Maria Bueno, and Ann Jones, the latest Brit to shoulder the country's annual yearning for a Wimbledon title. I didn't exactly tee myself up to be a crowd favorite when I beat Ann in the Wightman Cup the week before, on our way to the title. Some of the British tabloid reporters accused me of faking the cramp I suffered in the third set before I rallied to win. I admit I can be a ham, even a drama queen at times, but I would never pull a stunt like that.

The adverse coverage affected my reception by the crowds a week later at Wimbledon. I told myself to shove it out of my mind. As nice as it was to be the top-ranked player in America, you couldn't truly be No. 1 in the world unless you won Wimbledon. When my old friend Harold Guiver told me he couldn't make it from Long Beach to London, I sent him a note back that said, "You'll be sorry, because this is the year."

Larry, who had finished his undergraduate degree from L.A. State in June, joined me at Wimbledon for the first time, which was exciting. We were staying at the Lexham Gardens off Cromwell Road in Earl's Court. Like many English hotels then, the shared bathroom was down the hall. The only source of warmth to fend off the dank, rainy days was a wall heater that required dropping a constant supply of shillings into a slot to keep it cranking out hot air.

The room rate was right, though, and they had a terrific staff. I loved how quaint the hotel looked outside with its Corinthian columns, blond brick, and potted petunias. I loved hearing the *clip-clop* of horse hooves on the cobblestone streets as the milkman made his rounds early each morning. It was still dark outside then, and Larry and I knew we had a little more time to stay in bed. Then, once it was time to go, what could be more deluxe than ignoring the nearby tube station and getting picked up right outside our door by a magnificent Rolls-Royce or Daimler flying the Wimbledon flag? The All England Club sent the top-seeded players a chauffeured ride.

Larry watched my matches from the competitor's box as I progressed through the draw, but he was so anxious he began devouring entire bags of the bonbons they sold on the grounds. On a subsequent trip, Larry also tried speaking play-by-play of my matches into a tape recorder—anything to calm his nerves. He told me, "I couldn't do what you do."

My name on the Wimbledon scoreboard now read "Mrs. L.W. King," which I considered just another All England Club tradition, same as the curtsies and the flower bouquets. But Larry was so progressive it bothered him. When we were talking about getting married, he had actually suggested changing his last name to Moffitt instead because, he said, "King is so common." Later, when fans began asking him for his autograph, he would sometimes sign, "Mr. Billie Jean King."

"Why do you do that?" I asked him.

"Well, that's how everyone really thinks of me," he said with a laugh.

Larry never had problems with his own identity.

I DIDN'T LOOK like a world beater during the first week of Wimbledon. I had to rally from significant holes in three of my first four matches. I had asked seventeen-year-old Rosie Casals to be my regular doubles partner earlier that summer, and we lost in the Wimbledon quarterfinals to Margaret and Judy Tegart. Soon, Rosie and I would start a long run as the top doubles team on tour, but for now my more immediate problem was the nausea, fatigue, and intestinal trouble caused by my undiagnosed illness. It continued to bother me off and on.

By the time Margaret and I met in the singles semifinals, her move through the draw had been far more powerful than mine. A reporter asked me how I intended to beat her and I said, "Simple. Chip and charge at her feet."

Actually, I had a few more strategies in mind. Doris Hart, our Wightman Cup captain, had been by my side all month and she became a secret weapon. She told me, "If Margaret attacks, you lob." For the plan to work, you have to have good touch and keep your opponent guessing when you're going to lob. Otherwise you're toast. But we knew if I could do it well, I could force Margaret from the offensive position she preferred, crowding the net, to a defensive position. The morning of the match I woke up extra excited, but in a good way. I was so focused I felt almost hyper lucid. The grass seemed greener, the sounds seemed sharper, my legs had spring. I could feel every hair on my head. I couldn't wait.

Once the crowd had settled in and the chair umpire said "Play," Margaret came out tight and she never relaxed. As Doris had suggested, I kept lobbing over Margaret's head, knowing when I could see the back of her shirt that it was time for me to rush the net. Also, that backhand volley of mine that Alice Marble had told me was special kept coming through. The two shots that Merv Rose improved most when I was training in Australia—my serve and my forehand—lifted me as well. It was as if everything I had been working on all those years were funneled into that moment and snapped into place. I felt that nothing could stop me, no situation was beyond my control.

Every tennis match is made up of hundreds of shots, and yet this match felt as though it tipped with a single blow: a running forehand in the second set that I ripped down the line and Margaret initially began to reach for—and then let it go. She groaned in surprise when the ball wasn't called out. She was never the same after that. One newspaper story on the following day remarked how I was all over the court, anticipating everything, while "the rangy Australian stepped uncertainly around and seemed to lack confidence . . . The Aussie's usual serve-and-smash game seemed adequate for most opponents but Mrs. King had no trouble handling it."

I erased a break point with that winner and held serve for a 4–3 lead. The rest of the second set went swiftly. I broke Margaret's serve in the next game, and for the final four points of the match Margaret mishit an overhead smash, drove a backhand volley into the net, missed a forehand down the line, and netted another backhand volley. I was moving on. I was one match away from No. 1.

In the Wimbledon final two days later, I fought it out for three sets with Maria, by now a three-time Wimbledon champion. After I dropped the second set, I was ticked off but it didn't occur to me that I would lose. Maria was an elegant champion with a strong serve. But she didn't have much footspeed and I exploited that. I wasn't as graceful as she was, but I had terrific lateral movement and could cover the court faster than just about everyone. I followed Doris's scouting report to serve wide to Maria's forehand, and to lob over her when she came forward. In the final set, it was my backhand that lifted me. In the fourth game I broke Maria's serve using back-to-back returns that left her stranded in the middle of the court as the ball flew by. She didn't win another game.

The final score was 6–3, 3–6, 6–1. I threw my racket high into the air, covered my face, stole a peek at Larry. *I just won Wimbledon!*

My heart was still pounding as a red carpet was rolled out on the court for Princess Marina of Greece and Denmark, the Duchess of Kent, and she presented me with the silver-and-gold Venus Rosewater Dish. I knew that the trophy is engraved with the names of all the previous women's winners, so I did a quick look to find Alice, Althea, Maureen Connolly, and Doris Hart's names. It felt overwhelming to realize, *Now my name will be there forever too.* I kissed the trophy and held it above my head, acknowledging the crowd. I wished my parents and Randy and everyone back in Long Beach could be there with Larry. I was as happy as I'd ever been in my life.

The next night at the Wimbledon Ball, I took the traditional first dance with the men's champion, Manuel Santana of Spain, before Larry politely asked to cut in. Then Larry took my hand with a smile. For the next few minutes we went swirling around the ballroom floor feeling we'd come a very long way from being two kids who spent their first date at a dance club in Long Beach, California.

———

MARGARET STEPPED AWAY from tennis after I defeated her at Wimbledon. She later wrote in one of her memoirs that she had lost her lust for tennis. She moved to Perth, Australia's westernmost big city, and opened a boutique on a quiet street, happy to be anonymous again. I was deeply disappointed. I always wanted to play the best to be the best. She wasn't at the U.S. Nationals a month later when I tried to win my first title there, and I didn't know if she'd ever be back.

I was seeded No. 1 in all the grass court tournaments I played in the States that summer before arriving at Forest Hills. I was also still taking antibiotics and sick to my stomach many days. I followed doctor's orders and missed a couple of matches in August because I just couldn't move. Otherwise, I kept on grinding, because that's what I do. As far as I'm concerned, it's never an excuse to say you lost a match because you were sick or injured. We all play hurt. So either you win with grace or you say the other person beat you and move on.

That was my mindset when I stepped out to play Kerry Melville, an up-and-coming nineteen-year-old from Australia, in my second-round match at Forest Hills—until I looked up at the umpire's chair and saw Al Bumann, the same Texas USLTA official who had helped the effort to make me share the No. 1 ranking with Nancy Richey. I started thinking about the nasty politics of the sport. I shouldn't have let it distract me, but I did. I stopped everything and complained heatedly that Bumann should be removed, to no avail. Which only incensed me more.

Rather than suck it up after that, I got so angry I basically blew the match. I hit balls to the back wall of the court so often I lost count. It wasn't fair to Kerry, who played well and beat me, 6–4, 6–4. A reporter who remembered that I had defeated Kerry two weeks earlier asked me what happened and I said, "She just outplayed me, that's all." Which was true. I also behaved like an ass, and everyone knew it.

I was feeling so bad physically I went home to Long Beach to have my mother take care of me. It was so great to start feeling better, and to be back in the neighborhood and hanging out with Randy. He was about to turn eighteen, he now stood six feet three, and he had been named Long Beach's athlete of the year for 1966 after pitching a string of no-hitters. He was on his way. Though I was a married woman now and the top player in tennis, in Bill and Betty's house they still called me "Sis" and expected me to be at the dinner table with Randy at 5:30 sharp, do my share of chores and be in bed by 8:30 p.m. And it all felt . . . *perfect*.

Larry was to start law school that month and he found us a tiny, one-bedroom apartment near campus. When it was time to move, all we had to pack were our clothes, a few pots and pans, some tennis gear, and Larry's collection of Andy Williams records. I was more into Aretha Franklin and Motown music myself, especially the Temptations and the Supremes. We had the car radio tuned to KJH, and I was singing along with the Supremes' Diana Ross as Larry and I hit the freeway, headed north.

Our new apartment was near the grand old Claremont Hotel at the foot of a forested canyon. I loved living in Berkeley at that time. The neighborhood was like heaven under a canopy of oak and fragrant eucalyptus trees. I was feeling better because I saw yet another doctor for what had been afflicting me since I was in South Africa and I was finally diagnosed with colitis and put on a nondairy diet. It took me only three minutes to walk to the Berkeley Tennis Club. On a typical day I would hit the courts by 8:30 a.m. to practice, usually with a male player such as Don Jacobus, a former University of Pacific star. If Rosie was in town—she lived across the bay in San Francisco—we'd have lunch together and then practice a few hours.

I had first met Rosie when she was a tiny thirteen-year-old playing doubles with Gloria Segerquist against Carole Caldwell and me at the Pacific Coast Championships at the Berkeley Tennis Club. She was riveting even then. Rosie stood only five feet two and a quarter—don't forget the quarter, she'd say—and she had just about every shot you could imagine. She might've been the best all-around athlete on tour. Her acrobatic game and hustle made her a crowd favorite, and she was feisty.

Rosie's biological parents had emigrated to San Francisco from El Salvador, but less than a year after Rosie was born they decided they couldn't care for her and her older sister, Victoria. The girls went to live with their great-uncle and great-aunt, Manuel and Maria Casals. It was Manuel who started Rosie in tennis by driving her to the public courts at Golden Gate Park. Rosie used to sit in the driver's seat and Manuel would run down the San Francisco hills alongside his car waiting for her to catch it in gear and then jump in once the engine started. Still other times, the two of them made their rides to the tennis courts on Manuel's scooter, with Rosie clutching his waist and her racket slung over her back.

By her own admission, Rosie was often self-conscious about her roots and lack of money after she graduated to the clubby, ultra-white world of tennis. She had a frank sense of humor and disliked pretense as much as I did. Together we became frequent champions and fellow rabble-rousers, best friends, and confidants for life.

When we began playing doubles together, Rosie was the same age I was when I made my first visit to Wimbledon. On our initial trip there together, it was as if I was seeing everything through new eyes. I introduced Rosie to the clotted cream and strawberries. I showed her the locker rooms and explained the unofficial caste system: past winners and the top sixteen ladies seeds were in the more luxurious members' dressing room on the upper floor, where the attendant would launder your tennis clothes, polish your sneakers overnight, even draw you a bath in one of the three clawfoot tubs if you asked. The other established players were assigned to a second locker room that was two flights down. The basement changing room was for the lowest-ranked entrants. I had Rosie close her eyes and I took her to the top of Centre Court before the tournament began, just like Gerald Williams had done for me five years earlier, and I said, "Okay. Now open your eyes."

"It's so beautiful," Rosie said quietly. "It *is* like a cathedral."

It was great to have Rosie become part of the life I settled into in Berkeley that fall. I enjoyed the break from constant travel. I continued to cook and clean for Larry, and I loved the thought of being a lawyer's wife once he graduated. But I already had this gnawing realization that I could never fit into a "normal" or "conventional" mold, whatever that meant.

THE BAY AREA HAD become the center of the radical universe in America by the time Larry and I arrived late in the summer of 1966. Sometimes when we met for lunch at the student union in the middle of campus I could see where the police had cordoned off streets to stop the protest marches. Larry would tell me about smelling pot or tear gas on his way home, or how the National Guardsmen would be chasing hippies as the hippies were yelling things over their shoulders like, "The revolution is coming! The revolution is coming!" That was about as close as Larry or I got to the serious action, but you couldn't help being struck by the spirit of rebellion.

Berkeley was being transformed by students who had traveled to Mississippi in 1963 and 1964 to help increase African American voter registration. They came back versed in civil rights movement tactics like civil disobedience. Some even acquired a taste for confrontation, which eventually led to sit-ins and contributed to a ban of on-campus political organizations.

Just a few miles away from Berkeley, tens of thousands of draftees were being processed and shipped to Vietnam through the port of Oakland, and Berkeley students joined the antiwar protests that were in full swing. The Black Panther movement had taken hold on campus during that time, too, and Dolores Huerta and César Chávez were deep into their labor organizing work for the striking migrant (and mostly Latinx) workers in California, which led to the establishment of the National Farm Workers Association. Dolores became one of my heroines, and I would get to know her decades later. She told me she wished she had not acquiesced when Cesar came to her and suggested, "It would be better if we had one person speaking for us, not two." That's how he became the public front man for the movement while Dolores was the skilled negotiator and organizer who coordinated the consumer boycott of grapes and many other actions that eventually led them to victory.

On the other side of the bay, the flower-child crowd had flocked to Golden Gate Park for the Human Be-In in January 1967, a counterculture event that drew the likes of psychedelic drug advocate

Timothy Leary, the Beat Generation poet Allen Ginsberg, and the activist/comedian Dick Gregory. It was the precursor to San Francisco's "Summer of Love" that left the Haight-Ashbury district hailed as an epicenter of America's hippie movement and drug use.

That lifestyle was completely foreign to me, but insatiably curious as I am, I would engage the hippies in discussion. I've never seen difference as a bad thing and I always want to learn more. Ever since I was a child watching African American children my age turned away from schools, and then when I felt discrimination myself because of gender, I've harbored a deep sense of outrage as well. I can't stand injustice or unkindness of any kind. In Berkeley, it seemed like everything in American life was being reexamined, including what it meant to be a woman and women's roles in the workplace and society. I was questioning where I fit in too.

The National Organization for Women was founded by twenty-eight activists at a national conference on the status of women in Washington, D.C., while I was winning my first Wimbledon singles title in 1966. I played Virginia Wade in the 1968 U.S. Open final on the same night that feminists held their famous protest of the Miss America pageant in Atlantic City. That uprising was conceived by Carol Hanisch, the radical feminist who coined the phrase "The personal *is* political."

Hanisch and the other organizers saw the pageant as an opportunity to gain publicity for their protests against America's treatment of women by rejecting the "vapid" symbolism of Miss America, an image they said "oppresses women in every area in which it purports to represent us." They favored threatening to burn their bras instead.

My stand on feminism—even whether I should publicly use the word—evolved over time. When Larry and I first met, he was probably more sophisticated than I was about politics in some regards. In the beginning I could be very literal, too black-and-white. When I'd remark that, say, "I don't get what burning our bras would accomplish," Larry might counter that sometimes it takes the people on the extreme edges to move everyone toward the middle. Which is true.

What I've also found is when you're actually doing advocacy work from the inside, you have to be strategic to get things done. You have to realize that sometimes success comes incrementally. I often felt radical inside, but outside I tried to be pragmatic and measured. I wanted to take strong stands without alienating the people I was trying to persuade, and it was a constant high-wire act. As an activist, it's a continual challenge to find the right balance.

That said, I already had great clarity about where I stood on my sport by the time I arrived in Berkeley. By 1967, everyone sensed that change was finally coming in the business of tennis, and I had a choice to make: I could step aside, or I could help lead. Ever since my epiphany at the Los Angeles Tennis Club when I was twelve years old, I had thought tennis could be my platform to help create a more equal world. Now that I was No. 1, I decided it was time to raise the volume and see if anyone would listen. Walls were coming down everywhere I looked, including the one that usually separated politics and sports.

I BEGAN SPEAKING OUT more just a few months after the heavyweight boxing champion Muhammad Ali refused to go to Vietnam as a soldier, but more than a year before the Black Power protests at the 1968 Mexico City Olympics led by the American sprinters John Carlos and Tommie Smith. They were expelled from the Games for their clench-fisted salute from atop the medal stand. Carlos and Smith attended San Jose State, which is just a forty-five-mile drive from Berkeley, and they were involved with Dr. Harry Edwards, a sports sociologist and activist who was helping athletes organize protests of human rights abuses against people of color. The UCLA basketball star Kareem Abdul-Jabbar, another ally of Dr. Edwards, skipped the 1968 Summer Games completely. Soon, another African American athlete, Curt Flood, would take on the reserve clause in Major League Baseball that bound a player to his team, memorably saying, "A well-paid slave is nonetheless a slave."

In my mind, nothing illustrated the multilevel conflicts going on within America by the spring of 1967 as much as the firestorm surrounding Ali. As Cassius Clay, he had shocked the world by knocking out Sonny Liston to win the pro heavyweight title in 1964. That's the fight where Ali jumped the ropes and began screaming, "I *am* the Greatest!" He often told a story about coming home to Louisville from the 1960 Rome Olympics and throwing his boxing gold medal into the Ohio River because he was refused service in a restaurant because he was Black. After being mentored by Malcolm X and others, he changed his name and converted to Islam. He refused to be inducted into the U.S. Army, on religious and moral grounds, uttering his famous line, "I ain't got no quarrel with them Viet Cong." Eventually, he was stripped of his heavyweight title.

I read and admired Malcolm X's autobiography, but I was too much of a pacifist to totally buy into his "by any means necessary" credo. I had been raised in a religious tradition that advocated the sort of nonviolent actions that Dr. King favored. I didn't agree with everything Ali said then, either, but I strongly supported his choice to speak out against the war and to declare himself a conscientious objector, even if nobody was asking me at the time.

I hated the Vietnam War. It made no sense to me. Why were we fighting there? What would "winning" even look like? Every week there were photos in *Life* magazine and news coverage on TV that brought home the horrors of the war—bloodied soldiers lying facedown in the mud, mothers weeping over their lost children, caskets coming home draped in flags.

Larry and I talked about Vietnam a lot. American soldiers were dying at a rate of more than two hundred a week in 1967. I was thankful that both Larry and my brother were in school. For the time being, they had student deferments from the draft. But if I didn't want my brother and my husband drafted, how could I fault Ali? There was something about Ali's manner and message that I connected with immediately. Once we began running into each other years later at charity banquets and sports events, we became quite friendly. We often talked about how you never know if you're going to touch someone's life or they're going to touch yours, regardless of gender, creed, or color, so you have to be open and alert. Every time I saw Ali, he would lean toward me with that mischievous look on his face and make me laugh by whispering in his raspy voice, "Billie Jeeeean, you're the Queen."

Muhammad paid dearly for his activism. He was suspended from boxing for three years, stripped of his title, and called a traitor by his critics. Yet he never let bitterness gain a foothold in his heart, at least that I could see.

Around the same time Ali's saga was playing out in 1967, another sports story caught my attention. A twenty-year-old university student named Kathrine Switzer registered as K. W. Switzer to run the all-male Boston Marathon. Racing authorities had always claimed that the 26.2-mile distance was too strenuous for women. I was tired of hearing that nonsense—and Switzer was determined to prove them wrong. About two miles into the course, a race official named Jock Semple saw her and tried to rip off her bib number while screaming, "Get the hell out of my race!" Photographers captured the moment.

Semple was knocked to the ground by Switzer's boyfriend, Tom Miller, a 235-pound former All-American football player and nationally ranked hammer thrower who was running beside her. Switzer completed the race about an hour behind the first female finisher, Roberta "Bobbi" Gibb, who raced unregistered for the second straight year. (Gibb wore nursing shoes because running sneakers weren't made expressly for women then.) The Switzer-Semple story made international headlines.

It would be another five years before women could officially enter the Boston Marathon, and twelve years before the women's marathon was finally added to the 1984 Summer Olympics and won by America's Joan Benoit. Chauvinistic attitudes in sports are slow to change. In 2005, Gian Franco Kasper, head of the International Ski Federation, was still saying that women should be banned from Olympic ski jumping because the hard landings might impact their ability to have children. A women's Olympic ski jumping event wasn't added until 2014. And *that* change came only two years after the ground shook, the azaleas parted, and the Augusta National Golf Club, home of the Masters, admitted its first two women club members. Civilization did not end.

When I looked around tennis, I thought the USLTA's treatment of women and its stance on amateurism were both outdated. Lawn tennis started in the English countryside as a social pastime for wealthy Victorians, and women had always been part of the tradition. And yet we were treated as second-class citizens, even if we played on the same size courts and in many of the same tournaments as men. To a lot of us, merely allowing women in the door wasn't good enough.

As far as amateurism was concerned, the traditionalists always resisted allowing professionals to compete at the major tournaments. As early as 1960, some progressive officials brought a proposal to the International Lawn Tennis Federation to annually sanction a dozen or so "open" tournaments, meaning that both amateurs and professionals could be in the same draw. The measure lost by five lousy votes.

I often wonder how different my life would have been if I could have played pro tennis from the beginning of my career. I remember sitting in my dressing room cubicle at Wimbledon at ages eighteen and nineteen, looking at the older women and thinking, *Why are you happy to be amateurs when the guys can be pros? You retire from hitting balls for ten years and you've never had any income coming in, you're not trained for anything. What are you going to do with your life?*

I didn't see a pathway. In 1964, I quietly tried to organize a group walkout at Forest Hills when a few other American women were complaining about various things, including the seedings and how the USLTA was giving more under-the-table money to foreigners than us to participate. I was only twenty, but I said, "Well, I'm willing to refuse to play." I was seeded third and had more to lose than some of the others, but none of the unhappy players would join me. They were afraid.

By 1967, the push for open tennis intensified. Jack Kramer's traveling pro tour continued to dangle rich contracts and consistently siphoned off the best male amateur talent. Not that he helped any women. While Dennis Ralston, a top male player then, could turn pro and deflect the purists' complaints about taking money by pointing out that he had a wife and kids to support, I didn't have the pro option. I was putting my husband through law school by hoarding every dollar of expense money I could get, and we were barely making it. As usual, Larry worked hard. Now he was a pot scrubber for $100 a week at a sorority on campus where they also gave him dinner.

It bothered me greatly that if I was an Australian, European, or South American player at my level, I wouldn't have had to worry about money. The USLTA's international counterparts were far more lax in their definition of an amateur. A top seed could make a thousand dollars just to be in the draw of some overseas tournaments, which is why so many Americans wanted to stay in Europe before and after Roland-Garros or Wimbledon. Yet the USLTA kept yanking the choke chain.

The Australians were particularly brazen about supporting their stars. Bob Mitchell paid for Margaret's apartment and gave her a weekly salary with no job requirement other than to play tennis. Volkswagen loaned her cars to drive. Slazenger paid her to use its rackets. Her countrymen Roy Emerson and Tony Roche were among those who had lucrative consulting jobs for equipment makers or other companies. When Kramer offered Australia's Neale Fraser a $60,000 guarantee for two seasons on his professional tour, Fraser turned him down, saying it wasn't worth it after the aggravation, expenses, and taxes he'd face as a barnstorming pro. He could make nearly as much as a phony amateur. It was a sweet life.

I was raised to be honest, and I took integrity seriously. But now I was taking money under the table too—"the Green Handshake," we called it—from tournament promoters, national association officials, and their sidemen. Every time I'd walk into a tournament I'd think, *We've got to change this.* I had to be my own agent and negotiate the payments I landed for me and sometimes Rosie, if we were playing doubles. I hated the wink-and-a-nod hypocrisy, but unless you had a rich spouse there was no other way to survive.

The system became known as "shamateurism." Arthur Ashe once said, "We all deserve Oscars for impersonating amateurs." When purists complained that the pros Kramer signed were corrupting the sport, he scoffed, "A tennis professional is just an amateur who has started to pay taxes." It was true, and everyone knew it. (Larry and I always reported my expense money to the IRS as income.) Tennis association officials were behaving like feudal overlords. They told us where to play, when to play, what not to say. They maintained power by keeping the amateur players dependent on the crumbs they rationed out. And sometimes, you couldn't even count on crumbs, especially as a woman.

My former doubles partner Karen Hantze Susman wanted to retire from tennis gradually, on her own terms. She was still the fourth-ranked woman in the U.S. by 1965 even though she'd cut back on her schedule as she and her husband were setting up a post-tennis life in St. Louis. Even in her finest moment, she had endured being diminished by the press as the "twenty-two-year-old housewife who won Wimbledon" in 1962. Now, when she entered the U.S. Nationals, she was left unseeded. That was a problem because only a handful of the top seeds got expense money. When Karen said she'd have to withdraw from the tournament if they didn't pay her the $28 per diem, USLTA officials called her bluff. Karen then defaulted her opening match against Margaret. The USLTA retaliated by suspending Karen from competition for six months.

Karen was so disgusted and hurt she didn't play singles again on the national level for thirteen years and never won another major. I never forgot that. Larry and I invited her to make a comeback when we started World TeamTennis, and Karen played one season with us.

BY THE TIME I returned to the circuit in March 1967, I'd had it too. I did some newspaper interviews before taking off for the South African Championships, my opening tournament of the year, and now I said what a lot of us had been thinking for a long time: The amateur tennis system in America had to change or we would continue to get our butts kicked on the international stage. I added that America was wasting its young talent and there wasn't enough expense money for established amateurs like me to continue. "The

My brother, Randy, and me.

My parents, Randy, and me in our front yard, West 36th Street, Long Beach, California.

My neighborhood playmates and me (far left) at age four. We look like extras from *The Little Rascals*.

I loved playing for our softball team that won the fifteen-and-under Long Beach 1953 city championship. That's me wearing my glove, second on the right.

Susan Williams, Jerry Cromwell, Allan Robbins, and me at the Virginia Country Club, where Susan invited me and I hit my first tennis ball.

My first coach, Clyde Walker, always made extra time for Jerry Cromwell and me.

Perry T. Jones, who was nicknamed "the czar" of Southern California tennis, has a chat with me.

Uncle Art, Aunt Gladys, and my dad, Bill Moffitt.

My parents and I on a visit to see my mother's family: back row, left to right, my grandmother, Dot; Aunt Doris; and, to the right of my parents, my grandfather James Kehoe. My cousin, Donna Lee, is on the front left, next to me.

Althea Gibson, the first Black woman to play the U.S. National Championships (now the U.S. Open), is accompanied after her 1950 opening win at Forest Hills by the two-time champion Alice Marble, my future coach, who fought for Althea to have the right to play.

The summer I spent with my 1959 Southern California Junior Wightman Cup teammates was the most fun I'd ever had in tennis by then. Left to right: Kathy Chabot, Karen Hantze, Carole Caldwell, me, Barbara Browning, and Pam Davis.

Eighteen-year-old Karen Hantze and I were unseeded when we became the youngest duo ever to win the Wimbledon Ladies' doubles title by upsetting Jan Lehane and Margaret Smith in 1961. I was seventeen.

When Carole Caldwell, Darlene Hard, and I won the inaugural Fed Cup competition for the U.S. in 1963, we accepted the trophy from the International Lawn Tennis Federation president, George de Stefani. "You guys, this is history!" I said.

I dropped everything in 1964 and accepted an offer to train in Australia with Mervyn Rose (shown here as a player). That's how much I burned to be No. 1.

It was a thrill for me to meet Senator Robert F. Kennedy after playing Margaret Smith in the 1965 U.S. Nationals final at Forest Hills. Even though I lost that day, for the first time I knew I could be No. 1.

Larry King and I at our wedding on September 17, 1965. I still smile about how happy we were.

The first time I met my future coach and adviser Frank Brennan (shown here at Forest Hills), he said something no one had ever said to me: "You're going to be No. 1 someday."

Althea Gibson, Arthur Ashe, and me at a 1969 Philadelphia tennis clinic. Althea was one of my sheroes from the first time I saw her play at the Los Angeles Tennis Club more than a decade earlier, at the height of her career.

Before I lifted the Venus Rosewater Dish after winning my first Wimbledon singles title in 1966—my wildest dream come true—I snuck a peek at the names of the other champions I knew were listed there.

My dream to become a pro tennis player finally became a reality on April 1, 1968, when I signed with George MacCall's barnstorming troupe, the National Tennis League, along with, left to right, Ann Jones, Françoise Dürr, Roy Emerson, and Rosie Casals. Before us, four women had never toured together as pros.

This photograph of the Original 9 captures the birth of the women's professional tennis tour. It was taken moments after we decided to risk our careers and sign $1 contracts with the magazine publisher and promoter Gladys Heldman in Houston and compete in the first Virginia Slims Invitational Tennis Tournament. Bottom, left to right: Judy Dalton, Kerry Melville (Reid), Rosie Casals, Gladys, Kristy Pigeon. Top, left to right: Valerie Ziegenfuss, me, Nancy Richey, Jane (Peaches) Bartkowicz. Missing from this photo is Julie Heldman.

I felt I had to beat Chrissie Evert in the 1971 U.S. Open semifinals to protect our new women's pro tour because she was just sixteen and still an amateur. I won, but Chrissie's dramatic run at the Open established that she was our next superstar.

Australians always are the best in amateur tennis because there is a whopping financial payoff," I said. "They'll always have the edge on us until the tide changes."

Later that year, I was part of our winning Wightman Cup and Federation Cup teams. I also swept the singles, doubles, and mixed-doubles titles at Wimbledon, the pinnacle. My compensation at Wimbledon for all that was a £45 gift voucher.

I kept up my steady drumbeat of protests. I was derided as cranky and impertinent for telling a *Chicago Tribune* reporter that women's sports stories needed to be moved off the society pages and onto the sports pages. When I came home from my Wimbledon sweep, not a single photographer or reporter was waiting to ask me a thing about it.

I watched with great interest as the staid old All England Club, of all places, hosted an all-male pro tournament as a trial balloon event shortly after Wimbledon in 1967 to see how the public would respond. Centre Court was made available for the competition, another huge break with tradition. The event was a huge success. Thirty thousand people bought tickets. The BBC televised it live. This could be the answer that tennis needed. But again, where were the women?

I kept pushing for change. I told reporters in the States, "There is no way amateur tennis is going to be available to everyone if only rich kids could play." I said the USLTA, a nonprofit organization run by volunteers, had no incentive to grow the sport, adding, "They seem more devoted to their five o'clock happy hours at their clubs." The USLTA was content to keep amateur tennis "pure," which to them meant no salaried jobs, no lifeblood endorsement money for players, no reward for playing in tournaments other than the glory of the title and another trophy for the shelf. I could never understand it.

Everybody wanted to interview me now. I was No. 1 in the world, and I kept talking. When Perry T. Jones publicly ripped all players who wanted open tournaments—the Czar said he wished he could drop an atom bomb to stop the effort—I spoke up again, even though I was in the middle of the U.S. Nationals. I said tennis was "fifty years behind the times." I asked how anyone could live on the $28 per diem I was earning at Forest Hills despite being a Wimbledon champion and the world No. 1.

At one point during the tournament, I took a walk down a gravel path and around the grounds with the USLTA president, Bob Kelleher, a federal judge whom I respected and liked. He said he wanted me to win the Sullivan Award that year, which annually goes to America's best amateur athlete. I told him as much as I appreciated that, I couldn't worry about amateur honors when I didn't know how long I could even afford to keep playing tennis. I wanted our game to be pro. He told me I had to be patient. Soon we were raising our voices.

"Let me tell you something," Bob said. "You've got to keep quiet or you're going to be suspended."

"Fine! Go ahead!" I shot back. Then I went on to sweep the singles, doubles, and mixed-doubles titles at Forest Hills with Rosie and Owen Davidson, the same as we had at Wimbledon. I did not shut up. I was not suspended. Your racket can do a lot of talking for you.

I was in Australia in December 1967 when Wimbledon officials, buoyed by the summer trial event they had run, dropped a bombshell: They announced that Wimbledon would be the first major to welcome pros and amateurs, starting in 1968, in defiance of the International Lawn Tennis Federation. The All England Club president, Herman David, called amateurism "a living lie" and said even the pros who had been banned before could return. When I heard that, I yelled, "Yes!"

The other big news at the Australian Nationals was that Margaret decided to end her brief retirement after marrying Barry Court, a merchant and yachtsman who came from a prominent Perth political family. She took his last name, so I beat Margaret *Court* in the Australian final. I had now won the last three Grand Slam singles titles and I had a total of five major singles championships overall. But my ability to make an honest living or gain financial security for Larry and myself had improved very little.

Other than Margaret's return to the tour, the talk of the 1968

Australian Nationals was *Who's turning pro?* A New Orleans tennis promoter named Dick Dixon reacted to Wimbledon's decision by announcing that he was starting an all-male professional troupe called World Championship Tennis. The Texas oil tycoon Lamar Hunt was the WCT's financial muscle. The first players they signed, led by John Newcombe, were called "the Handsome Eight."

By January 1968, George MacCall, a former U.S. Davis Cup captain, declared that he was starting a rival pro outfit called the National Tennis League, and he'd signed Rod Laver, Ken Rosewall, Fred Stolle, Pancho Gonzalez, and Andrés Gimeno. George was in Melbourne to recruit more talent, including Roy Emerson and, to my surprise, me.

Revolutionary change in tennis was coming. The ILTF, rather than picking a fight with Wimbledon, said in March 1968 that each national association could decide how to operate for itself. The rest of tennis had joined the revolt Wimbledon started, triggering the most significant event in tennis history: The Open Era had begun.

I was twenty-four, and I had been playing on the amateur circuit for nearly a decade. When the news became official, I danced around our apartment in Berkeley and said, "Larry, isn't it great?"

Larry set his jaw and shook his head no. "Just watch, Billie Jean. Once men get open tennis, they're going to squeeze the women out."

"C'mon, Larry!" I said. "We're all friends! Why would they do that?"

Chapter 10

I T TOOK ME about two seconds to tell George MacCall I'd
play on his National Tennis League tour. George had hoped to
sign Margaret as well, but she demanded to be paid more than
me, which George wasn't willing to do; I was now the world's
top-ranked player and Margaret's comeback had begun unevenly.

When George asked me who else he should approach, I suggested Rosie, Ann Jones, and Françoise Dürr, whom everyone called
Frankie. They all jumped at the chance. I knew we were all good
communicators as well as top players, and our mix of nationalities
and personalities would have appeal wherever we went. We knew we
had to be able to sell our sport. No women had toured as pros since
Althea and Karol Fageros nearly a decade earlier, and four women
had never been featured on the same card at once.

My last match as an amateur was an unforgettable three-set collapse against Nancy Richey at the newly renovated Madison Square
Garden. That defeat was on a Saturday, and on Monday, April 1,
1968, I was back in Los Angeles with Rosie, Frankie, Ann, and Roy
Emerson. We held a press conference to sign our exclusive pro contracts with George. I felt like a mountain had been lifted off my
back. Larry and I could actually breathe a little. The shamateurism
hypocrisy was over, and we could finally earn a living in tennis out in
the open, the way it should always have been.

I quickly landed my first endorsement, a radio deal with Maxwell
House that I wouldn't agree to until I tried their coffee. I was also
provided with a Hertz VIP card and my first charge card (American
Express). To me, the cards were a sign of stature. At the time, even

working women continued to have trouble getting a credit card or loans unless their husband, father, or employer signed for it. It was one of the injustices Ruth Bader Ginsburg helped change.

Bob Kelleher, the same USLTA official who had urged me to pipe down during the 1967 U.S. Nationals, was now involved in making Forest Hills an open tournament, and he negotiated my two-year, $80,000 contract with George MacCall. I was promised more earnings if I surpassed a certain level of prize money at the events we played. George lured Emmo to our group with a guarantee of $75,000 a year, and I read that Rod Laver had signed with us for even more.

Was I worth only half of what the top men were paid? You can guess my answer. But I was finally getting a living wage for doing what I loved, and I knew I couldn't take on all the issues at once.

The NTL's opening professional tournament was scheduled to start at the L.A. Forum six days after we held our press conference in Los Angeles, and we sold fourteen thousand tickets by mid-week. Four thousand tickets were bought by area businesses for under-resourced kids from Inglewood and the surrounding neighborhoods, which thrilled me. It felt as if another dream I'd always had—moving big-time tennis out of the private clubs and spreading it everywhere—was finally coming true. Before our event at the Forum, our MacCall pros were going to offer free clinics in Watts and East L.A. The plan was to mark courts on the streets in chalk, pass out free rackets, and have the pros show the kids some basics.

Then everything came to a crashing halt. On Thursday, April 4, we heard the news that Dr. Martin Luther King Jr. had been assassinated that evening in Memphis. The shock and pain I felt was overwhelming. Dr. King was standing on the balcony of the Lorraine Motel and turned to grab his coat when he was shot dead by a sniper. The next day I saw the now-famous newspaper photo of him sprawled on the ground while three aides pointed in the direction of the rifle shot. The horror of the moment was piercing.

I loved Dr. King and his vision and the spellbinding way he spoke. Just the day before he was murdered, Dr. King had given his incredibly moving "I've Been to the Mountaintop" speech and eerily alluded to perhaps not living long enough to see his dreams come true. Now the country was convulsing with grief and anger. He was dead at thirty-nine.

Riots broke out in more than two hundred cities and towns across America for days, though not in Los Angeles, where we were. The only thing I can guess was that maybe the city's ongoing recovery from the 1965 Watts riots helped keep the lid on the violence. Thirty-five people died in the Watts uprisings and more than $40 million in damage was done as L.A. raged and burned for four days. Dr. King had actually come to Watts forty-eight hours into the riots, hoping to ease tensions. Maybe that memory lingered.

The Sunday after Dr. King's death was declared a day of mourning in Los Angeles, and events were canceled everywhere—including ours. I used the free time to listen to a recording of Dr. King's "I Have a Dream" speech over and over. Years later when Martin Luther King Day became a national holiday, a TV station in New York used to air his speeches in chronological order. What a gift.

Keep moving, Dr. King once said, "and if you can't fly, then run, if you can't run, then walk, if you can't walk, then crawl, but whatever you do, keep moving forward."

OUR MACCALL GROUP FLEW from America to Europe to kick off a month-long stay in France and Britain. Before I joined the National Tennis League, I'd heard tales for years about barnstorming pros hopping from town to town, setting up a temporary court in a gym or a rec hall—or even on a rooftop—to play an exhibition match, then pulling up stakes and moving on to the next gig. It's the sort of thing that sounds romantic, like running away to join the circus once seemed. But I couldn't really imagine what it was like until I lived it.

Within two weeks, I wondered what I had gotten myself into. I knew it was going to be hard work, but at one point I counted eighteen matches in twenty-one days. My knees, which were wonky even in the best of times after my car accident, were soon barking from the wear and tear. Every day, the pattern was the same: Arrive. Play. Move on. Repeat.

We began by hopscotching all over the south of France, then up to Paris, Lille, then back to the south again to Pau and Aix-en-Provence. It was a blur. We were often flying in or out of some little regional airport that had a windsock flapping on a pole, and we were always connecting through Toulouse. If I never sit on a runway in Toulouse again, I'll be happy. Then our troupe would pile into a van for some hours-long drive that was often spent teetering on the edge of some winding mountain road with no guard rails. Once at the venue, we'd jump out, hustle to change into our tennis clothes, then head straight to the court. We never knew what we'd find. Often, there wasn't even a locker room.

Cannes was the site of my first professional match. It was played in a tin-roofed gymnasium in a thunderstorm. The downpour was so deafening we couldn't hear the umpire, let alone the ball hitting our strings. The air was so humid my glasses fogged up. We were playing before a hundred people, if that. At one point I walked up to Vic Braden, George MacCall's second in command, and shouted over the machine-gun patter of the rain, "This is really exciting, Vic. I'm sure it will all be worth it someday!"

Vic nodded and laughed.

In the Po Valley, we played outdoors one night on a just-made black asphalt court that was laid to the exact dimensions of the playing surface and not an inch more, leaving a three-inch drop to navigate when we had to chase the ball to the out-of-bounds areas. Did I mention that the balls also turned sticky and charcoal black right away? In other venues, we had to brush cobwebs off the showerheads and toilets, or the water ran brown. Some places smelled of mildew, or worse. We woke early, ate on the run, and slept in hotels with faded sheets and lumpy mattresses, if we slept at all.

As shaky as the conditions often were, those were cherished days for us. Everyone was figuring out this new world order as we went, and it was so much fun traveling together, learning from each other, discussing our vision for our sport. Laver, Rosewall, Gonzalez, and

Gimeno had toured for years with Jack Kramer's pro outfits, and they were like soldiers on a battlefield. They could sleep anytime, anywhere. Stolle, Emerson, and the four of us women had more adjusting to do. We all grew closer. Sometimes we were so wired after our matches we'd go to a local bar to wind down. The Aussies badgered me until I finally sampled beer, but my limit was one and done. Sometimes we'd drop coins in the jukebox and dance till 2 or 3 a.m., get up by 6 a.m. and do it all again.

The only two autographs I ever asked for when I was a starstruck kid were from Pancho Gonzalez and Tony Trabert. Now I was playing mixed doubles with Gonzalez some nights and listening to his stories, including some about his own run-ins with Perry T. Jones at the Los Angeles Tennis Club. His given first name was Ricardo, and he disliked the nickname "Pancho," a patronizing nod to his Mexican American roots. Even at forty, Gonzalez remained a study in elegance and one of the most intense competitors in the sport. Gussie Moran once said that seeing Gonzalez play was like watching a god patroling his personal heaven. Seeing him up close, I understood what she meant.

Rosie, Ann, Frankie, and I became as tight as sisters during that tour. Rosie, who was still only nineteen, had been calling me "Old Lady" for a couple years now, ever since I stumbled clumsily during a match we played. Now she never called me anything else. Other people called her "Rosebud," or "the General."

It was also Rosie who nicknamed Ann Jones "Annie Oakley" after Ann fell off a horse at Maureen Connolly's ranch in Texas (she wasn't hurt). Ann was, at twenty-nine, the oldest woman among us and she didn't suffer fools gladly. She came from Birmingham, an English industrial city about one hundred miles north of London, and her working-class parents were both table tennis champions. Ann was a table tennis world finalist too, before she switched to lawn tennis. She said she wanted to get out in the sunshine.

And Frankie Dürr, well—Frankie might've been the most colorful of us all. She was born in 1942 to French parents in Algiers and her family had to dodge bullets to escape the Algerian uprising against France in the 1950s. While we were touring she was dating a tennis player from the Caribbean who moonlighted as a calypso singer on the French Riviera. Frankie had won Roland-Garros the year before the MacCall tour, so she was already a star in her home country, and an absolute godsend when we needed a translator in small towns where no English or Spanish was spoken.

Trouble was, Frankie still had such a heavy accent and eccentric English that sometimes we felt like we needed a translator to understand her. On the court, she made us laugh when she missed an easy shot because she would pound her racket into the ground while crying, "Sheet! Sheet! Sheet!" (Later, Frankie and the Dutch star Betty Stöve, who spoke six languages, used to kill time at our women's tournaments by playing poly-lingual games of Scrabble that were impenetrable to the rest of us but provoked some comical word challenges between them. "We know what we're doing!" Frankie would say.)

I suppose George MacCall could've mounted a smoother tour, but his heart was in the right place. He would turn out to be as disorganized as he was charming, and I never got paid all the money I was promised. I think most of us didn't. But this was an exciting first for women, and though we knew there would be more challenges ahead, we were on our way.

In late April we flew to England for the official kickoff of tennis's Open Era at the British Hard Court Championships in Bournemouth, the first sanctioned tournament where pros and amateurs could compete together. It should have been a great moment, but right from the start we had trouble with the lopsided purses. The men's winner would get $2,400 and the women's winner $720, a bad omen for women's tennis. George refused to enter the four of us. The prize money we won went toward paying our guarantees, so I couldn't blame him for letting only the guys play.

Still, it drove us crazy to sit in London watching the televised matches from the lounge at the Lexham Gardens Hotel. We all threw pillows at the TV when Virginia Wade won the singles title, beating Winnie Shaw, another Brit. The women's prize money went unclaimed because Virginia was an amateur and couldn't collect it. That was a good deal for the Bournemouth organizers. Not us.

George was soon threatening to have our entire troupe—men and women—boycott Roland-Garros in late May if the prize money didn't improve. When the tournament landed more sponsorships, bumping up the total purse from $20,000 to $64,000, with $3,000 going to the men's singles titlist and $1,000 to the women's champion, George decided to send us to Paris. Easier said than done.

That month, leftist students took over the city's universities and marched through the streets to protest an array of issues. Millions of French workers went out on sympathy strikes. The country was practically shuttered for nearly a month and the protests reached such an angry pitch that French president Charles de Gaulle had secretly fled to Germany at one point, fearing a revolution. Luckily for us, Frankie was accustomed to French strikes, and she knew what to do. We flew from London to Amsterdam, rented two cars, and drove the 320 miles to Paris. The Champs-Élysées was flooded with demonstrators when we got there. There had been clashes elsewhere between protesters and police. It was unnerving, even scary, as we drove to our hotel.

At Roland-Garros, the grandstands were nearly deserted. I was the top seed for the tournament and had little trouble getting through to the quarterfinals, where I was matched against Maria Bueno. We were scheduled to play on Wednesday, June 5. When I woke up that morning, I switched on the television in my hotel room. I knew that in California, where it was just after midnight, the Democratic presidential primary had concluded and I wanted to see if Robert F. Kennedy, whom I loved, had won. I met Bobby in 1965 when he was a New York senator and he presented me with my finalist trophy at Forest Hills. I believed that he was our country's best presidential candidate. He said he was going to end the war in Vietnam and continue to support the civil rights fight. Despite all the chaos going on, he filled me with hope.

As I watched the news, I couldn't understand what the French TV newscaster was saying but from his expression it seemed that something was wrong. First they showed video of Bobby smiling and waving after his victory speech in a Los Angeles hotel ballroom. I could see Rosey Grier, the retired defensive linesman for the L.A. Rams, towering over Bobby's wife, Ethel, who was standing behind her husband. Then the footage cut abruptly to pandemonium in the crowd, horrified faces, and the image of Bobby on the floor of the Ambassador Hotel's kitchen with a busboy crouching protectively over Bobby's bleeding head.

I was panicked as I dialed Larry in Berkeley. It seemed to take forever for the international call to go through. Larry had been watching the news, too. He told me that Rosey had wrestled the gun out of the assassin's hand and held him down until the police arrived. Bobby Kennedy was now in surgery at a Los Angeles hospital. By midday in Paris we were told that he was in a coma, barely clinging to life.

I had a match to play, and I didn't know what to do beyond move forward. I shut out the sorrow long enough to get by Maria, 6–4, 6–4.

When I went to sleep that night Kennedy was still clinging to life and when I woke up the next morning he was dead. Gone at forty-two. I sat there alone, sobbing softly in my hotel room.

The rest of my tournament was forgettable. I felt like I was sleepwalking. I was having trouble getting the assassination out of my head. It was one of those days in life—much like 9/11 would feel decades later—when you literally wondered if the whole world had gone crazy. It was painful and disorienting to add up all the killings: Medgar Evers and JFK in 1963, Malcolm X in 1965, now King and Bobby Kennedy gone two months apart.

That evening, I thought I had settled down enough for the semifinals. I was scheduled to play Nancy Richey, which helped me refocus a bit. We hadn't played since March when she rallied to beat me at Madison Square Garden. Nancy had chosen to remain an amateur, and I wanted to prove what I had been saying all along: Professionals are the best of the best. But if you let yourself think of the outcome rather than each ball coming over the net, you're inviting trouble.

I took the first set. But Nancy played brilliantly the last two sets and smartly moved the ball around so I couldn't chase much down.

She deserved her comeback victory. The next day, she did the same thing to Ann Jones, reeling off fifteen straight points after falling behind 2–5 in the second set to take the title.

My hope of owning all four major titles at once—a non–calendar year Grand Slam—was gone. The exhaustion of playing the NTL schedule seemed to be catching up to me as well. I had known for a while that I had chondromalacia, or trouble with the tissue behind both of my kneecaps, as a result of my car wreck. Plus, I was still on antibiotics and a nondairy diet for colitis. Now I was also diagnosed with stress-induced asthma. It was all I could do to last two sets some days.

I withdrew from the Kent Open to recover for two weeks, which touched off speculation that I would not be able to play Wimbledon. There was no way I was going to miss it. I was now the two-time defending champion and the top-ranked player in the world, and my parents had agreed to join me in London for the first time.

It took a lot to convince those two homebodies to fly to England. Bringing them there was a small way for me to thank them for all they had done for me. They had been hearing me go on about Wimbledon for years. I wanted them to see the center of the tennis universe for themselves.

MY PARENTS WERE taken aback by the size of the stadium crowds and the elegance of the Wimbledon grounds. Mom couldn't get over how the spectators seeking tickets for the next day's matches lined up all night on the road outside the All England Club swaddled in blankets or sleeping in makeshift tents. I was a little worried that Dad's temper might show during one of my matches, but I needn't have been. Dad was on his best behavior, perhaps in part because of the unlikely new pal he made on the trip, a Roman Catholic priest named Father Roland, who was a dear friend of my coach, Frank Brennan, and his family.

It was hilarious to see my dad, who refused to vote for John F. Kennedy on religious grounds, become fast friends with a man who doled out communion. Go figure. Larry and I had installed my parents in a room down the hall from us at the Lexham Gardens Hotel. My dad and Father Roland began taking the London tube together with my father clutching a rolled-up copy of each day's tennis schedule. He would study it each morning and use a red pen to circle the names of all the Americans who were playing that day. "Gotta see the Americans!" he would tell me as he bustled out the door.

Wimbledon's decision to become an open tournament that year had sparked the rest of tennis to follow along, but that didn't end the heated debate about whether allowing professionals was a good idea. There was a backlash in the press and among the public that the pros made tennis too "commercial," as if that's a dirty word. There was handwringing that money would bleed the honor out of the sport, as if we could eat or survive on "honor." I still loved Wimbledon as much as ever, but I began to feel that Wimbledon had stopped loving me back.

I could hear a change in the tone of the reporters' questions. When Rosie, Ann, Frankie, and I got to the women's locker room, we got the cold shoulder there, too, from most of the women who had remained amateurs. That hurt more than anything. When you can see things so clearly and everyone looks at you like you've got six heads, it's hard on you. There was a transition going on in our sport and I felt an urgency, bordering on a sense of panic, that the women would be left behind. The idea that our pro foursome's success might make the sport better for all women players seemed to get lost.

I was trying to become the first woman to win Wimbledon three consecutive years since Maureen Connolly, a significant achievement. But the crowds' polite clapping as I made my way through the draw began to feel halfhearted, maybe even a little passive-aggressive at times—never more so than when I saved a match point in the second set against their home girl, Ann Jones, and rallied to win our semifinal in three sets. I'd have almost preferred to hear boos. At least that would've been honest. I was no longer the spunky little underdog who amused everyone on arrival with her stream-of-conscious chatter and giant-killing upsets. I was one of the invading pros. But I wasn't about to apologize for it. As I told a British TV interviewer who suggested that my ambition might turn people off, "I'm out here to win . . . In America, we're brought up very differently than English children. 'Did you win or did you lose?'—that's all that they ask at home. They don't care about the rest. You're a loser and that's it." By the time I edged Judy Tegart in our tense final 9–7, 7–5, I told myself I had to get thicker skin. But it helped to know I wasn't the only pro who felt vindicated. All of us felt we had something to prove that year.

Rod Laver was playing Wimbledon for the first time since he'd been suspended six years earlier for turning pro on one of Kramer's tours. Though Rod won his third career Wimbledon title by beating Tony Roche the day after I beat Judy, he said he actually felt the proudest on the opening day of the tournament. Then he explained why.

Rod said when he captured his first Wimbledon title in 1961 he received an All England Club necktie, the same as all the men's winners did then in lieu of prize money. When he turned pro two years later, he received a stern letter from the All England Club ordering him to never wear the tie again. He'd been banished.

"I took enormous satisfaction from dragging out my old purple and green Wimbledon tie that had been unceremoniously yanked from my neck, and putting it on," Laver said after he won the 1968 title, adding that he wasn't the only former champion who felt that way. Thirteen former winners in the men's field had returned to Wimbledon now that it was open to all. Pancho Gonzalez was in the men's draw after two decades away, and Ken Rosewall and Lew Hoad appeared for the first time in twelve years.

I think Mom and Dad had to leave the United States and experience Wimbledon to truly understand the scope of our fight to transform tennis, not just the thrill of seeing me win the most important tournament in the world.

Chapter 11

THE NEW PROFESSIONAL LIFE I was leading had repercussions for Larry and me beyond putting me back on the road for weeks at a time. When the ILTF opened pro tennis in March 1968, a lot of the promoters were caught flatfooted. Larry and I had anticipated the need for more professional tournaments, especially for women. He and a group of his law school friends quickly got together with another Bay Area pal, Hap Klopp, who had just bought the North Face outerwear company, to stage an event at the Oakland Coliseum Arena.

We called it "Tennis for Everyone," a progressive play on the old country club cliché "Tennis, anyone?" In coming years, Larry and I would stage more of them, pairing the pro tournaments with free clinics we'd hold during the week, often on public courts in communities where tennis wasn't usually played. Larry and I had been wanting to do something like that for under-resourced youth in the Bay Area since we moved to Berkeley. Our idea was to get children involved early and give them a lifetime sport to care about.

Our first event in Oakland offered $10,000 in guaranteed prize money, and the field was built around our players from the MacCall tour, four men and four women. (Given the debt I felt to Althea for being my long-ago inspiration as a child, we invited her to play with us as a pro, and we were thrilled when she appeared in three 1969 events, starting in Oakland. Even at forty, Althea was still lean and athletic. The fans who came out for those TFE events saw African American and Latinx champions playing our game, not just white people from effete clubs, which is something I had always wanted. Larry did too.)

Larry didn't tell me until afterward that he had taken $5,000 of our money—in fact, *all* of our savings—and risked it on the 1968 tournament. I couldn't believe it. Why didn't he discuss it with me? By that point I had never made more than $7,000 a year and Larry was still a year away from graduating law school. I take chances, but I'm a big believer in financial stability, and having at least some "rock" money on the side that you only touch in an emergency. I was stunned and alarmed at the risk he unilaterally took.

Luckily for us, that first Tennis for Everyone tournament was a success on every level. It earned about $5,000. And that's how Larry the Lawyer became Larry the Promoter. Larry always said it was a curse to make money on his first tennis event because he immediately thought he was an expert. And he had the bug.

The next year we lost $10,000 on the same tournament because it rained so hard in Oakland the authorities were warning motorists to stay off the Bay Area bridges. The bad weather virtually eliminated our walk-up ticket sales.

When we first got together, Larry had told me he never wanted to be broke, as his father was always struggling. I took that as a sign that Larry would be frugal with money, the same as me. I was wrong. To Larry, avoiding his father's fate meant taking risks to try to get ahead. There was something he liked about having ten balls in the air and being right on the edge of disaster, figuring it out as he went along. As soon as he had money in his hands, he was chasing the next big idea. He always thought he'd win. In the coming years, he invested in such things as inventing a smokeless ashtray and a national roller hockey league, in addition to all the ventures that were ultimately successful.

We were already apart for weeks at a time now because of my touring schedule and Larry's law studies, and we thought if Larry became a promoter it might draw us closer together. But from that very first Oakland tournament in 1968 we realized we needed to book two hotel rooms when we were both working. He needed to be on the phone night and day, and I needed my rest. Sometimes we'd get adjoining rooms so we weren't completely separated. But it was another sign that we were starting to spin off in different directions. Sometimes our lives felt like Irresistible Force meeting Immovable Object.

When Larry was washing pots at the sorority, he told me he used to go to their mixers for something to do while I was gone and dance with some of the girls because, as he said with a laugh, "They considered me 'safe' because I'm married." But he never once told me not to pursue a tennis career. I, in turn, never wanted to stand in the way of him chasing fulfillment. I think we both felt that's part of loving someone. It was just excruciatingly hard at that age to know how to reconcile it all as a couple.

When Larry accepted a summer internship with a white-shoe law firm in New York City he was entertaining the idea that Manhattan might be a good place to settle down and build a practice. After a few weeks of staying with one of my former host families on Long Island Larry came to dislike the grinding commute and took a room in the city to be nearer his office and save time. Unfortunately, that was the summer the city's garbage truck workers went on strike, and the Manhattan streets were a steaming, pungent mess. He decided that the concrete canyons of New York City weren't for him.

I advanced to the final of the first U.S. Open, as the U.S. National Championships were now called. I spent the night before my match against Virginia Wade in my hotel room with my left knee propped up on a guitar case while tears rolled down my face because of the pain. It took Virginia only forty-two minutes to dust me off in the championship match the next day. The only bright spot of those two weeks for me was watching Arthur Ashe become the first African American male player to win the tournament. It was moving to watch Arthur make history with his father and brother present, and later to see him land on the cover of *Life* magazine.

Knowing I couldn't put off knee surgery any longer, I checked into Pacific Hospital in Long Beach that September. When I woke up from the operation, the pain was excruciating. It made sense when my terrific surgeon, Dr. Donald L. Larsen, came into my room and told me how much damage they had found behind my left kneecap. But when he added, "Don't count on playing Wimbledon again," I was stunned. Then I became upset. I sat in bed thinking, *This can't be the end. It can't be. Pro tennis has just begun, I'm still a month away from my twenty-fifth birthday and I'm going to miss out on my dream? After fighting so hard?* For a few days, I remained distraught. Then I said to myself, *No. No way it ends here! I am going to play again. And I'm going to win.*

I was back on the court in a month. I returned to Berkeley to recover, and Larry would soft-toss me tennis balls as I stood leaning on a crutch I held under my left armpit while swinging my racket with my right hand. Sophisticated rehab regimens didn't exist in those days, so I followed what the doctors told me to do, like taking hot baths to improve the range of motion in my knee. Years later we learned it was better to apply ice after workouts. Still, I felt good enough by January 1969 to enter the Australian Open. I knew I wouldn't win it, I just needed match play. That meant hitting the road again, and more weeks apart from Larry.

We were spending even more time talking about the Vietnam War now because Larry's student deferment would end in June 1969 when he graduated. It was a stressful time. Both of our fathers had enlisted during World War II and the idea of service had been drilled into us: When you are called, you go. After a lot of long, late-night discussions, Larry decided to join the Army Reserve. If he volunteered rather than wait to be drafted he had a chance of staying out of Vietnam and could begin his law career. I saw the wisdom in that. But I was unhappy when Larry accepted a job with the Honolulu law firm of Pratt, Moore, Bortz & Case.

Larry had fallen in love with Oahu on a past visit there, but his desire to go to Hawaii was problematic. I wanted him to be happy, but practically speaking, living in Hawaii meant I'd have to fly five or six hours to get to tournaments on the West Coast, twelve hours to get to the East Coast, and Europe was half a world away. Also, there was no top-flight pro tennis culture in Hawaii. Who would I practice with?

I began to feel conflicted, a bit unsettled, unsure where we were headed when he refused to reconsider. The philosophical fault lines that were starting to show in our relationship, our communication breakdowns, the long separations from each other, had all been in play with Larry and me for months. I was starting to wonder if Larry and I would have been better off if we had been able to live together first instead of marrying so young, before we'd even seriously dated anyone else. We had always agreed we wanted to have kids, but we were always putting it off for some reason. Now it was the advent of open tennis and waiting for his career to start. I still loved Larry and he loved me, but I was starting to question what I was doing—even who I was.

When we first began dating, I had told Larry that I sometimes felt attracted to women as well as men, and that a woman and I had kissed once in college. I had never told anyone that before. I felt there *was* no one safe to confide in. But after Larry and I became very serious, very quickly, I thought I had to tell him. I didn't know how to make sense of it myself. I don't know if younger people today realize how shame based and dangerous it was in the 1960s to be gay, how complete the curtain of silence was, how insidious the fear of scorn and reprisals was, how deep the closet went.

Every message we got then—from therapists, teachers, law enforcement, our families—was that homosexuality was "deviant" behavior. It was a huge leap of faith for me to risk telling Larry about the kiss, and an enormous relief when Larry told me that he would always love me, no matter what, and that he didn't care what happened before he was in my life, so long as I loved him.

But when I came back to Berkeley to rehab my knee in the spring of 1969, Larry and I had another heartfelt talk. Larry later said it felt like "the most poignant cry for help" I'd ever made to him. He could see I was distraught about something and asked me, "What's wrong?"

I said, "Oh, I'm going to ruin you, Larry. I'm going to ruin you."

"Why?"

"I've had some relationships in my past," I stammered.

Then I told him for the first time that I had gotten involved with someone on the road, but it was over. And I told him that my confusion about being attracted to both women and men still existed.

"That doesn't have anything to do with me. That won't ruin me," he said.

"How can you be a lawyer if somebody says I've had other relationships or feelings for women?"

"It won't bother me, it won't affect me," he insisted. "Don't be distraught on my account, Billie Jean."

"I never want to hurt you, Larry, and I'm afraid I'll ruin you," I repeated.

I felt telling the truth was the right thing to do, but confessing that I had had an affair stung and angered Larry, and he came to believe that it gave him license to see other women—discreetly at first. I knew about some of them (*Sports Illustrated* printed the name of one), but I felt I had no footing to protest. I had betrayed him first. I wasn't even sure we should still be married, but being together was the only thing either of us had known since we were seventeen and eighteen.

In a paradoxical way, our problem wasn't that we were out of love. Far from it. We cared about each other so much that we kept straining for a way to negotiate a growing list of challenges that never felt totally in our control. Neither of us wanted to countenance the idea that those challenges doomed us as a couple. Some magical thinking set in instead. *Maybe if we wait things out, our problems will somehow resolve themselves...*

I kept playing and Larry finished his law degree by summertime, but it turned out to be a miserable year for both of us. I didn't win a major in 1969 (or 1970, for that matter). We still were not getting along great by the time we went to Wimbledon in 1969, and then we foolishly agreed to allow a BBC-TV crew to follow us for two days.

When word came just before the tournament started that Maureen Connolly had succumbed to ovarian cancer at the age of thirty-four, I took a long, soul-searching walk through the streets of London, thinking about how life can be cut short at any minute, and how you have to make the most of it. Was I doing that?

Watching the BBC segment on Larry and me painfully drove home how unhappy we were. Larry said a few awkward things on camera—at one point tweaking me for not cooking for him as often as other wives—and the footage cut to me wincing at a few of his remarks. Larry claimed to be the more emotionally available person in our relationship. That irritated me because we had discussed it in an argument we had the night before the interviews started and Larry had agreed that the opposite was true: He had said he knew he wasn't great at talking decisions through, and that he could be emotionally remote, even occasionally oblivious, traits he conceded created "a certain amount of conflict."

The night before the first day of filming, I told Larry for the first time that I wanted a divorce.

He said no.

The tournament was in full swing. I backed down. But it was excruciating.

I was trying for my fourth consecutive title at Wimbledon, something that hadn't been done since Helen Wills Moody accomplished it in the late 1920s. I made it to the final opposite Ann Jones, who had upset Margaret in the semifinals. Once again I was playing against both Ann and the Wimbledon crowd, which was cheering wildly for their local hero. I got cranky when some fans crossed the line and yelled "Out!" as I began to swing at balls that were in. At one point, I stopped, stared at a heckler, and then curtsied to him, which was a smart-ass thing to do. Ann told the press afterward that she was embarrassed by the fans' stunts, but nonetheless, I had let myself get too irritable and distracted. As a pro, that's an unacceptable excuse. I sprayed shots all over the plot. On match point I double-faulted—an inglorious end that touched off a national celebration. The Wimbledon title was the crowning achievement of Ann's career and I was sincerely happy for my friend. She deserved it. But I was deeply unhappy with myself.

Larry and I settled back into our patterns. I threw myself into the circuit. Larry returned to his law firm in Hawaii and building TennisAmerica, the small but growing empire of tennis camps and clinics, tournaments, and pro shops we started with our friend Dennis Van der Meer, a well-respected teaching pro. We still had Tennis for Everyone. It wasn't long before Larry was called to serve occasionally with the Army Reserve, sometimes on the mainland. We still loved kicking around ideas, dreaming of where things could go. That never, ever changed. But most of the time we were living apart, maintaining appearances, pretending to others that nothing was wrong.

Larry bought a condo in the Kalani Valley, a nice neighborhood east of Honolulu. When I was in town, Larry was expected to bring me to his law firm dinner parties and I dutifully went, the same as the other wives. We were often invited to the home of Daniel H. Case, one of the firm's partners. One of Daniel's sons, Steve Case, was later among the founders of America Online. I might've enjoyed having an extended conversation with Daniel or others after dinner, but while the men retired to the living room to talk business and politics I was expected to trundle off with the women to talk about whatever it was women were supposed to talk about. They were very nice, but we had little in common. This was not what I had in mind for the rest of my life.

IT'S INTERESTING FOR ME to look back at how I came to the women's movement gradually. What began as a struggle for equal opportunities and pay equity for women had mushroomed by the late 1960s into a full-blown fight over other important issues, especially access to birth control and legal abortion.

The idea that women wanted control over their bodies, their reproductive rights, their careers, and their definition of fair treatment, with the freedom to make those decisions without men's approval, were controversial concepts when I came of age. Married couples didn't even have the "right" to use birth control until a 1965 Supreme Court ruling, *Griswold v. Connecticut,* said the choice was protected under the Constitution as a right to privacy. Still, that decision was no help to unmarried women, who remained denied full access to contraceptives by twenty-six states. It took another seven years before the Court legalized birth control for everyone, irrespective of their marital status, in 1972.

Roe v. Wade, the case that legalized abortion, was decided in 1973. But women could still be fired from their jobs for getting pregnant until the 1978 passage of the Pregnancy Discrimination Act. Spousal rape—being coerced or forcibly compelled to have unwanted sex with your partner—wasn't criminalized in all fifty states until 1993. That's still hard for me to believe. The first time any court in America recognized sexual harassment as grounds for legal action wasn't until 1977. But many workplaces, as well as college and university admissions offices, were slow to end discriminatory practices. Many Ivy League colleges were still only open to men and operating on admission quotas deep into the 1970s.

Rosie thought the women's protest movement was great and she was ready to have women's tennis hop on the bandwagon. I thought we had to be more strategic. I wanted to speak out in a way that was strong, but I also wanted people to listen, not tune us out. To me, that meant being disciplined about everything: my tone of voice, the words I used, the pragmatism of our goals. I was always asking myself, *How can we win? How can we open a dialogue, and then keep it going?* While I strongly supported the women's movement, it was not in a wholesale way early on. Parts of the early feminist movement felt too extremist or elitist to me, too devoid of women of color.

The movement was initially unfriendly to lesbians as well. The phrase "Lavender Menace" was first used in 1969 by Betty Friedan to describe the threat she said lesbians posed to the emerging movement. Friedan, who had become the president of the National Organization for Women by then, even alleged in a *New York Times* essay that lesbians were among a handful of "infiltrator" groups that were "trained by the FBI and CIA" to hijack women's liberation. The distancing didn't save feminists from being called lesbians or man-haters anyway. The straight women acted as if being associated with lesbians infringed on heterosexuals' rights, rather than seeing how their behavior was adding to the stigmatization of gays.

The gay liberation movement started the same year Friedan made her "menace" remark with an uprising outside the Stonewall Inn in Manhattan's West Village. The gay club was raided by police in the wee hours of June 28 and, as usual, there was some roughhousing and arrests. But this time it touched off two days of rioting to protest the cops' routine harassment and brutality against the LGBTQ+ community. (The New York Police Department officially apologized in 2019, on the fiftieth anniversary of Stonewall.)

I was so homophobic myself then, I didn't say the word *lesbian* even in private company. I thought a lot about uttering words like "I'm a feminist" or "feminism" in my public interviews because I knew the words alienated many people, especially in the early days of the movement. Many people then thought that feminists advocated female supremacy or special treatment. I've always defined feminism as advocating equal rights and equal opportunity for everybody. For a long time, I thought you could argue for equal opportunity without having to use a charged word like feminism and, if your reasons were sound, you could still prevail. Semantics are so powerful. One word can alter everything.

Often, if I did discuss feminism, I took great pains to make sure my definition of the term wasn't misconstrued. My goal was to win hearts and minds. My intent was to make transformational, long-lasting change. To do that, I knew we had to bring men along with us to help us, not drive them away. Sometimes I'd turn my post-match press conferences into consciousness-raising sessions with sportswriters if they mentioned feminism. I'd say, "Before I answer your questions, I want to go around the room and have all of you tell me first what feminism means to *you*."

I'd tell them I had actually looked up the term *feminist,* and they were often surprised when I'd continue, "Do you know the word was created in 1837 by a man, the French philosopher Charles Fourier?" I'd explain that Fourier believed all important jobs should be open to women on the basis of skill and aptitude rather than closed on account of gender. He also wrote about how society was ordered in ways that could potentially hurt women's rights as human beings. "Who here is okay with that?" I'd ask, looking around the press room. "I think people misinterpret the women's movement, in that they think we want to dominate or advocate separatism. In my mind, it's really to create equal opportunity, to share. There's a big difference in those two words—dominate, versus share."

PUTTING FEMINISM ASIDE, it's important to remember that the politicization of sports and the role of the athlete-activist like Muhammad Ali was new, and there had never been a *female* athlete-activist by then who was advocating for women athletes as a group. Sports superstardom was the near-exclusive domain of men.

Sure, there had been a few sportswomen who became sensations—Suzanne Lenglen, Alice Marble, Althea Gibson, and Maureen Connolly in tennis; the golfers Patty Berg, Mickey Wright, and Kathy Whitworth; the figure skater Peggy Fleming; the sprinter Wilma Rudolph; and the all-around athlete Babe Didrikson Zaharias. But none of them was overtly political except Alice, through her advocacy for Althea's inclusion. Alice was a feminist too. She used to talk at length about how every woman athlete owes a debt to the women before her. Althea was enormously inspiring, but she didn't seek the spotlight. She let her performance speak for her.

I knew, of course, that I was treading on new ground. Today it's often hilarious to me when I see old videos of myself talking in soft, measured tones, or imperturbably fielding provocative questions when I must have been growling inside. I have to laugh, too, when I see more recent sportswomen/activists such as Megan Rapinoe, the U.S. soccer star and out lesbian, sprinkle a few f-bombs into their conversations when they're publicly making their points. It's a sign of the wonderful freedom they feel and the surer footing we've gained. But in my time, I would've been a pariah. Even feminism was an f-word for many back then.

As it was, I was called radical anyway, even if not in the bra-burning sense of the word, because of my outspokenness. Whatever I did it was magnified, dissected. Things were constantly shifting and I felt I couldn't ignore them. I felt an urgency, even a certain sense of alarm, that we could drop off the face of the tennis world because so many men didn't want to work with us. It took a personal toll. Once I began to pipe up more, there were a lot of days when I'd act in public as if the criticism or cold treatment didn't bother me, but it stung.

Looking back, I was probably too naive and idealistic in thinking we could persuade men at the time to willingly share their power and privilege, especially when they had never known anything else. Frederick Douglass knew what he was talking about when he wrote, "Power cedes nothing without a demand."

One of the factors that made me and even our most reluctant female tennis peers willing to ramp up our protests was the realization that our status didn't improve by sitting out the gender or cultural wars, or by refraining from calling out sexism. We all encountered discrimination, lousy experiences, and remarks, regardless of our individual differences.

Even the concept of woman breadwinners was still new to people then. Jeanie Brinkman, a publicist and marketing director who worked in the tennis world, says she'd get strange looks on airplanes simply because she carried a briefcase. Rosie said, "People ask us all the time, 'Why aren't you in the kitchen? Why aren't you getting married?', We'd say, 'Why should we?'"

The press coverage of the day was routinely centered on our looks—the "splendidly conformed" Gail Chanfreau, "the pretty, well-meaning" Ceci Martinez—or descriptions of Margaret's "near-virile" serve, Nancy Richey Gunter's "tomboy style," my "manful" resolve. A *New York* magazine writer wrote that Ken Gunter spoke of his wife, Nancy, "like a Western hero who prefers his women, like his horses, to display a little spirit." Seriously? Other writers spent a few paragraphs asserting that I made being flat-chested "sexy" or that my wardrobe choices trended toward "last year's conventions."

The attacks on our femininity were a constant. When the *Sports Illustrated* writer Edwin "Bud" Shrake visited the women's tour a couple of years after we launched, he wrote, "The players were an amazingly good-looking group of people, especially when one thought of the stereotype of the woman athlete. Nobody had a beard . . . Nobody waddled. Not a lumberjack in the group."

Jim Murray, the Pulitzer Prize–winning columnist at the *Los Angeles Times,* called me "Little Miss Popoff" and wrote about my alleged bitterness at not being born a boy: "King has never forgiven Nature for the dirty trick it played on her in preventing her from being a free safety for the Green Bay Packers . . . Around Long Beach, they say her father got her into tennis so she wouldn't be a lady wrestler." The idea that women simply wanted to see what we could be seemed incomprehensible to some people.

Grace Lichtenstein, one of the few women who covered sports at the time, expertly captured just how ingrained such attitudes were when she wrote, "These women were defying all the false tenets of femininity that had plagued me and so many other girls. As a kid growing up in the 1950s, I accepted the concept of women athletes as freaks. I had been taught that to want to become an athlete of any kind was unacceptable. Girls were passive, non-competitive, dependent. The notion of a sexy woman athlete was a contradiction."

Ingrid Löfdahl-Bentzer, our top Swedish player, was an accomplished woman who spoke seven languages and served as one of our first players' association officers. On a trip to Italy once, Ingrid used a rolled-up magazine to swat away the numerous men who catcalled her or tried to pinch her rear end as she walked down the street. She was a formidable woman. And yet, when Ingrid reminisced about her tour experiences decades later, she told an American writer, "Back then, so many things could prick you. The most stupid things would come up. I always remember my first husband had a girlfriend before me with skin like porcelain. She always smelled like perfume. And here I was, I smelled of Ben-Gay liniment and I had calluses on my hands. I thought, '*Ahhh, Bentzer—you're a jock.*' As a woman, you'd get put into these funny, funny positions. Nowadays it's easy to look back and say, 'Well, that treatment was crap!' But at the time . . ."

I had been taking questions about when I was going to stop being a tennis bum since I was a sixteen-year-old marooned at those tournament country club mixers. From the mid-1970s to this day, I can't tell you how many women have approached me somewhere to tell me they admire my game or my activism—and then introduce themselves as "Mrs. Joe Smith" or say, "I'm just his wife," and point to a man across the room.

I look at them and say, "That's great, but who are *you*?"

NOW THAT THERE WAS open tennis, so much more was theoretically in play for women players. Yet the resistance we were encountering was getting stiffer. Larry's prophecy that the men would try to push us out of the game was coming true.

When Rosie, Frankie, Ann, and I became the first troupe of women pros to travel the world for two years with the MacCall tour, we enjoyed a warm relationship with the six men in our group, Rod Laver, Roy Emerson, Fred Stolle, Ken Rosewall, Pancho Gonzalez, and Andrés Gimeno. Now that shamateurism was exposed and everything could be aboveboard, we were all fighting for better pay from tournaments and promoters. All of us wanted more freedom to set our own playing schedules and loosen the control of the national associations like the USLTA. And yet, when I tried to enlist the male players' support for our fight for better treatment and prize money by arguing that a united front would benefit us all, I was stunned at the male players' responses. We were less welcome than before.

I went to the men's leaders before they started the Association of Tennis Professionals in 1972 because I couldn't believe the men left women out. They never bothered to respond to me. It was the same in 1969 when John Newcombe organized the International Players Association. I asked them, too, if they planned to include women, and I was told, "You must be joking." It still hurts me to talk about it. Newcombe and I played mixed doubles during the months I trained in Australia. I would later become good friends with Arthur Ashe, the first president of the ATP, but he was backward on gender issues before he married his wife, Jeanne Moutoussamy, an exceptional photographer and strong professional woman.

Arthur told *The Boston Globe,* "The women are going to disappear because they don't draw flies." Clark Graebner said, "I'm just as happy to never see the girls. They're not very attractive. I wouldn't want my daughter playing on tour." The American star Stan Smith told *The Daily Mirror* of London, "These girls would be much happier if they settled down, got married, and had a family. Tennis is a rough life and it really isn't good for them. It de-feminizes them . . . [They become] too independent and they can't adapt to anyone else, they won't be dependent on a man. They want to take charge, not only on the courts but at home."

I couldn't believe it. These were my friends and contemporaries and they didn't want us around. It was crushing. Fred Stolle, one of the Aussies, told me, "No one wants to *pay* to watch you birds play."

While the disparities between the men's and women's prize money remained a problem from the first open tournament in Bournemouth, we soon had another issue. The number of tournaments where women players were invited was shrinking as well.

By 1970, George MacCall couldn't make the NTL work anymore, and the rival WCT bought the contracts of all six of our male teammates—but none of us women. Every woman player around the world was again at the sole mercy of our national associations and promoters for opportunities to compete.

Larry and I were worried enough that Larry drafted a confidential letter that we circulated in February 1970 to eight of the top women's players and Gladys Heldman, the publisher of *World Tennis* magazine, who was also a promoter. We offered a proposal for how we could set up a pro women's tour as a group. The proposal argued that we should take control of our futures, and it suggested that the players we approached could share 10 percent ownership of our events, with another 20 percent going to whomever was hired to manage the circuit. The remaining 70 percent would go to the promoters for their operational costs and prize money.

We couldn't get enough of the other women to take the leap, so we tabled the idea. Three months later, a handful of us thought about organizing a protest during the 1970 Italian Open in May when first prize was $7,500 for the men compared to just $600 for the women—an appalling twelve-to-one disparity. We complained that our treatment was getting worse, but we didn't walk out.

Things were really starting to rumble now. We learned that the men's U.S. Open winner would get $20,000 compared to just $7,500 for the women's champ, which mirrored what the other Grand Slams were offering. Our concerns spiked again when Jack Kramer, never one to conceal his contempt for female players, convinced the ILTF to set up a $1 million International Grand Prix tennis circuit for 1971 with Pepsi as a sponsor. Only a handful of the twenty-five new Grand Prix events would be open to women, and at those events we weren't eligible for perks like the $229,000 in year-end bonuses the men could earn. In fact, under Kramer's plan, the few tournaments women did play would have to send 10 percent of the proceeds into the *men's* bonus pot. Unbelievable. We got only the scraps for prize money, but now we were also supposed to subsidize the men's tour at the limited Grand Prix events they did let us play in.

Worse, when I asked USLTA officials how their 1971 schedule for us was shaping up, they told me there were only two tournaments scheduled for women between October 1970 and March 1971. That was a deeply troubling moment. The livelihoods of women players everywhere were at stake.

We were finally fed up when Kramer announced that the prize money he was offering for the 1970 Pepsi Pacific Southwest Championships two weeks after the U.S. Open would be a disparity of eight to one. He planned to offer a $65,000 purse to the men versus $7,500 for the entire women's field. None of the women would be paid a dime for their work unless they made the Round of 16, but every man who entered would get a paycheck.

This time, there was an uprising. It started at Forest Hills in September 1970, and it is no exaggeration to say tennis—and, eventually, the business of all sports for women—would never be the same.

Chapter 12

I WASN'T PLAYING at the 1970 U.S. Open because I was recovering from my second knee surgery, this one to my right knee. I only survived my semifinal match against Rosie at Wimbledon a month earlier by chipping and lobbing strategically against her. Before our final, Margaret had a doctor shoot six or seven syringes of painkillers into her badly twisted ankle. I wish I had done the same to my knee.

The brutal two-hour twenty-seven-minute match that we played was the longest in the history of the ladies' championships to that point. My run of three Wimbledon titles had been snapped the previous year, and I wanted to start a new streak. Margaret arrived at Wimbledon determined to keep alive her chance for a Grand Slam sweep of the majors that year, the same as she was trying to do when I upset her in 1962.

This time she outlasted me 14–12 in the marathon first set that took eighty-eight minutes to play. In the second set we blasted away at each other for another hour. At times we looked like two escapees from an orthopedic ward. Margaret kept tripping on her numb foot and even fell down once. I could barely stand on my shaky right leg. We had been in each other's crosshairs as the two best players in the world for years now, and each of us refused to give an inch. I was up 8–7 in the second set, but she won the next game by knifing a backhand volley by me. At least I went down fighting, rescuing seven match points before she won the epic second set, too, 11–9. Tennis historians still call it one of the finest matches ever played on Centre Court. But for me, it was a crushing defeat.

I had the knee surgery the following week. I was still on crutches by the U.S. Open, so I agreed to work the tournament as a television commentator for CBS. Sports broadcasting was just opening up to a few women. Maureen Connolly had announced some Wimbledon matches on BBC broadcasts, and the Olympic swimmer Donna de Varona retired from competition at the age of seventeen and in 1964 became the first female sports broadcaster on an American network when she joined ABC's *Wide World of Sports*.

I spent a lot of time in the tiny women's locker room at Forest Hills gauging the players' mood. Rosie and I started polling the women players to see if we could agree to protest Kramer's prize money decision. I called Larry for advice, and he suggested we talk again to Gladys Heldman. Rosie and I had already met with Gladys about it at a tournament in New Jersey the week before the Open.

Years later, when Gladys was asked who was responsible for starting the women's tennis tour, she often smiled slyly and jokingly said, "Jack Kramer did." Gladys was a brilliant, self-made, well-connected power broker in a male-dominated world who founded her magazine at the age of thirty-one and turned it into the bible of our sport. She was tireless, generous, glamorous, eccentric, narcissistic, creative, and just plain wonderful. She could also be imperious if necessary and would go toe-to-toe with anybody. She was an outsider in the WASP-dominated tennis world, a Jewish woman who couldn't join some of the private clubs where we played, and she often used the pages of *World Tennis* to advocate for causes. In short, she was not someone who easily took no for an answer, or the kind of woman you told to be quiet and go away.

Rosie, Nancy Richey, and I had lunch with Gladys on the West Side Tennis Club terrace during the U.S. Open and asked her for help. We all agreed that a boycott of Kramer's tournament wouldn't work unless all the women were united, and that wasn't true yet. It was decided instead that Gladys would try to persuade Kramer to increase the women's purse. She spoke with him twice. The first time, he refused to talk to her about it. The second time he told her, "Fine, if the women players don't like it, I won't give them *any* prize money." Gladys's report back to us was "Kramer's an ass."

Gladys started making phone calls. Meanwhile, one of our smart-est young players, Ceci Martinez, decided to apply her psychology training from San Francisco State University to the problem. We were constantly told that paying spectators weren't interested in women's tennis. We faced a Catch-22: Our visibility was sabotaged because women's matches were routinely shunted to the back courts and received little or no publicity or coverage, then we were blamed for not drawing bigger crowds.

Ceci decided to test the competing premises. She designed a one-page questionnaire that she and her doubles partner, Esmé Emmanuel, of South Africa, handed out at Forest Hills during the U.S. Open. The mimeographed survey asked fans questions includ-ing "Do you think women players should (1) play their own tour-naments separate from the men, (2) play along with the men at the same tournaments, (3) not play professional tennis?"

The results were encouraging. Of the 278 people who returned the questionnaires—94 women and 184 men—about half said wom-en's tennis was just as interesting as men's. Eighty-two percent of men preferred seeing men and women play in the same tourna-ment. One third of the men and half of the women thought the prize money distribution should be equal. This was something we could build on. This was data, not hearsay.

On Sunday, September 6, Rosie and I led a locker room meeting to discuss whether to boycott Kramer's event. Everyone hated the prize money disparity, but once again a lot of women were afraid. What if we upset our national associations? What if we were banned from Wimbledon or the other majors? We were pretty hotly divided, and I was getting pretty exasperated, when Gladys burst through the door with a big smile on her face and almost sang, "Ladies! I've got news!"

Gladys and her family were moving back to Houston after years of living in New York and she said she could organize an eight-woman tournament at the Houston Racquet Club from September 23 to 26, the same week as Kramer's 1970 Pacific Southwest tournament. She said the total prize money would be $5,000. It seemed like an ele-gant solution. We could forget having to ask all the women to join the boycott, and yet still send a message to Kramer and the establishment that we would seek other options if they continued their inequitable treatment of us.

The next day, Rosie, Ceci, and eight other players announced our intentions to reporters from around the world at the annual Lawn Tennis Writers Association luncheon. I had business commitments in Manhattan and couldn't attend, but they were terrific. They distributed a three-point manifesto in which we said we were seeking "prize money commensurate with that of men, equal exposure in center court matches, and better treatment by the news media, which subordinates women's tennis to the men's game." We weren't even arguing for equal pay at that point. Rosie suggested that a three-to-one ratio could be acceptable. Rosie also dropped the word *boycott* for the first time and said some of us might skip Kramer's event because of the "ridiculous" disparity in prize money. "It's discrimination," she said.

The news of our revolt made headlines around the world, including on the front page of *The New York Times.* Numerous other outlets printed the results of Ceci's survey. It was the first time a large segment of the general public had an insight into how unfairly the women players were being treated.

Once again, most of the top male players abandoned us. Arthur Ashe told reporters, "Men are playing for a living now. They don't want to give up money just for girls to play. Why should we have to split the money with them? . . . We're supporting families and we're the drawing cards." Rod Laver, Pancho Gonzalez, and Stan Smith, who would soon overtake Arthur as America's best player, said similar things. Marty Riessen complained that "women's events just clutter up tournaments" and Cliff Richey—whose sister, Nancy, was on our side—said, "Women ride on the coattails of the men and then complain."

I wasn't about to remain quiet. When Bud Collins reached me, I fired back in *The Boston Globe,* "I sell more tickets than Stan Smith. I think I'm a more exciting player and more people want to see me play."

Kramer later insisted in his autobiography that the diminished women's prize money was "just good business sense" on his part, not prejudice. "People get up and go get a hot dog or go to the bathroom when the women come on," he wrote.

THE PLAYERS WHO AGREED to compete in Houston that week were Rosie Casals, Nancy Richey, Kerry Melville, Judy Dalton, Val Ziegenfuss, Peaches Bartkowicz, Kristy Pigeon, Patti Hogan, and me. Julie Heldman, Gladys's daughter, attended but, because she was injured, played only a token point with me as a show of solidarity with us. It was clear to me that what we were doing was historic. My surgically repaired knee was still mending and I was hobbling around pretty badly, so I originally planned to play only the mixed-doubles pro-am. The club's male members bid for the opportunity to play with us, and I donated $500 so the women pros earned some prize money for participating. But when Patti withdrew and we needed another singles player, I took her place.

Gladys thought Margaret would also play singles, but Margaret, never an eager suffragette, later said she never intended to play. She said her ankle had not yet healed after our match at Wimbledon and she was exhausted from finishing her Grand Slam sweep at Forest Hills. CBS had deigned to broadcast only the last ten minutes of Margaret's landmark victory there even though Maureen Connolly was the first and only other woman to ever accomplish a calendar-year sweep of the majors. Even that slight didn't change Margaret's mind. Rather than join us in Houston, she went fishing in Florida with her husband, Barry.

The Friday before our tournament week in Houston, Stan Malless, the chairman of the USLTA Sanction and Schedule Committee, began calling our American players to threaten us with indefinite suspensions if we played, a vague threat that implied we could be banned from making a living at the U.S. Open, Wimbledon, or anywhere else. The Australians among us feared that their association might do the same to them.

Malless upped the pressure on the Houston Racquet Club by refusing to sanction our event. That was a surprise to the Texas

Tennis Association president-elect Jim Hight and the tournament organizer Delores Hornberger, president of the club's Women's Association. Tickets had been sold. The bleachers had already been set up. When Hight called, the USLTA made up a couple of rules on the fly to justify its threats, at one point telling him that our event and Kramer's couldn't be sanctioned during the same week, which was untrue. Hight pointed out that overlaps had happened before and treating us differently was discrimination. He and Delores bravely decided that under no circumstances would the tournament be canceled.

Gladys was still trying to reach USLTA officials herself. She urged all of us players to travel to Houston and promised to cover our airfare. We'd figure things out when we got there. The USLTA's threats were obviously about controlling women players. But something that Jack Kramer did showed the extreme lengths some men were willing to go. Kramer convened a meeting of the Pacific Southwest tournament's all-male board, and then sent a telegram to the USLTA attributed to his longtime ally Perry T. Jones—who was in a coma on his deathbed at the time—condemning our "illegal" tournament. The Czar passed away the next day.

Kramer had battled the USLTA from 1952 to 1967 when he was promoting his own breakaway events for male pros, and now he was dictating USLTA policy with his objections against us. Gladys kept trying all weekend to reach the USLTA president, Alastair Martin, with whom she had worked closely in the past, but Martin didn't respond to the two telegrams she sent. Nancy finally reached Martin by phone on Monday evening—forty-eight hours before we were supposed to begin—and Martin confirmed that we risked suspensions if we played.

By the following day, all but one of our players had arrived in Houston. Gladys had never quit working the phones and finalized another coup on Tuesday morning, hours before our pre-tournament cocktail party at the Houston Racquet Club began: Philip Morris, whose CEO was her longtime friend Joseph F. Cullman 3rd, had agreed to give $2,500 to sponsor our tournament on behalf of its two-year-old Virginia Slims brand, a cigarette marketed to women.

The Houston Racquet Club gratefully accepted the offer from Slims brand manager Steve Korsen and agreed to change the event's name from the First Houston Women's International Tennis Tournament to the Virginia Slims Invitational of Houston. Slims assistant brand manager Bill Cutler and the Philip Morris publicist Dallas Kersey booked flights to Houston to arrive in time to attend the party.

Having the backing of such an influential corporate sponsor was extremely important. But while Gladys was getting the Philip Morris commitment, Malless had phoned Delores and said the USLTA would now sanction our tournament if we made it an event with no publicized prize money and paid us nothing beyond our air travel, food, and lodging expenses—a return to shamateurism. Delores agreed to that concession before talking to the players, which I was very unhappy to learn after Peaches and I, the last to arrive in Houston that day, made it to the pre-tournament cocktail party. To me, the USLTA's offer was yet another insult. If we agreed to return to shamateurism, where or when would it ever stop?

We called a players' meeting for the following morning to revisit taking the prize money off the table. The gathering took place in a conference room at the Houston Racquet Club after an instructional clinic we held but before the first match of the tournament was scheduled to begin. Gladys, the tournament organizers, and the two Slims marketing officials joined us.

I argued that we should defy the USLTA, and Rosie agreed that reverting to shamateurism was unacceptable. Patti Hogan expressed amazement that the USLTA was actually encouraging "a return to the very evil that open tennis was supposed to have eliminated." But if we rejected that condition, the other issue we would have to address was how to transcend the USLTA's threats to suspend us or withhold sanctioning our event. Then the answer came to us: Gladys could sign us as contract pros for that week, same as George Mac-Call and Lamar Hunt had done for the men on their tours. Past precedent suggested that both the club and our tournament should be considered outside the USLTA's jurisdiction, although given the present climate, who could be sure?

"But I can't pay you," Gladys said.

"Then make it one dollar," I told her. "A dollar contract is as binding as a trillion dollars."

Our livelihoods hung in the balance. The stakes were huge. It was 2:45 p.m. now, forty-five minutes before the first match was set to begin, and reporters were in another area of the club waiting to talk to us. The players asked everyone but Gladys to leave our meeting room. We voted unanimously to defy the USLTA—to play and risk being suspended. Then Gladys dictated a one-sentence agreement that Patti Hogan wrote down on a notebook. It read "We, the undersigned, declare ourselves under contract to *World Tennis* magazine, at a guarantee of $1 per player." As each of us added our signature, Gladys handed us a dollar bill.

I can't remember if my hand was shaking as I took my turn signing, but I do recall that my heart was thumping and my stomach was churning. This was revolutionary. We had finally decided to control our own destiny.

I hurried out to a pay phone and called the USLTA's Alastair Martin. I wanted to do things right, so I asked him one last time if the USLTA would offer any more tournaments for women to play that year. He told me nothing had changed. So I told him, "Well, then I'm sorry, Mr. Martin, but you've left us no choice. I didn't want you to read this in the newspaper tomorrow without me calling you. We've decided to play."

I hung up the phone, ran to where the others were, and said, "We're a go!" And that's when we lined up and *The Houston Post*'s Béla Ugrin snapped a photo that became iconic: It shows Gladys holding up our contract and eight of us players holding up our $1 bills and smiling. We became known as the Original 9.

We had no idea what the future held. But what's that saying, Faith is stepping off a cliff and hoping you grow wings? That was us. And grow wings we did.

THRILLED AS I WAS that we didn't back down, my mind was already racing ahead to the landscape we'd encounter once the euphoria of the Houston tournament waned. Remember, October was just days away and there were only two USLTA tournaments scheduled for women during the next six months. We desperately wanted to start our tour in three months and yet we had no infrastructure, no sponsorships or promoters. The pressure was on.

I lost my first-round Virginia Slims match to Judy Dalton, but Rosie, fresh off her terrific runner-up finish to Margaret at the U.S. Open, was moving toward Saturday's final. She was as concerned as I was about our future as a group. Gladys felt the same, so she was back to working her connections as only Gladys could.

Rosie and I had asked Gladys several times if she would consider running an expanded tour for us beyond Houston, and she always told us that she was too busy with her other work. During the U.S. Open a couple of weeks earlier, Dennis Van der Meer, a partner in TennisAmerica with Larry and me, had attended Gladys's annual *World Tennis* party at her Manhattan apartment, which was the social event of the fortnight, and openly told people about our willingness to promote some tournaments. Rosie mentioned the possibility to some reporters the next day during a tournament rain delay. Now I called Larry and asked him if he could fly from California to Houston to present a plan before we disbanded, and then I told a *Houston Chronicle* reporter that Larry was on his way.

Larry arrived in time to join us at Gladys's house on Friday night for the spaghetti dinner party we had to celebrate the tournament's success. When we finished eating, we asked if Larry could present the proposal that he and Dennis had devised about what to do next, and we moved to one of the large bedrooms. Gladys didn't join us.

Larry admitted that he didn't have any sponsors lined up yet but he'd chase them. He was willing to start by promoting three or four events on the West Coast because we needed places to play going forward. When we voted unanimously to hire him, Gladys became upset when her daughter Julie left the room and told her the news. I'm not sure if Julie knew that Gladys had kept telling Rosie and me that she didn't want to run a new tour. Now Gladys claimed we were pushing her aside.

Larry found Gladys in the kitchen and told her, "Gladys, I'm only here because we thought you didn't want to run a new women's tour! We'd much rather help you than undertake the project ourselves."

Then Gladys said what we'd hoped for all along: "I do want to run it!"

There was no precedent on how we should construct a women's-only tournament circuit. That same night, we discussed what would be a reasonable amount of prize money per event. The players agreed to be honest with each other about what we were making under the table. I said I got $1,100 a week, and I thought that was a huge payday. Val Ziegenfuss said, "Are you kidding me? I'm lucky to get a plane ticket!" Many of the others didn't get anything beyond nominal expense money.

I said I didn't give a damn if the trade-off for going our own way was that I'd never play another Wimbledon. Nancy and Rosie said they didn't care, either. But some of the other women were still saying, *We have a lot to lose.* Finally I said, "Lose? *Lose?* What do *we* have to lose? What do we have now? We have fewer and fewer places to play. When we do play with the men, it's an eight-to-one ratio of prize money even though we're playing in front of a packed house. So you think they're giving us something? Me personally, I think they're giving us absolutely *nothing.* I think we have *nothing* to lose!"

"We could fall flat on our faces if we start a tour," I continued. "There's a great chance we are never going to make the big bucks ourselves or enjoy the adulation that future generations might. But are you willing to do this just because it's the *right* thing to do?" We took our vote, and it was unanimous. Gladys would run a breakaway tour in which we all committed to play.

THE HOUSTON TOURNAMENT WAS a success despite being thrown together in under two weeks, and Rosie was proud that she won that first title, beating Judy in straight sets. We had also made sure that our winner earned $1,600, $100 more than the women's singles champion at Kramer's Pacific Southwest event could make. Two weeks after that, four of us held a press conference at the Philip

Morris headquarters in New York to announce the Virginia Slims/ World Tennis professional women's circuit for 1971, and Gladys uttered a memorable line to the assembled press: "You've heard of Women's Lib? This is Women's Lob."

For us, a tour with women in charge was a dream come true. Our stated goals, from the start, were three-fold: We wanted to make sure that any girl in the world, if she's good enough, would have a place to compete; that women and girl athletes would finally be appreciated for their accomplishments, not just their looks; and that we'd be able to make a living.

In the short term, we still had a few more skirmishes. We had threatened to boycott the Pacific Coast Open in Berkeley—the tournament right after our Houston event—because the total women's prize money there didn't meet our new $10,000 minimum. This time the promoter, Barry MacKay, agreed to get another $7,600 for the women's purse, making it $11,000 compared with $26,000 for the men. We were showing what women players could do when we stuck together and others were willing to champion us. The additional money came from the San Francisco native Alvin Duskin, a left-leaning social activist and clothing designer whose popular sweater dresses were favored by fashion icons like Twiggy.

The USLTA did make another attempt to divide and conquer our group. A little over three months after the Houston tournament, the USLTA said it would forgo suspending everyone who played there—except for Rosie and me. The USLTA's excuse for singling us out was that we had already been reinstated once after turning pro on the MacCall tour, and twice was not possible. Once again, they were making up rules on the fly to pressure us. We had only forty-eight hours to respond before play began at our first 1971 Virginia Slims Circuit stop in San Francisco. Once again, our players' response was unanimous: The USLTA would reinstate all of us, or none of us would play their events. We were again speaking as one voice, and it made all the difference in the world. We were all reinstated.

Philip Morris had a lot of promotional money to spend because all cigarette advertising on television had been banned, and so they chose to invest a significant amount in us. We zigzagged around the country that first year putting on an ambitious slate of nineteen tournaments that offered a total of $310,000 in prize money. By 1973, our prize money had grown to $750,000, and sixteen-year-old Martina Navratilova had joined eighteen-year-old Chrissie Evert on the tour. The two of them alone combined to win a staggering $30 million by the time they retired. From our $1 rebellion, women's tennis grew into a profession where the U.S. Open singles winner earned $3.85 million in 2019.

It's hard to exaggerate how game-changing Joe Cullman's help was. Philip Morris didn't bankroll the entire 1971 tour—tournament organizers were responsible for their own events—but the company contributed a great deal beyond boosting the tour's prize money. In addition to throwing Philip Morris's corporate weight behind us, Joe expended some personal capital when he backed us. Beginning in 1969, Joe had served a two-year stint as chairman of the U.S. Open and helped the tournament land its first national TV broadcasting deal with CBS. Now he was putting his influence to work for our breakaway protest. That validation mattered greatly to the other people and companies we were approaching for support.

Joe obviously wanted to sell more cigarettes, but he cared deeply about social justice as well. Like Gladys, Joe had experienced discrimination for being Jewish, and he once said he became involved in tennis in the 1960s because when he looked at the players and fans in the stands, "I was not happy with the lack of diversity—racial, religious, gender, and economic . . . Tennis wasn't moving fast enough."

It was the first time women athletes had ever had that much power and money invested in us—let alone more money and power than those we were fighting at the USLTA. And Gladys was outstanding. She felt personally responsible for the players and fiercely advocated for our interests, paid some tour expenses with her own money, created a slush fund to help struggling players stay on tour, and often worked for us for free, sending us telegrams and holding monthly meetings to update us on tour business.

At the start of Virginia Slims' involvement, I had relayed my reservations to Gladys about partnering with a cigarette company, let alone a brand that was irking feminists with its slogan, "You've come a long way, baby." I knew that numerous male sports stars such as Joe DiMaggio had been featured in ads for tobacco products. Throughout the 1960s, Philip Morris had four tennis players on staff as brand ambassadors: Arthur Ashe, Manuel Santana, Rafael Osuna, and Roy Emerson. Gladys herself smoked at least two packs a day. Nonetheless, I told her, "We're athletes. This bothers me."

She looked at me and said, "You want a tour or not?"

Excellent point.

I still say our partnership with Philip Morris was the greatest in the history of sports. They never asked us to smoke, and never asked us to endorse their product. They told us we could say whatever we wanted—and we did. Without their support, I'm not sure how we would've made it. The company provided us with an expert staff that helped us create and stage events, and do our marketing, public relations, signage, TV coverage—you name it. They committed to growing women's tennis and making us known and relatable. They emphasized turning us into celebrities, not just tennis players; today it's called personal branding. They made our tour possible and then ensured its growth into the global big business it is today. No other women's pro sports undertaking has been more successful or longer lasting.

Initially, I—a lot of us actually—didn't want to break off from the male players. I still think all of us would've enjoyed more self-determination if the men and women had stuck together. (The idea was revived by Roger Federer when tennis was shut down during the pandemic in 2020, but it didn't immediately go anywhere despite widespread support from other players on social media.) Because we're a global sport, we could do so much good by setting an egalitarian example.

The start of the original Slims tour was not the only time we were forced to empower ourselves as women because the men refused to work with us. In fact, the rejections pushed us to take control of our future. I was learning that you can't build a movement without incurring opposition, and we often gained a bigger foothold each time it happened, gathering strength as we went. Some of us were feeling empowered for the first time in our lives.

Chapter 13

OUR GREAT EXPERIMENT in women's pro tennis kicked off in San Francisco, on January 6, 1971, with the BMC Pro Women's Championship, a tournament with nineteen players and a $15,000 purse. The sponsor was British Motor Car Distributors, which was owned by a Norwegian American named Kjell Qvale. When Larry and I spoke to him about backing all-women tournaments in San Francisco and Long Beach, he saw it as a great marketing opportunity. He said he would give us the money, but only if Jerry Diamond, his gifted publicist, ran the events. At the outset, Jerry wasn't thrilled by the prospect.

Jerry had Bronx roots, a thick New York accent, and a tough-guy manner. He grew up in a walk-up apartment over a jewelry store and started out as an automotive writer, then switched to representing racetracks and major motorsports events. I don't think he had seen a tennis match in his life before we met. When he called a newspaper buddy of his in Los Angeles for advice, his friend made a call to . . . Jack Kramer. How do you suppose that went? But Kjell wouldn't let Jerry off the hook.

The San Francisco Civic Auditorium held about nine thousand people and it cost $10,000 to rent for the championship. Our total paid attendance was less than five thousand. When Jerry went to Kjell to tell him the first event had lost $25,000, Kjell told him, "Jerry, you did a *great* job!" Jerry said, "Huh?" Kjell continued, "We've had the front page of the newspapers every day, the TV news—everything! I think I got about $250,000 worth of exposure for British Motor Cars. Let's commit to doing it again."

For the first two years, Jerry remained so annoyed to be working on the event that he would wheel and walk away when he saw Larry coming, as if it was Larry's fault. But in the third year the tournament made $50,000, and Jerry—who owned one-third of it, the same as Kjell and Larry and me—became one of our biggest believers and assets. In 1974, I hired Jerry as executive director of the Women's Tennis Association and he negotiated terrific deals for us over the years with big-name sponsors who helped us go from an experiment to an industry.

After our inaugural San Francisco stop, we put together the Billie Jean King Invitational in my hometown of Long Beach, and Larry and Dennis Van der Meer staged it. We drew more than nine thousand spectators over four days, with weekend crowds much larger than the recent men's pro tennis tournaments that year, even though ours was a bootstrap operation. My mom and dad helped us with ticket sales, and Larry, Rosie, and I slept at their house. It was my first tournament in Long Beach in ten years, and we had a blast. The city had decided in 1968 to rename Recreation Park, one of the public courts where Clyde taught me, the Billie Jean Moffitt King Tennis Center. Larry and I donated our tournament's proceeds to build permanent seating for the main court.

Now that the Slims tour had Philip Morris's backing, we negotiated a truce, of sorts, with the USLTA: We agreed to pay them a fee in exchange for sanctioning the Slims tournaments. But then—infuriatingly—the USLTA and its overseer, the International Lawn Tennis Federation, added more women's events to their 1971 summer and fall calendar.

If they had just done that when I called the USLTA chief Alastair Martin from Houston in September 1970, we might have never broken away. The result now was messy and confusing to fans. The other circuit featured Margaret, England's Virginia Wade, and sensations like nineteen-year-old Evonne Goolagong of Australia and young Chrissie Evert, who was already getting a lot of attention.

We still held out hope that Margaret would join us on the 1971 Virginia Slims tour even though she had stayed away when we risked our livelihoods to create it. But she denounced us in the fall of 1970 in a press release. "If you worry about money you become hard. It's a bad thing," she wrote. "Besides, men play five sets, women play three, and by and large the biggest crowds turn up to watch the guys play. So I don't think women should be paid the same as men. We aren't equal."

Thanks, mate.

We were used to hearing Margaret pander to the male tennis establishment, but what surprised me was her attempt to put us down as money grubbers. She had happily taken Bob Mitchell's largesse in Melbourne. We all knew she was making a bundle playing tournaments for high appearance fees. Her stance was regrettable. Again, we moved on without her.

At the beginning of the Slims tour I found an extra gear I didn't know I had. I was playing really well again, with no knee pain for the first time in three years. It made a huge difference that I wasn't playing just for myself. We all felt like we were carrying the future of women's tennis onto the court each night. In my case, that sense of mission that I had had since I was a child now had a concrete focus, and it brought out the best in me.

We racked up fourteen tournaments in the first three and a half months of 1971 alone, almost one a week. I won the first five, beating Rosie each time in the final. The pace was grueling, but it helped Rosie and me to have had the MacCall tour experience. Our Slims events were played everywhere from college gyms and rec centers to Caesars Palace in Las Vegas, which felt like the big-time even though sand came blowing off the desert onto our outdoor court. For the first time, a lot of women players were making real money, and we were determined to keep it going.

We picked up a lot of support from women who wanted to promote our tournaments. Two months after we got our start in Houston, Dorothy Chewning, a longtime tennis fixture in Richmond, Virginia, welcomed the Slims players to her tournament, the Westwood Racquet Club Invitational. By 1972, Nancy Jeffett annually hosted the Maureen Connolly Brinker Invitational in Dallas. Cindy Trabue and Sandy Lecklider of the Junior League of Birmingham, Michigan, convinced the Kresge Foundation to foot the prize money for what became the K-Mart International, and persevered when our portable court went missing until the last minute while in transit by train. Joyce Turley ran our stop in Oklahoma City, and personally recruited one hundred sponsors herself for $100 apiece. "I'd start out in the morning and I wouldn't go home until I had three sponsors," Joyce told the historian Donn Gobbie.

Everybody pitched in enormously. As our top-ranked player, I was most often cast as the main spokeswoman, the standard setter, the biggest agitator. It was always, "Billie, over here . . . Billie, what do you think?" By the time I had won seven of our first nine singles titles, the demands were constant. I would wake up before dawn to be interviewed on the morning TV and radio shows, and I'd sometimes lie on my hotel bed and dial up reporters until midnight or later to promote the next stop on our schedule.

My friends said I was too intense. Larry said I paid a big price, often to the point of getting sick. But I couldn't relax. Practically overnight, we were trying to change a tennis structure that had existed for a hundred years and buck chauvinism at the same time. When things didn't happen as fast as I felt they should, I was driven to find out why.

I so badly wanted us to be a locked-down, airtight, professional-looking operation. I would take the balls and show the ball boys and ball girls the correct way to throw them to the other side of the court. One night I stood in the lobby before playing my final and counted the fans coming in. At every stop, I wanted to know if the promoter was doing enough, if the publicist was effective, if the fans were happy. The tour came first, and everything had to be exactly right. When it wasn't, I admit I often got pretty impatient.

Jeanie Brinkman, whom Philip Morris hired to do public relations for the tour in 1973, later said of those years, "Billie Jean was a magnet, attracting and repelling with equally strong force. The tour used to fluctuate with her. If Billie was on a rampage, tension was high. If she was happy, everyone was. It was never tranquil with Billie around, but that's what it took to make the sport . . . These women are professional tennis players, and it's not a release from the tension—it *is* the tension."

Sometimes we had good advance sales, but other times, when sales were lagging, our players would visit high school assemblies, or stand in the street outside our venues the day of the matches and hand out tickets to random motorists or pedestrians passing by. We were taking world-class tennis to brand-new places and sometimes the uninitiated crowds would applaud during points. But I loved that too. When Rosie was asked once if the noise was a distraction after the sepulchral atmosphere we were used to, Rosie joked, "I could care less if they got stoned."

In Chattanooga, one of our most challenging stops, the first indoor facility we used was a metal-roofed hangar with lighting so dim the balls we used were fuchsia—the better to see them, I guess. To sell tickets on the day of the finals, we stopped cars by waving signs that read "Women's Tennis Here!," some of us wearing Davy Crockett–style coonskin caps. In the end, we packed the place with about a thousand people. When I won the tournament, they gave me a squirrel gun along with the winner's check. When I took another title in Oklahoma City, they handed me a ten-gallon cowboy hat with $2,500 emblazoned in foil numerals on the front. At our tour stop near Birmingham, Michigan, Frankie caused a sensation at our pre-tournament cocktail party by showing up in black fake-fur hot pants. When she played, she often had her dog, Topspin, carry her racket out between its teeth.

On days like that, we would look around and blink in amazement at what we'd started. It was glorious, side-splitting, outrageously good fun. It felt like we were spinning straw into gold, or we were extras in one of those corny Judy Garland–Mickey Rooney movies where the overcaffeinated kids band together to save their home-town, telling each other, "Whaddaya say, gang? Let's put on a show!"

ONE OF THE MOST exciting things about building our women's tour from scratch was that we were able to shape it the way we wanted. From the start, we made a conscious decision to break away from tennis's staid image and have our events be more freewheeling

and engaging. I've always maintained that tennis players are entertainers, and, as such, we should be paid the same regardless of how
many sets we play or what our gender is. We never claimed that we
were better than men. What we said was that women put on just as
good a show. Now we were proving it.

Philip Morris was an absolute marketing machine, and they sent
us Ellen Merlo, a public relations specialist and event planner who
worked for the company's Marlboro brand, which sponsored Indy
Car races. Ellen never played tennis, but she was a brilliant strate-
gist and she helped shape us into a polished, professional group. She
set up advertising, offered media training for the players to help us
with interviews, wrangled reporters to cover our events, and phoned
in scores to make sure we made the local papers. Often a few people
were sent ahead of us to our next tour stop to do advance promotional work. The players did everything we could to help. If the print
reporters or TV stations wouldn't send someone to us, we'd often
get in a car and drive to them. If a sports editor balked at sending a
writer, I'd sometimes get on the phone and say, "Well, do you have
a stringer? And if they do a good job, would you consider using the
story then?" They often did. We were good copy.

There were no full-time athletic trainers to help us in the early
days. Nancy Richey once had a root canal in Denver in the morning, then played her match at night gargling Scotch to kill the pain.
Rosie worked another match crouched by the net as a ball girl
because we needed the help. To help defray costs, Ann Jones's husband, Pip, used to roll up the Slims' carpeted indoor court and drive
it on a truck from town to town himself. When the USLTA banned
its officials from working our tournaments for a while, Peachy Kellmeyer, our tour director, sometimes had to recruit people in the are-
nas. "One time we talked the Xerox repairman into calling the lines
but he gave himself away when he yelled 'Foul!' instead of 'Out!,'"
Peachy said years later.

We added some new twists to our format. At some stops we
spruced up the introductions and had our players walk out one by
one from behind a curtain to spotlight us to fans. When we grew

tired of hearing that men deserved to be paid more because they play the best-of-five sets at the majors, we made our year-end Slims Championship final the best-of-five sets from 1984 to 1998.

It was Joe Cullman who had the inspired idea to hire the dress designer and tennis historian Ted Tinling, the colorful Englishman who was banned from Wimbledon for thirty-three years for designing Gussie Moran's lace panties in 1949. Ted stood six feet five, he was bald as a honeydew and thin as a shoelace, and he knew everyone in the sport dating back to Suzanne Lenglen. Wimbledon still hadn't allowed Ted to return by the time he joined us, and he liked to brag, "I put the sin in tennis!" Bud called him "the Leaning Tower of Pizazz." Ted designed our Slims players' eye-catching outfits and treated us like show-biz celebrities. I absolutely loved him. Nobody told better stories.

By the start of the Slims' second season, all of us had personally fitted, hand-sewn Tinling originals. Ted would set coordinated color schemes for us each season, and Margaret Goatson Kirgin, Ted's seamstress and longtime assistant, carried out the labor-intensive details of each garment's final design; Rose Stevens contributed too. Frankie Dürr told Ted she wanted her décolletage to look good. Rosie's sequined dresses usually weighed about ten pounds. I used to argue with Ted to give me more sparkle. "More, more, more—you're not giving me enough, Teddy!" I'd say.

Ted's affectionate nickname for me became "Madame Superstar." Considering his many witticisms about other players, I got off easy. During Martina Navratilova's career, Ted memorably said, "She swings from arrogance to panic with nothing in between." Ted said Gabriela Sabatini, the rangy Argentine beauty, "looks like Marilyn Monroe, walks like John Wayne."

THE RISE OF the Virginia Slims Tour touched off a flurry of other ventures or firsts that Larry and I soon undertook together. Sometimes it was hard to keep up with all there was to do. Larry had given notice to his law firm in Hawaii when he finished his Army Reserve obligations in June 1970. He felt better suited to be an entrepreneur, and he threw himself into expanding the TennisAmerica franchise as well as building what would soon become King Enterprises. He enjoyed the action so much that Rosie nicknamed him "the Kingfish."

By then, I had had deals with Keds and Adidas sneakers, and a clothing line with Head sportswear. We always had ideas percolating. It felt like a new world was bursting open at the seams, and sometimes all we had to do was say the word and a first was spoken into existence. How about a team tennis league? Okay! Me: Why doesn't *Sports Illustrated* cover us more? Larry: "Women deserve their own sports magazine." Done! How about a players' association for women so we can fend for ourselves, and speak with one voice? It came to be in 1973. I wanted to do everything and Larry wanted to help make it happen.

While my marriage with Larry was still listing, he and I were becoming more entangled in business than ever. It gave me pause, but our latest rationalization to keep powering ahead was that we had to ensure that the Virginia Slims Circuit succeeded. It was still a challenge, especially with the USLTA adding tournaments to its competing set of women's events featuring stars like Margaret and Chrissie.

Larry and I kept our condo in Hawaii but took an apartment in the Bay Area as well, a sparsely furnished one-bedroom in Emeryville. That was the closest thing we had to a base. We were literally living out of suitcases in different cities and different hotels. We hardly saw each other. Other people were beginning to wonder about it, and reporters even asked us directly about our "unconventional" marriage. Rumors that we might split had started surfacing in print as early as 1970, and we always denied it.

At one point, Larry sat for an interview with British television that later appeared in a BBC documentary about me called *Rogue Champion* (a title that tells you a lot about how the media regarded me then). The commentator asked Larry how we arrived at our "unusual" arrangement, and Larry said, "She's put fourteen years into her career. I can't tell her, 'Stop your career. You're married. I'm ready to settle down.' It wouldn't hardly be fair, I don't think."

"I don't quite understand that," the male interviewer said.

"You don't understand that?" Larry repeated patiently. He paused. Then he tried again: "I don't let a preference override what I think is her destiny."

That was Larry. The hardest thing was that we had pictured being with each other forever, and it was heartbreaking to consider that it might not work out. Even when our relationship was rocky, even once I realized I was conflicted about my sexuality, Larry and I could still spend hours talking about anything. Larry's mind always fascinated me. People with a legal or scientific mind, like he has, tend to work through things systematically, relying on logic and facts. I was more of a big-picture thinker. In so many ways, our relationship was symbiotic. We always enjoyed pitching ideas or discussing the state of the world. I'd talk about my dreams and he'd come back with how to make it happen. We still had a strong connection in life, in values, and, sometimes, in bed. When we finally did end up in the same city for a night or two, our time together could still be sweet. That's how I got pregnant six weeks into the Virginia Slims tour after Larry and I spent a night together during our tour stop near Boston.

I knew it almost immediately. I had stopped taking birth control pills after Larry showed me a magazine article that said it was dangerous to stay on them for more than five years. Maybe it was just more magical thinking on my part, if I was thinking at all. After our rare night together, I played two more tournaments and nearly threw up on the court at the second one, in New York City. That's when I called Larry and flew back to California to take a pregnancy test. It came back positive. *Oh, dear God,* I thought. *Now what do I do?*

WHEN THE WHOLE WORLD learned nearly a year later that I'd had an abortion, I was accused of sacrificing motherhood for the sake of my career. I can honestly say that tennis had little to do with my decision. A few women had temporarily stopped playing after childbirth and returned to competition. Margaret did it twice.

I'd always wanted to have children and still did—but not then.

Our marriage was too shaky, and our lives were so complicated and unpredictable. Also, I now realized my attraction to women wasn't going away. I didn't know what I wanted, and I didn't know what Larry and I were doing. We discussed my pregnancy for days. It was a deeply personal conversation as well as a moral and political one. Larry and I agreed that a woman had the right to decide if and when she wanted to be pregnant, and the government had no right to interfere. He ultimately left the decision to me, and when I told him my choice to have an abortion, he said he supported me. In the end, I couldn't imagine bringing up a child in such chaos.

I took ten days off, skipping a tournament in Puerto Rico in late March. We told the press I was recovering from the flu. I had begged Larry not to tell anybody what was really going on, but he told Gladys, "We're a little bit pregnant." He might as well have used a megaphone, because it soon felt like everybody on the tour knew. But like so many other secrets within the tennis world, nobody said a word to the press at the time.

When I see hard-won reproductive rights being reargued and rolled back today—during the COVID-19 pandemic, for example, it took a 2020 federal court ruling to stop some states from seizing the chance to try to limit legal abortions—it makes me wonder if people remember how difficult things were before, even when a woman's pregnancy was caused by rape or incest. How short our memories are.

When I became pregnant in 1971, abortion was still a felony in most states and it would continue to be until the *Roe v. Wade* decision two years later. California was one of a handful of states that had legalized the procedure before then, as long as it was a "therapeutic" abortion performed by a doctor in a hospital. But any woman wanting an abortion had to go before a medical committee first and explain why she believed that her pregnancy would "gravely impair" her "physical or mental health." So that's what I had to do. Explaining to a panel of ten or fifteen strangers why I qualified for an abortion was probably the most degrading thing I've ever experienced. When Larry and I walked into the room and saw them looking back at us, Larry said to me under his breath, "This is ridiculous."

The fee for the procedure was nearly $580, an enormous sum back then. I could afford it, but what about a poor woman stuck in a desperate situation who wanted an abortion? She would still have to rely on a dangerous back-alley abortion mill—if she could find one.

When the morning arrived, I spent most of my time in the waiting room trying to comfort a terrified fifteen-year-old girl from Alabama, where abortion was illegal. We sat there for a while.

"How are you doing?" I asked.

"Not good," she said quietly. I was five weeks pregnant. She was farther along because it had taken her months to get to California for the procedure, and it had been a nightmare. She had one relative in Oakland who had taken her in and made the appointment for her.

Before my procedure there was one more indignity. Because I was married, Larry had to sign the consent form before we could proceed. Whether it was access to financing, credit cards, or the right to govern my own body, men were still in charge.

The abortion procedure itself was quick. When I woke up in the recovery room, Larry was there to take me home. I felt a sense of relief, but also a sense of emptiness and sadness over losing a dream that we once held as a couple. I also felt sorrow for my parents, who wanted a grandchild so badly. They didn't know about my pregnancy or my decision. I was afraid my choice to end my pregnancy would gut them.

Three days later, I was playing the Virginia Slims Masters in St. Petersburg, Florida. It was foolish, I know. I went because Gladys was pressuring me to go, saying, "If you don't show, Billie Jean, there is no tournament." When I called the tournament director, Don Kaiser, intending to withdraw anyway on Wednesday morning, just forty-eight hours after leaving the hospital, he also pleaded with me to reconsider, and I caved. I got on a 10 p.m. red-eye flight that night and arrived in St. Pete at 6:30 a.m., rested a bit that afternoon and played my opening match that night.

I could tell some of the other players were surprised to see me walk in. I don't blame them. What was I thinking? It was yet another one of those times I shouldn't have played, but I was driven to make the tour succeed. I even somehow made it to the semifinals two days later, where I was matched for the first time against Chrissie, then sixteen. Kaiser added six hundred more seats for our sold-out match.

Chrissie still looked like a little girl with her sweet, serious face and ponytail, but I wasn't about to underestimate her just because of those eyelet-and-lace dresses or hair ribbons she favored. She was still an amateur, but she already had upset Margaret. Her father entered her in St. Petersburg because it wasn't far from their Fort Lauderdale home, and he wanted her to gain more experience. Even at that age, Chrissie had sensational shot placement, a strong lob and a crisp two-handed backhand. She was amazingly perceptive, unyielding, and frighteningly consistent. The British press nicknamed her "Little Miss Metronome."

The Florida weather was blazing hot and humid the day of our match, which was unlucky for me. The sun felt sharp on my skin, and I quickly began to dehydrate. When Chrissie noticed I was a little slow, she remorselessly ran me back and forth along the baseline, as she should have. I remember how I could feel the total concentration behind her shot selection, a correctness and intelligence in her game. We hadn't had a player like that at her age since Maureen Connolly broke records in the 1950s.

I kept up with Chrissie in the hour-long first set, rallying from a 1–4 deficit to eke it out in a tiebreaker. In the second set, Chrissie again held me in rallies that frequently lasted twenty shots or more and she won it, 6–3, to level the match. By then I was feeling so sick from the heat and from cramps that I had to forfeit. All I can remember is leaning over the sink in the locker room, heaving and splashing cold water on my face. Chrissie came over and asked, "Are you all right?" She seemed genuinely concerned, and I was touched by how considerate she was.

As trying as those circumstances were for me, the next time Chrissie and I played would be even more challenging, for different reasons.

Chapter 14

A FEW MONTHS LATER at the 1971 U.S. Open, I was walking across the grounds at Forest Hills when I decided to pop in on Chrissie's second-round match against Mary-Ann Eisel, an accomplished veteran. I wanted to watch Chrissie a bit because she had been on a months-long winning streak after beating Margaret. When I arrived, she had narrowly lost the first set and was trailing Mary-Ann in the second, 6–5.

Bud Collins was calling the match on CBS-TV with Ann Jones. Years later, Bud loved to retell how Mary-Ann was preparing to serve at 40–love, triple match point, and he and Ann were trying to be "very gentle" because "Chrissie was so young, you know? We were saying, 'Why, she hit some good shots today . . . She'll be back, just you wait and see!' Then, almost as an aside, we said, 'Oh, look. She saved a match point. Why, good for her!' But then, Chrissie saved another one—and another one, and another one! Six match points in all!"

The crowd went nuts when Chrissie rallied to take the second set from Mary-Ann in a tiebreaker. The fans roared again as she ran Mary-Ann off the court 6–1 in the third. The atmosphere was electric. When I arrived back at the women's locker room, I excitedly told anyone who would listen, "You guys, that kid is our next superstar! She is it! She's the one!" A star was born in my eyes that match.

I knew Chrissie had come into the Open having won forty-six straight matches. Now I could see why. And she kept the magic going. She had two more comebacks to beat Lesley Hunt and Frankie Dürr after losing the first set to each. Frankie wiped away tears afterward. "Chrissie had pros—hardened pros—crying!" Bud said.

I was two months shy of my twenty-eighth birthday, and I knew we needed a boost of fresh talent on the Virginia Slims tour. Chrissie was perfect for the job—and she was American! What she had accomplished by the time we played our semifinal match was a turning point for tennis. You could feel it as it was happening. But when Chrissie walked into the locker room after each win, all that was missing were the snowdrifts. Virtually none of the other players said a word to her. She was just a nice, shy kid, but they were irritated because she was getting so much attention. They were also upset that the prize money they could be winning wouldn't even go to her since she was an amateur. I think Val Ziegenfuss had the class to congratulate her, but most of them were just awful, and they got colder as Chrissie advanced through the draw.

When I heard what was happening, I was not happy, so I called a players' meeting at an out-of-the-way table not far from the West Side Tennis Club terrace. Once we were huddled around, I said, "Listen, you guys, Chris Evert is the greatest thing that could happen to us. Look at her—she is it! She's our next superstar and you're going to be passing the baton to her. She's already helped women's tennis, and she's going to put more money in your pockets, not less. And forget all that—she's just a nice kid. So, I don't even care if you like her. We've got to make her feel welcome. It's not about 'like.' It's about doing the right thing."

Someone said, "Well, she's not that nice to us either."

"You guys—c'mon! She's *sixteen*!" I yelped.

The fact that Chrissie was playing the rival USLTA events posed a threat to the Slims circuit. But I reminded everyone that it was her dad, Jimmy Evert, who made those career decisions, not Chrissie. Then I said, "Do you think you're going to get her on our tour if you're not nice to her? We need her more than she needs us."

By the time Chrissie and I were to play in the semifinals, she was a national sensation. Bud was hauling her on CBS after every match for live interviews. Billy Talbert, the U.S. Open tournament director, joked that he scheduled all of Chrissie's matches on the stadium court after she beat Mary-Ann because "there'd be a riot if I didn't." *The New York Times* called her "Cinderella in Sneakers," and Barry Lorge gushed in *Tennis* magazine, "For 10 wonderful days, New York was a sentimental place and the U.S. Open was a great romance."

I feared if an amateur challenger—a teenager, no less—won the U.S. Open during the first year of the Slims circuit, we might not survive another season. We were the upstarts who were trying something new. The USLTA was the Establishment trying to flick us off before we got traction. I was the only multiple Grand Slam singles winner on the Slims tour. If a kid like Chrissie ran away with the crown against our best player and then went back to playing against Margaret, Virginia Wade, and Evonne Goolagong on their rival tour, our circuit could be endangered. Evonne was only nineteen years old herself then, and she had just won Roland-Garros and Wimbledon. So, as much as I already liked Chrissie personally, I knew it was up to me to stop her. Now.

After warming up for our semifinal, I felt so much pressure that I went into a shower in the women's dressing room, blasted the water as high as it would go so no one would hear me, and began sobbing uncontrollably as I contemplated the stakes.

BY THE TIME we were ready to walk out for our match I had regained my equilibrium. Letting out all my emotions had been cathartic. Then I moved on. I visualized exactly how I wanted to play Chrissie. I went through the phrases I wanted to embed in my mind like a string of mantras: *One ball at a time, Billie . . . Leave everything on the court . . . Nothing matters except this. Here. Now. Let's go, let's go, let's go!* Then I was out the clubhouse door. Chrissie was already there, waiting.

As she and I walked together down the fenced path to the stadium, hundreds of fans were calling out to us. Chrissie stared straight ahead and never said a word, which I learned was her way of preparing for a match. I found out later that she thought what talking I did was gamesmanship, but, in fact, I was just trying to encourage her to soak everything in. I knew it would never be quite like this for her again. Just as we reached the court, I turned to her and said, "You're riding the crest of a wave. Enjoy every moment of it."

The stadium was overflowing with a crowd of 13,647 that included Vice President Spiro Agnew and his Secret Service detail. You could feel the crowd's anticipation as we warmed up, and the atmosphere stayed charged. This was what we'd always wanted—real excitement for women's tennis, a sold-out stadium, top billing on the marquee, a huge TV audience, money to be made.

When we began to play, my strategy was to disrupt Chrissie's game with a constantly changing medley of shots to throw off her excellent timing. She hadn't lost in seven months and I was determined not to let her get control of this match. I think she expected me to charge the net, but I stayed at the baseline more than she anticipated and rallied, using a variety of spins, chips, and dinks. Her passing shots were deadly, so I stayed back and fed her drop shots and soft stuff to keep her off-balance. It helped me a lot that we were playing on grass. The surfaces were so uneven in those days, even at Forest Hills, that you never knew when the ball was going to skid or die once it bounced, especially when I hit my slice. They had groundskeepers who replaced the divots in the grass between matches.

I remember letting out a few blasts of emotion as we went—spiking my extra service ball after I won one game; baring my teeth and yelling *"Yeah!"* after another point, then pacing in a circle, pumping myself up. In later years, Chrissie told me that she trained herself never to look at me during a match because my intensity could overwhelm her. (Julie Heldman said the same thing.) But I didn't know any of that then. Chrissie was remarkably cool even when I outlasted her in some groundstroke rallies, her strength.

The first crack in her game didn't appear until the seventh game of the first set. She double-faulted on the first point and I ended up breaking her serve. That was the turning point. I took the first set, 6–3. Chrissie fought valiantly, and by the time I won the second, 6–2, the crowd was cheering for both of us, the veteran and the new kid. When we shook hands over the net I could see that she hated losing as much as I did. So I whispered, "Don't let it bother you—you've got your whole life ahead of you."

The win set up the only Grand Slam singles final that Rosie and I ever played, but we had to wait three days because of unrelenting rains. Rosie had only beaten me once in nine previous tries, and I could hardly look at her when I won again in two tight sets. During the days-long delay to play our match, I was still feeling bad for Chrissie, so I sent her a telegram that read: "When you left New York, the skies opened up and it poured rain. The heavens weren't happy you were gone." She told me she teared up when she read it. That match was a thunderclap start to a deep, lifelong friendship.

Chrissie went home that week to a heroine's welcome at St. Thomas Aquinas, her Fort Lauderdale high school. The governor of Florida declared her homecoming "Chris Evert Day." As I got ready to move on to our next tour stop, I could only shake my head in wonder, remembering how my high school couldn't have cared less when I won Wimbledon for the first time. We really had come a long way. I felt encouraged about what we were building more than ever. I knew we had just seen another glimpse of how glimmering our future could be.

I CASHED A $5,000 CHECK for winning the 1971 U.S. Open, a payday that didn't sound all that bad unless you knew that Stan Smith, the men's title winner, won $15,000 and was given twice the $2,500 I received in expense money. (*That has to change,* I told myself.)

Money was on the mind of the media, too. I had played so well on the first year of the Virginia Slims circuit that the press started keeping count: If I won $20,000 more before the end of 1971, I would be the first woman athlete in history to earn $100,000 in a single year. I had predicted that it was possible before we launched in December, and again in March. The second time, Margaret told *The New York Times*, "She'll have to win it from me." She had no intention of being eclipsed, and I welcomed the added drama. I had announced my $100,000 goal thinking that it would increase interest in our new tour. Throughout the year, I made it a calculated strategy to talk openly about the money and embrace the milestone. Like it or not, in this culture money is a measuring stick. I was always thinking, *How can we tell our story and get people to care about us, follow us? What will start them talking?* As I told Larry, people understand money whether they're a factory worker or a CEO. Women athletes were fighting desperately to be taken seriously. For me, it was about the message we were sending more than the money.

It would've been sweet justice if I got within a whisker of the milestone by winning Jack Kramer's tournament, the Pepsi Pacific Southwest Open, the next stop after Forest Hills. As I said earlier, I would come to see Kramer's sexism and contempt for women's tennis as a gift that motivated us to rise up, but I didn't feel that way yet. There were hard feelings all around. I was grateful we were rarely in the same room, he felt the same way, and things got much worse between us for years before they got better.

The total women's purse for Kramer's event had been raised from $11,000 to $18,000 after some pressure from our Slims players and an infusion of cash from Joe Cullman. Still, it grated on me that the men's total was bumped up to $65,000, a gaping difference. Plus, being back at the Los Angeles Tennis Club was unpleasant for me. It always evoked memories of Perry T. Jones tossing me out of the photo when I was ten, the Czar ominously summoning me to his office with a hooked finger, the Czar characterizing anyone who wanted pro tennis as crass moneygrubbers. Over the years, outsiders like Pancho Gonzalez and I never totally fit in at the club. We talked about it.

Joe Bixler, the Wilson rep who had been so great to me as a kid, had taken over the Southern California Tennis Association when Jones died the year before, and he had moved into Perry's office at the club. I appreciated Joe for his kindnesses toward me before, but I disliked how he now sided with Kramer and the sexist old-boy network. Joe also didn't see anything wrong with the all-male, all-white makeup of the association's thirty-six-member board.

The outside world was changing fast, but the club was stuck in a time warp in many ways. Tennis players had become professional, many tournaments had not. The umpires, referees, and line judges were still well-meaning volunteers who got little to no training, and some of them were glaringly incompetent. It was a pet peeve of mine that they were unpaid while we now were playing for our livelihood.

The bad calls piled up that week at the Pacific Southwest, and my anger had been on a slow boil for days by the time Rosie and I played the final before a sellout crowd of 3,200. With the first set tied at 6–all, there had already been six or seven bad calls by the same line judge when Rosie ended a long rally by overshooting the baseline. The inept linesperson called it in, giving Rosie a 3–0 tiebreaker lead.

I flipped my racket in the air, threw up my hands, and yelled something at the sky asking to be saved from any more of this. (If my dad had been there, he might've sawed off my racket handle right then.) Then I kept yammering. I stomped over to the chair umpire, John Coman, for the third time, but this time I said, "I want that linesperson out!" Rosie walked over and backed me up, agreeing that the calls were terrible.

John refused to do anything, so I asked to see Kramer, since he was the official tournament referee. John should've told me then that Jack had designated him to be both the umpire and referee for our match since Jack was doing the TV broadcast, which made John the final judge. But John explained none of that. He just sat there, looking down at me from his elevated perch, saying nothing.

I was so disgusted I began packing up my rackets and I looked at Rosie and said, "I am outta here."

She said, "No, Old Lady, don't go!"

"Rosie, you stay here. Stay so you can win this match."

"I'm coming with you."

"No!"

Back and forth we went—"Yes! *No!* Stay! *No!*"—until I steamed off. Rosie was right behind me, her jaw clamped shut in anger too. I'm not proud of it—but it was hysterical when she blinked and told me that she forgot we weren't playing doubles and she left because she was thinking we were a team.

The crowd booed us on our way off and we deserved it. The press massacred us too. We were fined by the USLTA. And that's how Rosie and I became an infamous footnote in tennis history: We're still the only two singles players to default *after* we both took the court. As you can imagine, Kramer was not charmed.

My brother, Randy, who was sidelined because of a knee injury, was in the stands that day, and so he hobbled over to the clubhouse to catch Jack's angry press conference. He said he wanted to deck Jack when he overheard him ripping women's tennis in general—and me in particular. Randy held off, thank goodness.

I PASSED THE MILESTONE of $100,000 by beating Rosie at the Virginia Slims Thunderbird Tennis Tournament in Phoenix, the last stop on our tour that year. Making that kind of money in our first year was another victory for women's tennis, and Rosie and I ended up dousing each other with champagne to celebrate. The final stop on the 1971 Virginia Slims Circuit originally was scheduled to be played in mid-April in Las Vegas, but the response to us was so enthusiastic Gladys was able to add six more Slims-sponsored tournaments as the year went on, giving us a total of nineteen. We were exploding the lie that people weren't willing to come out and pay to see women play.

The day after I won in Phoenix, the Philip Morris folks, always alert to a smart marketing opportunity, had me standing in a persimmon-red pantsuit for a press conference at their corporate headquarters in New York City before a crowd of print media and a bank of television cameras. There was an expectant hush as I looked at a telephone intercom onstage and the amplified sound of a call being placed crackled and buzzed. Then a woman's voice came on the line saying, "This is a recording . . ."

We all laughed.

Finally, after several attempts, the familiar baritone of Richard Nixon came through the speakerphone.

"Hello?"

"Hello, Mr. President," I said.

"Yes, yes, I just wanted to congratulate you for your great successes this year," Nixon told me. "I'm glad to see a fellow Californian get over $100,000."

"Thank you, Mr. President," I said, adding that I was especially proud to be the first woman to do it.

"Well, that's the most important thing," Nixon replied.

It was amazing how far we had come. My dad and mom had been flown in for the occasion and they were standing nearby, flushed with pride. The president of the United States was recognizing me the same way he would a returning astronaut or a Super Bowl–winning quarterback.

I earned more in the Slims' first season than all but five players in Major League Baseball, including the Cincinnati Reds all-star catcher Johnny Bench, who made $90,000, and the Oakland A's outfielder Reggie Jackson, who made $45,000. Willie Mays's $150,000 salary led baseball that year. I also outearned some of the biggest stars in the other major sports, including the National Basketball Association's Jerry West, the National Football League's Dick Butkus, and the National Hockey League's Bobby Hull. When I ran into Reggie later at a luncheon, he told me he "just about fainted" when he saw what I had made. "You guys are making some serious bread," he said.

By the time I finished playing out the year in England and New Zealand after the Slims schedule ended, I had won $117,000. Despite the relentless schedule, I took seventeen of the thirty-one singles titles I played for and had a 112–14 record. If you tossed in the twenty-two doubles titles I won, nearly all of them with Rosie, I easily played more matches that year than Johnny Bench played baseball games (149).

Most of the women on our tour sincerely congratulated me. But there was a segment of players and fans that disliked the disproportionate share of the attention I was getting. I tried to push other players out front more, often to little avail. I was making news. Still, I caught a lot of flak for being a greedy or self-centered professional. The funny thing is, I've genuinely never cared much about material things. The rented apartment Larry and I had in the Bay Area was laughably simple. Early in our marriage, I measured my prize money by how many Big Macs it would buy Larry and me. He and I put nearly all our money into expanding our businesses or helping causes. Ilana Kloss, my life partner of four decades, and I are the same way. As long as I'm healthy and I can take care of the people I love, I have a roof overhead and I can order whatever I want in a restaurant, maybe stretch out my short legs on an airplane headed somewhere interesting, I'm happy.

I'm not saying money isn't important. It gives you freedom from worry, and the liberty to walk away from things. In business, money creates power and influence. Sometimes it's a means to accomplish an end. But money has never dominated my life and never will.

I will concede that I was exhausted by the end of the year. I had played more tennis than any human being should. Then I kept over-doing it for years. It took a toll on my body and mind. Life outside of tennis seemed to blur like scenery outside a train window. One incident in particular illustrates how lamentably true that was.

SOMETIME IN LATE 1971, Larry and I had a lunch conversation with the editors of a new magazine called *Ms.*, which was set to launch in early 1972. The magazine was the brainchild of the women's activist Gloria Steinem, the publisher Pat Carbine, and a group of other women writers and editors, many of whom were sick of working for male-run publications that didn't take them or their ideas seriously.

A year earlier, one hundred women had held an eleven-hour sit-in at the *Ladies' Home Journal* demanding, among other things, that the magazine replace the editor-in-chief, John Mack Carter, with a woman. He refused to resign, but he did let the women produce one section of one issue—the crumbs, not the pie.

Gloria and the others wanted *Ms.* to become the voice of the women's movement. That sounded great to me. Later, I used to swing by their office and watch them sit in a circle on the floor and discuss the makeup of their next issue. Sometime after our first get-together, an envelope from the magazine arrived at the apart-ment that Larry and I had in California. It was in a stack of mail that Larry handed me after I got home, and he told me I would probably want to support the petition inside the envelope because, he said, "It will help legalize abortion." The Supreme Court's *Roe v. Wade* ruling was almost two years off.

I said okay, that I would take a look. But it was Larry who actually signed my name on the petition and sent it back without telling me he had done so—or me knowing that the petition allowed *Ms.* to publish my name along with a list of other prominent women signees under the headline "We Have Had Abortions." The fifty-three others included Steinem, the playwright Lillian Hellman, the historian Barbara Tuchman, the singer Judy Collins, and the writers Anaïs Nin, Susan Sontag, and Grace Paley. I was blindsided when the list was printed.

I supported the pro-choice abortion movement wholeheartedly, and I'm glad I was on the list. It was important. As the companion article noted, at the time women could get therapeutic abortions in just two states; the rest of the time they had to seek illegal procedures that were often unsafe. Legalizing abortion was a cause that I believed in strongly. But it is my body, my privacy, my decision, and the choice to make my abortion public should have been mine, not Larry's. I couldn't even prepare my parents for the news.

I know it's hard to imagine in this age of Twitter and the 24/7 news cycle, but it took a few weeks before Bud got wind of the petition and devoted a few lines to my abortion in his column for *The Boston Globe.* In late February, Mark Asher, a sports reporter for *The Washington Post,* asked me about it while I was promoting a tournament in Maryland. I told him how I truthfully felt: "If every woman who had an abortion would come out and say so, then it wouldn't be such a social stigma." I also asked him not to make the story about my procedure. He did. The article was picked up all over the country, including in the *Los Angeles Times,* the newspaper that slapped down on my parents' doorstep each day. The headline was "Billie Jean King Defends Her Abortion—and Women's Rights."

I got tons of hate mail. But the worst part was that I still hadn't told my parents about my abortion. It was another one of the many times where my inhibitions about not wanting to hurt them left me shrinking from emotional conflict. Even Randy suffered. He told me only recently that angry people sent letters to him at Candlestick

Park, where he pitched for the San Francisco Giants, calling me a "baby-killer," a "murderer," and more. One package that arrived was filled with plastic fetuses.

A month went by, then two. The *Ms.* story never came up in my weekly call with my parents, and I didn't have the stomach to mention it myself. By the time I went home for Mother's Day, of all days, Dad was working at the firehouse, so it was just Mom and me at dinner, chatting about a lot of things but not the elephant in the room. Then we settled in to watch *60 Minutes* because they were running a segment about me that night.

In addition to saying plenty of good things about me, the show included the usual footage of my antics on the court. I laughed when I was shown getting ready to serve in a match in San Juan, Puerto Rico, as the chair umpire admonished the raucous crowd, "Quiet, please"—only to have me stop bouncing the ball, look up, and say, "Awww, I *like* the noise." The crowd laughed.

The correspondent Morley Safer made a lot of the fact that I was twenty-eight years old and suggested that I was entering my twilight as an athlete. I smiled, because I felt I had a lot of miles left. Then the mood changed when Safer caught up with Larry on camera at a TennisAmerica camp in California and asked, "What about children, Larry?" Larry said, "Not until our lives become more stable. It would be too selfish to have children now, and not be able to give them the proper amount of time and attention. Billie Jean is a perfectionist on more than the tennis court. If she couldn't be a good mother, I don't think she'd want to be one." I looked over and saw that tears were puddling in my mother's eyes.

I was shown next sitting with Morley at an outdoor table in a Florida country club three thousand miles from my husband, and Safer said, "Was the decision to have an abortion that clear-cut? It's no family now, it's tennis now?"

"No, that wasn't the reason," I said, managing to stay poker-faced. "The main reason I had an abortion was that we didn't want a child at this time . . . Even if I wasn't playing tennis, I still would have had the abortion." I didn't tell Safer that my shaky marriage was the determining factor.

After the segment ended, my mother and I sat in silence in the living room. Finally, she said, "I cried for three days when I heard." All I could do was stare at the floor and let her talk. I felt terrible shame—not for the abortion, but for the way she found out. I could only imagine the pain she was feeling. "Don't you love children?" my mother asked me. "Don't you love Larry?"

I apologized for being gutless. I told her I did love children and I still loved Larry, but it was not the right time. She shook her head. "I still can't understand," she said, her voice trailing off.

Neither my mom nor my dad ever sat in judgment of my decision. Growing up in the Great Depression taught them some hard realities. Sometimes people's reasons for getting an abortion have zero to do with not wanting to have children. My mother was pro-choice, though she didn't express it then. The point, for me, was that I had let my family down and they were dragged into my public controversy. I was haunted by that later when I began to grapple with other secrets of mine that I feared might emotionally tear us apart.

Chapter 15

I spent much of 1972 feeling like a hamster in a spinning wheel. Often I would catch a morning flight from a tournament city, spend the whole day in business meetings, then catch a flight back and get to the court just in time to change and play without warming up. We were so determined to keep the tour growing that I was saying yes to every request, finding less privacy away from the court, and not practicing or training properly. My tennis suffered. In early February, I played Chrissie again in Fort Lauderdale, her hometown, and won only one game. Bud cracked in print that it was like the playboy quarterback Joe Namath going all the way to Sweden and getting kissed only once despite all the beautiful women there.

It wasn't funny to me. It was one of the worst matches of my life. I actually wondered if I should quit. I even told Larry that one day when I was back in California. I was so exhausted I had decided to take a couple of weeks away from the circuit. The phone never stopped ringing. When I finally dragged myself back to a court near our place to hit with Larry and prepare to come back, I changed my mind with every stroke I smacked. *I can't quit. Thwack. I'm finished. Thwack. But what about the tour? Thwack. I can't do it anymore.*

I called Larry over and said, "I'm retiring. Let's go home and make some calls."

He said, "Okay. But are you sure?"

I was supposed to catch a flight the next day to play in Dallas. By the time we reached our front door I had changed my mind again and said, "What am I talking about? I'm turning this around!" I think merely reminding myself that I did have a choice to play or quit helped me refocus on what I loved about the game rather than the grinding work it sometimes took to compete plus juggle everything else.

Chrissie again beat me in straight sets the next time we played, this time in St. Petersburg. God, she was already great, and getting better all the time. Larry and I visited Chrissie's dad, Jimmy, several times, hoping to get her to join the Virginia Slims circuit. The first time I walked into their house in Fort Lauderdale it felt like home. Jimmy was a strict disciplinarian, the same as my dad. Colette, Chrissie's mom, was a cheerful, leavening influence. All of the Evert kids played tennis at Holiday Park, the public courts where Jimmy was the teaching pro, as soon as they could hold a racket. They were all rock-solid people who put family first.

Jimmy was a USLTA loyalist and did not let Chrissie join our circuit until she was eighteen, but we respected each other and became friends. Jimmy and Chrissie even agreed to help me when I decided to focus on winning Roland-Garros for the first time and Chrissie decided to skip the 1972 tournament because of school. (Thank God for proms, right?) I was tired of hearing that to be considered truly great, I had to win at least one Roland-Garros singles title because it was the only major held on clay. I had about a month to get ready, and I spent nearly a week with the Everts in May. Their help was invaluable. We hit for four, sometimes six hours every day, and the preparation contributed greatly to my success once I got to Paris. Chrissie was amazing. She would ask me, "What do you want?" and deliver every shot I asked for, the full repertoire.

In our ensuing years on tour, Chrissie and I would sometimes practice together and she would get impatient with me because I couldn't maintain the precision on my groundstrokes that she could. She'd get this glare and I'd have to stop, stifle a laugh, and say, "Chrissie? Don't you *dare* get mad at me, or I am *out* of here. *I am doing the best I can, all right?*" It was hysterical. I was so curious about the secret of her unshakable mindset that I asked her once what she thought about during matches. She looked at me as if to say "Duh" and deadpanned, "One more ball."

I won Roland-Garros in 1972, beating Evonne Goolagong in the final in straight sets. It was my one and only career singles title at Roland-Garros and I didn't drop a set the entire tournament. I defeated Evonne again in the final at Wimbledon for my fourth career title there. Scalpers were getting $100 for the $9 seats to that match, and the Wimbledon crowd was again so openly against me that Evonne said afterward, "When she hits a short shot or hits out and everybody claps, it upsets me. I just don't think it's fair."

Margaret was back on tour now and playing well after a long break during which she gave birth to her first child, Danny. Her husband was traveling the circuit with them to help. It bothered me that Margaret would put down progressives or call women's libbers "masculine and non-traditional," while she was now the breadwinner in her family and her husband supplied the child care.

I beat Margaret at the 1972 U.S. Open in the semifinals and went on to win the tournament without dropping a set. It was my third singles win in the three 1972 majors I played, my best year ever. I was again ranked No. 1 and probably could've won the calendar-year Grand Slam that year, but I didn't go to the Australian Open because I chose to remain loyal to the Slims circuit instead. The majors weren't the end-all like they are now. A lot of us often skipped one or two of them. It was the price we were willing to pay for the tour because we wanted to be able to make a living the other forty-four weeks a year. We cared more about creating jobs. That's why I maintain that it's hard to compare the career Grand Slam titles of more recent champions to the stars of our era, especially someone like Rod Laver, whose total of eleven majors was suppressed because Rod was banned for five years for turning pro. That's twenty opportunities he missed. Chrissie and Martina sacrificed a lot of chances to play in all four majors as well because they supported the women's tour and, later, World TeamTennis.

As it was, I almost didn't go to the 1972 U.S. Open either. The Slims players had voted to boycott the tournament a month beforehand because the men's winner's share of $25,000 still far outstripped the $10,000 that the women's champion received. Gladys talked us out of it, saying we should give the U.S. Open tournament director, Billy Talbert, more time to raise some extra cash. Billy was a terrific guy, even if he was unconvinced women should earn as much as men. I felt we were at another crucial moment. If we backed down completely, our push for equity across the board could fall short.

I met with Billy—just the two of us sitting on facing chairs in the small officials' hut near the courts at Forest Hills—and told him that we would show up in 1972, but I wouldn't play in the 1973 U.S. Open if they didn't level the prize money, and most of the top women would walk out with me. I reminded him about the results of Ceci Martinez's fan survey, and asked him if tournament organizers really thought that the men were bigger draws or more entertaining than Chrissie, Rosie, Evonne, Margaret, and the other great women we had.

Then I told him I had lined up a sponsor—a Bristol-Myers brand, Ban deodorant—to kick in the extra $55,000 to achieve the equal prize money we were seeking. He made the deal. As a business-woman and an activist, I never forgot that lesson. Billy couldn't believe that I'd brought money to the table, not just rhetoric. I had concrete proof that we added value. By the end of our talks, Billy was persuaded, maybe more strongly than we knew. In 2019 when we went combing through the minutes of the USLTA meetings to find the exact date where the equal prize money vote took place, we couldn't find proof that it ever did. I think Billy might have just told the board, "We're having equal prize money. Case closed."

We agreed not to announce the arrangement until just before the 1973 tournament. And that's how the U.S. Open became the first major to pay women and men the same.

MY PUBLIC PROFILE HAD been rising sharply for a few years now, and I started to get involved in more issues beyond sports and the reproductive rights debate. In September 1972, I agreed to play an exhibition match for the National Women's Political Caucus to raise money for women running for office. In October, I was honored by the Manhattan Women's Political Caucus. That event was also a fundraiser, and it drew Gloria Steinem and other feminist movement leaders such as Muriel Siebert, the first woman to buy a seat on the New York Stock Exchange, the civil rights lawyer Eleanor Holmes Norton, and Bella Abzug, the U.S. congresswoman whose nickname was "Battling Bella." She showed up in her trademark floppy hat and auctioned it off.

Supporting political candidates was activism I could embrace. The voting age in America had just been lowered from twenty-one to eighteen, and there was a push to capture the ballots of the new voters and hopefully have Congress look more diverse, like the rest of the country. Bella's campaign slogan was "This woman's place is in the House—the House of Representatives." The 435-member House had only fifteen female members at the time, less than 4 percent. Shirley Chisholm had become the first African American woman elected in 1968.

One of the bills the women's activists were championing was the Equal Rights Amendment, which banned any discrimination on the basis of sex. Twenty-two states had ratified the ERA by the end of 1972, but a two-thirds majority of thirty-eight states wasn't achieved until January 2020. Even then, after the Democrat-controlled House of Representatives voted to make the amendment law, it touched off arguments in the Republican-controlled Senate about whether the deadline for ratification had expired. Majority Leader Mitch McConnell refused to schedule the ERA for a Senate vote.

I should've lobbied harder for the ERA at the outset. Until the word *woman* is included in the Constitution so it reads "all men *and women* are created equal" our rights can't be fully guaranteed. Early on, I felt I didn't have enough information and I wish I had asked for help, or that the feminist leaders had pulled me aside and explained why I should fight harder for the amendment. But all they asked me to do was help them raise money or march. I was rarely invited to speak from the podium. Some feminists thought sports overly reflected the dog-eat-dog ethos of the patriarchy. I thought some feminists sometimes intellectualized things too much.

I asked Gloria why she didn't use more athletes to promote equality. She said, "Billie, this is about politics." I told her, "Gloria, we *are* politics. You're not using us right! We can sell this movement! We're on TV, we sweat, we're real! We're out here doing and proving all these things that so many feminists are only talking about!" I maintained that the women on the Slims circuit were the embodiment of independence and empowerment. We challenged the male-dominated system to demand a living, and we were out there every day making it on our own.

Throughout that year I was also tracking the work toward a new law called Title IX, which was one of the 1972 amendments to the Higher Education Act of 1965. I think Title IX is the third most important piece of U.S. legislation in the twentieth century after the Nineteenth Amendment, which assured women's right to vote, and the Civil Rights Act of 1964.

The push started when Bernice Sandler, a part-time lecturer at the University of Maryland, applied for a tenure-track position in 1969 and was told she came on "too strong for a woman." She began to research the laws on gender discrimination and found a footnote to a law on federal contracts that prohibited discrimination based on sex. She filed a complaint against her university. Then, after running an ad in the *Saturday Review* literary magazine looking for other examples of discrimination in higher education, Sandler gathered enough material to file 250 complaints against colleges receiving federal contracts. She sent copies of the complaints to members of Congress, asking them to urge the secretary of labor to enforce the law. One of the recipients was Edith Starrett Green, a Democratic congresswoman from Portland, Oregon.

Edith, a former educator and longtime champion of equal opportunity and women's rights, had wanted to address sex discrimination in education after she sat in on a congressional hearing where school superintendents were praising a program for under-resourced boys and she asked what the superintendents were doing for girls who walked the same streets. Edith was told only boys needed the program because "they're going to have to be the breadwinners." She was astonished to learn the Civil Rights Act of 1964 didn't provide any protection on the basis of sex, and eventually hired Bernice to be part of her staff. Together, they drafted the proposed legislation that became Title IX.

A version of Edith's original bill passed through Congress with bipartisan leadership from another U.S. congresswoman, Hawaii Democrat Patsy Mink, and two senators, Democrat Birch Bayh of Indiana and Republican Ted Stevens of Alaska. Patsy was the first Asian American woman elected to Congress. Stevens helped Alaska earn U.S. statehood in 1959 before turning into a guardian angel for Title IX during his forty-year career in Congress. Birch's first wife, Marvella, had been shut out of the University of Virginia because she was a woman. Birch never forgot that, or something his father, an athletic administrator and coach, told him and his sister when they asked their dad what he planned to say when he testified to Congress in 1940 about educational opportunities: "I'm going to tell them that little girls need strong bodies to carry their minds around just like little boys."

Bayh wrote the thirty-seven words that compose Title IX, and it is only one sentence long: "No person in the United States shall, on the basis of sex, be excluded from participation in, be denied the benefits of, or be subjected to discrimination under any educational program or activity receiving federal assistance."

His remarks on the Senate floor when he introduced the measure captured what women were up against.

We are all familiar with the stereotype of women as pretty things who go to college to find a husband, go on to graduate school because they want a more interesting husband, and finally marry, have children, and never work again. The desire of many schools not to waste a "man's place" on a woman stems from such stereotyped notions. But the facts absolutely contradict these myths about the "weaker sex" and it is time to change our operating assumptions . . . [and] provide for the women of America something that is rightfully theirs—an equal chance to attend the schools of their choice, to develop the skills they want, and to apply those skills with the knowledge that they will have a fair chance to secure the jobs of their choice with equal pay for equal work.

I still get chills reading that. Making a government serve its people is what statesmanship is about. Bayh always put the country before party politics and I wish more elected officials were like that today.

Title IX was signed into law by Richard Nixon on June 23, 1972. Those thirty-seven words sparked a sea change for women in the U.S. and eventually around the world. But anyone who tells you that they realized immediately that Title IX would lead to the resultant boom in women's sports opportunities, participation, scholarships, jobs, and other advances isn't remembering those early days correctly. The full impact became clearer only after the Office for Civil Rights was asked for interpretations of how, or even if, the law applied to sports. Compliance guidelines were set, challenged, and threatened again and again over the years. The law is still vulnerable to clawback attempts today.

I was part of a panel discussion at the Fordham School of Law in 2019 about Senator Bayh's work for Title IX, as was the Indiana Pacers executive Kelly Krauskopf, the first woman to be an assistant general manager in the NBA. Kelly told a story about inviting Bayh to the first WNBA game that the Indiana Fever played in Indianapolis after she had moved to his home state to start the franchise as the Fever's general manager.

Bayh accepted Kelly's invitation to attend opening night, and she told him, "Look at this, look at this . . ." as they stood together on the court, scanning the arena in wonder, absorbing the sight of the sellout crowd of sixteen thousand, the excitement, the players running through their pre-game warmups as rousing music played. When Kelly turned back to look at Bayh, he had tears in his eyes. "We didn't know—*I* didn't know what Title IX would mean for sports," he told her. "When I meet women and girls like you is when I understand."

I WAS WORN OUT again by October of the second year of the Slims tour. I was pushing my body beyond reason and working dozens of hours off the court. In Boca Raton, I staggered to a straight-set loss to Chrissie in 90-degree heat, at one point throwing up into a hat that the chair umpire handed me. My doctor had me tested afterward for mononucleosis. I had always imagined that when I became No. 1 I'd have a fuller life, and in many ways I did. But 1972 was the year I really became a celebrity, and I was discovering that fame created complications. "[People] know my name," I had told *60 Minutes*. "They know I play tennis, and I feel I owe it to them to give them time."

By now I had been drawn into the highly politicized worlds of women's rights, abortion rights, and electoral politics, not just sports. To the outside world, it seemed I was either a curiosity or a disrupter—sometimes both. People wanted a closer look at me. For years it was hard for me to eat in a restaurant. One day a fan pulled up a chair to my table and sat down as if he intended to join me for the meal, uninvited. Variations of that were common.

The questions about my marriage to Larry hadn't stopped, either. At one point I described our hectic lives to someone as two circles that intersect occasionally, and my friend countered that the two circles looked more like smoke rings evaporating before everyone's eyes. I had achieved most of my competitive goals, but I didn't have peace of mind.

Larry has said he felt lonely during that period, but he was also happy because he was "doing my own thing . . . doing what I wanted, and I felt actualized." Decades later, he told the journalist Selena Roberts that his view of my divorce requests, which I repeated over the years, was that "I was her husband, good, bad, or [in]different, you know . . . The bottom line was I didn't see any reason to get divorced because Billie Jean had identity problems. I felt that when it all got sorted out, she would be much better off growing old and gray with me than any other person on the planet."

I originally thought we'd be lifers, too, and that idea paralyzed both of us. We were breaking each other's hearts because we couldn't face the reckoning.

I finally concluded that I needed to take a personal inventory, so I did something I hadn't done since college. I took three months off. I decided I would use it as a time of reflection, and from the start, it was absolute bliss. I divided my time between the Bay Area and Los Angeles. It felt like such a blessed freedom to simply get back to doing everyday things. I'd wake up in the morning and ask myself, *Should I see a movie or read a book today, try some new restaurant or drop in on a friend?* Sometimes I'd visit Fort Scott, which is part of the Presidio national park in San Francisco. I spent a lot of time in Marin County, driving over the Golden Gate Bridge to the windswept headlands there, then traveling the switchback-filled roads and hairpin turns that carved a path down the cliffs until, finally, I hit the glistening Pacific Ocean.

One of my favorite destinations was Stinson Beach. I returned there repeatedly and found a spot on the long crescent of sand where I could lean against a tree stump and let my mind wander. Sometimes I'd bring a book to read, or something to write on. Mostly, I'd just meditate. I'd listen to the sound of the waves crashing, breathe deeply, feel my heartbeat slowing down.

At times, I thought a lot about how far my sport had come and what we could still do. I also thought about how the journey had changed me. The point was driven home when a tour friend, Vicki Berner, handed me a copy of *Atlas Shrugged* by Ayn Rand and said, "Billie, you've got to read this! You're Dagny Taggart!"

Taggart is an unconventional protagonist: a workaholic woman who runs her family's railroad company and is treated like an outsider. I could relate to that. But another theme of the novel—the idea that self-sacrifice for the good of society is immoral, and that unproductive people are parasites—was too cold and heartless to me. I liked how the book reinforced my belief that an individual can make a difference. But unlike Rand, I believe that all of us can make a difference, not just the strongest or most gifted or privileged among us.

Still, the book came at the right time in my life, when I was spread too thin and stuck in my years-long impasse between loving Larry and being conflicted about who I was. The book helped me see that self-interest can be a healthy thing. I realized, with some regret, that from the time I was young I had thought happiness always depended on pleasing the people dearest to me—an impossible task, to be sure. I often negated what I needed or felt. I buried my emotions, yielded to my fears. Sometimes I'd overindulge in food to comfort myself after a loss or when I was just feeling bad, then put myself on strict diets. My weight was a constant concern.

I asked myself, what would have happened if I hadn't taken charge of my life in the past? Where would I be if I had not ignored what I was told about what couldn't or shouldn't be possible? Years later, when I'd gotten serious about therapy, I started figuring things out even more. But during my sabbatical in the fall of 1972, something else I was learning about myself was scaring me half to death. I was falling in love with a woman.

IT BEGAN WITH a haircut. A friend on the Slims tour named Tory Fretz kept telling me about a terrific stylist at a salon in Beverly Hills who might be able to help me with my thick hair and was used to dealing with celebrity clients. "I want you to meet her," Tory said. "She's really nice and gives great cuts." So one day in May 1972, Tory took me in for an appointment with Marilyn Barnett. She was a slender woman with fine features, feathery blond hair, and a soft, lilting voice. She worked fast—a few snips here and there and I was out of there in twenty minutes, looking better.

Marilyn and I didn't meet again until I was taking my break from competition in the fall of 1972 and spending lots of time on my own. I'm not much of a partygoer, but one night in Los Angeles I thought it might be fun to drop in at a friend's gathering. Marilyn and I saw each other across the room right away, and she walked up to me and asked me if I was going to come in for another haircut.

We started talking and I found her funny, and more than a little flirty. She was laidback and into yoga and halter-top dresses then, and she had a disarming smile. Best of all, she knew nothing about tennis. I had just won the Roland-Garros, Wimbledon, and U.S. Open titles and she didn't have a clue or a care about what any of it meant. It felt *wonderful*.

Talking to Marilyn was refreshing after years of nothing but tennis, tennis, tennis. She suggested that we have dinner one night. I said, "Sure." That's how it started—casual, relaxed. I visited her a few days later at the funky little wood house that she rented in Hollywood on Doheny Drive, just off Sunset Boulevard. She was dating a rock musician at the time.

The house felt like a comfortable and cozy escape, far from tennis, far from the crowds, far from the strains in the rest of my life. I could relax around Marilyn and talk about my frustrations on the tour or about anything else. Marilyn was a good listener—what hair stylist isn't?—and enjoyable to be around, so I would see her whenever I was in Los Angeles. It wasn't the first time I had been drawn to a woman, but the intensity of this attraction seemed so natural and right. It didn't take all that long for our relationship to become physical. Our first time making love was scary but also wonderful.

Being with Marilyn at first was like floating in a bubble detached from outside responsibilities but connected to another person in an intimate, liberating way. It was the first time I had been with someone outside of my sports world and I wasn't being judged as a player, a businessperson, an outlier, or anything at all. I could be vulnerable. And at first, I let myself get lost in her.

On a typical day together we'd sleep in late and she'd cook eggs or oatmeal for breakfast. Sometimes I would just read or we'd sit around and listen to music, which we both loved. Some afternoons we'd hop into her Karmann Ghia convertible and fly along the freeways, blasting music on the radio. There's a scene in the 2017 *Battle of the Sexes* film when Marilyn and I dance to the song "Crimson and Clover"; it gave me chills when I first saw the movie because I had never told the screenwriter or directors it's the song I most associated with Marilyn. One of the lyrics is "I don't hardly know her, but I think I could love her." I remember hearing it on the car stereo while we drove through the city, the wind whipping wisps of Marilyn's blond hair around her face.

By the end of that year I was living a double life, right out in the open. At the start with Marilyn, I only told a few close friends what was happening, but it became pretty obvious what was going

Once the Original 9's breakaway tournament in Houston was a success, our next challenge was creating a full tour schedule. Dorothy Chewning, one of the few women tournament organizers at the time, agreed to rebrand her Westwood Racquet Club Invitational in Richmond, Virginia, as the Virginia Slims Invitational of Richmond, and Philip Morris provided the entire $8,200 in prize money. More players joined us. We were on our way! The ten of us who played there in late November 1970 included, left to right, Kristy Pigeon, Valerie Ziegenfuss, Nancy Richey, me, Stephanie DeFina Johnson, Mary Ann Curtis, Denise Carter, Rosie Casals, and Darlene Hard. Missing is Ceci Martinez, who was en route from San Francisco.

I purposely announced my quest to become the first female professional athlete to earn $100,000 in a single year the day we launched the Virginia Slims Tour in 1971 to draw needed attention to us. "It proves women can earn a respectable living in sports," I said after I'd achieved my goal in Phoenix, our last tour stop that year.

The British fashion designer Ted Tinling with, left to right, Virginia Wade, Evonne Goolagong, Rosie Casals, and me wearing outfits that Ted designed for each of us in 1973. Virginia Slims, our sponsor, hired Ted to add glamour to our fledgling tour.

I've always said the trailblazing support that women's pro tennis received from Philip Morris CEO Joseph Cullman 3rd (shown here with me and Gladys Heldman) led to the best business sponsorship in the history of sports.

I considered it part of my job to constantly promote women's tennis and talk to the media, because without the media, how would people know our stories or care about us? I enjoyed the give-and-take with reporters.

Seeing the joy on our faces in this photograph reminds me of how I always found it uplifting and empowering to brainstorm with Gloria Steinem. In the fall of 1972, we were part of an effort to get more women elected to political office. She was always generous to me with her insight about the women's movement and the publishing business.

My brother, Randy, told our parents when he was ten years old that he wanted to be a major-league baseball player, and he did it. R.J. spent ten of his twelve big-league seasons pitching for the San Francisco Giants.

Senator Birch Bayh wrote the thirty-seven words that constitute Title IX and cosponsored the landmark 1972 federal legislation that revolutionized access to educational opportunities, funding, and scholarships for women and girls in the U.S.

Ted Tinling, the tennis historian and fashion designer, chats at a tournament cocktail party in the Egyptian Section of the Penn Museum in Philadelphia with, left to right, Bonnie Logan, Sylvia Hooks, and Ann Koger, the first African Americans to play the Virginia Slims tour. That week's competition was the 1973 Max-Pax Classic at the Palestra.

I used the $5,000 check I received from host Bob Hope and presenter Tony Randall when I was named the 1973 Female Athlete of the Year to fund the creation of the Women's Sports Foundation in 1974.

My vision of creating an organization for our pro players to speak with one voice, establish a global tour, and secure more sponsorships became a reality when more than sixty of us met on June 21, 1973, at the Gloucester Hotel in London and voted to form the Women's Tennis Association. Among the attendees leaving the room with me after the vote was Indonesia's Lany Kaligis, left, and my future life partner, Ilana Kloss of South Africa, at far right.

The U.S. Open tournament director, Billy Talbert, presents the mixed-doubles trophy to Owen Davidson and me in 1973, the year Talbert kept his privately negotiated promise to me that the tournament would be the first major to offer equal prize money for women and men. As an American, I'm proud we can claim that distinction.

Bobby Riggs and I mug for the cameras in July 1973 after our New York press conference at the Town Tennis Club to announce our Battle of the Sexes match.

The promoter Jerry Perenchio surprised me moments before my entrance into the Houston Astrodome for the Battle of the Sexes match by suggesting that I ride into the stadium on this flashy litter carried by four men in togas. I said, "Jerry, I *love* it! It's showtime, baby!"

Playing serve-and-volley tennis fit my personality from the moment I took up the sport. It requires terrific movement and being comfortable anywhere on the court. Here, I'm hustling at the 1972 U.S. Open to hit a backhand volley, my strongest shot throughout my career.

The month after I beat Bobby Riggs, I was invited to testify at the Senate Education Committee hearings on programs to eliminate discrimination in education. I talked at length about the challenges women and girls faced. "We are wasting half the potential in this country," I told the senators, and urged them to act.

Muhammad Ali and I had so much fun when we appeared on *The Mike Douglas Show* in 1973, and wherever our paths crossed after that. I respected many of the stances Ali took, particularly his opposition to the Vietnam War and his work to empower Black people and combat prejudice. He was one of my all-time favorites.

Larry King and I proudly show off our first issue of *womenSports*, published in June 1974. A sports magazine devoted entirely to women was unprecedented.

Larry and I always felt that taking tennis to communities where the sport wasn't often played was important. Here, I'm having fun with children at a clinic sponsored by the Philadelphia Freedoms, my first WTT team.

on when she started traveling with me in the spring of 1973. Some tour insiders knew that I had questioned my sexual orientation for a while. Larry also knew, of course.

Marilyn and I didn't shy away from spending time together in public, dining in restaurants, going to movies, listening to music in coffeehouses. I'd take two or even three days off, which was a lot for me then. If we ran into anyone I knew, I'd just introduce her as my friend or, later, my personal assistant and road manager. I was paying her $600 a month to handle those two jobs and picking up all her expenses when she was on the circuit with me. Marilyn had dated women as well as men before, so hiding in plain sight wasn't new to her. But I did ask her not to speak about our romantic involvement to anybody. It was too risky.

Even the rumor that I might be gay nearly cost me an important honor, though I didn't know it at the time. *Sports Illustrated,* the magazine I had read and admired since I was a teenager along with *World Tennis,* was internally discussing choosing me as its first Sportswoman of the Year in 1972 after decades of honoring only men. In the end, I shared the award with UCLA's legendary basketball coach John Wooden, whom I deeply admired because of his success and the person he was. Taking incremental steps is often how progress goes. The first generation pushes the door ajar, and the next generation kicks it open. Chrissie had the honor all to herself four years later.

It took three decades after my selection to learn the rest of the story behind *SI*'s decision. My friend Frank Deford told me that when I was being considered he ran into André Laguerre, the magazine's managing editor, in the hallway. André asked him, "What's this I hear about Billie Jean King being a lesbian?"

Frank said he smiled and said reassuringly, "Oh, André, they say that about all women athletes." Had Laguerre's suspicions been confirmed, I never would have had a share of the 1972 award.

I think other sportswriters also protected me more than I realized. I had many other good friends in the press corps—Bud, Barry Lorge, Bob Martin at the *Long Beach Press-Telegram,* Neil Amdur at *The New York Times,* and Mike Lupica at the New York *Daily News,* to name a few. Women sportswriters were still rare. The Associated Press estimated in the early 1970s there were only about twenty-five women covering sports for America's 1,700 newspapers. The legendary Mary Garber covered sports for the *Twin City Sentinel* and then the *Winston-Salem Journal* (both in North Carolina) beginning in 1944, and continued to work part-time until 2002. It was Melissa Ludtke's 1978 lawsuit against Major League Baseball for equal access to locker rooms that cleared the way for all journalists, men and women, to do their jobs more effectively. That opened the floodgates for more women. Title IX contributed too. The first female sportswriting pioneers—Garber, Ludtke, Robin Herman, Lesley Visser, Jane Leavy, Stephanie Salter, Claire Smith, Tracy Dodds, Susan Fornoff, Christine Brennan, Michele Himmelberg, Jane Gross, and Helene Elliott—soon had a lot more company. Le Anne Schreiber eventually became the first female sports editor at the *Times,* and Robin Finn covered tennis.

I think I got along with journalists because I admired what they did and I understood that they needed access to us in time to meet their deadlines. The writers called me out when I deserved it, but they were almost always fair. I've always made sure to thank the traditional media, especially in this digital age, because without them our stories would never have been told, and we'd never have made it. I also liked asking them questions, learning about them, their jobs, their travels. It was a two-way street.

I FELT SAFER with Marilyn when we were inside the tour. In women's tennis we protected each other whether we were gay, straight, the biggest star, or the lowest qualifier. We were like a traveling family, complete with all the overlapping storylines, dramas, loves, and neuroses, and we kept things in-house. Nobody talked about the handful of gay women on the circuit. It's always been a myth that the women's tour was and is overrun with lesbians and men's sports is completely free of gays. I doubt there were more LGBTQ+ people on the tour percentage-wise than there are in the general population.

Feeling safe beyond the tour was a different story. It's hard to convey how oppressive it was. Hardly anyone in public life was out then that I can remember, except a handful of authors and activists such as James Baldwin, Audre Lorde, Gore Vidal, Rita Mae Brown, Larry Kramer, and, later, Harvey Milk, the first openly gay elected official in California. (Milk was assassinated at City Hall eleven months later, along with San Francisco Mayor George Moscone, by a political rival who opposed Milk's activism.) The AIDS scourge that outed the actor Rock Hudson, the first major American celebrity known to die of the virus, was still more than a decade away. Otherwise, lesbian and gay sexuality—let alone the BTQ+ part of the abbreviation—wasn't part of the public discourse. It was arguably one of the few ways that homophobia kinda sorta worked *for* us. Unless there was a messy divorce or arrest involved, a person's sexuality was hardly mentioned in the press, and publicists at the time protected us by saying our personal lives were nobody's business.

Of course, knowing that didn't make our lives any less terrifying. There were no guarantees. Gays had scant legal protection. Contracts with sponsors and employers often included morals clauses that allowed them to drop you on the spot. One scandal and your livelihood could be destroyed overnight. On the occasions people were outed, the label was used as a cudgel to mock, fire, ostracize, demonize, or even to justify physically injuring gays.

Hardly anybody then was saying, You're gay, so what?, and handing you a rainbow. LGBTQ+ people were beaten up, raped, arrested, and even killed. Families were torn apart, children were disowned, lives were thrown asunder. It still happens, but I'm not sure people truly grasp how bad it was then, or the internal war such ritual shaming can create. One of the most exhausting things in life is pretending to be someone you're not.

I was in a delicate position because I was our fledgling tour's leading player and spokesperson, a woman known for calling out hypocrisy. "Mother Freedom" was Bud's tongue-in-cheek nickname for me. My reputation was built on being a truth-teller and pioneer. Now I was living a lie and hating myself for it. The fact that I felt I was lying out of necessity didn't lessen my shame or dissonance about it. I didn't even feel that I could go to therapy to sort it out.

The psychiatry manuals still said gays were "deviants." There was this taint.

The conventional thinking then was that straight is okay but gays and lesbians are consigned to unhappy, dysfunctional lives on earth and damned to hell after that. My parents were homophobic. My religious upbringing told me that homosexuality was wrong. And yet, if I was being honest, I didn't feel like a sinner. So what *did* that make me? All I knew was that I was still married to a man but in a relationship with a woman and if it was revealed, it would be a catastrophe.

Unlike now, there was very little talk in popular culture then about sexual orientation being something nuanced that resides on a continuum and can change over the course of someone's life. That would've helped. I was attracted to men and like men's bodies, but I feel like I connect with women more on an emotional level, not just a physical one. I guess the clearest way I can say it is I didn't end up a lesbian because of the sex alone—it was a whole constellation of feelings that had to do with connectedness, tenderness, how you experience everything *besides* sex with another human being. Sometimes the sex is the least of it. I know that's hard for a lot of people to understand, but it's only once anyone genuinely tries to grasp those distinctions that they begin to see how I could love Larry dearly and even feel attracted to him, and yet ultimately prefer to be in a life relationship with a woman.

In the 1970s, it was nearly impossible to trust that the public would understand. I feared the fallout if I was not who I seemed to be. The psychological switchbacks were so tough at times I wondered if there would ever be a place in this world for someone like me. I can relate to something Dave Kopay, who retired from the NFL before he came out as gay in 1975, said: "I feel too gay for the straight world, and too straight for the gay world." Dave had hoped to go into coaching after his eight-year NFL career. No one would hire him. He ended up running the family linoleum business instead.

After I began seeing Marilyn, I talked to some people I respect about coming out. They warned me not to do it. "It won't just hurt the tour—we won't *have* a tour," I was told. As a result, my fear of exposure became greater, not less, as time went on. My estimation of the bad consequences soared. Dread or anxiety sometimes dogged me. Sometimes my anger at having to hide my authentic self would come out in inappropriate ways. Food remained something I turned to for comfort. I couldn't really talk about who I truly was because I thought if I did, I'd cause problems for myself and a lot of people who loved or relied on or believed in me. It had already happened before.

So I did what was second nature to me: I tried to power through it, not give in to the emotional turmoil. When I began seeing Marilyn, everything went well between us. But things sometimes take awhile to become evident when you're in a long-distance relationship. My perceptions began to change once Marilyn and I were together all the time on the road that first year and I got to know her better. Doubts crept in. Did I trust her enough to keep seeing her? Did I want to be gay, straight, divorced, married? I didn't know myself. It could depend on what week you asked me. Everything felt so up in the air.

Grace Lichtenstein sensed it during the months she spent on the 1973 tennis tour to report her book, *A Long Way, Baby*. She wrote that nobody, not even Larry and I, knew why we didn't get divorced. I told her, "We probably should've lived together before we were married but we were hung up on Puritanism. We'd be better off divorced and living together. I'm tired of the idea that you have to stay together because of a contract." Larry told her our arrangement was a matter of "love, convenience, understanding. We've loved each other for a long time even though we're not really husband and wife. We had our separate careers, and when people don't see each other much, the relationship has to change."

And so it did. But sometimes my head and my heart literally felt like they were being squeezed in a vise. *I can't make this right, I can't make that right. I'm in a bind.* I always felt like I had to keep all the plates spinning in midair because any sort of crash—even one misstep—could be disastrous. The pressure I felt was extraordinary. I don't know how I kept it all going.

Chapter 16

W HEN MY MONTHS-LONG BREAK came to a close and I returned to the Virginia Slims circuit in January 1973, Marilyn and I shared a suite or a room with two beds when we were on the road, which wasn't unusual for women on the tennis tour. There was still a lot of infighting going on between the USLTA and the Slims. Our schedule was up in the air, and I wanted to end the uncertainty. By spring, some good news came.

USLTA officials had been pushing back hard against the Slims tour, which had signed more than sixty players, by reviving the threat to ban us from the majors and by strong-arming sponsors and tournament directors to drop us. It got so bad that Gladys Heldman incorporated our group as an autonomous body she called the Women's International Tennis Federation, and then sued the USLTA in federal court. I joined the lawsuit. The USLTA and the Virginia Slims circuit knew that staying apart was self-sabotage for both tours, and Joe Cullman was able to broker a truce at an April 27 meeting in New York. Julie Heldman, Frankie, Betty Stöve of the Netherlands, and I took part in the negotiations, and by the end, I was greatly relieved. We dissolved the short-lived WITF, and a plan was put in place for a single women's circuit that would be called the Virginia Slims Tour and operate with the sanctioning of the USLTA and ITF, with our first full schedule starting in 1974. Chrissie had just turned pro on her eighteenth birthday, and she was such a sensation that spectators lined up around the block to see her play the first time she appeared at our Slims San Francisco stop.

Unfortunately, one condition of the settlement was that the USLTA insisted Gladys had to go. They felt she was a polarizing figure. Gladys was deeply disappointed. So was I. For us, she had been magnificent.

At about the same time Gladys was leaving, something that had started as a minor irritant for me was shaping up as another assault on the legitimacy of women's tennis. Bobby Riggs, the former tennis champion and incorrigible hustler I'd been hearing about since I was a kid in Long Beach began pestering me to play him in a high-stakes challenge match. As I mentioned earlier, Riggs had the pedigree of having swept all three Wimbledon titles in 1939 and winning the U.S. Nationals singles championship twice, all as an amateur. He was now playing on the senior circuit, where there was no prize money either, but it kept Bobby in the mix. He made a living hustling rich club players and celebrities after his second wife divorced him. I had genuine respect and empathy for Bobby. I know he felt he had never gotten his due as a great champion, and he was probably right.

I had never met Riggs until 1971, when he hopped over a low fence around the club court at Forest Hills where I was practicing. He had been phoning for weeks, trying to get a match with me. I wouldn't take his calls. So he tried the direct approach.

"C'mon, Billie Jean! Why don't you play me?" he said. "You know you can beat an old man."

"Not interested," I told him. I knew there was nothing in it for me or women's tennis.

Every few months after that, another offer from Bobby would float up and I'd turn him down. At first it was kind of humorous. Then it became an annoyance—especially when he escalated things two years into his overtures by going to the media with his challenge to me.

"I don't believe that women deserve the same prize money as the men, as Billie Jean has been saying," Bobby said at a news conference. He shared a telegram he sent me: "You insist that the top women players provide a brand of tennis comparable to the men. I challenge you to prove it on a tennis court." He announced that he'd put up $5,000 of his own money for a winner-take-all match with me, and if I wouldn't play him, he'd offer the same deal to any of the top women players. I still wouldn't take the bait.

In late February, I was playing in a tournament in Indianapolis and beat Margaret in the semifinals, snapping her twelve-tournament winning streak. When I stepped into the arena elevator afterward, there was Margaret. As the doors closed, she smiled at me and said, "You know, I've decided to play Bobby Riggs. They've offered $10,000."

I couldn't believe she fell for it. I'd just turned down Riggs again two days earlier. I smiled back at her and tried to sound supportive, but all I could come up with was, "Okay, Margaret, if that's what you want to do. But I'm begging you, please—you *have* to win. You know that, right? This isn't just about tennis. You have no idea how important this is for women's tennis."

She looked at me like I had six heads. For Margaret, it was just another exhibition match with a nice paycheck to tuck in her wallet. It burned me that for years she had been telling everyone money was ruining tennis and now she was risking the reputation of our tour for money—and not that much of it, at that. Before we separated, I pleaded with her one last time, "Margaret, please win."

Rosie let Bobby Riggs have it in an interview with *Sports Illustrated*. She questioned why any pro woman player should have to answer to "an old, obnoxious has-been like Riggs who can't hear, can't see, walks like a duck and is an idiot besides." I had to laugh. Rosie always spoke her mind.

Margaret later admitted that pride was one of the reasons she agreed to play Bobby. "It rubbed me the wrong way when he not only lampooned my sport but proclaimed Billie Jean the best player in the world when I had beaten her many more times than she had beaten me," Margaret wrote in her 1975 memoir.

As I mentioned earlier, after I went to Australia to become a full-time player and train, our record was dead even over the next twenty-four matches. I was ranked No. 1 at the end of 1972, but by the time Margaret agreed to play Riggs, she had drawn close to overtaking me. But this wasn't about the rankings or head-to-heads anyway. Bobby was challenging me first because I also represented women's liberation, not Margaret. She was the first to admit that she "was nobody's idea of a women's libber . . . I am playing this match for me. A woman is not supposed to beat a man, so I've got nothing to lose."

Nor did Margaret think she *would* lose. At five-feet-nine, she was two inches taller than Bobby, and at thirty-one, she was twenty-four years younger. Years later, she admitted that she expected the match to be an "inconsequential novelty," just "a bit of fun" as she geared up for Roland-Garros and Wimbledon. She didn't prepare in any special way or even develop a game plan to play Bobby. She said the biggest impression Riggs made on her before their match was that "here is a man who has quite a big mouth."

The showdown took place at the San Diego Country Estates, a half-built resort community looking for a boost, on May 13, 1973—Mother's Day. CBS decided to broadcast the match on live TV and added $10,000 to the winner's payday. I couldn't watch because I was thirty thousand feet above the Pacific Ocean at the time. That week, a group of Slims players had flown to Japan for the first-ever women's pro tournament there. I wrapped up the finals in Tokyo the night before Margaret's match for a very nice $8,400 prize—nearly as much as Margaret was making against Riggs, but with none of the gimmickry or headaches. Then I hopped a red-eye back to the States with Marilyn, Rosie, and the other American players.

All we talked about during the long flight was how great it would be if Margaret wiped out Bobby and silenced him forever. We hoped to catch some of the match when we stopped in Honolulu. Once the jetway door swung open, we raced off the plane and fanned out across the arrivals lounge hunting for one of those coin-operated television sets that used to be attached to rows of seats in airports. I fed a quarter into one TV and groaned, "C'mon!" when all it would play was the previous week's *Gunsmoke,* a popular Western. Rosie pulled out her portable radio and turned the dial until she found a local news station. We held our breaths when the broadcaster turned to sports and said, "And in California this afternoon, Bobby Riggs defeated Margaret Court, 6–2, 6–1."

She lost in a rout? We couldn't believe it. I looked at Rosie and said, "Now I have to play him." Then I called Larry and said, "Let's set it up."

RIGGS'S DEFEAT OF MARGARET became known as the Mother's Day Massacre. When I watched the videotape for the first time and saw Margaret curtsying to Bobby before the match as he handed her a bouquet of roses, I thought she had lost it right then. Bobby disarmed her first, and then he dissected her. The oldest hustler trick in the book.

I was not surprised when Bobby's representatives phoned us before we could get to them. There had been nothing in it for our tour if I beat the 1939 champion of Wimbledon, but everything changed when he beat Margaret, one of the best, perhaps most physically imposing female players that tennis had ever seen. Now we had something to prove. I confess that there were moments once the negotiations for our match began when I'd get a churning in the pit of my stomach as I imagined the increased hype, the pressure, the responsibility that was coming if I played Riggs. I'd think, *Oh my God. I have to win.* It wasn't just about my pride or reputation. I imagined that our tour could be threatened or might disappear, Title IX could be damaged, and so many causes that we were still working for—starting with equal prize money and equitable treatment—would falter.

It was late June when we agreed to the basic terms for the match: a $100,000 winner-take-all purse from the promoter Jerry Perenchio, plus more from related ventures to be negotiated. I insisted that we play the men's standard best-of-five sets so there would be no excuses.

I knew that announcing the match was on would create a nonstop avalanche of publicity and free Bobby to start yammering again, which he did, saying things like, "I don't think women can stand up to the stress . . . Women's tennis stinks! . . . Women who can, do. Women who can't become feminists." So I insisted that we hold off announcing the deal for a few weeks so that I could concentrate on Wimbledon.

That decision felt even better when the ATP, the men's ten-month-old players' union, decided to boycott the tournament because one of their members, Yugoslavia's Niki Pilić, had been suspended by the International Lawn Tennis Federation for refusing to play the Davis Cup. I reached out to Arthur Ashe and the other men's leaders yet again, to see if they wanted our support, and I reiterated my long-held belief that we would be stronger if we all banded together. As usual, the men wanted nothing to do with us, even though we'd now proved that we could attract big crowds and major sponsors on our own. Once again, their rejection ended up empowering us.

I had been trying to organize all the women players since 1964, and now I was determined to make my idea happen. The men were positioned better than ever to assert that they deserved most if not all of the prize money, and I knew we had to protect women's interests as a group. I also knew that the decision of the top seventy male stars to boycott Wimbledon would help us and our women's tour by shining an unprecedented spotlight on us for the entire fortnight.

During the Queen's Club tournament the week before Wimbledon, I put in hours of meetings between my matches talking to other players. At first we were all over the place. Some of the women, including Frankie and Rosie, favored threatening our own Wimbledon boycott over the unequal prize money (£3,000 for the ladies' champion versus £5,000 for the men's champion that year). But a number of our top players, including Chrissie and Evonne, refused outright to join a boycott, so it would have been pointless.

As the women players started gathering in London in advance of Wimbledon, we benefited from a stroke of luck. The logistics of getting everyone together were simplified because the new Gloucester Hotel, which had ambitions of becoming an official tournament hotel, was providing free lodging to the women players in the main draw. We made the Gloucester our base of operations, and on June 21, 1973, we were able to round up sixty-five of us in a large meeting room at the hotel. Rosie, Ann Jones, and Val Ziegenfuss were among those highly involved. I asked Betty Stöve, who stood six feet one, to guard the door and told her, "Betty, nobody gets in and nobody gets out until we have an association. Got it?"

We had Larry draw up the organizational bylaws before we met so we could take a vote right then. In addition to his involvement in the Riggs negotiations, Larry was churning out so many business deals for the two of us I had trouble keeping track. We were into publishing, business management, event promotion, tennis pro shops, and TennisAmerica camps in fourteen locations with about two hundred instructors and three thousand students. Most exciting of all, we had just joined forces with a group of businessmen to start the team tennis league that Larry and I had been dreaming about for years. Now, Larry was in London to inform players about the league, in addition to trying to help us push through the women's players association.

When the meeting began, Rosie joined me at the front of the room for a few remarks. Then we opened the floor for discussion. Julie Anthony, our Stanford scholar who played the tour part-time while studying for her psychology PhD, asked, "Why do we need an organization?" I love Julie, and we still laugh about this today, but the glare I gave her said everything. I felt like screeching, *Are you kidding me?*

Instead, I took a deep breath and patiently laid out one more time the benefits of having an association. The most important aspect was that we would have the power to call the shots on our own tour, and not be dictated to by the national associations or the ATP. We could speak as one voice. I explained the suggested bylaws Larry had created, and there was some discussion about why we had to pay 10 percent of our prize money to fund the new organization. I noted that we had already paid that much to Gladys; it was just the cost of doing business. Then we talked a long while about what we should call ourselves. It could've gone on forever, and so I said, "You guys, this is it. If we don't get this done now, I give up." I asked everyone who wanted to vote yes to raise their hands. The tally was nearly unanimous. We were now the Women's Tennis Association.

There were some whoops and scattered applause around the room, and then a small rush to the door, but Betty continued to block the way as I said, "Whoa! Whoa! We're not done yet. We still have to elect officers." Frankie was voted secretary, Betty was chosen treasurer, and I was made president. Virginia Wade, a USLTA and ILTF loyalist who had been our most reluctant recruit, was elected vice president. She resigned two weeks later. To promote unity, I had advocated for someone from the USLTA's women's tour to be one of our officers. Like Chrissie and Evonne, who weren't at the Gloucester meeting, Virginia was not playing our Slims tour yet.

When Betty opened the doors, we spilled out into the lobby and I announced to the waiting press, "We have an organization!" Judging from their questions, it didn't seem like they cared. They were more interested in knowing whether we were supporting the men's boycott of Wimbledon. But word spread somehow. A year earlier, one of my heroes, Marvin Miller, the groundbreaking executive director of the Major League Baseball Players Association and an avid tennis player, had led the baseball union's first-ever strike against the owners and won better pension funding and salary arbitration for the players. Now Miller sent us his congratulations in an interview with United Press International. His endorsement meant the world to me.

We still needed someone to run the WTA's day-to-day operations. I met with Gladys and offered her the job as our first executive director. I thought she would want to run our association.

"Absolutely not," she said.

I was surprised and disappointed. But Gladys was used to running her own show and she didn't want to work for anybody else. It felt like the end of an era. Her work to make women's tennis viable had been indispensable, and she's a historic, sometimes underappreciated giant in our sport's lore. The Original 9 honored Gladys's memory at our fiftieth-anniversary celebration in 2020.

I WAS EXTREMELY GRATEFUL that we had our players' association organized when Wimbledon began four days later, because

I was chasing my fifth career Wimbledon singles championship, a milestone that hadn't been reached since Helen Wills Moody in 1932, and my mind felt so much lighter. I'd walk through the gates at the All England Club every day thinking, *We have an association! It's done!* We all knew that it was so important for our future.

Because of the men's boycott, the top men playing were the Czech star Jan Kodes and Romania's Ilie Nastase, both of whom were following orders from their Communist-run tennis associations. Sweden's Bjorn Borg, then only seventeen, made his All England Club debut that week and quickly achieved rock star status, especially among the hordes of young girls who shrieked at him the way others did for the Beatles. Borg soon needed security just to walk across the grounds.

Otherwise, the women were the unchallenged stars of the show. People wanted to see us. The total attendance of 300,172 was the second highest in the championships' history to that date. We had all our best players in the draw and our top four seeds—Margaret, Chrissie, Evonne, and me—advanced to the semifinals. Better yet, both of those matches were terrific. Chrissie knocked out Margaret in three sets that were decided 6–1, meaning Margaret pried away a total of just two games in the two sets she lost. Chrissie called it the best match of her life—all eighteen years of it so far.

I played Evonne the same day, and it was one of the most exciting matches of my life. Evonne fought off seven match points before I won in three sets. I couldn't believe some of the trouble spots she escaped. In the end, I just had a better day, but Evonne reminded the world of her grace and the caliber of player she was.

When Chrissie and I played our rain-delayed final two days later, I shut her out in the first set in only seventeen minutes. She had still never beaten me on grass, but there were some tense moments before I closed out the second set, 7–5, to take my fifth title. As happy as I was, I had to stay focused because my tournament wasn't done. Rosie and I then won the doubles title by defeating Frankie and Betty in three sets, and Owen Davidson and I beat Raul Ramirez and Janet Newberry for the mixed-doubles title, giving me my second triple crown at the All England Club.

I was too exhausted to attend the Wimbledon Ball that night. And anyway, my mind was already racing ahead to Bobby Riggs.

A few days later, I found myself sitting side by side with Bobby at a press conference at the Town Tennis Club in Manhattan. Jerry Perenchio, who had had enormous success staging the 1971 Fight of the Century between Muhammad Ali and Joe Frazier at Madison Square Garden, told the press the Ali-Frazier bout "was 'The Fight'" and "this is 'The Match.'" Then Bobby and I traded banter like we were prizefighters at a weigh-in.

"She's fighting and carrying the banner for women's lib," Bobby said, "and I'm carrying the male is supreme, the male is king, no matter what the difference in age is. We can beat the girls on and off the court in almost anything . . . I can kill her."

"I don't think so," I said. "The one thing I can't stand is what Bobby has to say, that men are supreme. First of all, people are people, and people are supreme in different things. It's not 'men are supreme in everything.'"

"They want the same kind of money as us . . . It's ridiculous," Bobby said.

"Without women, *you* wouldn't have these opportunities," I told him. "Since 1939, you've never had it so good."

Our two-month buildup toward the Battle of the Sexes had begun.

Chapter 17

A T THE REMOVE of a half century, it might be difficult to understand why so much import and hype was centered around a tennis match like the one that Bobby and I played. But the significance was real, and the aftereffects were seismic. Knowing the context explains a lot.

The America I returned to from England that summer was gripped by live television coverage of the Senate Watergate hearings that eventually led to President Richard Nixon's resignation. American troops pulled out of Vietnam that year, but the feeling that we had lost the unpopular war and the suspicions that our government had lied to us were sobering. There was soaring inflation, a roiling stock market, and a looming energy crisis. People waited in long lines to fill up their gas tanks and they were worried about their jobs. In short, American exceptionalism was being challenged on many fronts and so were gender roles—specifically, white men's unquestioned superiority. For the first time, the U.S. government approved using the appellation "Ms." as a substitute for Miss or Mrs. in official government documents.

Riggs wasn't the only man saying that women belonged in the home, or that we were constitutionally incapable of handling tough jobs and stress. By the mid-1970s, only 9 percent of the physicians in America were female because medical school admissions had been withheld from them for years. Women's representation was also abysmally low in law, politics, CEO positions, piloting a passenger airline plane, and countless other endeavors.

Bobby's male chauvinist pig act tapped into anxieties about

men's changing status in a transformed world. A lot of what he said wouldn't be tolerated today. When I agreed to try to avenge Margaret's loss, I became a symbol for people who were tired of seeing women dismissed en masse, demeaned as second-class citizens and shut out of opportunities everywhere, not just sports. Women were still earning only 56.6 percent of what a man earned for the same job by 1973, the biggest difference since the government began measuring the wage gap in 1960, and the gap was worse for women of color. The roles men and women occupied were in flux, but men still had the upper hand and the power. Sexism and racism abounded. The glass ceiling was real.

"We've kept those women where they belong," Bobby said in one of our press conferences.

"I like the idea that I'm playing for someone besides myself—and I feel I am in this particular case," I said.

In the two months after we announced the match, we were able to settle on the rest of the terms and payments. Jerry booked the Houston Astrodome for September 20, 1973. The ABC network won the auction for the broadcast rights, paying $750,000, and the Astrodome paid another $300,000 to host the event. That was an unbelievable amount of money for tennis.

Bobby and I didn't share in any of those windfalls, but Jerry helped us both get additional endorsements to make sure the loser didn't go home empty-handed. Bobby signed individual deals with Hai Karate aftershave, American Express, and Nabisco, the maker of Sugar Daddy lollipops, a play on his chauvinist pig shtick that earned him $50,000. He was even chasing a deal with Clairol because he had been using Miss Clairol hair coloring to hide his gray hair for years. (His shade was Sunlit Brown, Nora Ephron reported in *New York* magazine.) I got an endorsement for Sunbeam curling irons. I also made a point to wear the special blue suede sneakers that I convinced Adidas to make for me the year before. "We're on color TV, let's do something that stands out," I told them.

ABC assigned Howard Cosell, the most famous sports announcer in the business, to call the play-by-play. Rosie would provide color analysis from the women's perspective. ABC wanted Jack Kramer to provide the male point of view, but there was no way I was going to give him such an enormous platform to run down women's tennis; I had Larry tell Jerry that weeks before the match. When Jerry balked, Larry flew to New York to tell Roone Arledge, the head of ABC Sports, that I'd refuse to play if Jack stayed.

"When I delivered the message," said Larry, "I could see the blood rise from Roone's collar to the roots of his hair. I've never seen a human being turn that crimson in my life."

"No one tells ABC who their network talent is!" Roone said.

Larry remained calm and said, "Roone, Billie Jean isn't saying who your talent is. Just who it *isn't*."

Once Larry explained my background with Kramer and my reasons for wanting his removal, Roone simmered down. Larry walked out of the meeting thinking he had convinced Roone to make a change.

In the eight-week run-up to the Battle of the Sexes, I made a concerted effort to avoid the press and stay away from Bobby. Tennis is in significant part a head game, and Bobby was an expert at getting into his opponents' psyches. It worked with Margaret, who was always susceptible to nerves anyway, and Bobby repeatedly tried to plant the idea that his mind games would work on me, too. "I'm not Margaret," I'd answer him with a smile. "I love pressure." Still, I lay low while he ran all over the place promoting himself and whipping up attention for the match by spouting more sexist things: "The best way to handle women is to keep them pregnant and barefoot . . . I love women—in the bedroom, and the kitchen, in that order." His remarks made me wince. The media lapped it up.

One show I did agree to appear on was *The Tonight Show* with Johnny Carson on July 31, nine days after we announced the match. Johnny loved tennis and I had been on his show before. He asked about the Battle of the Sexes and Riggs. The actor Tony Randall, Johnny's previous guest, sat next to me on the couch and interjected little jokes here and there about women's tennis. It was all in good fun, and a few months later Bobby and I taped a guest appearance on Randall's hit TV show, *The Odd Couple*. A few months after that,

Tony and Bob Hope handed me a check for $5,000 as an award winner of the Gillette Cavalcade of Champions—money that I announced I would use to start the Women's Sports Foundation, in part to protect Title IX. The chain of events was a reminder of the power of relationships. You never know when or where a significant one will begin, or new allies will appear.

I PLAYED ONLY three tournaments in the two months between Wimbledon and the Battle of the Sexes and my health became an on-again, off-again issue that left people speculating that the pressure of the Riggs showdown was getting to me. They were wrong, but that didn't stop the chatter.

I strained my right knee at a tournament in New Jersey in mid-August and dropped out after the first round. Luckily, I felt healed enough to play the U.S. Open, which was a big deal because we would be playing for equal prize money for the first time. Some of the men gave the tournament director, Billy Talbert, grief about it. Billy was asked by a reporter if he had anything to say to them, and I loved it when Billy said, "I'll just tell the men to go sell their product better." How great was that?

The 1973 U.S. Open began in the middle of a brutal heat wave. The day before my fourth-round match with Julie Heldman I woke up with a headache, fever, and chills that were so bad I couldn't get out of bed. A doctor came and gave me a shot of penicillin. The day of the match, I was still weak but I dragged myself to the court. It was 96 degrees and so humid I felt I was sucking hot air through a wet towel. I managed to take the first set, but the heat began to get to me by the time I had stretched out to a 4–1 lead in the second. First I had the shakes. Then I got so wobbly I thought I was going to pass out. Every time I looked up the sky started whirling.

Julie won the next nine games. I knew I was done. But because nobody likes to win or lose by default, I was trying to finish the third set on my feet. I was taking my time during the one-minute change-overs to keep from puking or collapsing—which aggravated Julie.

Like her mother, Gladys, Julie was smart, passionate, and sometimes difficult. She was leading 2–1 in the third when she saw my legs buckle and asked, "Billie Jean, are you all right?"

"I think I'm going to faint," I said.

I lost the next two games as well, and on the ensuing changeover I sat down on the bench and put my head between my knees, hoping to pull myself together. "Is a minute up?" Julie asked the umpire. Then she turned to me and said, "The minute is up! You've got to play or stop the match!"

I felt so lousy that I looked at her and snapped, "If you want it that badly, Julie, you can have it!" Then I walked off the court to go lie down in the locker room.

I was out of the U.S. Open.

Julie, who had beaten me only twice before, told the press, "I wanted it any way I could get it. I would have kicked her, I wanted it so bad."

As soon as I gathered myself enough to leave the locker room, I was ambushed by reporters on the terrace. "Does this mean you're backing out of the Riggs match?" one asked.

"Of course not," I said.

The doctor who treated me told reporters that I had been suffering from influenza for two days and I probably had a reaction to the heat and penicillin. But that didn't stop the freight train of rumors: Billie Jean King was in trouble. Women can't take pressure. "Billie Jean Wilts!" read a typical headline. More than one columnist wondered if I was faking the illness to avoid playing Bobby. The speculation didn't stop even after Rosie and I advanced to the U.S. Open doubles final (we lost) and Owen Davidson and I won the mixed-doubles title.

The rumors that I was succumbing to the tension were so persistent that advance ticket sales at the Astrodome plummeted. Five London theaters canceled their live, closed-circuit showings of the match. I was supposed to share the cover of *Newsweek* with Bobby but I was dropped at the last minute. The magazine instead ran a goofy cartoon of Riggs under the headline "The Happy Hustler."

Bobby was raking in endorsements with his boasts. I had that one new deal with Sunbeam.

There were four weeks gone in the buildup for the Battle of the Sexes, a little over four weeks to go.

AFTER FOREST HILLS I flew to Hilton Head, South Carolina, where I was the touring pro for the Hilton Head Racquet Club. Dick Butera, a thirty-nine-year-old real estate developer from Philadelphia, had hired me to promote his club and help him design the tennis facilities. He was a charming guy and we became great friends. He set me up with a condo next to his on the edge of the club, near a beautiful stand of pine trees. It was the perfect getaway to get my body and mind right for the match against Bobby. I've often said pressure is a privilege, but this was one of those times I occasionally felt overprivileged.

I saw very few people that week as I prepared. "I just want to be peaceful and focused," I told Dick. I narrowed my world to a small circle that included him and Pete Collins, the resident teaching pro, who hit with me whenever I wanted to practice. Larry flew in and out of Hilton Head a few times with papers for me to sign. I didn't have my own publicist then, so Larry's assistant, Annalee Thurston, set up camp at my condo too. Her main job that week was to turn down all requests for interviews and public appearances.

Usually Marilyn filled that role, but she had flown back to Los Angeles and wasn't to join me in Hilton Head until six days after I got there. I needed a break from her. She had been making me uncomfortable for months. She had become possessive and extremely controlling within the first few months we were together. Friends and business associates began to tell me she was blocking their calls or messages, unbeknownst to me. During tournaments, she made sure she was a conspicuous presence near me, especially when the TV cameras were around. At first I thought she was a little overzealous but just trying to be helpful. I came to see that it was actually her way to draw attention to herself. She told the media she was the gatekeeper in charge of my schedule, my mail, even my diet. One time she interrupted an important interview to try to feed me an avocado. She did a lot of odd or inappropriate things like that.

It had also become clear that Marilyn expected me to take care of her financially, not just on tour but for the rest of her life. That was not something I'd ever said, and I certainly didn't have that in mind by the time our relationship started to fray before the end of our first year.

By early summer in 1973, Marilyn and I were no longer sleeping together. Whenever she felt me pulling away, she got agitated and tried to make herself more indispensable. By the time September arrived, I had decided to put some distance between us. I knew she wouldn't handle it well if I suddenly broke off the relationship completely, and honestly, I couldn't invite any added drama; I had quite enough just preparing for Riggs. Nor did it help that I'm bad when it comes to emotional confrontations in personal relationships. Avoidance often sets in. I'm most happy when everyone else is feeling happy and emotionally connected. So I kept Marilyn on the payroll, took her phone calls while she was in Los Angeles, and didn't fight it when she said she planned to fly to Hilton Head and accompany me to Houston.

Shortly after I arrived in Hilton Head, Marilyn called me from Los Angeles to say that she'd heard a rumor that Bobby was telling people around town that he had made a side deal with Jerry Perenchio for a piece of the huge expected gate at the Astrodome. That would've been a violation of our agreement. I slammed down the phone and told Dick Butera, who was visiting for lunch, what Marilyn had told me. "That's it!" I said. "I'm out! Call Jerry Perenchio and tell him the match is off!"

Dick said, "Now wait a second, Billie. Before you cancel, let's call Jerry and make sure it's true."

"It's not true," Jerry insisted when Dick reached him. Jerry heard me in the background spouting off as I paced around the kitchen, so he told Dick, "Listen, I'm on my way." Jerry hopped on a private jet from Los Angeles, even though it meant bringing along a group of boxing managers, as he was in the middle of delicate negotiations for a heavyweight title match. Dick drove Jerry and me to lunch. Jerry convinced me that the rumors that Marilyn had passed on were untrue. Believing her would've been a high-stakes debacle.

I POURED THE REST of my energy that week into preparing to play Bobby. I spoke on the phone with my former coach, Frank Brennan, who urged me to forgo rallying from the baseline, something Margaret had done. He suggested hitting behind Bobby because slower or older players tend to cheat toward the open areas of the court more. It was good advice. Dennis Van der Meer had coached Margaret a bit for Riggs, and he told me that Margaret didn't take Bobby seriously enough. That was not going to be my problem.

My father had always taught me never to underestimate my opponents and be respectful, even if I disliked them. Being fifty-five years old had slowed Bobby down, but he was still spry and he had the know-how and array of shots to hurt me. He had proved it when he wiped out Margaret.

To go five sets with Bobby, I worked to strengthen my legs and be at peak fitness. I still didn't have a personal trainer or a science-based routine, hard as that is to imagine today. I just made it up as I went along. I did two hundred sit-ups and four hundred leg extensions a day using homemade ankle weights. I began staying up later every night and waking up late in the morning so my energy would be at its peak for our night match.

During that summer I had run into Margaret. "Would you mind if I ask you a few questions about Bobby's game?" I said. I was nervous about bringing up such a sore subject, but she was kind enough to tell me, "His backhand was surprisingly weak." So I planned to attack it.

On the court, I didn't want to overdo it so I limited myself to a few hours of practice each day. I asked Pete Collins to play like Bobby and vary his speeds, toss me lots of junk shots with heavy spin. Poor Pete must have hit me three hundred lobs a day while I worked on sharpening my overhead smashes. Then he and I would play a practice match.

By the end of my preparations for Bobby I had a strategy. I was down to 135 pounds, my ideal weight. My abs were ripped and my arms were toned. Between practices or in the evening, I spent a lot of time alone in my condo. Sometimes I'd just lie in my bed listening to the distant ocean, the birds chirping in the trees. I'd slow my breathing and meditate. I always had a tennis ball in my hand or pocket as a sort of talisman, and from time to time I would hold the ball or look at it as a reminder of all the blessings the game had already given me.

When I wanted to pump myself up, I'd listen to music like Elton John's "Take Me to the Pilot" or the title song from *Jesus Christ Superstar,* the popular rock musical. I used the Maureen McGovern song "The Morning After" to imagine how I'd feel once the match ended and I was the winner. I visualized myself playing Bobby and doing everything right. I beat him in my head a thousand times.

By Saturday afternoon, the day before I left for Houston, I was as ready as I would ever be. When I walked over to Dick's condo that day to say hello, I found him lying on the floor in front of the television watching Penn State play Stanford in college football. I happened to get there just in time to see the Stanford band march onto the field at halftime. They were playing Helen Reddy's anthem "I Am Woman," and then, to my surprise, the band snaked around to form my initials, BJK. Dick and I looked at each other and we both had tears in our eyes. Neither of us said a word.

The faraway show of support left me with a range of emotions—happiness, gratitude, astonishment at how much the match was capturing the public imagination. The next day when Dick, Pete, Marilyn, and I packed up my gear and boarded our flight to Houston, it felt like we were deploying on some kind of special ops mission. And in a way, we were. Losing was not an option.

Chapter 18

B Y THE TIME I resurfaced in public in Houston, Bobby
had been in town for a week and the city was already a
madhouse of media, overheated hype, and money.

I persuaded my parents to fly in for a few days because
they hadn't seen me play in person for five years and I wanted them
near me for this match. I knew it would be historic. I put them up
at the Houston Oaks Hotel, the same place where the rest of our
party—Dick, Marilyn, Pete Collins, Larry, and I—were staying.
We might've been one big, mixed-up family but we were all pulling
together. Randy couldn't attend because the San Francisco Giants
schedule wouldn't allow it, but he watched the match on his water-
bed at home, yelling at the television.

The Oaks Hotel was a safe distance from the circus atmosphere
of the Astroworld Hotel where Bobby had set up his carnival act.
While I was playing tournaments or training, he had been gallivant-
ing around Beverly Hills and elsewhere, making the rounds of the
nightclubs and talk shows, usually in the company of a rotating cast
of beautiful young women. At a Hollywood function, Frank Sinatra kissed Bobby on the cheek. Now that Bobby and I were both in
Houston, I figured the less Bobby saw of me, the more it would drive
him nuts because he would have no opportunity to try to psych me
out. Two could play that game. He hadn't seen me in a month.

Crazy as it sounds, I had another commitment to juggle that
week, of all weeks. I had promised to play the Virginia Slims tournament in Houston long before I agreed to play Bobby. I had wanted
to withdraw, but Gladys kept saying, "We'll get killed on ticket sales

if you do. And you signed a contract. You have to play." At least they scheduled my first two Slims matches on Monday, and I won both easily. Then I took off to the hotel to make final preparations to play Bobby on Thursday night. Seventy-two hours to go.

A few friends told me Bobby was keeping the press and himself entertained by playing celebrity challengers in the practice bubble they had set up for us in the Astrodome parking lot. That was his idea of practicing. Otherwise, Bobby's only preparation seemed to be laying off the booze for a few weeks before the match and taking, he claimed, 415 vitamin pills a day. He made a great show in Houston of squiring around Sandra Giles, a young actress he was dating, and taking endless calls from bettors looking for a piece of the action. Bobby was so sure he could win that he didn't bother to rest much or change his schedule. To the last, his hotel room door was always open and his suite filled up nightly with cigarette-smoking reporters, random hangers-on, and a stream of women.

It's hard to overstate how much Margaret's loss to Bobby colored things. When they played, eighteen of the twenty-four reporters who covered the match predicted that Margaret would win. After that? The Las Vegas bookmaker Jimmy "the Greek" Snyder installed Bobby as a 5-to-2 favorite to beat me.

At first it was kind of amusing to watch the boundless energy that Bobby threw into hawking our showdown. Some of it was just a put-on, and I told myself it was all part of the promotion. He was saying the grating things he always said—"I'll tell you why I'll win. She's a woman and they don't have the emotional stability! She'll choke, just like Margaret did . . . The man is supreme!" Other things Bobby did were harder to dismiss. The day before our final press conference, he showed up at his practice wearing a T-shirt with two circles cut out to expose his nipples, and then cracked to reporters that he thought the shirt would look better on me. That crossed the line.

I knew some people actually did believe some of the sexist things he was spouting and I wanted to be forceful and crystal clear: It was not okay. The day before the match, when one of the reporters at our final joint press conference asked how I felt about Bobby, I told the truth: "That creep runs down women . . . I like him for many things, but I hate him putting down women, not giving us credit as competitors."

That seemed to strike a nerve in Bobby. We were sitting elbow to elbow and he ignored a question put to him and turned to me instead. "Please don't call me a creep," he pleaded. "You don't mean that, do you? Won't you take that back?"

As I studied his face I wasn't sure if he was truly pained or if this was another of his cons. And frankly, I didn't care. I could feel the dynamic in the room shift when I looked him in the eye, smiled dismissively, and said, "No way, baby. 'Creep' stands."

The next twenty-four hours were a blur. I do remember the Smithsonian Institution asking for the dress I would wear during the match. Everywhere I went—the practice bubble, the hotel lobby, a last-minute run to a grocery store in Houston—women kept approaching me and saying, "I hope you win . . . I hope you shut up that S.O.B. . . . I want you to kick his pompous ass."

People were divided over who was going to win, and they were arguing it out at their kitchen tables, around the vending machines at work, inside beauty salons and corner bars. Countless wagers were made. Husbands promised their wives to take over the ironing for a week if I won; bosses vowed to make the coffee for their secretaries. Viewing parties were planned, and people had fun with it. (My partner, Ilana, was then a young touring pro, and she watched the match at the home of friends on Long Island.)

The media kept canvassing experts for predictions. Eleanor "Teach" Tennant, Bobby's former coach, told the press that Bobby was such a shot-making genius, "He knows the air inside a tennis ball." When I ran into Bud Collins, he said, "I went with Riggs." That hurt, but it stung me even more when I overheard some Slims players in the bathroom at our Houston tournament telling one another that they wanted me to win, but they thought Riggs would beat me. They didn't know I was there until I walked out of one of the stalls, looked at them without saying a word and left after washing my hands.

While I was busy strategizing with Dennis Van der Meer and watching at the last minute a bit of film from Bobby's win against

Margaret, Bobby kept playing celebrity challengers in the practice bubble for $100 or more a set. Over the years, Bobby had burnished his hustler label by cooking up gimmicks like placing thirty-two chairs on the court, playing in galoshes, attaching himself to a dog on a leash as he played. He still won. In Houston, he was selling buttons that read "Pigs for Riggs."

We were so totally different. A big part of my preparation for a match—or a speech, or any event, really—has always been running through everything that could happen ahead of time. Every detail is important to me, from having a backup pair of sneakers to familiarizing myself with the venue. For the Battle of the Sexes, I especially left nothing to chance. I arranged for a guard to let me into the Astrodome the day before the match to show me around. The stadium looked like an enormous flying saucer on the outside. It was nicknamed the Eighth Wonder of the World when it opened in 1965 because it was the first domed stadium of its size anywhere. Inside, it was a cavernous, echoing space.

I knew I'd have to get used to the lighting, the depth perception, and finding the ball fast in the steel girders of the 208-foot-high webbed ceiling. Then again, so would Bobby. The Sportface carpet court we were using would be laid out at one end of the stadium, in the middle of the Houston Astros' baseball diamond between first and third base. I reminded myself that I wouldn't have the luxury of getting acclimated beforehand because the court wasn't being assembled until the day of our match. But it would be the same for Bobby.

Just like my ritual at Wimbledon's Centre Court, I climbed up to the nosebleed seats and took in the Astrodome scene from above. I spent a lot of time just sitting there, thinking about what I was playing for and how charged the stadium would be the night we played. Before other matches I usually prayed, "Please God, let us both play to the best of our abilities." This time, I may have slipped and said, "Please God, let me win."

THE DETAILS OF the ABC broadcast were supposed to have been worked out weeks ahead of time, but early Wednesday—less than forty-eight hours before the match—I learned Jack Kramer was still scheduled to be in the booth with Howard Cosell and Rosie. "No way!" I told Larry. "Call Roone Arledge and tell him the match is off!" Roone agreed to meet with me at the Astrodome, and as soon as I walked into his office I could tell he thought I was bluffing. So I got right to the point.

"Roone, if I step out on that court tomorrow night and I find out that Kramer is in the TV booth, I will put down my racket and walk. We told you that weeks ago."

"C'mon Billie Jean, you'll play," Roone said. "Would you really give up this chance just to keep Kramer off the air?"

"Yes," I shot back. "Why would I give Jack Kramer three hours of prime time to run down women's tennis?"

I didn't think Roone would blow up the whole thing over an announcer, but you never know. And I would have walked. Roone did agree to remove Kramer—but only if Larry would make a televised statement in my stead that would air before the match, explaining why I wanted Jack out. I agreed to that, and to letting Kramer save face with his own taped statement. As it turned out, both statements that aired were untrue. Kramer said he offered to pull out so I wouldn't have the excuse that his presence distracted me into losing. Larry, who hadn't cleared it with me, went along with it. Kramer wouldn't have affected my performance if he threw a bomb on the court. But at least he was out of the booth. Roone replaced him with Gene Scott, a well-spoken former Davis Cup player.

I still hadn't seen the dress I was going to wear, but I wanted something special and I trusted Ted Tinling to come up with the perfect outfit. The week of the match, Teddy flew from London to Houston and spirited it into our hotel. He always kept his designs as secret as royal wedding gowns. When he took it out of the garment bag for me, I saw that the dress was an absolute work of art. It was made from a gorgeous material that was as luminous as mother of pearl.

"Cutting edge! The latest from Paris!" Teddy announced.

I slipped it on, and it fit perfectly. But when I tried to move, the fabric crinkled and scratched. It was stiff. I sighed and shook my head.

"I am so sorry, Ted. I'm afraid I can't play in this."

"No worries, Madame Superstar!" Ted said cheerfully. He knew me well enough to have made a backup outfit and showed it to me with a flourish. It was a soft menthol-green dress with a cutaway collar, light blue yoke, and a royal-blue bodice strip that matched my blue Adidas shoes.

"Oh, Ted, it's perfect!" I said.

"Mmmm . . . almost," Teddy said, eyeing how it looked on me. He spent the next day hunting all over Houston for tiny round mirrors to sew on the fabric. He wanted me to sparkle when the world tuned in and the lights went up in the Astrodome.

The closer I got to a big match that I knew I was well prepared for, the calmer I somehow became. In the final twenty-four hours, I was already running on autopilot. I don't remember a phone call that my brother swears took place soon after I got back to the hotel Wednesday night. Randy says I called him in San Francisco, and that our conversation after he picked up went like this:

"Hey, Sis! How's it going? Should I bet on you to win tomorrow?"

"R.J.? Bet the house."

The next morning my brother hung a sign over his locker at Candlestick Park that read "Taking bets." Every Giants team member bet against me. The Vegas odds were still 5 to 2 for Bobby, meaning a $5 wager on him would return only $7. Bobby was personally offering all comers 8-to-5 odds he'd win. When Jimmy the Greek arrived in Houston the day before the match, he told the Associated Press, "King money is scarce—it's hard to find a bet on a girl."

My father wagered on me with his firefighter pals in Long Beach. When *Sports Illustrated*'s Curry Kirkpatrick interviewed him, Dad said, "Sissy will murder this Riggs . . . I hope Sissy shuts him up good." That made me laugh. Dad sounded like he was ready to play the match himself.

Nora Ephron, Grace Lichtenstein, and a few other women

reporters also had money on me. ABC had its network camera crews all over the country, asking celebrities who they favored. I wasn't surprised when Pancho Gonzalez, John Newcombe, and the retired NFL legend Jim Brown took Bobby. To this day, Chrissie needlessly keeps apologizing for saying she thought Bobby had the edge because he beat Margaret. The Olympic decathlete Rafer Johnson, the retired NFL lineman Rosey Grier, and the heavyweight champ George Foreman sided with me.

I slept well the night before the match and woke up late, as planned. I ordered room service and spent the day with my feet up, mostly listening to music. When we arrived at the stadium around 4 p.m. I got my first glimpse of the wooden basketball court that was being laid over the baseball field. The work crew was stretching out the long rolls of carpet on top of the floorboards to create our tennis court. Festive bunting and rows of yellow chairs were set out for the VIP crowd on all four sides of the court—the worst possible backdrop for tennis.

Jerry Perenchio wanted it to feel like a prizefight, and so he had flown in a planeload of celebrities to sprinkle some glamour among the spectators who had paid $100 for courtside seats. (The lowest-priced stadium seat was $6.) There were some pretty big show-biz names: the singers Andy Williams and Glen Campbell, the talk show host Merv Griffin, and the actors Robert Stack, Rod Steiger, and Janet Leigh. Jerry brought in the 170-piece University of Houston marching band to liven things up. There was a carving station and bars where the high rollers could buy the champagne they were now sipping out of plastic coupes.

When ABC's Frank Gifford arrived to tape an interview with me for broadcast that night, he looked handsome in his tuxedo, even if it was strange attire in which to cover a tennis match. But then, everything about the event was surreal or high theater. A crowd of 30,472—the largest ever for tennis—attended that night, and an estimated 90 million people watched worldwide on TV even though the match aired after midnight in Europe. Advertising cost $90,000 a minute.

Frank and I found a quiet spot for the interview. He asked about my health, and I told him I was 100 percent. The few times I've watched the tape of our talk in the decades since, it's always striking for me to hear how carefully I modulated my voice as Frank continued. Some people had trouble with my politics, and I knew that. I was being called "militant" pretty regularly by then. So how do you lead if people hate your guts? I knew people expected me to be aggressive, so I gave them reasonable, calm, soft-spoken. When Frank asked me the inevitable at the end of the interview—"The feminist thing, how important is that, Billie?"—I chose my words carefully.

"The women's movement is important to me, as long as it stays practical," I said. "I think the women's movement is really about making a better life for more people than just women."

I was a feminist, of course. Still am. But again, I was thinking strategically. I was playing this match to change hearts and minds, after all.

When I was done with Frank's interview, Pete Collins and Dennis Van der Meer helped me warm up and I had my first chance to assess the court. The acrylic carpet had played reasonably fast when it was laid over the asphalt in our parking lot practice bubble. Now that it was stretched over wood flooring in the Astrodome, the surface was springy underfoot as I ran, but when the balls landed there was a lower bounce—an observation I would exploit later to make Bobby work harder.

After warming up, I went to the baseball visiting team locker room to shower and get ready. I liked that my brother, Randy, used the same dressing room when his team was in town. There were still about two hours to go before the 8 p.m. coin toss. Telegrams were piled up on the training table, so I read some of them. My parents swung by to wish me luck. They were dressed to the nines and having a wonderful time. Larry and Dick Butera, Marilyn, and Dennis were also in and out. With about an hour still to go I finally got antsy. I thought about how hard we had fought to get a women's tour and WTA, and I visualized how losing could take away from everything we'd ever done. I began reliving all the big matches in my past, won and lost, how much importance was loaded into this one night.

I thought again about how my life would be different if I lost. Every place I'd go it would be, *She's the one that got beat by that old guy.* They might not even remember Bobby's name but it would haunt me forever.

The loneliness of the moment started to feel overwhelming. When Dick popped in again I said, "Dick, I've gotta get out of here. Let's go."

"Where?"

"To a party."

Dick was shocked. As I've said, I disliked parties, but I knew the Virginia Slims team was throwing a going-away bash for Gladys in one of the Astrodome suites. So that's where we went. You should've seen the double takes I got as we rode up in the elevator, and again as we strode through a public restaurant on the way to the suite. Inside, it looked like an episode of "Billie Jean King, This Is Your Tennis Life." I wanted to thank everyone who had supported me. Most of the players and executives from the Virginia Slims Circuit were there, along with some colleagues past and present, including George MacCall, who had given me my pro start.

When Ted Tinling saw me he said, "My dear, what *are* you doing here? You're on in an hour!"

"Ted, I just want to thank you for my beautiful dress," I said. Then I found Gladys and told her how much I appreciated everything she had done for tennis, and for me. I said hello to a few other friends after that, but I could sense a certain awkwardness, as if most of them were worried I was headed for a humiliating defeat. This was not the time for bad vibes, so I signaled to Dick, *Let's go.* It was time to be alone again.

The remaining minutes until we had to play were melting away faster now, and slowly, surely, I was getting calmer, almost serene. As the moment to take the court arrived, it had always been like a switch went off in me and I was in the zone. *Done. Gone.* Later, I didn't even remember that Rosie came down from the TV booth to check on me before she went on the air. She told me she said, "Old Lady, how are you feeling about this match? Are you going to do it?"

She said when I looked up at her, she was struck by how steady my blue eyes were as I said, "Rosie, I'm going to win it in straight sets."

When Jerry came to the locker room to walk me to the staging area under the stands he asked me, "Are you ready, Billie Jean?" I laughed and said, "Are you kidding, Jerry? I was born ready." The corridor he led me down was a cross between Mardi Gras and the back lot at the MGM studios. There were two mascots dressed as dancing pigs. A bearded man was wearing an apron. A gaggle of cheerleaders wearing hot pants was milling about.

Jerry stopped me unexpectedly by a gilded Egyptian litter—the kind Cleopatra might've used. It was festooned with giant red, orange, and white ostrich feathers, and surrounding it were a half-dozen bare-chested athletes wearing gold arm bands and togas. Jerry had recruited them from Rice University to carry me into the arena. Not a word about this had been mentioned to me earlier, and Jerry seemed kind of sheepish as he stammered, "We weren't sure if you'd want to do this but—"

"Are you kidding? I *love* it!" I said, scrambling into the red velvet seat.

"You do?" Jerry said with a grin. He was just finding out that if I say I'm in, I'm all in. We both laughed after I added, "Feminists like fun and entertainment too, Jerry. It's showtime, baby!" And in thirty seconds, away we went.

I made my grand entrance to surprised roars and an explosion of camera flashes as the band played "I Am Woman," and the television audience was treated to this commentary from Howard Cosell: "And here comes Billie Jean King . . . A very attractive young lady. Sometimes you get the feeling that if she ever let her hair grow down to her shoulders, took her glasses off, you'd have somebody vying for a Hollywood screen test."

Really, Howard? I used to watch Cosell stick up so forcefully for Muhammad Ali and wish I'd had an announcer of similar stature to help me fight my causes. The support would've been so welcome. But right then, Howard judged my looks and made not one mention of my accomplishments—my championship titles, the pro tour we had built, how I had earned more than $100,000 in prize money two years in a row, putting me on par with star male athletes. If there was any doubt why women were fighting to change things, here was a classic example. As I was carried through the crowd toward the court, the noise was ear-splitting. But I felt good, even calmer, when I quickly spotted the curly hair and familiar face of Pam Austin among several other players. They were shouting encouragement to me and holding up signs that read "BYE BYE BOBBY."

Riggs rode in after me on a rickshaw pulled by members of "Bobby's Bosom Buddies," a contingent of young Houston women who were chosen in a contest that week using a tape measure to determine their bust sizes. Bobby was wearing a yellow and red warmup jacket emblazoned with the Sugar Daddy logo and carrying one of the caramel lollipops. It was about the size of a car door. He presented it to me when we met at the net, and Marilyn and some helpers handed me my gift for him—a squealing brown piglet with a pink bow that I named Robert Larimore Riggs, Bobby's full name. Jerry's wife, Jackie, had come up with the pig idea. I said I'd go along with it on one condition: They had to promise me that that little piggy would never be sent to market. The pig later escaped the pandemonium and was eventually found, shaken but unharmed, in a corner of the Astrodome. And he did live happily ever after on a farm. (I checked.)

Now the stunts were done. Finally, we were ready to play.

Chapter 19

Most great athletes will tell you that there are moments in a game or a match when you can feel in your bones what you must do, and then trust it completely. Champions, especially, learn to adjust. In a solitary sport like tennis, the need for that skill is especially acute because the game tests you so much mentally, physically, and emotionally. You have to find your way on your own out there.

By the time Bobby and I met on the floor of the Astrodome, something inside told me to make a last-minute change of strategy. I wouldn't charge into the match and serve and volley on almost every point as Bobby and everyone else expected. I was going to run him around for five points and see what happened. *He's older,* I thought to myself. *I'm going to hit the ball as softly as possible. I won't give him any power, and so he'll have to generate his own pace . . . If I do charge, I'm going to hit little dink shots and make him rush and bend and strain to run them down. He's not expecting that. I'll wear him out.*

If that didn't work, I could always change it up again. But I was going for it. I ran through my mental checklist for the match one last time: *Keep your mouth shut, Billie. Don't let anything upset you, including bad line calls—and you know there are some bad ones coming. Look at the people they've got on the lines, men in white shoes and checkered pants, women in bell-bottoms. Not many professionals here. Ignore it. Don't get upset by how close the spectators and chairs are, the people walking around and talking even during points. Stay in the moment. Let's go!*

I win the toss and choose to serve first. I'm purposely not hitting it as hard as I can to him. The first point goes to Bobby on an unforced error. *Let it go.* Bobby lobs and I hit a smash out of bounds. I hardly ever miss overheads. I'm not getting my first serves in yet either. I can feel myself walking under the ball and it's throwing my timing off, so I tell myself, *Get up to the ball, Bozo! Let's do it!* I'm still figuring it out, getting acclimated, but I have a great second serve so I'm fine. *That's better.* I'm testing him, taking my time. I dump a backhand volley into the net, but I'm not worried. It's my steadiest shot. I win the next rally and the first game, 1–0. *Yes!* Now I can breathe. I'm off to a solid start.

Bobby serves. I'm making him run already, and now he tries to get me moving too. He later confesses that he had no idea how fast I am. I run down a crosscourt lob behind the baseline, flick a backhand lob at him with my back to the net that he smashes, but I get to that shot, too, and pass him with a stinging forehand down the line. Love–15. *Bring it on!* I'm raring to go.

For all the pre-match hype about Bobby's skills, many folks forgot I was a versatile shot maker and shrewd tactician too. Now I'm trying different shots, seeing what works. If I have it, I use it. I stay on the baseline and take my time hitting steady, soft returns. (Pete Collins, who is watching from the audience, thinks I have lost my mind: *What happened to our game plan?*) Some of my shots land long, but again I'm not concerned. I'm making Bobby work for every point. The score is even through the first two games, and now I change it up—I come to the net and put away a sharp backhand volley. Now I'm playing my game, and Bobby is already soaked in sweat. I've held this game so far at love and now I'm serving for game point. I wind up slowly, then hasten the tempo and slam the ball into the corner, leaving him lunging at air. *Ace.*

On the changeover I'm up 2–1 and Bobby peels off his warm-up jacket, which he had kept on to give his sponsors an extra bump. On the air, Cosell notes that Bobby has discarded it and says that in addition to Riggs's wardrobe, "Maybe the braggadocio is a little reduced too." My coach Dennis sits to my right, looking calm. Marilyn is next to him, ready to pass me Gatorade and towels. Larry sits next to them, staring at his feet. As usual, he's so nervous he can't watch.

When Bobby comes out after the changeover I see that his blue knit shirt is darkened with sweat. I feel fresh. We go back and forth for the next few games. The champion shows up in Bobby and he hits some terrific shots. He breaks my serve in the fifth game, and leads, 3–2. I'm still not worried. I'm running him around, dinking shots back to make him bend over, depriving him of air as he has to jackknife down to dig out each low-bouncing ball. From the beginning of the match, I had noticed that Bobby couldn't hit a backhand down the line, which forced him to play to my backhand—my strength. I remind myself to methodically construct each point, each game, each set. *One ball at a time.* I break him right back in the sixth game, blasting an overhead for another winner.

At 4–4 on my serve, Cosell remarks on television, "The comedy seems to have gone out of Bobby Riggs." *No curtsies here.* I take the ninth game and lead 30–all. I hit a high backhand volley and Bobby lunges, shanking it to the right. *Break point and set point.* The crowd is roaring but I'm not paying much attention. I'm crouched in my stance, watching, waiting. Bobby's first serve is a fault. Then . . . double fault.

I do soak in the crowd roar now. It's deafening. *He's choking.*

Winning the first set, 6–4, is huge psychologically. It was also vital strategically, because I had never played more than three sets in competition. I'm on the right track, but I also keep telling myself, *Stay in the now. Don't look around. Keep doing what you're doing.* I ignore what is happening on Bobby's side of the umpire's chair during the four-minute TV break. When I see the videotape later, I find out that Frank Gifford had come over between sets to interview Bobby, who was toweling off sweat and popping salt pills to try to stay hydrated. Bobby drops all the playacting and delivers an analysis of the match to Frank that is honest and smart.

"This is a net player's court, and she's very good at the net," Bobby says. "She's making a lot of wonderful volleys, and I missed a lot of first serves . . . She's playing better than I am right now."

To me, that showed who Bobby Riggs really was—not just a hustler, a dealmaker, but a champion. Then he added, "It's just the first set. There's a long way to go. All I can tell you is I'm going to have to pick the pace up or change my tactics or play a little faster. She's awful quick."

I start the second set by walking to the wrong side of the court, which was worth a laugh. It's a good sign. I'm still locked in the zone.

Bobby and I exchange service breaks again to start the second set. I win the second game with a running backhand crosscourt, one of my favorite shots. I start the third game with a backhand half-volley that brings Bobby forward, and he hits the ball into the net. I'm mixing things up and forcing him out of his comfort zone. *Where are those famous lobs?* When he does lob, I kill him with my overhead, just as I practiced. I'm loosening up now, serving down the middle and then hitting behind him, wrongfooting him like Frank Brennan suggested. Between points, Bobby is panting. *That's what I want to see.* I'm putting slice on the ball to make him run three or four extra steps. People around us are jumping up and down in their seats, but I'm still lost in what I'm doing, barely aware of anything beyond the court, just focused on the next ball. Early in my career I might've played to the crowd, but tonight the court is my only world. I have tunnel vision.

When I'm up 2–1 in the second set, I pass him with a topspin forehand I hit with both feet off the ground. *I'm throwing everything I've got at him now.* I'm taking in information and processing it, understanding fully what's going on. Bobby is showing me that he can't hit over the ball to generate much topspin and he has no speed, but he's still got some fight in him. Up in the booth, Gene Scott observes, "When Bobby wins a point, he has to win it pretty much on Billie Jean's error. When Billie Jean wins it, she wins it clean." The pattern held all night. I was ending points with outright winners, meaning Bobby never got a racket on the ball.

When I pull ahead 4–3 in the second set, I know the next game is crucial. If I win this set Bobby knows he has to endure five sets to beat me. Bobby serves. I chase down everything. He can't offset the ground I cover. I break his serve by passing him with another backhand. *I own that shot.* It's 5–3, and in the TV booth Rosie is dryly saying, "Looks like I'm going to win some money on this match."

Riggs is wiped out and showing it. I don't need to look at him, I can sense it. It's a boost to know I'm *making* it happen. I'm generating all the energy and force now, and he can feel it too. These are crucial points coming up, but I say to myself, *Play each ball like any other.* At 40–love, triple set point, I get my first serve in and Bobby flops a backhand into the net. Second set: 6–3.

Frank Gifford comes up to me during the break and asks me if the match has been easier than I expected. "I didn't know what to expect," I said. "I never think it's won until it's over."

Bobby comes out for the third set with a different attitude. I didn't expect anything less. He finally realized that hitting to my backhand was a mistake and tries probing my forehand. Doesn't work. I break his serve in the opening game. Then I tell myself, *Now is the time to turn up the flame. End it. Finish him off.*

For the rest of the match, the effort both of us are expending—me to finish it, and Bobby to stay alive—results in some occasionally ugly tennis. Again, I don't care. My only job here is to win fair and square, period. I just have to win. That's what people will remember.

From the start of the match I had made sure to switch my racket to my left hand between points. That's a tension-busting trick that Margaret Osborne du Pont taught me to give your racket hand a rest. Bobby doesn't do that. I'm up 4–2 in the third set when I see that he's pulling his fingers, rubbing his hand. Cramp. It's a bad one. We've all been there, and I actually start feeling sorry for him now. I have a flashback to all those times I was so conflicted about beating men or boys that I lied to protect their egos, and I start ruminating. *What happens to Bobby when I beat him in front of millions?* Then: *Stop it! What happens if he beats you? Think of the pain that you'll feel for years. Get back to one point at a time. One ball at a time. Nothing else. Execute!*

Bobby asks for a ten-minute injury timeout for his hand cramp, and though a cramp is not technically an injury I let him have it. I don't look, but over on his side, Bobby gulps down another handful of salt pills and gets a hand massage from his coach, Lornie Kuhle. I've got to make sure I stay loose and avoid cramping during the long break myself, so Dennis stands up and I put my feet up on his chair. What I didn't expect was that Marilyn, without being asked, starts massaging my calf. *Oh boy, is this inappropriate. What is she doing?* I want her out of my space. I'm not happy with her. But I don't want a scene so I let it go on for a little and then pull away. *I want to get out of this relationship, but I can't deal with it now. I have to play.* I swig some more Gatorade. I get my mind back to the match.

The last few games are tormented, which often happens when so much is at stake. I fault on a first serve and chew myself out. *What are you doing, Billie? Hit it!* Then I drive a topspin shot into the net. *Lord have mercy on my soul.* Bobby breaks me to win the game. I break right back, and I've got him in trouble again. One game away from a straight-set victory. Bobby can barely move. He can barely serve. On my first two match points I can't put him away. At 30–40, we fall back to deuce because I miss a forehand. I look calm, but I'm screaming at myself inside, *That forehand was the embarrassment of the world! Enough is enough!* This game has already lasted fifteen points.

Third match point for me, Bobby winds up and his first serve is a fault.

When I went to Australia as a young woman to learn how to be No. 1, one of the first things the Aussies taught me was to just get the ball back in these situations. Make them play, no matter what. So that's what I'm going to do now. Just get the ball high over the net to his backhand. Give him a chance to miss. *Make him play.*

Fans are on their feet screaming, but all my senses are trained on Bobby as he rocks back to serve again. I don't even hear my dad booming, "Close him out, Sissy! Close him out!" Bobby serves to my forehand, and I hit it up the middle. He tries a backhand volley, but he can barely lift his arm anymore. My racket is already flying through the air when I see his ball is floating weakly into the net. I cover my face for a second—happy it's over, ecstatic I won—and Bobby has already jumped the net and come to my side of the court to congratulate me. *How the heck did he summon that?* I hug him and throw an arm around him as we walk off the court. It's bedlam, but I can hear him anyway as he leans in and tells me "You're too good. I underestimated you."

People are rushing at me from all sides now. The first to reach me is Dennis, and I kiss him on the cheek. Then comes Dick Butera, and I kiss him too. What the hell. Finally there is Larry, and I throw my arms around his neck and collapse against him for a moment. My relief is so great, the satisfaction so complete.

With Larry's arm still around me and friends forming a scrum to keep me from being crushed, we make it to the award area. George Foreman has muscled his way there, too. He presents me with the winner's check for $100,000 and a towering gold-plated trophy. Larry lifts me onto a nearby table so I can hoist it to the crowd. At one point I stick out my tongue and laugh, feeling absolutely giddy. That's when I finally see my mom and dad, and so I tilt the trophy at them and scream, "Thank you!"

"Way to go, champ!" Dad yells back at me. My mom is nodding and absolutely beaming.

On the way to the locker room I could only think of two things I'd given up for training but wanted desperately now—cold beer and ice cream, in that order. I was still so wired when I arrived at my post-match press conference that I paced the dais in my bare feet with a beer in my hand. As we waited for Bobby, I took some reporters' questions and someone told me the final count of outright winners I hit was 70 of the 109 points I won—a remarkable 68 percent.

So much for the rap that all women choke. Curry Kirkpatrick emphasized the same point in his article, writing that my play was "a brilliant rising to an occasion; a clutch performance under the most trying of circumstances. Seldom has there been a more classic example of a skilled athlete performing at peak efficiency in the most important moment of her life."

"This is the culmination of nineteen years of work," I told the press that night. "Since the time they wouldn't let me be in the picture because I didn't have on a tennis skirt, I've wanted to change the game around. Now it's here."

After the press conference I swung by Jerry Perenchio's hotel suite at the Astroworld for a few minutes. Dick was showing everybody the $10,000 check that Bobby had just written him to settle their bet. Right away, a few of the old male pros started griping that Bobby must have thrown the match on purpose. I heard that was a hot topic at the Los Angeles Tennis Club, too, where Jack Kramer, Pancho Gonzalez, and a bunch of other male players had watched the telecast. Some of them couldn't believe Bobby had lost to a woman. But Arthur Ashe wasn't among them. After playing doubles with me in Hilton Head a few weeks before the Riggs match, Arthur wrote in his diary that he had gained a greater appreciation for my game, and he won an $80 bet on me as he watched the Battle of the Sexes in a crowded bar.

Forty years later, ESPN broadcast a bogus story reviving the tanking question and suggesting that Bobby lost to pay off mafia gambling debts. The charge never made sense and Bobby always denied it. First of all, he bet heavily on himself for the match. Dick's check was just one of many Bobby had to pay out. Second, Bobby's coach, Lornie, who knew him better than anyone, says the allegation that Bobby tanked is preposterous because Bobby had plenty of money and he was never in debt to any mobsters. Lornie insisted that Bobby's greatest undoing was his ego. Bobby admitted that too. Before the match he told *New York* magazine, "I'm overconfident and undertrained. I'm completely ridiculous."

Most important, Bobby thought he had a lucrative franchise going if he beat me. It wasn't widely known, but Jerry Perenchio was already angling to put together an astonishing $1 million winner-take-all match between Bobby and Chrissie, and there was talk that perhaps Bobby would play Rosie after that. That alone should've killed any talk of a fixed match.

Years later, Bobby even took a lie detector test on the attorney F. Lee Bailey's talk show, hoping to prove once and for all that our match was legitimate. In 1990, he told *World Tennis* magazine, "I didn't let Billie Jean win. I bet on that match and I bet on Bobby Riggs and I lost. It was a bitter, bitter defeat. Throwing the match couldn't be further from the truth. Losing to her was the most disappointing, disheartening experience of my life."

Besides, a pro tennis player knows when a fellow player tanks. I knew this wasn't a tank. Bobby wanted to beat me; he just couldn't. "She was too good—she was never extended," he said, classy in defeat. "She was playing well within herself. It was over too quickly."

Chapter 20

I T WAS NEARLY MIDNIGHT in Northampton, Massachusetts, when the news that I'd won 6–4, 6–3, 6–3 flashed on television screens all over Smith College. News reports said five hundred women streamed out of their dormitories, unlocked the school tower to ring the bells, and marched across the campus with victory signs. One read, "Today, tennis—tomorrow the world."

Other celebrations happened all over the country. Millions of women—and quite a few men—applauded my victory. I knew it would be big if I beat Bobby, but it really sank in when I flew to Philadelphia a few days later on a promotional tour for the city's new World TeamTennis team, the Freedoms, who had made me the first player taken in the league's inaugural draft. As soon as I stepped out of the limo in front of my hotel, a city worker popped out of a manhole and shouted, "Way to go, Billie!" Then a police officer apologized for asking for my autograph and added, "If I didn't, my wife would kill me." The Philadelphia fire department made me an honorary chief, complete with a white fire chief's hat. When I walked into the newsroom of *The Philadelphia Bulletin,* everybody applauded. Then a group of women ran across the office to greet me, and one of them said, "Billie Jean, we've been wanting to ask for a raise for ten years. But we never had the courage to do it." Another said, "After you won that match, we decided to go for it."

"That's great, but did you get the raise?" I asked.

"Yes!"

"Well, right on!"

The phenomenon the match created surpassed my wildest

expectations. Remember, by the time Bobby and I played, I had already marched for women's liberation and the world had found out I had an abortion, I'd carved out a path on my terms as a new kind of career woman and wife, I'd endured questions about my "unconventional" marriage, battled with powerful men like Jack Kramer and the tennis establishment in very public standoffs, and helped lead a breakaway movement to build the first all-women's tennis tour despite threats and predictions that it couldn't be done. Taking stands was nothing new for me. But Bobby was mocking women across the board, and it was as if I was every woman's stand-in that night at the Astrodome when I backed up what I said. In America, especially, I think we've always had a romance with mavericks who call their shots or engage something on principle, and then deliver. I think that's partly what happened with me after I played Bobby. Even people who didn't agree with me nonetheless respected the way I performed. Skeptics were willing to give me another look. And the fans who already liked me now seemed to like me far more.

Suddenly I was catapulted to the forefront of social justice movements that were effecting great change. I found myself with influence that leaped the firewall of sports and spread into the worlds of entertainment, business, and politics. This was the biggest platform I had ever had, and I intended to keep championing the cause of equality. I wanted any little girl to have the same dreams as any little boy. I gave interview after interview to newspapers and magazines for months. I cohosted with Mike Douglas for a week on his popular TV talk show, I did a cameo on Sonny and Cher's variety show. There were many other invitations. I sometimes got standing ovations now *before* I played a match or said a word at public appearances. It started to feel like I was on a victory lap that showed no sign of ending anytime soon.

Of course, the flip side of the massive attention was an almost total loss of what privacy I had left, an even crazier schedule, and a flood of requests from folks asking me to personally deliver them from whatever challenge they might be facing. That was new. It was as if people thought I had a magic wand. I've always had a difficult time saying no—I want to be kind and good, I understand that yearning not to feel erased or invisible, and I probably said yes too often. Chrissie used to joke that I had become a "mother to millions." Girls and women, moms and dads, school administrators and coaches, people from all walks of life would contact me to see if I could personally intervene in their lives to right some wrong, slay another dragon. It still happens. I do as much as I can.

In the five decades since, it is not an exaggeration to say not a day has gone by without someone talking to me about the Battle of the Sexes match. Women still tell me about where they were when they saw it, how happy and empowered they felt when I won. So many women approach me choked with emotion to say, "Thank you . . . You made things possible . . . You changed my life." They tell me they finally felt it was okay to compete and win, how much self-confidence it gave them to think that they didn't have to be one of the boys to beat the boys. Some women tell me that for the first time they believed that anything was possible for them.

People are often surprised to hear that the men who approach me often have tears in their eyes too. They say, "Billie Jean, I was very young when I saw that match and now I have a daughter. It changed me." One of those men was Barack Obama. When I met him for the first time in the Oval Office after he became president, he told me, "You don't realize it, but I saw that match at twelve. Now I have two daughters and it has made a difference in how I raise them." Hearing that was just the best. Many other men admit to me that they had never absorbed or even considered the sexist treatment of girls and women until they had a daughter, and they found themselves asking, *Is this the hard life she'll have to face as well?* Often, they're motivated to push for equality for the first time.

Little boys were coming up to me after the match and saying, "I want to be a great tennis player like you." They didn't think of me as a woman as much as an athlete.

AS I MENTIONED BEFORE, when Senator Birch Bayh and others successfully pushed Title IX through Congress the year before our Battle of the Sexes match, few people recognized how much the law could affect sports. But in late May 1973, *Sports Illustrated* ran a terrific cover story titled "Sports Is Unfair to Women." The writers, Nancy Williamson and Bil Gilbert, compiled page after page of infuriating examples of how boys' and girls' sports programs were kept separate and unequal:

- By 1973, an estimated fifty thousand men attended college on sports scholarships. Fewer than fifty women had them nationwide.
- In 1969, a Syracuse, New York, school board budgeted $90,000 for boys' sports and $200 for girls'. At the University of Washington, where enrollment was 41 percent women, less than 1 percent of the sports budget went to women's sports.
- Many of the girls surveyed had trouble naming even a few women athletes.

When I read that article I felt both outraged and vindicated. Then *Sports Illustrated* published two more scathing pieces on sex discrimination in sports. The additional stories made the case that there indeed was a great hunger among girls to participate in sports even though the men who ran the institutions insisted that girls weren't interested. The articles also made clear that few people seemed keen to watch women's sports because there were hardly any women's sports to watch.

It was a point we had been making in women's tennis for at least a decade, and we were debunking it more forcefully each passing year. In 1976, just five years after I became the first sportswoman to win $100,000 on our Slims tour, Chrissie became the first female athlete to top $1 million in career prize money. The velocity at which things were moving for us in tennis was stunning. Especially since men had a one-hundred-year head start in the sports marketplace.

The *Sports Illustrated* writers asked what could be done to give women and girls everywhere more athletic opportunities, and found that the remedy already existed—it was Title IX, a lawyer in the Office for Civil Rights of the U.S. Department of Health, Education, and Welfare told the magazine. If a school was spending far more money on male sports than on female sports—and it was nearly impossible to find a co-ed school then that wasn't—the federal government could withhold funds to those institutions until the discrimination was remedied.

You could feel the fear and loathing spike in the male-dominated athletic offices and locker rooms across the country. Title IX was seen as an existential threat. Many schools, particularly those in the NCAA's Division I (or biggest) conferences, were raking in cash from their men's football and basketball programs with virtually no money going to women's teams. The spending balance would now have to change. Once again, nobody was demanding overnight equality or a 50/50 funding split; rather, Title IX mandated a "proportionally" fair allocation for girls and women based on a series of criteria laid out for institutions.

Title IX's opponents complained that the law constituted political correctness and could lead to the end of college football and basketball's March Madness. Women's advocates countered that one group's "grand old traditions" often happen at the expense of another group's continued repression. Our proof was in the math. At the time, major college football programs routinely warehoused players and handed out 120 or more full-ride scholarships per year per team, meaning that one major college football team exceeded the *total number of athletic scholarships available to women in the entire country*—fifty by *Sports Illustrated*'s count in 1973. The imbalance was indefensible.

Three weeks after I defeated Bobby, on November 9, 1973, I appeared before a U.S. Senate subcommittee to talk about the Women's Educational Equity Act, a proposed adjunct to Title IX. The WEEA legislation would create federal grants to help institutions fund Title IX requirements.

I'd come a long way from my grade school public-speaking panic attacks. Here I was in our nation's capital talking with seven senators on an all-male committee about what they should do with regard to federal legislation. It was an opportunity for me to contend that we should reshape our institutions to make sure they're places where all of us are supported, so all of us can excel. I spoke from the

When Elton John said he wanted to write a song for me with his longtime lyricist Bernie Taupin, I thought, *Wait! Did I just hear that right?* The amazing result was their No. 1 hit "Philadelphia Freedom."

Elton wearing the Philadelphia Freedoms jacket that I asked Ted Tinling to make for him because Elton was such a tennis fan. We're having a few laughs here at the Queen's Club in West Kensington, London.

One of my favorite life experiences was joining Elton with his band and backup vocalists in front of fifty-five thousand fans at Dodger Stadium in 1975.

Ilana and I joined Elton and David Furnish to help celebrate David's fortieth birthday in Venice in 2002. They were married in 2014.

WTA Executive Director Jerry Diamond, second from right, and I met with Wimbledon officials and Ann Jones, then a player and Wimbledon committee member, in February 1975. We told them our women pros wouldn't play Wimbledon the following year if the tournament didn't close the gap between men's and women's prize money. We left with a bump from 70 to 80 percent of what the men earned, and an agreement with Wimbledon to revisit the pay issue annually.

Ilana with her mother, Ruth; sister, Merle; and father, Shlaim. This photo was taken nearly a decade after I first met the Kloss family at the 1966 South African Championships in their hometown of Johannesburg. Ruth was a tournament volunteer and Ilana was a ball girl whose dream of playing the women's tour came true.

Linky Boshoff (left) and Ilana Kloss play Rosie Casals and me in 1975, the year before they finished as the No. 1–ranked doubles team in the world.

I had the privilege of visiting the Oval Office for the first time in 1975 when President Gerald Ford invited Arthur Ashe and me after our victories at Wimbledon. The date was July 21, 1975, the same day that Title IX officially went into effect in the U.S.

This is one of my favorite photographs because the purist in me likes that I'm balanced and fully extended as I reach for this forehand volley at an indoor match in 1975. I'm one of the few players who love playing indoors as much as outdoors. To me, the caliber of indoor play is often better because of the controlled conditions, and I love the acoustics—the crowd noise is louder, more exciting. I never liked quiet in tennis.

Former congresswoman Bella Abzug, left, invited me to address the huge crowd at the finish of the 2,610-mile torch relay run from Seneca Falls, New York, to Houston, where the 1977 National Women's Conference was held. Standing next to us on the right are Gloria Steinem and New York lieutenant governor Mary Anne Krupsak.

I supported Dr. Renée Richards's court fight to play on the women's tour and asked her to be my doubles partner at the 1977 Lionel Cup in Port Washington, New York.

I didn't think I'd recover from surgery in time to try to win a record twentieth career title at Wimbledon in 1979. I'm forever grateful that Martina Navratilova, then my doubles partner, refused to give up on me. Here we are, accepting the trophy.

This is Lucy, who was a gift from my brother, Randy, sitting on a 1922 bench from Centre Court, Wimbledon.

My parents, Betty and Bill Moffitt, stood with Larry and me as a show of support following the painful Los Angeles press conference that I called after Marilyn Barnett outed me in 1981.

Peanuts creator Charles Schulz became a dear friend after he agreed to serve as a Women's Sports Foundation trustee. He'd often surprise me by writing me into his comic strip.

Martina Navratilova, Mary Carillo, and I became the first all-women's broadcasting team to call matches at Wimbledon when we worked for HBO Sports.

I first saw Venus and Serena Williams at this April 1988 Domino's Pizza World Team Tennis clinic in Long Beach, California, when the girls were seven and six, respectively. Their mother, Oracene, told me that day that she and her husband, Richard, taught the girls to play and they all came to the clinic from their home in Compton to pick up some pointers. I remember thinking, *WOW. These girls have the ability to be the very best.*

The popularity of women's tennis was so huge by 2001 that the U.S. Open moved its Saturday women's final to prime time—a first. It seemed fitting that Venus and Serena Williams, who drove so much of the excitement, played the title match. Venus won in straight sets.

The U.S. Olympic team assistant coach Zina Garrison stands with Lindsay Davenport, Venus Williams, Monica Seles, Serena Williams, and me the year we competed at the 2000 Sydney Summer Olympics. I served as team captain. I always called this group tennis's version of the Dream Team because all four players had been ranked No. 1 in their careers.

Ilana Kloss and me on our first family vacation to Provincetown, Massachusetts, in 2003 with Ilana's mother, Ruth; sister, Merle; Merle's husband, Richard Blackman; and their children, Josh and Lara.

This keepsake photo was taken backstage the night the U.S. National Tennis Center was named after me in 2006, proving it wasn't an out-of-body experience—it really *did* happen! Left to right: Franklin Johnson and Arlen Kantarian, two of the USTA executives who sponsored the renaming effort; Jimmy Connors; Chrissie Evert; New York mayor Michael Bloomberg; me; Ilana; Venus Williams; Mary Carillo; and John McEnroe.

Fireworks explode overhead during the naming ceremony for the USTA Billie Jean King National Tennis Center on opening night at the 2006 U.S. Open. One of the many reasons the honor meant so much to me is that the national tennis center sits on forty-six-and-a-half acres of public-park land, and I was a public-park kid.

Democratic presidential hopeful Senator Hillary Clinton and I share a laugh during our appearance at a New York town hall hosted by Women for Hillary in June 2007.

heart. I told the committee how often I could've been dissuaded from becoming who I was. I shared my childhood stories about the boys getting expense money while I was given nothing. I suggested that the Senate should take the word *women* out of the title of the bill. "I think it should be changed to the Education Equity Act," I said, noting that the grants would be given to both men and women, so women weren't seeking special rights, just fair treatment.

I talked about how a lack of facilities and funding impeded girls and women athletes, and how social mores and psychological conditioning worked against us too. "We're considered freaks, we're considered masculine . . . that boys are not going to like us," I said. "It is tough enough to guts it out on a tennis court other than to have to worry about all the other aspects of society accepting you as a human being. We are just now being accepted—I had to wait this long. [And] what about the boy who is not athletically inclined? Why should he be put down, too?" I said people should be able to do their own thing, whatever their abilities or interests are.

I also let the senators know I didn't like the NCAA. "As far as I'm concerned, we should get rid of this monopoly because they [athletes] are going to school because of their excellence in sports. Who's kidding whom? College athletes today are professional athletes." It took the NCAA another forty-some years to begrudgingly allow athletes to be paid something beyond their room, board, and classes for the use of their name, image, and likeness. But it was obvious even in 1973 that major college football and basketball had their own version of shamateurism. So I said so.

A couple of months later, Congress passed the Women's Educational Equity Act. I was heartened to see how many men in Congress were willing to work with women to safeguard our rights. The vote was an example of how many men will do what's right if you can engage them as allies rather than reflexively dismiss them as enemies. Title IX remains intact, but we have to remain watchful. There are still legal challenges to the law and a stubborn lack of compliance to this day.

To keep the equality-for-all conversation going, I started the Women's Sports Foundation, as promised, eight months after the

Battle of the Sexes match, using the $5,000 award that Gillette gave me on its *Cavalcade of Champions* TV show. The WSF was originally created to fight for gender equality in sports from the grassroots to collegiate and professional levels. At the outset, it was the only national organization dedicated to assisting and funding the development of sports for women and girls. The foundation soon evolved into providing research, education, legal referrals, grants, coaching, and leadership development. The WSF works with the National Women's Law Center. In 1987, the WSF executive director, Deborah Slaner Larkin, succeeded in soliciting enough support from all fifty states to convince Congress and President Ronald Reagan to establish National Girls and Women in Sports Day, an annual day of observance that is celebrated with events across the country to recognize the importance of female athletic participation and achievements. Women's sports leaders and athletes also meet with congressional leaders on Capitol Hill to discuss issues and legislation.

By the fiftieth anniversary of Title IX in 2022, the WSF will have raised and invested more than $100 million to expand opportunities for girls and women in all sports. Part of our work has been documenting the extraordinary effect of Title IX. In 1972, only 3 percent of American girls played high school sports; the number was 43 percent in 2020. Fan interest in women's sports has grown enormously too. NCAA women's basketball teams drew 11.5 million fans during the 2018–19 season, and the women's college softball championships averaged 1.57 million viewers a game on ESPN that academic year.

The dominance and popularity of the U.S. national women's soccer team, starting with its dramatic 1999 World Cup victory before a sellout crowd of 90,185 at the Rose Bowl, a record for a women's sporting event, sparked the growth of women's soccer around the world. At the American team's fourth World Cup title victory in Lyon, France, in 2019, the crowd broke into spontaneous, thundering chants of "Equal pay! Equal pay!" in the waning minutes of the final. The U.S. team was so admired that their Swedish opponents had taken the extraordinary step of taping a video that was played on the scoreboard before the championship game thanking the American team they were about to play for all they had done for the sport. It was well known that the U.S. women had filed a lawsuit against their federation charging unequal treatment compared to the U.S. men's team.

ANOTHER OF MY DREAMS since I was a young woman was to make tennis a team sport. To me, team sports are where it's at in terms of jobs, maximum audience size, participation slots, and money. I also knew many kids quit playing tennis because they missed the camaraderie that team sports provide. After I signed to play Bobby in the summer of 1973, Larry and I were approached by a group of businessmen led by Dennis Murphy, a sports entrepreneur who had cofounded maverick leagues such as the American Basketball Association and the World Hockey Association. Murphy and his group initially wanted to start another women's tennis tour because they believed that the Virginia Slims Circuit's viability was still doubtful. Larry said, "Not interested." When Murphy came back to us with the idea of a team tennis league, we jumped. The basic concept had been knocking around for decades, and Larry and I had been shaping and refining our version since college.

We told them our idea was to create a World TeamTennis league with women and men on the roster in equal numbers, playing matches that made an equal contribution to the final score. Everything equal, see? Owners could buy franchises and set up teams in different American cities, the same as the NBA or NFL.

We were convinced that our World TeamTennis format offered something for everybody. Players would have a guaranteed salary for several months, with time carved out to play the majors. The networks would find World TeamTennis more TV friendly because a match would reliably last two hours or so, about the same as an NBA game. World TeamTennis would be great for fans because they were almost guaranteed to see the stars they bought tickets hoping to see, unlike traditional single-elimination tennis tournaments. Our fans also would have home teams to cheer for and they could get to know their players instead of having a tournament visit only one week a year (if their city even had a pro tournament). We also envisioned integrating World TeamTennis teams into their communities, supporting local charities, establishing programs, and holding clinics to grow the game at the grassroots level.

By then, tennis was the fastest-growing sport in the country, according to Nielsen surveys. Ten million Americans said they played tennis in 1970, and by 1974, the year after the Battle of the Sexes, the figure was 34 million people. It was the most amazing time ever for our sport. So many people took up the game that players reported it was often hard to get a court. Suddenly there was a gold rush in tennis. And money follows money.

Dennis Murphy and Larry set out to find thirteen investors willing to pay $50,000 each for the right to buy a league franchise. Before long, they had raised $500,000 and marveled that their only upfront expense was a $3 map of the U.S. that Larry would stick a pushpin into every time they sold another franchise. Three more teams were reserved for our founders, which is how Larry and I ended up owning a piece of the San Francisco Golden Gaters.

From the outset, World TeamTennis offered numerous innovations for our sport, such as music during matches and branded multicolor court surfaces. We used a simpler scoring system that eliminated advantage points so the next point after deuce wins a game. The no-ad scoring and the responsibility of playing for your team and your city added a lot of pressure that players didn't experience playing tournament tennis; many of them said it helped their performance when they returned to the tour.

We also permitted substitutions that were limited to one player per set, per gender. We were the first to pay linespeople, and among the first to use an all-electronic line-calling system when that technology came along. Each World TeamTennis match consisted of five sets—one set of women's and men's singles, women's and men's doubles, and mixed doubles—and a doubles set always opened and closed the match until Andre Agassi played for us in 2002. Andre persuasively argued that our format too often prevented teams from using their very best player in the final set, when the match was often decided. It made sense, so we made a new rule to allow the home team coach to determine the order of play—the better to get more strategy involved. We also encourage fans at World TeamTennis matches to hoot and holler, and they get to keep balls that are hit out of play.

"But what if people grumble about music and cheering at a tennis match?" a reporter asked me at the start.

"The players can't have all the good of the past and all the good of the future," I said. "Cheering and noise is where it's at. Some of them want the country club life and nobody hassling them and $200,000 a year. They've got to become more professional like other team sports."

When we launched, our friend Dick Butera bought the World TeamTennis franchise in Philadelphia on one condition: I had to agree to play for him and coach the team. I was willing to do just about anything to get World TeamTennis going. Plus, my role would be historic. This would be the first time a woman was coaching men in pro sports, and the first time women and men played on the same professional sports league teams. I even helped pick our Philadelphia team's name, the Freedoms, after we held a contest with *The Philadelphia Inquirer* that attracted more than fifteen thousand entries. *Freedom* is one of my favorite words, because of the infinity of possibilities it suggests.

Larry initially took the title of vice president of operations, and Rosie made history, too, as a player/coach for Detroit. We were thrilled when John Newcombe agreed to play for Houston for $75,000 a season, particularly since Jack Kramer was trying to block the ATP men from signing with us and Arthur Ashe, still president of the ATP, ran down World TeamTennis even though he had privately tried to negotiate a multiyear contract with us; I told the press that only after they mentioned Arthur's criticisms. Kramer disliked our format. He complained that there was "too much emphasis on dames." But in our first season our sixteen teams drew 5 million fans.

Some of our original owners remain familiar names today. Dr. Jerry Buss owned the Los Angeles Lakers and our Los Angeles Strings. Robert Kraft cut his teeth as an owner with the Boston Lobsters before he bought the New England Patriots and launched their NFL dynasty. Many of our other owners knew almost nothing about sports. They were car dealership owners or furniture moguls caught up in the excitement of the moment, and it showed when we held our first player draft on August 3, 1973, in New York. Some of our teams ignored the availability list we gave them and wasted draft choices on Chrissie, Rod Laver, and Ilie Nastase, though all three said they wouldn't participate that first year. Maria Bueno and Pancho Segura were drafted though they hadn't played in years. Chicago took Bobby Riggs in the ninth round, just for laughs. Young stars such as Chrissie, Martina, and Bjorn Borg all played in our league eventually. Pittsburgh was thrilled to land Evonne Goolagong.

World TeamTennis ran into interference almost immediately from the European promoters who weren't happy that our May-to-August schedule pulled players off their tours. In retaliation, Philippe Chatrier, the head of the French Tennis Association and a friend of Kramer's, banned all World TeamTennis players from Roland-Garros in 1974. That was particularly devastating for Jimmy Connors, who won the other three majors that year in addition to honoring his contract to play for our Baltimore Banners. Jimmy and his agent, Bill Riordan, sued on Jimmy's behalf, but a French court refused to grant him an emergency injunction to play in the tournament.

The best male player on our World TeamTennis squad was Fred Stolle, my Aussie mate from our barnstorming days. Dick Butera moved heaven and earth to trade for Julie Anthony, the brainy and beautiful PhD student at Stanford who was still a part-time player. I had introduced them at Wimbledon the year before, and Dick developed a major crush on her. That I knew. What Dick did not tell me was that he had shipped out Laura Rossouw from our roster to get Julie. For a perfectionist like me, who was taking my coaching job very seriously and doing everything from giving players tips to arriving at the arena hours early to make sure they had every little thing they needed, Dick's decision was grating.

"Why did you do that without telling me?" I said.

"I guess it's because I knew you'd yell at me?" Dick answered.

I had to laugh. It was his money, and soon he was telling everybody he had bought the team just to get a date—and Julie *still* didn't go out with him. But he was a charming devil. Eventually, he did win her heart and they married.

I DON'T KNOW how we thought we could do it all, but *womenSports* magazine was born in the months following the Riggs match alongside the Women's Sports Foundation and World TeamTennis. God bless Bobby Riggs.

Larry and I could've chosen an easier path than launching a glossy magazine from concept to newsstand in six months in the middle of a recession. Magazines are capital intensive, and the economy was shrinking along with advertising budgets. Not only would we need a bundle of start-up money from investors, but the costs of paper, ink, postage, and transportation were skyrocketing with inflation. One banker asked us, "You've worked too long and hard. Why risk everything on a magazine?"

We persisted anyway. Our marketing research showed that participation in sports among girls and women had increased 175 percent in the previous three years, compared to just 5 to 10 percent among males. We also learned that *Sports Illustrated* had at least 100,000 female readers despite devoting very few resources to covering women's sports. There was definitely a market.

Our idea was to give women the same exposure that male athletes already enjoyed. When I was a kid, I never saw or heard of any women athletes beyond tennis and golf. Changing the paradigm drove me. We figured if readers, particularly young girls and boys, got to know female athletes through more in-depth coverage, it would go a long way toward normalizing and promoting the idea of women's sports in the culture as a whole.

Larry and I were again able to quickly raise the start-up money from a variety of sources because I remained in demand. The pop singer Helen Reddy and her husband/manager, Jeff Wald, thought the magazine was a good fit for them. They introduced us to other investors, and we ended up with about $700,000. A lot of that came out of our own pockets because we didn't want corporate control.

Larry and I had a tremendous amount of help from established magazine publishers, especially Pat Carbine and Gloria Steinem, who had gone the maverick route to start *Ms.* I had gotten to know them even better after I hired Pickwick, a public relations company that shared office space with *Ms.* in Midtown Manhattan. Pat Kingsley and Lois Smith, the partners at Pickwick, were the gold standard, representing entertainment superstars of the day including Robert Redford, Raquel Welch, and Mary Tyler Moore. Whenever I came by for a meeting with Pat and Lois, Peggy Seigal, or Gerry Johnson, I would often poke my head into the *Ms.* offices to say hello. Sometimes I would listen in on their story meetings, soaking up the process of how they put together an issue. I couldn't wait to get started with our magazine.

As was often the case, Larry and I were learning another new business on the fly. Who knew you needed to buy a three-year supply of paper when you started publishing? Gloria and Pat were big supporters since our project was geared toward women's empowerment, and so they opened the books of *Ms.* magazine and walked Jim Jorgensen, the business manager we hired, through details like print runs and ad base rates. Larry was the hands-on publisher. I wrote a first-person column and appeared on the masthead as a publisher, too.

We held our launch party in New York City at Gallaghers, an old-fashioned steak house known for drawing the likes of Joe DiMaggio and Joe Namath as well as a mix of local wiseguys, sportswriters, and horse racing touts. The choice of location was intentional. We aspired to be part of the big-time sports landscape.

We started *womenSports* with a print run of 115,000 and soon moved up to 200,000. We would later learn that only six of the seventy-seven magazines that launched along with us in 1974 survived. As a business, it was a roller-coaster ride for us as well, but as an editorial product, it gave us moments of great elation and pride. Our first iteration of *womenSports* was just what we hoped:

progressive, creative, original, informative, edgy, empowering, irreverent, and fun. There was a monthly column from a male perspective called "A Pig's Eye" and we playfully called our results scoreboard "Who Did What to Whom." Our "Foremothers" feature celebrated women's sports history, another long-neglected area. We devoted an entire issue to "The Revolution in Women's Sports," which included an action manual on how to fight schools that didn't comply with Title IX. We covered everything from backpacking to basketball to women's tackle football.

A glossy, mass-circulation sports magazine entirely devoted to women was unprecedented. Anne Lamott, now a celebrated author, was among our brilliant young hires. Another was the tennis player Tam O'Shaughnessy, who remains a dear friend. Tam still talks about the parade of top women athletes who visited our offices and the camaraderie and sense of mission the staff shared, especially in the magazine's early days. "We all felt like we were doing something important," she said. "We'd go to lunch together. Play volleyball after work. Then go back to work and stay as late as we needed to. We came back in on weekends. It felt very exciting to be part of a first in history." Tam went on to start a couple of businesses with the astronaut Sally Ride, a childhood friend of hers, including Sally Ride Science, which encouraged girls to get involved in math, science, and technology. I had known Sally since she was a terrific junior tennis player. Tam later thanked Larry and me "for showing us how to make a difference and how to be brave if you see something that isn't right. You *can* make a difference."

Many *womenSports* readers told us how inspirational, even galvanizing, it was to finally have a place where other athletes looked like them and faced the same challenges. They said we became an indispensable resource—sometimes the only resource—where girls and women could research which opportunities existed and learn what colleges and universities were offering athletic scholarships. One of those women was Shellie Pfohl, who became executive director of the President's Council on Fitness, Sports, and Nutrition in 2010. She told me that as a young girl in rural Iowa she would run the length of her family's long driveway to check the mailbox to see if her monthly *womenSports* issue had arrived, and then run back home once it did because she couldn't wait to read what was inside.

Stories like that were what we were hoping for with all the projects we did. I always say I want things to be better fifty years from now, one hundred years from now. I want to create change that lasts.

Chapter 21

SO MUCH HAPPENED in the months immediately before and after I played Bobby Riggs, I remember laughing and telling someone once, "Do you know how much more exciting my life became in the '70s?" Several weeks before the Riggs match, Jerry Perenchio invited me to a large dinner party that was held in Los Angeles. I asked, "Who's the party for?" Jerry said casually, "Oh, it's for Elton John."

Elton was my favorite recording artist in the early 1970s. The first time I heard him sing the ballad "Your Song" over my car radio, I had to pull over on a busy San Francisco street to listen to it. I loved his voice and keyboard playing. I couldn't believe how poignant the song was, how much it moved me. I bought *Tumbleweed Connection*, *Madman Across the Water*, and all his other records. What I didn't know before Jerry invited me to the dinner party was that Elton was a tennis fanatic, and he was a big fan of mine.

The thing I remember most about that night is that Elton and I were seated at opposite ends of a large room, and Tony King, Elton's manager, came over to me as the plates were being cleared and said, "This is ridiculous. Elton's been dying to meet you all night, but he's too shy." I said, "Ditto." Tony said, "Come with me," and led me to a seat across from Elton and introduced us. We only had a chance to chat for a few minutes, but as we parted Elton said, "When are you coming to London?"

I had already gotten a big taste of the Los Angeles celebrity swirl by then—"*Have your people call my people, kiss, kiss! Seriously, you look great!"*—and I wasn't sure if he really meant that he might want to get together.

Fast-forward to Wimbledon, late June 1974. When I checked into the Gloucester Hotel, the desk clerk handed me a note: "Billie—Call me—Elton." When I dialed the number, Elton picked up and offered to come by. For privacy, he suggested I meet him outside in his car, which turned out to be a shiny new Rolls-Royce Phantom VI limo. "Would you like to listen to some music?" he said after I got into the cavernous back seat. "I've got thirty-six speakers." This I had to hear. Elton cued up some tunes, and we sat there for hours, listening and talking.

Elton and I quickly developed a sweet rapport that night. We discussed how music and sports are great levelers that can bring everyone together regardless of their race, gender, or social caste. I told Elton how much I loved his music. He told me he had watched the Battle of the Sexes match in a hotel room in Los Angeles. "When I saw you come out on that litter thing, I thought, 'Wow! She's copying me!'" he teased.

The more we talked, the more we found we had in common. We were both working-class kids at the peak of our fame and we weren't sure how to handle it. We both carried secrets about our sexuality, though we didn't discuss it that night. We were both riven with contradictions—introverts who nonetheless wanted people around us. As shy as we were, we felt most alive onstage.

Once Wimbledon started, Elton came to see me again, and played tennis with Larry at the Queen's Club, which was then the official practice site for the tournament. Elton came back on the day I played in the quarterfinals against eighth-seeded Olga Morozova, the Soviet Union's top player, and I was knocked out in straight sets. The loss not only killed me, it also left Elton convinced he was bad luck; he never came to see me play at Wimbledon again. It was the first time I had lost before the semifinals there since 1962, a streak of twelve years.

Hoping to cheer me up that night, Elton insisted on taking me out on the town. First, Italian food at our favorite hole-in-the-wall restaurant in Wimbledon village. Next, a working-class pub in Brixton where I saw my first drag show and we stood at a bar that was four deep with customers. I drank soda and Elton drank beer and led us all in sing-alongs. From there, it was on to an infamous members-only nightclub called Tramp, where we walked down a flight of stairs, made a couple of turns, and—*is this really happening?*—Mick Jagger and his wife, Bianca, were waiting for us at a back table. There was a dance floor at Tramp as well as a posh dining area, and the club was known for attracting celebrity musicians, actors, even royals. One night when we were not there, Keith Moon of the Who swung from a chandelier until it came crashing down. Such things happened at Tramp a lot.

(On another visit to London, Martina and I went to see Elton perform at Wembley Stadium. Afterward, back at the hotel, he offhandedly mentioned, "Oh, some friends might be coming by in a bit." I thought nothing of it until there was a knock on the door, Elton opened it, and there stood Paul McCartney, his wife, Linda, and their baby daughter, Stella.

"Hi," Paul said casually as they walked in.

A couple of minutes after that, Harry Nilsson and Dino Martin arrived.)

Elton and I bonded for life on that first visit. Forty years later, we're still like a pair of nomads who constantly fly off in different directions but always find each other again. When we were both in the States late in July 1974, Elton agreed to play a celebrity match for us in Philadelphia. It was a favor to our World TeamTennis team, and a dream come true for a tennis nut like him. I asked Ted Tinling to fit Elton for a Freedoms uniform and Elton loved it. We were playing Toronto and our crowds had been lagging at the Spectrum, but almost ten thousand fans turned out that night, mainly to watch Elton play (and beat) Bill Cosby, a Philly native.

Elton was also in town to play a concert at the arena. On the way to the Spectrum that night, he turned and said to me, "I want to write a song for you."

"C'mon," I laughed, thinking, *I didn't just hear that.*

I only realized he was serious when he added, "What should we call it? How about Philadelphia Freedom?"

"That would be a great gift to the people of Philadelphia," I told him.

The next time I saw Elton, I was in Denver about a month later to play another World TeamTennis match and he was recording his latest album at a studio outside the city. When I went out to warm up, he was sitting in a courtside seat wearing his Freedoms shirt. He said he had something he wanted me to hear, so I took him back to our team locker room. He was carrying a small tape deck and smiled at me as he set it down and hit Play.

I used to be a rolling stone, you know
If a cause was right . . .

As soon as I heard Elton singing those first two lines after the trilling flutes and opening horns and strings of "Philadelphia Freedom" I was awestruck. So was our entire team. I still think it's unbelievable. He looked relieved and told us, "Oh, I was hoping you would love it." He added that every time he belted out each syllable of "PHIL-A-DEL-PHI-A" in the refrain, he imagined me stomping around and yelling at a chair umpire. That made me laugh. The song is a wonderful, completely original work by Elton and his amazing longtime lyricist, Bernie Taupin, that they styled as a tribute to the Philadelphia soul sound. The tune became a source of pride for the city as well as Elton's first hit to cross over to No. 1 on the R&B charts, which was doubly rewarding for him.

Elton sat with us on the team bench that night in Denver. Later that year, he gave me my first of several chances to experience his rock 'n' roll life onstage. He had a concert at the Spectrum. We were sitting in his dressing room beforehand and he said he wanted me to be one of his backup vocalists that night. "That's not happening," I said. When it was time for him to walk out onstage, I took off running down a hallway and a bodyguard was sent to chase me down. The man literally dragged me back to Elton, who then lifted me in his arms and carried me out, kicking and screaming.

The crowd screamed and cheered, thinking it was all part of the act.

I WAS NEVER CRAZY about the "Old Lady" nickname that Rosie jokingly hung on me in my early twenties, even though I laughed and played along. By 1974, I was starting to feel younger players like Chrissie, Evonne, and Martina gaining on me. I was nearly thirty-one, my knees were again killing me, and I couldn't run and jump like I had before. As an elite athlete, you're always poignantly aware that your run has to end sometime.

I had always mentored up-and-coming players or invited them to practice with me, just as others had been kind enough to do for me. I knew we had to prepare our next generation to keep the momentum rolling. Chrissie still jokes about the day I told her that I wanted her to succeed me as WTA president, so she needed to start preparing right away—at age nineteen—by serving as vice president that year. She gulped and said, "*Me?* Why me?"

"Because you're our superstar," I said. "It's easier for the star players to lead because the media will listen to you." I assured her that the other veterans and I would help her, plus she had the WTA and Slims support staff to call on. The next year, Chrissie succeeded me as president and served a total of eleven years over two stints, doing a terrific job. She put in the work, informed herself about the issues we faced, and was an articulate spokeswoman for the tour.

Passing the WTA presidency to Chrissie was more proof that my role in the game was changing. Another sign was that at both Wimbledon and the U.S. Open in 1974, the tennis world was fixated on the Jimmy Connors and Chrissie soap opera.

It made total sense that Jimmy and Chrissie would find each other. They were both public-park kids from middle-class Catholic families who were raised to be tennis champions. Jimmy's colorful mother, Gloria, was a gifted amateur who had twice played at Forest Hills as a teenager before she became Jimmy's hard-driving coach. (When Jimmy debuted at Wimbledon in a 1972 match, Gloria had to be asked to stop shouting, "Kick him in the slats, Jimbo! *Whoo hoo!*") As a young woman, Gloria was courted by Pancho Segura and asked on a date by Jimmy Evert, Chrissie's father, before he met his wife, Colette. Gloria Connors coached stars like Mickey Rooney and Errol Flynn after leaving Illinois and settling in Los Angeles. The

Connors and Evert kids naturally ran into each other over the years on the junior tennis circuit.

Jimmy is three years older than Chrissie, and they didn't start dating until 1972, when she was seventeen. At the time, they were still both traveling with their mothers. The tabloids were onto their romance from the beginning. I mean, how could they resist? It was made to look like a classic case of the good girl falling for the incorrigible bad boy. By 1974, they were engaged and headed toward the finals at Wimbledon. But even then, Chrissie was having second thoughts. Her reservations hadn't gone away by the time we arrived at the U.S. Open at Forest Hills.

One day as we were both sitting in the locker room, Chrissie asked me how it was being married and having a tennis career.

"I think you have to be a full person," I told her. "I was young to be married at twenty-one. But a woman was expected to get married back then. I was the last among my friends to marry. I really wanted to get married. We had dated for two years."

Chrissie was the first to admit that she had led a sheltered life. She was clearly struggling. I asked gently, "Do you love Jimmy?"

She sighed and said, "Yes, yes. It's not that."

Tennis meant so much to Chrissie, and she knew that she would be the one pressured to give up her career. Even Jimmy had suggested as much. She and Jimmy had both gone on to win Wimbledon, which only highlighted how realistic their individual tennis ambitions were.

Chrissie lost to Evonne in the U.S. Open semifinals, and Jimmy won the men's championship. I wasn't surprised when they called off their wedding a few weeks later after a long, late-night phone call. Chrissie was still only nineteen. Both of them went on to spend the next decade at or near the No. 1 spot.

I faced Evonne for the 1974 title at Forest Hills, and it was probably the best tennis we ever played against each other. The match was filled with scintillating exchanges and went to a third-set tiebreaker before I reeled off eight of the last nine points to win. It was my fourth U.S. Open title, and I had to rally again and again to do it. When I walked into the press room afterward, the reporters applauded me. Then Rosie and I won the doubles title in another epic match.

It doesn't get much better than that. Then I thought, *Maybe it never will.*

When the year-end world rankings were released for 1974, Chrissie was No. 1 and I was No. 2, knocked off the top in the *World Tennis* magazine and Lance Tingay's London *Daily Telgraph* lists for the first time in three years. By then, I felt like I was running out of goals as a tennis player and my priorities had shifted. I announced at a news conference in December 1974 that I intended to leave tournament singles competition in a few weeks. After that, I planned to play only doubles and mixed doubles at a few events because I was juggling three or four full-time careers. "I'm having the time of my life, but it's not fair to the sponsors and the public if I can't give them my best at all times," I said.

I signed a contract with ABC in late 1974 to be a sports commentator. I had a lot to learn about broadcasting, but there was no training provided before they put me on air, so I tried to pick up the technical aspects as I went and booked elocution lessons on my own. I still laugh at how I had to cram for some of my early assignments, like the World Wristwrestling Championships in Petaluma, California.

Some of our World TeamTennis owners wanted to bail after our inaugural year, in part because their cost of player procurement had been driven higher than they expected. We decided to contract by six teams before we started again in 1975, and my Philadelphia team was among them. I agreed to be traded to the New York Sets, and some of our other players were folded into the Boston roster. I eventually took an apartment on West Sixty-Sixth Street, across from Lincoln Center, that had a tennis court in the building, and it became my East Coast home. I could see the American Ballet Theatre rehearsing in the high-rise across the street. I had fallen in love with ballet after I'd seen the Bolshoi and Kirov companies perform on one of the trips I made to Russia.

The West Coast headquarters of King Enterprises had moved to a suite of offices in San Mateo, just south of San Francisco. Larry and

I bought a condo near the office, though we didn't spend much time there since we were both constantly traveling. We now had at least twenty-five employees working on our various businesses, and we were both so busy we wanted something low maintenance. The one exception was a half-Labrador, half–Old English Sheepdog puppy that Randy wanted to give Larry and me that winter. I talked Larry into taking her, and she often came on the road. It was easier to fly with pets then, and we named her Lucy after the Beatles' song "Lucy in the Sky with Diamonds" and the Lucy character in the *Peanuts* comic strip.

One time Larry flew to San Francisco without me, drove to San Mateo, fell asleep at the apartment for a few hours, and then woke up and called out for Lucy. No response. He tried again. Still nothing. That wasn't like her.

Then Larry bolted upright in bed and thought *Oh my God!*, realizing that he'd been so distracted by everything he had to do that he had left Lucy in her airline travel crate at baggage claim. It was another example of how crazy everything was. Larry raced back to the airport, and when he opened the crate door to check on Lucy, she bounded out of the cage wagging her tail.

She lived to be fifteen and a half. The stories she could tell.

IN JANUARY 1975, *Seventeen* magazine released a poll of teenage girls in which I was voted "The World's Most Admired Woman," capturing 37 percent of the vote. Former Israeli Prime Minister Golda Meir was second, followed by Mary Tyler Moore, the Olympic gymnast Olga Korbut, Barbra Streisand, and Chrissie Evert. I was thrilled that three woman athletes were in that elite group, which showed that young people were choosing us as role models.

"This was a tremendous departure from past surveys," Ray Robinson, *Seventeen*'s managing editor, told *Sports Illustrated*. "There is something going on out there with young girls. There are new heroines, but not the high lamas of feminism. It seems to be important to the girls that Billie Jean did it all on her own, just her and that damn tennis racket."

Winning the *Seventeen* poll dovetailed nicely that same month with the first *Women's Superstars* show, a made-for-TV event that we created to bring together the greatest female athletes of the day. It was a two-part competition that consisted of a qualifying round and then the finals. Both aired nationally on ABC. The network already had a male *Superstars* program when Larry took the idea of having a female version to Sidney Schlenker, the vice president and manager of the Houston Astrodome, whom Larry had gotten to know because of the Riggs match. Sid offered the Astrodome as the venue and partnered with us on the *Superstars* fifty-fifty. Then we signed up twenty-three women athletes from eighteen different sports to $1,000 guarantees. When ABC Sports and the sports talent agency IMG found out what we were doing, they tried to stop us. Once they realized we already had so many top women under contract, they offered to sign on with us as coproducers instead, so we were able to demand that the women be given the same prize money as the male superstars. That was a coup that hiked our total available prize money to $69,000, with $34,000 going to our winner.

Many of the women athletes we brought in had never dreamed of being able to chase that kind of payday. Our invitees ran the gamut from four-foot-eleven gymnast Cathy Rigby to the pro tackle football quarterback Barbara O'Brien, the jockey Robyn Smith to the towering volleyball spiker Mary Jo Peppler. We had the golfers Jane Blalock and Sandra Palmer, the surfer Laura Blears Ching, Olympians such as the sprinter Wyomia Tyus, the diver Micki King, and the swimmer Debbie Meyer. We competed in events that were not our specialties, such as an obstacle course, a sixty-yard dash, swimming, and so on. The idea was to show us at our athletic best and perhaps even our most vulnerable. (That would be me in the rowing competition, where I just kept going in circles. I couldn't stop laughing.)

To me, one of the most meaningful things that happened at the Superstars occurred away from the playing field. We knew we were introducing the national audience to many of the athletes, but we were surprised at how many of the women superstars had never heard of each other before they arrived in Houston. (Even today, women's sports receive only about 4 percent of all sports media coverage.) The ABC announcer Donna de Varona, who later served as the Women's Sports Foundation's first president, Jane Blalock, and I organized some social gatherings for the athletes. Our conversations revealed how many of us had experienced the same struggles to make it and how deeply we craved a regular forum to exchange ideas, find fellowship, and access financial support that could help us stay in our games. I felt there was a lot the year-old WSF could do to make all of that happen, and the *Superstars* event helped us sharpen the foundation's mission. Later that year, the WSF established our annual Salute to Women in Sports gala to keep bringing everyone together and raise funds. (In 2020, we held the forty-sixth version as a live-stream event because of the coronavirus pandemic.)

The tennis tour's winter season opened the same month the *Women's Superstars* aired, and it quickly became clear to me that my announced plan to stop playing tournament singles might not stand. For a lot of pressing reasons, retirement would have to wait.

Chapter 22

I DON'T THINK my roles as a businesswoman and a tennis player ever overlapped with as much urgency as I felt in 1975 once a few of our ventures started going sideways. Three young enterprises were now up and running—the magazine, World TeamTennis, and the Women's Sports Foundation—and all three would experience fits and starts. Like most things Larry and I did, we established them to be vehicles for transformative change, so making sure they kept chugging along meant more to me than amassing titles. We thought we could do it all.

The wave I began riding after the Riggs match showed little sign of slowing. For every commitment I turned away, two took its place. We were accomplishing enough to convince me that we had made important inroads, and yet everything remained so fragile I'd think, *I can't stop pushing now.*

I initially planned to play two events in January to say goodbye to tournament singles. I suffered a painful 6–1, 6–1 loss to Chrissie in the first one in San Francisco. I remained upset going into the next tournament—my announced singles swan song—and when I was to play Chrissie again in the final, I told myself if this was indeed it, I was determined to go out fighting. I worked myself into such a pitch I routed her in straight sets, losing only five games. "That's the best I've ever seen her play," Chrissie said. After that, I seriously started questioning if I should step away.

By February 1975, the WTA was considering boycotting the Wimbledon championships over unequal prize money, just as we had discussed the year before. This time, Chrissie embraced the idea. She was now No. 1 in the world, she had just ascended to WTA president, and, at twenty, she was on her own for the first time in her life—no fiancé, no mom traveling with her, no father calling all the shots regarding her career. When reporters asked her where she stood on boycotting Wimbledon, Chrissie said, "I'd like to play at Wimbledon, but not if it throws women's tennis back a few years. What's the point of the WTA if we don't stick together?" Perfect.

Jerry Diamond and I flew to England that month for talks with Wimbledon officials about averting a boycott. Jerry had replaced the WTA's Martin Carmichael as executive director in 1974, and he stayed on the job eleven years. He was one of the best hires the WTA ever made. When Jerry took over we were $35,000 in debt and offered less than $1 million in annual prize money; when he left in 1985, the total pot was $14.2 million. He was a brilliant negotiator, and Ann Jones and I were among those who got to witness that during our Wimbledon discussion with Sir Brian Burnett, chairman of the All England Club.

"Jerry, I'm just going to say a few opening words and then it's all yours," I told him as we traveled to the meeting. "It's the All England Club. It's all men. They don't want to hear from me."

We knew Wimbledon would lose its lucrative contract with NBC if there was another boycott a year after the men stayed away. To show Sir Brian how much leverage and unity we had, Jerry produced a contract that was signed by more than eighty women players, obligating us to compete the following summer in another tournament to be held the same time as Wimbledon. We told Sir Brian the contract for us to skip Wimbledon and play elsewhere would be binding only if the women didn't receive at least 70 percent of the prize money the men were paid at Wimbledon in 1976. The second condition: Our percentage would have to be negotiated upward each succeeding year, until equal prize money was achieved.

Sir Brian accepted the proposal; he had little choice. When we announced that the WTA was calling off its boycott because of the increased prize money we had been promised, I told the media another bit of news: "I'll be playing singles at Wimbledon this year, too."

My change of plans started in earnest when TennisAmerica, our tennis instruction business, developed liabilities of $400,000 after Larry and Dennis Van der Meer hired a Stanford University economics lecturer to run it the previous year. The business filed for bankruptcy in early 1975. (It was eventually bought and revived by Nike.) When Frank Deford came to interview me for a profile in early 1975 I confessed to him that I would probably have to abandon my plan of selective play. I admitted for the first time that I played Chrissie not only to avenge the beating she gave me in our previous final in San Francisco, but because I needed to enter every possible tournament to win enough prize money to keep *womenSports* from folding. "I probably played so well because I had to, for the money," I told Frank.

To Larry and me, TennisAmerica was a business, but *womenSports* and World TeamTennis were our babies. And World TeamTennis was struggling too. It fit my utopian vision of a nonsexist sports world where everything was equal, and I've never given up on the concept. But World TeamTennis lost $12 million in 1975, our first year; that was less than projected but still scary. When we cut the league back from sixteen to ten teams by the start of our second season, only three of the original owners were still in place. We could argue that the league was a good investment because most of the owners who bailed had sold at a profit. But there was no certainty that we'd meet our projection to be out of the red by year four.

Our magazine *womenSports* was considered a success even though it lost a million dollars in its first year, hardly unusual for a start-up. Unlike our involvement in World TeamTennis, though, the money Larry and I were risking on the magazine was mostly our own. Larry eventually found *womenSports* an angel investor, Charter Publications, the owner of *Redbook* and other magazines, and that temporarily saved the day. Larry and I reclaimed ownership three years later when Charter closed the magazine and we relaunched it through the Women's Sports Foundation with the slightly altered title, *Women's Sports*. It lived on another twenty years until Condé Nast bought it in 1998 and folded it into *Self* two years after that.

I had only been making big money for a few years by 1975, and our business misadventures were noticed. There was speculation about how financially overextended I was, and reports of how I was playing "to keep the wolf from the door." As Frank wrote in *SI*, "The unkindest remark going around the tennis community is that Billie Jean may not only be the Jackie Robinson of women's sports, but the Joe Louis as well." It was an allusion to how Louis, the iconic heavy-weight boxing champion, had to go work as a casino greeter in Las Vegas late in life because he had gone broke.

In the same article, Frank wrote about another growing concern of mine: "Some of the interest in her most private life is more than genially searching; it borders on raw inquisition. Alone, perhaps, of any public figure, she has been asked point-blank if she is a Lesbian."

THE SOURCE OF the "inquisition" Frank was referring to was *Playboy*. Joe Hyams was a Hollywood writer and an avid club tennis player who was married to the actress Elke Sommer, and he had written an instruction book with me, *Billie Jean King's Secrets of Winning Tennis,* that we published the year before. The *Playboy* Interview, as it was called, was a major event back then that reached millions of people. Cultural figures from Dr. Martin Luther King Jr. to the Beatles had agreed to do it because of its reach. But only a few women or athletes were asked when Joe approached me. I wanted the opportunity to use the interview to reach men who might not ordinarily hear a woman talking about women's liberation, sports, and politics.

My publicist Pat Kingsley and I discussed the interview before I agreed to do it. I said, "Pat, you know they're going to ask me about my sexuality." She told me she was confident I could handle it. In early 1975 I agreed to the interview, and when Joe asked about sex, I easily dismissed some of his questions, including whether I had ever seen a porn movie, but others made me uncomfortable. Joe mentioned the rumors about my sexual orientation and asked me—on the record—if I was a lesbian. That was a first.

"My sex life is no one's business," I said, echoing the same pat answer that many publicists at the time, including mine, gave. I should have stopped there. But I added, "If I don't answer your question, people will think I have something to hide . . . [so] I'll give you the answer. No, I'm not a lesbian. That's not even in the ballpark for me."

It was yet another example of the mental gymnastics I was doing at the time regarding my sexuality. Today, after forty years of loving Ilana, I know I am a lesbian. But before that, I told myself that declaring what I was came down to labels, and I wasn't willing to accept any of them with any finality. I was attracted to both women and men, so I didn't think of myself as a lesbian. When I was on and off again with Larry, which was still happening, I'd say I was straight.

I went on to tell Joe that I believed everybody should feel free to live however they wanted, as long as they didn't hurt anybody. "I'm for liberation at all levels," I said, "be it gay liberation or whatever."

That, at least, was true. But even that assertion was freighted with the unspoken reality of my life: I wanted my own liberation. My torment over my lack of clarity and having to hide the truth again led me to discuss with close friends the idea of going public about my sexuality. Everyone warned me not to do it. Ellen Merlo, who had ascended to brand manager for Virginia Slims, still believed that coming out would hurt the tour and destroy my post-retirement prospects in broadcasting as well as tennis. That was crushing to hear, even though I thought she was right. The *Playboy* interview drove me deeper into my closet. And it was starting to feel as if the walls were closing in.

It has taken a lot of therapy for me to understand the role that my own homophobia played in my reasoning. Though it may be a shock to straight people, the societal bias against LGBTQ+ people is ingrained in many of us, too, particularly in people from older generations. Some of us are still reluctant to talk freely about our sexuality. It's a legacy of so many things, including not knowing if you could trust anyone with the information. People in the closet often take consolation in the idea that at least they're controlling who knows the truth, when the real truth is that the closet is controlling them.

I'm still working on it. Even now, I sometimes get a churning in my gut when I talk about being a lesbian. The word itself can make me uncomfortable because for most of my life the words *lesbian* or *dyke* were hurled as a slur. I prefer using the word *gay* because it's a happy, joyful word, the nicest kind of double entendre.

Elton, who is three years younger than me, was wrestling with the same dilemma. He is gay, and married to David Furnish now, and they have two children. But as a younger man, Elton was attracted to both men and women. He discussed his sexuality publicly for the first time in a *Rolling Stone* article that was published in 1976, the year after my *Playboy* interview. "There's nothing wrong with going to bed with somebody of your own sex," Elton said. "I think everybody's bisexual to a certain degree. I don't think it's just me. It's not a bad thing to be."

The remark was poorly received. Elton was one of the biggest rock stars on the planet at the time, but according to *Rolling Stone,* hate mail started pouring in. He battled drug and alcohol addictions for years and, like me, had food issues. His career suffered as a result of merely peeking out of the closet. It was yet another warning that the world wasn't ready to accept us for who we were. And to my own detriment, neither was I.

I DEVELOPED my lifelong habit of announcing goals like wanting to be No. 1 or, in 1975, chasing my sixth Wimbledon singles title, because it usually made me perform better. I put in the work and by the end of June 1975 I had never felt more fit. I was told after I arrived at Wimbledon that I could achieve a couple of significant records. If I won my sixth singles title, I'd tie the career total of the great Suzanne Lenglen, as well as match Elizabeth Ryan's overall mark of nineteen Wimbledon titles (all of them in doubles).

Margaret was back after giving birth to a daughter, and her game was starting to peak again. In the semifinals she lost to Evonne. Chrissie had taken the first set from me easily in our semifinal match, and during the changeover I had a sharp talk with myself. I was trying to savor every moment, thinking this could be my last time on Centre Court, and it was hurting me. When I came out for the second set I was literally snarling. I snapped at the umpire, snapped at the line judges, and stomped around the baseline seething energy. I recaptured my form. I took the second set by the same wide margin that Chrissie won the first.

In the third, I was down 0–3, 15–40, and fighting for my life again in a service game that kept slipping back and forth to deuce before I finally held. I would win the next five games to take the match, but just as I began my roll, Jimmy Connors caused a commotion in the stands by arriving with the actress Susan George on his arm (she was still living with the singer Jack Jones at the time).

Though Chrissie and Jimmy had broken off their engagement, they were still seeing each other on occasion and she didn't know there was another woman. Chrissie insisted afterward that she didn't see them—she was too classy to detract from my win, and she didn't want to feed the papers' appetite for scandal—but years later, she admitted, "Oh, I saw them all right. Flashbulbs were going off. People were standing up. You couldn't miss it." Her concentration was broken and she never quite got it back. The fans were so astonished by my comeback they kept roaring and clapping for me long after we left. I had to retrace my steps and run back out into the stadium to take a curtain call. Everyone was still jammed around Centre Court.

Two days later, still riding that high, I swamped Evonne in thirty-eight minutes for the title, surrendering just one game. It was the closest I've ever come to a perfect match.

Arthur Ashe, who like me was thirty-one, faced Connors the next day in another battle of the generations, and I watched Arthur crush Jimmy in four sets. Some reporters suggested that it was karma coming back to bite Jimmy in the butt. In addition to the stir with Chrissie, Jimmy had sued the ATP after being banned from Roland-Garros, and the case was still pending when Arthur, the ATP's first president, beat him.

It was stirring to see Arthur become the first Black man to win the Wimbledon singles title, and we had fun dancing together at the Wimbledon Ball. "What a great way to end my career here," I told the press, insisting again that I was done as a tournament singles player. I honestly thought that was it. When the U.S. Open rolled around in late August, I wasn't in the singles draw. But the tournament would be best remembered for something else, because it shaped the next generation of our tour.

MARTINA NAVRATILOVA WAS BORN in Prague in 1956 at the height of the Cold War and the Soviet occupation of Czechoslovakia. She came from a tennis family. Her grandmother had been the country's No. 2–ranked player before World War II, and Martina's mom, Jana, was a tennis player as well as a gymnast and ski instructor. Martina's father, who was also a skier, left Jana when Martina was three. Martina was raised by Jana's second husband, Mirek Navratil, and took his last name. Mirek also played tennis and encouraged Martina to compete. She was a national champion by age fifteen.

Chrissie and I had looked out for Martina ever since she joined the U.S. circuit in early 1973. Chrissie knew what it was like to be young and under the microscope. Martina and Chrissie played doubles together for a while and I became an informal coach and mentor to Martina. By that summer of 1975, she had grown incredibly powerful and stood five feet eight. But she was at least twenty pounds overweight, which I could relate to. She was also a deeply emotional player, which could hurt her as much as help her. She was already chewing out umpires and line judges. Besides tweaking her backhand, I wanted to encourage her to learn self-discipline, something I had also lacked at her age as I battled both my temper and my weight.

When Martina first started playing in the States, tournament announcers would inevitably mangle her name: "And from Czechoslovakia . . . Marina Navatova!"

"Mar-TI-na Nav-RA-TIL-ova!" she'd yell back in frustration.

"Don't worry," I told her as we were playing doubles together at a tournament in Chicago. "Just keep winning. They'll learn to pronounce your name."

Everyone could see that Martina had the potential to be a star in women's tennis. She was an incredible all-around athlete, an acrobatic serve-and-volleyer with great hands and speed. She went on a winning streak in 1974 that included a straight-set victory over Margaret in the Australian Open quarterfinals. Some weeks later, as the two of us were sharing a ride in Detroit, I told Martina, "You know, you could be the best player ever."

She blinked and said, "You really think so?"

"Yes," I told her. "You're smart. You're an amazing athlete physically. But you have to really, really work for it. Just think about it."

Martina's lifestyle and independent spirit irritated the top Czech tennis federation officials who controlled her visas and travel. (Czech athletes had to return their passports when they reentered the country.) Martina fell in love with the trappings of Western capitalism—Gucci bags, Mercedes sports cars, McDonald's Big Macs. Her Czech handlers didn't like that, or how she was spending time with Chrissie and me. They grew irritated at Martina's other little rebellions, like not staying at the same hotels as her fellow Eastern Bloc players or delaying her return home once to play an extra U.S. tournament. The Czech officials told Martina she was becoming too Americanized and assigned the Czech coach Vera Sukova to be her chaperone. They almost didn't let Martina play in the 1975 U.S. Open, until her countryman, Jan Kodes, intervened for her.

By the time she arrived in New York that year, Martina had talked to Chrissie and me about wanting to defect to the West. We both avoided influencing her decision. There was too much at stake. She was just eighteen. The Berlin Wall was still intact. Who knew if or when she'd be able to see her family again if she left? What if she were injured and couldn't make a living in tennis?

Martina knew the dangers, but she was determined. Her parents had been allowed to travel with her to Wimbledon in 1975, but once there, Mirek and Jana backed out of defecting as a family. After that, Martina again contacted her manager and lawyer Fred Barman, who was based in Los Angeles. (Fred had helped us cofound World TeamTennis.) He set up a series of clandestine meetings for Martina with FBI and U.S. immigration officials in New York City during the Open. This time, she planned to seek asylum on her own. She feared that Czech officials would not let her leave the country again because they had ordered her to return home immediately after Forest Hills.

Only a few of us knew what Martina was considering, and we were afraid she would be snatched, drugged, and thrown on a plane back to Czechoslovakia. Stories like that floated around. The night that she lost to Chrissie in the U.S. Open semifinals, Martina and Fred went to the customs office in New York after hours and did some asylum paperwork. The next morning, Martina was awoken at 7:30 by the phone. The first call was from a CBS news crew, asking her for an interview in the hotel lobby right away. "Now?" Martina said. She didn't know why they called her. As soon as she hung up, the phone rang again. This time it was Vera Sukova crying, "How could you do it? Why did you defect?"

Vera told Martina there was a story about it in *The Washington Post* and that she was coming to talk Martina out of her decision, which touched off a panic. Martina called Fred, who told her, "Get out of there! Now!" She left the room with nothing and was standing in an alley near the hotel with something covering her head when Jeanie Brinkman, the Virginia Slims publicity director, scooped her up in a taxi. They stayed at Jeanie's Greenwich Village apartment until they took another taxi to Forest Hills a few hours later for a hastily arranged news conference. Jeanie figured they'd be safer there because of the security.

I didn't know something was happening that morning until I saw Martina walking around the Forest Hills clubhouse with Howard Cosell. I thought, *Oh my God, she did it*. Minutes later, Martina was standing in front of an enormous bank of photographers and reporters explaining how she thought the Czech Communist government was trying to control her life and stifle her career. Every time she showed a hint of emotion the camera shutters fired noisily in unison. She said she felt she had to leave and was grateful for the chance to live in America. "You don't know what you've got here," she told reporters.

"What's that?" asked one.

"Freedom," Martina said.

I was happy that Martina chose to defect, but it would be years before she was reunited with her parents and younger sister, and her beloved grandmother died before she could see her again. Martina moved in with Fred and his daughter, Shari, in Los Angeles and all of us on the tour became her extended family. Martina traveled with FBI protection for the first six months after she defected. Despite all the challenges, she still developed into the best all-around singles, doubles, and mixed-doubles player we've ever had. She and Chrissie would have a historic rivalry that is unsurpassed in individual sports for longevity, import, or drama. It lasted sixteen years and featured eighty matches between them. They ended with eighteen Grand Slam singles titles each.

People often ask me if I'm jealous that later generations have earned more or had it easier than we did, and I always say, "Not on your life." My reward has been watching women athletes who are freer now to concentrate on optimum performance rather than worrying about making a living or creating places to play. Chrissie and Martina were the first generation of women tennis pros who lived out the dreams my generation had about what the modern female athlete could be. Today, Ilana and I help other women athletes in sports including soccer, ice hockey, and cricket to grow their games. Yet tennis remains the leader in women's sports. Tennis has shown what's possible, and remains a model that other sports emulate.

Chapter 23

I SPENT MUCH of my next few years in tennis feeling like a woman plucking the petals off the daisy: *I'm going to stop playing singles. I'm not. I am. I'm not.* I would think I was done playing, then have a good practice with a tour player and the yearning would be back. No matter how much you know it's time to pass the torch, some residue of joy or ego, sadness or ambition, not to mention love—probably all of that—gets tapped back into, and you change your mind. Or at least I did. For much of my life nothing provided as much fun or sanctuary as performing on a tennis court.

After I won at Wimbledon in 1975, I made the mistake of listening to outside influences and giving in to the notion of going out on top. I skipped the U.S. Open when Martina defected because my knees had had it. A lot of the reporters there didn't believe me when I again said I was done with singles. One scoffed, "Frank Sinatra is always retiring and then coming back."

"Yeah," I told him, "but you don't sing with your knees."

I told myself if I quit then, I'd finally have the time to do things I'd always wanted to do. I bought a piano intending to get back into playing classical music. I wanted to take Spanish lessons. My love of dance had been rekindled when I met Dina Makarova, a photographer and writer who did some work for World TeamTennis as a Russian interpreter. Dina was the one who had taken me to see the Bolshoi and Kirov ballets when we were in Russia. Now she was writing a biography of Natalia Makarova (no relation), a prima ballerina who had defected to the West in the 1960s. Dina took me one day to see Mikhail Baryshnikov and Natalia dance *Swan Lake,* and again, I was captivated. I've always thought the feeling an athlete gets of shaping time and space isn't all that different from what a dancer must feel. There's a grace and a rhythm, a freedom and beauty involved that intrinsically appealed to me.

At about the same time, I was invited to meet another artist who fascinated me—Charles M. Schulz, the creator of *Peanuts*. Like tens of millions of other Americans, I had been a devoted fan of his comic strip for years. (At its height, *Peanuts* was syndicated in seventy-five countries and read by an estimated 355 million people.) Snoopy, the tennis-playing beagle, was my favorite character. Naturally, I related to Peppermint Patty, who was way ahead of her time when she was introduced in 1966. She could play sports better than any boy. I also had a huge soft spot for Charlie Brown, the shy, lovable kid who just wanted to belong and didn't care if he played with boys or with girls, as long as he could get into the game. Charlie Brown was a feminist, like his creator and alter ego. "I guess Charlie Brown *is* mostly me," Schulz once admitted.

I first started to recognize the inclusive message in *Peanuts* in 1973 after Bobby Riggs popped up in a Sunday panel devoted to how upset Lucy was that Riggs beat Margaret Court in the Mother's Day Massacre. After I defeated Bobby in the Battle of the Sexes that September, I began turning up in the strip, too. In March 1974, I opened my morning newspaper to find Peppermint Patty's little pal, Marcie, yelling at Patty to get off Snoopy's doghouse perch. Patty looks down and says, "Marcie, has anyone ever told you that when you're mad, you look just like Billie Jean King?" I couldn't stop laughing because it was true.

World TeamTennis had arrived in the Bay Area that spring, and Schulz became one of our biggest fans. He would regularly drive down from his home in Marin County to watch the Golden Gaters play in the Oakland Coliseum—Ilana was a young player on that team and remembers him well—and he made a point to come see me play, too, when I was in town with the New York Sets. Schulz and I didn't meet until Eva Auchincloss was putting together a board of trustees for the Women's Sports Foundation and asked me to accompany her to Schulz's Santa Rosa home for a meeting. The first thing

I noticed was his warm smile and crinkly blue eyes behind his large glasses. "You can call me Sparky," he said. As a baby he had been nicknamed after a cartoon horse named Spark Plug. Only people who didn't know him called him Charles or Charlie, he explained.

Sparky was a caring, unassuming man. He accepted the trustee position on the spot and supported the foundation and women's sports vigorously. He took me to his studio the first day we met and showed me where he illustrated his comic strip, which was a treat. Over the years I visited him often in Santa Rosa and we became dear friends. Ice hockey was among the many sports Sparky loved, and we'd talk for hours at the ice rink near his house, where he ordered the same lunch every day: a tuna fish sandwich, root beer, and a chocolate chip cookie. Sometimes I'd hit with him on the home tennis court he built, and I came to know his wife, Jeannie. He illustrated posters for the foundation, attended our board meetings, and hosted the Snoopy Cup and other tennis legends events that Rosie's company organized. I wrote the foreword for volume 12 of *The Complete Peanuts,* his definitive collection.

For twelve days in the autumn of 1979, Sparky used *Peanuts* to push for gender equality and forcefully call out the NCAA because Title IX was being debated again. He relied on research from the Women's Sports Foundation to show the huge imbalances between women's and men's collegiate sports but ended the storyline hopefully: "I think the day is coming when women will achieve equality in sports," Peppermint Patty tells Marcie.

In subsequent years, Sparky would mention me in *Peanuts* again, often with one of his characters saying some variation of perhaps Billie Jean would give them a call. I always took it as a sign I needed to phone Sparky, and so I did.

Larry and I were getting along better than we had since the early days of our marriage now that I'd slid back into my transition plan of playing only doubles. I was more relaxed. He was running World TeamTennis and I loved how he focused daily on that job instead of chasing a dozen other projects. We were spending a lot of time in the New York apartment and almost had a routine. In the mornings we walked our dog in Central Park. Sometimes we stopped for warm bagels. Later in the day we might take in the latest movie. I loved the rhythm I'd fallen into away from tennis—until I got to Wimbledon in June 1976.

I spent that week hitting with Chrissie and Martina before the championships, and even routed Chrissie in a practice one day while helping her prepare for the tournament as she'd once helped me prepare for Roland-Garros. When we were done, Chrissie motioned to me to meet her at the net and said quietly, "Billie! How can you not be out there this year?" Skipping singles at Wimbledon in 1976 remains probably the biggest regret of my professional tennis life.

When I got back to the New York Sets after Wimbledon, I resumed playing singles again, not just doubles. I was so glad I did. The Sets advanced to the World TeamTennis finals opposite the San Francisco Golden Gaters, and they were to be played the same week I had agreed to coach and play for the U.S. Fed Cup team. Some bicoastal flights and overnight drives were required for me to make both competitions. But our teams ended up taking both titles. Not bad for a thirty-two-year-old sometime "retiree" who was icing her knees during some changeovers. On the final weekend of Fed Cup and the World TeamTennis final I had played five matches in forty-eight hours—eight pressure-saturated sets of singles and doubles—without dropping a set.

Though both titles were hugely important to me, most of the media attention and live television coverage was focused on another tournament in the town of South Orange, New Jersey, which was ninety miles away from our Fed Cup site. The Slims publicity director, Jeanie Brinkman, was among the first to be alerted that something was happening there when a reporter called her one day and said, "Do you know there's a man playing the women's tour?"

Jeanie said, "Are you nuts?"

WHEN FORTY-ONE-YEAR-OLD Renée Richards turned up at the Tennis Week Open in South Orange, plenty of questions were raised that sports and society continue to grapple with today. When the rules for tennis and other sports were written, nobody thought about questions such as, Can a player compete as a woman if she had been born a male? Can hormone therapy and sex-reassignment surgery turn one sex into another? Is gender what you are assigned when you were born, or what you self-identify as later? What mix of physiological, psychological, and social forces are in play?

Before undergoing sex-reassignment surgery in 1975—an exceedingly rare procedure in those days—Renée had been known as Dr. Richard Raskind, a junior champion in high school and captain of the Yale tennis team who later served in the Navy, qualified five times for the U.S. Championships, and went on to build a career as a brilliant ophthalmological surgeon based in New York City.

Raskind seemed to have everything going for him—a thriving practice, a beautiful wife and young son, scads of dear friends who loved him—but he was also harboring a secret. Ever since he was a child, he had felt he was a female trapped in a man's body. He started crossdressing as a woman during college. Later, he began a course of hormone therapy, which was relatively new, and traveled to Morocco intending to continue transitioning—then canceled. When he again thought he couldn't continue as a man any longer, he got a divorce. After completing her transition, Renée—she chose the name because it's French for "reborn"—moved to California to start a new life with a new identity. She kept the details private from all but a few friends.

One of the first people to recognize her there was an old acquaintance from her amateur days, Bobby Riggs. When Bobby saw a six-foot-two woman practicing at the John Wayne Tennis Club in Newport Beach, he ambled over for a closer look through those thick glasses of his because he thought he recognized that distinctive forehand. When Bobby got close enough, he said, "Oh, it's you!" Though he hadn't seen Dick for years, there had been rumors.

In July 1976, Renée entered and won an important amateur tournament in San Diego. One of the losing players recognized her and tipped off a local reporter. The story made international headlines, and Renée was soon the most famous transsexual since Christine Jorgensen went public in the 1950s.

Jorgensen was an important person in LGBTQ+ history. Before she died in 1989, her advocacy for transgender rights and insistence

on living an out life contributed greatly to society's changing definition of sexuality, and the recognition that it can be something that
is not necessarily binary, or even static. Christine sparked important conversations about how, psychologically, some people's gender identity can be different than their biological sex. That kind of
public dialogue wasn't happening in America before she came along.
The fact that she professed herself to be happy in her new life made
an impact too.

Unlike Christine, Renée has always called herself a "reluctant
crusader." That changed when the USTA and the Women's Tennis Association banned her from all their tournaments, including
the U.S. Open. Renée said she never had any intention of playing
the Open *until* they told her she couldn't. She had gone through
an agonizing series of operations and hormone therapy and untold
emotional turbulence to be who she was. She owned a U.S. passport
that said she was female. She was licensed to practice medicine as a
female. What right did tennis officials have to reject her?

Renée told a writer from *womenSports* she wanted to show the
world she wasn't a "two-headed monster. A transexual, or anyone different, any minority, can still be a socially acceptable person." Gladys
interviewed Renée for *World Tennis* magazine as well and became
one of her earliest supporters. Another ally was Renée's friend Gene
Scott, who invited her to play his event in South Orange, and then
refused to back down even after Jerry Diamond, the WTA's executive director, pulled the event's sanction and most of the top players
withdrew. Renée's debut there was a spectacle. Howard Cosell called
her matches on TV, a capacity crowd of 3,200 was on hand, and hundreds of media members clamored to interview her. Hoping to add
a little levity and simultaneously underscore her determination not
to be cowed, Renée accepted Gene's offer to make an entrance by
arriving for her first match in his Rolls-Royce. "I'm here to make
a point," Renée told reporters. "It's a human rights issue. I want to
show that someone who has a different lifestyle or medical condition
has a right to stand up for what they are."

Renée made it to the semifinals, and the crowd gave her a standing ovation as she left the court when she lost. Renée cried, feel-

ing that she'd nonetheless let people down. She received hundreds of letters from all kinds of people, some of them hateful, more of them supportive, and many of them heartbreaking accounts of the discrimination and challenges they endured. (Significant hurdles remain. The 2015 U.S. Transgender Survey, the largest survey of transgender people in the U.S. to date, found that 81.7 percent of the respondents reported seriously thinking about suicide in their lifetimes, and 40.4 percent reported actually attempting suicide. Ninety-eight percent of those who experienced four or more instances of violence in the past year said they considered suicide that same year.)

Once Renée set her sights on the 1976 U.S. Open, the tournament committee announced a new rule requiring every woman entered to submit to a chromosome test to determine if they were genetically female. I felt the requirement was wrong then and I feel the same now. Renée refused the test and started a controversial legal battle for the right to play.

My instinct was to wait to take a public position until we learned more about the science and subject of sex reassignment, and I said so at one heated WTA meeting about Renée. (Today, many trans people prefer the term "gender confirmation" surgery over the term "sex reassignment.") At the start, the women players were almost unanimously opposed to allowing her on the circuit. Many people said they were worried that letting her compete would open the floodgates for other transgender players who were younger and stronger. Some even said that men would have the surgeries (it's actually a grueling *series* of surgeries) just to compete in women's tennis, which was absurd. It was more proof that ignorance breeds fear and contempt.

By March 1976, Renée was still snared in her legal battle and my knees felt strong enough to play tournaments again after another knee surgery. I asked the WTA to grant me a wild-card entry into the Virginia Slims singles championships in New York that month, and they initially said yes—then they said no. I was upset about their change of heart, so I decided to enter an unsanctioned four-tournament series that Gladys was running called the Lionel Cup. Gladys, generous as ever, had also offered a slot to Renée. The

WTA was not happy that I was breaking their boycott of Renée. That was okay with me. I wasn't too happy with them, either. Now that I was possibly going to play against Renée, I had to figure out my public stance on the issue of transgender players on the tour. I wanted to hear from Renée first, so I called her and said, "I need to meet you."

A friend of Renée's loaned us her apartment for our first conversation. We talked for four hours. Renée was open and warm and funny. She's a wonderful storyteller. She told me how she had always known she was female, and how she tried to overcompensate by taking up aggressive sports and acting macho in public. In private, she sometimes wore her sister's dresses. Her whole life had been a denial of her authentic self, and she finally couldn't live that way anymore. She fought depression and suicidal thoughts.

I was full of questions and, because Renée is a doctor, she was able to describe in clinical detail how her body had changed since her transition. Because of the removal of her testes and years of estrogen therapy, she was physiologically identical to a woman who had been through a hysterectomy and had her ovaries removed. Her muscles had lost their mass and were actually less efficient at supporting her large frame than most women of her height and weight. Renée weighed only 147 pounds, and she was nowhere near as powerful as Richard had been. The only thing about her that wasn't female was the Y chromosome lingering in her cells. Beyond that, doctors I spoke with confirmed to me she was physiologically female. By the time we parted ways that day, I was convinced that Renée was a woman.

As it turned out, we didn't take the court together until the second tournament that Gladys sponsored, this one in Port Washington, New York. I was entering singles and doubles, and so I asked Renée if she would be my partner. I knew my colleagues at the WTA would flip out, but she was becoming my friend, she was about to be thrown back into the maw of the New York media, and I wanted to make a very public show of support for her. I was thirty-three and Renée was forty-three and we didn't even have a chance to practice together before our first match because I got stuck in traffic, but we played like a couple of kids. At one point Renée foot-faulted on a serve and I turned around and joked, "Renée? Don't do that." She broke up laughing.

Renée was an incredibly smart player, and we rolled all the way to the semifinals. The day of that match, however, Renée had the flu. At several junctures she turned to me and said she wasn't sure she could play on. Every time, I told her, "Keep going . . . You're fine, Renée." (Easy for me to say.) We won the first set, but now she was panting when we sat down on the changeover and she told me, "Billie, I'm burning up." Again, I prodded her to keep going. "I won Wimbledon with a fever of 104!" I goaded her. She got up and limped through a few more games, but at the next changeover she was practically sprawling on the ground. That's when I turned to the stands, which were filled with her friends from Long Island, and shouted, "This is the last time I'm *ever* playing with a Jewish American princess!"

That drew huge laughs, including from Renée. She straggled back to her feet, we won the match and, thanks to her determination, we went on to win the tournament.

IN RENÉE'S LEGAL CASE against the USTA and WTA, her lawyers argued that the organizations were violating New York State's human rights laws against gender discrimination. She asked for a restraining order to prevent them from barring her from the 1977 U.S. Open. The case was heard in New York Supreme Court, with affidavits from doctors and other experts on both sides of the issue. Some of the tropes the USTA and WTA's attorneys invoked were stunning to read in a formal legal document. In one court filing, they wrote,

> We have reason to believe there are 10,000 transsexuals in the United States and many more female impersonators or imposters. The total number of such persons throughout the world is not known. Because of the millions of dollars in prize money available to competitors, because of the nationalistic desires to

excel in athletics, and because of world-wide experiments, especially in the iron curtain countries, to produce athletic stars
by any means undreamed of a few years ago, the USTA has
been especially sensitive to its obligation to assure fairness of
competition.

Seriously? The WTA and USTA attorneys were suggesting
that an army of Eastern Bloc drag queens might be rounded up
from every gay bar and cabaret between East Berlin and Moscow
and then trained for peak athletic performance to rake in millions
in tennis prize money, all for the glory of the Communist state?
They were equating transsexual people to "experiments." That was
unacceptable.

There was no recognition of the profound and complex factors
that push someone to declare a different gender identity than the
sex he or she had been assigned at birth, or the many surgical procedures, long-term psychological screening, counseling, and medical interventions necessary when someone goes through what Renée
did. Renée later wrote two books detailing her life and transition,
and portions are difficult reading. For me, trying to imagine the pain
and sense of displacement, the long recoveries, the feeling of being
in-process until the long journey is over, is heartrending. I can't
imagine people getting gender confirmation surgery merely because
they can. They do it because they can't bear *not* to go forward with it.

A few officials and players, including Frankie and Vicki Berner,
argued against Renée in the same court filing, claiming that she
would have an unfair advantage because she was born a male.

I submitted an affidavit that supported Renée and argued the
opposite: "From my observation of Dr. Richards and experience
with her on the court, as well as my total knowledge of the sport of
tennis, she does not enjoy physical superiority or strength so as to
have an advantage over women competitors."

On August 16, 1977, Judge Alfred M. Ascione found that Renée's
human rights had been violated by the USTA and WTA and
declared, "This person is now a female." She was cleared to play the
U.S. Open, which was now just days away.

Right after Renée won her case, I went to another WTA meeting and said to Chrissie, Rosie, Frankie, and the others, "Look. Renée is a woman, she's going to play and we should welcome her. And besides, she's great. You're going to love her."

I don't know if Chrissie knew I had used similar language when she was sixteen and our veteran players were icing her out. I wonder now if Alice Marble had a comparable talk with the other white players before she walked Althea Gibson through the gates of Forest Hills when Althea broke the color barrier there in 1950.

At the 1977 U.S. Open, Renée had the bad luck to draw Virginia Wade in the first round, to whom she lost. Renée and Betty Ann Stuart did advance to the doubles final before falling to Martina and Betty Stöve. What a thrill it was to see Renée contend for the title after her long fight and hear the band playing while the trophies were handed out. She retired in 1981 and coached Martina for a while. Renée is still a good friend, not to mention the best ophthalmologist Ilana and I have ever had.

I CONTINUE TO WORK hard to keep apprised of the latest ethics, science, and thinking about gender identity and expression, sexual orientation, and transgender rights, especially as they apply to the right to play sports. Figuring out the best way to include and protect the interests of all the athletes involved remains a hot-button discussion at all levels of competition. It's hard to see how we can arrive at a one-size-fits-all policy.

The Women's Sports Foundation tracks the transgender issue and publishes position papers and guides for athletes, parents, and sports organizations. What we know is constantly evolving, and so are the arguments about how to keep competition fair and yet available for everyone. Right now we have more questions than answers. How do we measure what physical advantages remain after trans athletes transition? What kind of testing or parameters should we have, if any at all? How should those standards change from sport to sport? Should trans athletes *have* to out themselves in order to compete? Remember, not everyone lives in a safe environment where being transgender is accepted or free of repercussions.

Defining the rules for hyperandrogenous (or intersex) athletes, people who are born with the anatomical or hormonal characteristics of both a male and female, is also challenging. In 2018, the Women's Sports Foundation honored the South African track world champion Caster Semenya for her accomplishments and example after she was ordered by the track and field's world governing body, the IAAF, to submit to hormone suppression therapy if she wanted to compete. Can you imagine someone trying to reverse-engineer Michael Jordan because he jumped too high or the Olympic champion Katie Ledecky because she swims too fast?

The IAAF said Semenya's naturally occurring testosterone levels exceed what a woman "should" have. But the IAAF has no such limit on how much naturally occurring testosterone a man can have. Apparently, the IAAF believes you can be too much of a woman but never too much of a man.

"This is the only area of sports I know where people are asked to undergo unnecessary medical intervention in order to compete," Katrina Karkazis, a bioethicist from Yale, told me. Katrina has consulted with the United Nations, the Women's Sports Foundation, and Semenya during her fight. Katrina added, "The IAAF acts as if the side effects of hormone suppression therapy are benign, and they're not."

The IAAF has been trying to police Caster ever since she won her first 800-meter world title in 2009 at age eighteen in a scorching time. Back then, word was leaked to the press that she was hyperandrogenous. It was a grievous violation of her privacy, and she didn't confirm the report. She won a temporary injunction lifting the hormone therapy order in 2010, but the IAAF successfully fought to reinstate it. As I write this, the IAAF has kept up its efforts to police Caster, most recently by passing rules that targeted only her events, the 400, 800, and 1,500 meters. Caster initially planned to adjust by trying to qualify for the Olympic Games in the 200-meter sprint, a steep challenge. However, she ended 2020 ranked 165th in the world, despite many top athletes sitting out the year due to the coronavirus pandemic. In February 2021, Caster, then thirty, filed an application to the European Court of Human Rights in a last-ditch bid to save her career and avert having to take more hormone suppression medication. If successful, she said she'd try for her third consecutive 800-meter medal at the Tokyo Summer Olympics, which were pushed back from 2020 to 2021; if denied, she'd attempt a long-shot bid in the 5,000. No ruling came. She missed the Games.

In my view, science matters, and research shows that there is no single biological measure that irrefutably places every human into one of two categories—male or female. The functions of genes and hormones in determining sex characteristics have been found to be more complicated than scientists knew in the 1970s. That's why a chromosome test or testosterone count or the sex a person is assigned at birth (most often by a visual examination) is not and should not be the sole determinant of gender.

It's incredibly tricky to know how this should apply to sports participation. As I write this, there is scant scientific research regarding the performance of transgender or intersex athletes. Until there is, we don't know if other athletes' concerns that they're at a competitive disadvantage are reasonable.

For now, the United States, like many countries, has no consistent state or national policies. Many cases wind up in court. In 2020, the Connecticut high school association's position as it was being sued for allowing transgender track athletes to compete was that multiple federal courts and government agencies have acknowledged that the term *sex* is "ambiguous," and historical usage of the word "has not kept pace with contemporary science, advances in medical knowledge and societal norms." In August 2020, Martina was among those who maintained that trans athletes' inclusion could pose an existential threat to women's sports. She was one of 309 athletes who signed a letter to the NCAA expressing support for an Idaho law that bans transgender female student athletes from competing in women's and girls' sports.

Still other sports federations from the high school to international level have passed rules mandating that trans athletes must finish gender confirmation surgery, or transgender and intersex athletes must take hormone suppression therapy before they can compete. The World Medical Association and the United Nations High Commissioner for Human Rights pushed back against such forced medical interventions in the summer of 2020, taking the position that they are a violation of an athlete's human rights. On that point, I firmly agree.

Nobody should make a decision about altering an athlete's body or decide their gender identity except that person. My hope and goal is that we can arrive at policies for intersex, trans, and cisgender athletes that protect everyone's right to play while also ensuring fair and safe competition. Championing everyone's human rights and factoring in the ethics and science involved is the correct thing to do.

Chapter 24

THE CONTRAST BETWEEN my clarity about Renée's situation and my long-running conflict about my own sexuality was an irony not lost on me. Here I was, terribly afraid of being exposed but pushing ahead to take a public stand for Renée even though it could attract more attention to my closeted existence. "Gay by association" was a common assumption then, and I used to get impatient late in my career when other players endured speculation about whether they were gay merely because they partnered with me. I thought, *Does this mean I can never have a female friend? Well, does it?*

I continued hiding my sexuality throughout the 1970s. I paid a steep price for that in my health and my relationships. At one point my stomach problems became so bothersome my doctor told me I might be developing ulcers, and he put me on a bland diet. Just about all I could eat was soft tortillas with a little butter. I was constantly on one diet or another because my weight fluctuated with my emotions. When I was still playing I might follow a strict 2,200-calorie-a-day regime. Then, when I had a tough loss, I might tell myself, *Forget it. I want a Big Mac.* My emotions often led to angry outbursts. Sometimes my moods could be overwhelming, especially if I was overtired—which was most of the time.

Rosie says I had gained a reputation among the other players for blowing matches because of my temper. Tennis officials often took the brunt of my anger. In Japan I got angry once over a really bad line call in a doubles match that Julie Anthony and I were playing. Julie was horrified when I literally threatened to "kill" the linesman if he didn't leave right after the match. I disrespectfully blew off an official dinner later that night, and when Julie came to check on me, she found me limping around because I had kicked something. She sat with me all night until I calmed down.

I lost another final in Austin, Texas, to Chrissie after another bad line call—this one on match point. Larry was there and ran ahead to the women's locker room and yelled, "Everyone out! Get out! She's going to go ballistic." He knew me, all right. The room was deserted when I got inside. I sent my rackets helicoptering into a set of lockers and they went clattering to the floor.

Peachy Kellmeyer, the first fulltime employee of the WTA and our first Virginia Slims tour director, reined me in sometimes. Peachy, whose given first names are Fern Lee, is a small but formidable West Virginian who speaks with a country drawl. Her good manners disguise that she has a spine of steel. Peachy had been a junior tennis champion in the 1950s and played in the U.S. Nationals at the age of fifteen. Later, she became the first woman to play for the men's Division I tennis squad at the University of Miami as well as the women's team. As a coach and physical education director at Florida's Marymount College, she also made history by successfully fighting to remove a rule barring scholarships for athletes at women's colleges. She's been a great advocate for equal opportunity and a defender of Title IX her entire career.

Peachy was also the only tournament director who never ticked me off when she came onto the court because I knew she was fair to everyone. She was also strong enough to stand up to me and even make me like her for it. That happened when we were playing a Slims tournament in Mission Viejo, California, at a tennis center surrounded by grass-covered hills. I was playing horribly against Robin Tenney in the first round and growing angrier with myself with each mistake. So I took it out on the balls. Every time I'd lose a point I'd knock a ball over the fence and into the hills. I was hitting moonshots. Pretty soon, all the ball kids were in the tall grass trying to find the balls and I was down to one ball—at which point I saw Peachy calmly walking out.

"Oh, hi Peach!" I said, thinking, *Here we go . . .*

"You cannot do that, Billie Jean," she said.

"I don't have a choice, Peach—I'm going crazy out here."

"Well, I'm not going to give you new balls. You'll have to serve with just one."

"You have got to be kidding me!" I barked.

She wasn't. "Fine," I said. I didn't miss a first serve the rest of the set. I even won the match. But it was another temper tantrum that qualified for my personal hall of shame. There were so many times when I was so mentally worn down. I remember telling Frank Deford, "I'm just not in the mood to fight anymore."

People had been pressuring me to run for political office by then, and I usually said I didn't have the heart for that. It was another thing I said that was untrue. I would have loved to run for office, but the country wasn't ready to elect someone who had a lesbian affair outside her marriage. I was still dealing with the Marilyn issue. She was not in any hurry to move out of the Malibu beach house, and things were not good between us. Trying to compartmentalize the secrecy and dysfunction made me anxious. So did not knowing when or how it might end.

THE LATE 1970S MARKED a generational shift for tennis that included the birth of some epic new rivalries just as a lot of former champions, including me, were moving on. Jimmy Connors was growling about his determination to chase Bjorn Borg "to the ends of the earth." Martina was on her way to overtaking Chrissie. Tracy Austin splashed down as a fifteen-year-old phenom, and her pigtails, braces, and pinafore dresses were a stark contrast to her advanced game. With her two-fisted backhand and fierce determination, she seemed like a younger, harder-hitting version of Chrissie, and playing such a mirror image of herself threatened Chrissie at first, by her own admission.

It was also an era when the top players were treated like rock stars. They were the first generation of professionals whose careers unfolded entirely in the television age. John McEnroe was on his way to join a rock band. Vitas Gerulaitis, John's fellow Queens native and a brilliant player, had an affection for Studio 54, the trendiest disco in Manhattan. Chrissie accepted Andy Warhol's offer to paint her portrait and dated the actor Burt Reynolds for a while.

By then, I was sometimes falling out of tournaments earlier than I had since I was a teenager. I finally found a way to accept that I couldn't be No. 1 forever and I allowed myself to experience the sheer joy of being out there, competing. One of the things that helped me a lot was reading Bill Bradley's 1976 book, *Life on the Run*, his first-person account of a few weeks in his life late in his career with a New York Knicks championship team.

Roger Kahn, author of *The Boys of Summer*, is usually credited with the oft-repeated line that a professional athlete "dies two deaths"—once when the person retires, and again when life ends. My takeaway from Bradley's book was that your career is indeed a separate lifetime, but only you should decide when to stop playing or what still brings you joy. You shouldn't listen to the outside world that's telling you you've faded, or that you're damaging your legacy.

Bradley's advice was a yardstick I started applying to myself and, later, to other athletes such as Chrissie and Martina when they asked my advice about retirement. "I don't care what people say or what your ranking is—do *you* still love it enough?" I asked each of them. My answer at that point was still yes, even as Margaret, Maria Bueno, and Arthur had all stepped away by 1979. My body was telling me my time was close. My mind kept saying, *Not yet, not yet.*

I needed orthotics and injections in my foot to allow me to play Wimbledon in 1978. I lost to Chrissie in the quarterfinals. I didn't enter in singles at the U.S. Open but won the doubles title with Martina. When I finally had plantar fasciitis surgery in December, my orthopedic surgeon, Dr. John Marshall, removed a golf ball–size chunk of scar tissue and a bone spur from my foot and told me he shouldn't have let me play that summer.

While I was still in a cast in early 1979, Martina asked me, "Are we playing doubles together at Wimbledon?"

"There's no way," I scoffed. "I won't be ready."

"I'm not playing without you," Martina said. Then she kept it up all spring, calling me at least a dozen times with the same offer.

She wouldn't give up on me, and I remain forever grateful. Prodding me to believe and giving me a goal to work toward were the greatest gifts she could've offered me that year. She wanted me to have the Wimbledon record of twenty titles overall, breaking my tie with Elizabeth Ryan, a fellow Southern Californian whom I had known since she watched me play junior tournaments at the Los Angeles Tennis Club.

I was able to work my way back in time to play Wimbledon with Martina. The day before our doubles final, news raced across the grounds that Elizabeth had suffered a heart attack as she was watching Martina win her second singles final. Elizabeth, who was eighty-seven, died on the way to a London hospital. I broke her record the next day, Martina carrying me most of the way. The minute the championship match was over, I glanced up at the stands where Elizabeth's customary seat sat empty. My victory felt so bittersweet.

There was someone else missing that day—Larry. Earlier that year, as the magazine and World TeamTennis were experiencing setbacks, Larry lost a lot of money on another venture, a smokeless ashtray. He had spent about $10,000 of our money on its development. Then, against the advice of our business manager, Jim Jorgensen, Larry invested more to manufacture and market thirty thousand ashtrays in time for Christmas 1977. They barely sold. The loss of more than $100,000 frightened me. I was thirty-six years old, worried about my future earning power and determined to have some untouchable money that would carry me through retirement. Not long after that, Jim set up individual bank accounts for Larry and me. The financial disengagement was the beginning of a long process of separation that would take us years to complete. The day I broke that Wimbledon record of a lifetime, Larry had chosen to run a one-hundred-mile ultramarathon back in the States.

SOMETIME IN THE SUMMER of 1979, Ruth Kloss wrote me a letter from South Africa asking me to check in as a friend on her daughter, Ilana. Ruth confided that whenever she heard from Ilana, she seemed lost.

Ruth and her entire family had been part of my life since I first met Ilana, by chance, more than a decade earlier. I was walking across the grounds at Ellis Park in Johannesburg at the South African Championships in 1966 and saw Ilana and her father practicing. I recognized Ilana because she and her friend, Renée Aucamp, had been ball girls for some of my singles and doubles matches with Rosie and they had done an excellent job. Now I could also see that Ilana, a shy but determined ten-year-old, had talent as a player, and so, as I did for many youngsters, I wanted to give her some encouragement.

"Do you mind if I hit with her a bit?" I asked her dad, Shlaim.

After ten or fifteen minutes, I told him, "You should make sure your daughter pursues tennis if she wants to. Here's the name and address of Frank Brennan. He's my coach back in the States." Then I said to Ilana, "I'm going to put the Wilson rep in touch with you, too, so you get free rackets. And when I leave, you can reach out to me if you want. Write to me."

Offering to help was just my way of paying forward the kindnesses that top players such as Doris Hart, Darlene Hard, and Alice Marble had shown me as a junior. It's something I still do. It was only years later that Ilana told me, "I decided I was going to be a professional tennis player that day."

I saw Ilana and her family at the South African Championships the following year as well, and I kept up my correspondence over the years with her and Ruth, who was in charge of the tournament's program sales. I'd send Ilana little notes about life on the tour, ask her questions about her game, maybe give her a few motivational tips. I had no idea that her parents were saving each handwritten letter in a large scrapbook they kept about Ilana's tennis career. Ilana still has it. It's fun to look at today. In one two-page letter I addressed to Ilana and Renée in June of 1971, I wrote,

The Queen's tournament starts Monday, a week from today, with Wimbledon to follow. My heart starts pounding every time

I think about it . . . Ilana, it seems as though your game is coming along in good form from what you write and from what I hear through the grapevine. As soon as possible you must start travelling and really start working on becoming a champion, if that is what you still desire. I could sit and talk or write to you all day trying to warn you about the various pitfalls along the way, but each person must experience their own adventure in life, the ups and downs, and the confusion of it all.

If you and Renée are meant to be any good, you will make it no matter what the odds. You will train, travel, fight, and struggle your way to the top. It is a good life and to be the best at something is worth a try, if you have that restless feeling deep down inside that keeps pushing and pulling to make you just a little bit better than the next person. Each new day will be a new challenge, a new adventure, never to be duplicated again. Think big.

Once Ilana traveled the pro tour, we occasionally ran into each other at tournaments or at World TeamTennis matches. She attended the Gloucester Hotel meeting where we founded the WTA and served as the African continent's representative on the WTA board. We didn't socialize together because I'm twelve years older and I was in another orbit of friends. But when Ruth wrote to me, I said I'd be happy to see what was going on in Ilana's life.

In late September 1979, Ilana and I were both playing in the Davison Classic in Atlanta so I asked Ilana to hit together, then grab some dinner. We hadn't had a heart-to-heart talk since she was a kid. Back then, I had usually done most of the talking. Now I listened to her for a change. She was a levelheaded twenty-three-year-old who had been on the road for tennis more or less since the age of sixteen. In some ways, she seemed older and wiser than her years; in other matters, she was innocent to the point of being naive.

"I'm in a rut," she told me that night. She wasn't sure where her tennis career was headed, or what the future held for South Africa, for that matter.

South Africa was still a very isolated country by then, with little news penetrating from the outside world. The radio was state run, and television (which didn't reach the country until 1976) was still censored by the government. The first day I met Ilana at Ellis Park, I asked her what she dreamed about most. "To play Wimbledon," she told me, even though she had never seen it live. She was limited to photos or listening to BBC radio broadcasts of the tournament.

By the time we had our dinner in Atlanta, Ilana had achieved her goal to get to London and more. In 1972, when she was sixteen, she won the Wimbledon juniors singles title. (I saw her early that day on the grounds at the All England Club, and motioned to her to come over to hit two-on-ones with Kristen Kemmer and me. That's how we both warmed up for our finals, and we both won.) The following year, Ilana became the youngest woman ever ranked No. 1 in South Africa. In 1974, she signed on to play World TeamTennis. She also won the juniors singles championship at the U.S. Open, and she partnered with her South African friend Linky Boshoff to play Rosie and me in women's doubles.

We defeated them in the early rounds in 1974, and again the next year. But in 1976, they beat Betty Stöve and me in a tough quarterfinal match and went on to win the U.S. Open title. It took me back to when Karen Hantze and I were teenagers just starting out and slaying the giants of women's tennis at the first Wimbledon we won.

Ilana and Linky took the Italian Open and German Open titles that year as well, earning themselves the year-end world No. 1 ranking in doubles. It was the high point of a great year for Ilana that included knocking off Martina in the second round of singles at the Family Circle Magazine Cup at Amelia Island. Ilana's highest career ranking in singles was nineteenth in the world. (Today, there's a two-tournament series in Potchefstroom, South Africa, called the Ilana Kloss International that offers players $50,000 in prize money and the much-needed opportunity to earn ranking points that can allow them to compete internationally. The best-performing South African player over those two weeks is also given a travel grant.)

By 1976, South Africa was imploding because of its oppressive apartheid system. In June, South African riot police killed hundreds of students and injured over a thousand more during the three-day

Soweto uprising, a protest against discriminatory education policies. The brutality stirred up more international hostility against
South Africa, which was already the target of international boycotts. South African artists and athletes became targets when they
ventured abroad.

Ilana is Jewish, and members of the South African Jewish community were among the leaders of the resistance working to change
the apartheid regime. One of the activists was Helen Suzman, the
lone anti-apartheid member of parliament for years. Suzman was
nominated for a Nobel Peace Prize.

Ilana's grandparents had emigrated to South Africa to escape
religious persecution in Lithuania before the Holocaust. Her family
didn't condone discrimination of any sort. The Klosses, like other
white South Africans they knew, disregarded the laws and tried to
help nonwhites when they could. When Ilana and her younger sister,
Merle, were growing up in Johannesburg, their parents risked allowing Christinah Mamonyaku Seema, their Black live-in housekeeper
and nanny, to keep her youngest daughter, Dipuo, with her during
her work week at the Klosses' house, even though it was illegal for
Blacks to do so. The Klosses were also very close to their handyman
Boenyene Joseph Morwa, who used to thrill Ilana, Merle, and their
cousin, Ian, by tucking them into the large basket on the front of his
bicycle and taking them on joy rides to the store when the Klosses
needed something.

I had gotten my first taste of how insidious apartheid was on my
initial visit to the South African Championships in 1966. When the
wife of the host family I was staying with came home and found me
talking to their Black maid in the kitchen, my host began chastising
the woman for speaking to me. She only stopped her blistering criticism when I hastily explained that it was my fault, I had initiated the
conversation, not knowing it was forbidden. That stopped her, but
I worried that the maid would have more hell to pay when I wasn't
around.

One day at the South African tournament site I was making my
way toward a section of empty seats to watch a match when a tournament official hurried over with a horrified look on her face and told

me, "Oh, no, Mrs. King. You mustn't go there." I asked, "Why not?" She said, "That's the nonwhites section." She told me to follow her to the whites-only seats. I noticed the drinking fountains were also labeled "Whites Only" and "Non-Whites."

"Being Jewish," Ilana told me much later, "I always had a strong sense of not being accepted everywhere. As Blacks and Jews, we had experienced something similar, but racism was so much worse because you can't hide your color. Growing up, I had a very deep sense of how terribly Black people were treated—that struggle, seeing how they lived in fear. My parents didn't do that, but I saw how tough the police were to Blacks, how they had to have a passbook to just be on the street. If you were Black, you could be arrested for any reason. There were very specific laws to follow. All of it was just so wrong."

Ilana and Linky's opposition to apartheid didn't spare them death threats and trouble once they were on tour. Japan was among the countries they couldn't compete in. At the 1976 Fed Cup in Philadelphia, the Soviet Union, Czechoslovakia, and Hungary withdrew their teams and more than a hundred people showed up to protest because South Africa and Rhodesia were allowed to play. The mood was ugly, and Ilana and Linky didn't realize that they were in any danger until a security detail arrived to protect them.

The anti-apartheid protests were worse the next year at the 1977 Fed Cup in Eastbourne, England, an outdoor venue. Rowdy demonstrators pelted Ilana's car as she drove to the tournament site and they stood outside both the South African team's hotel and the stadium, making noise to disrupt the tennis. There were bomb threats. During the opening ceremony, a demonstrator rushed the court and tossed an open bag of white flour in Ilana's direction. He missed her, but the close call was unsettling. Again, security was assigned to her hotel.

Apartheid was absolutely evil, and I totally understood why people were protesting against South Africa, but at the same time I thought it was a disaster to isolate people who needed more, not less, outside exposure to multicultural, democratic ideas. To the people who lived under apartheid, having foreigners visit gave them a glimpse outside their country, and proof that people elsewhere cared. That's why Arthur Ashe kept applying for a visa to South Africa for years until he was granted entry in 1973, when he broke the color barrier at the South African Open.

In his book *Days of Grace,* written with Arnold Rampersad, Arthur tells a bracing story about how he noticed a young Black boy staring at him intently on that trip. Arthur asked him why, and the boy replied, "Because you are the first truly free Black man I have ever seen." Arthur's visit impacted Ilana as well. She still considers him one of her heroes because, she says, "I saw tennis as my gateway to the world, but Arthur brought the world to us. I'm convinced he literally broke down apartheid by doing that. The scrutiny and excitement were unbelievable."

Arthur said he wouldn't play unless the tournament dropped the segregated seating, which they did, and that was a big deal. On days he didn't compete, Arthur made side trips to Soweto and other Black townships and the international media followed him and wrote stories about the conditions there. Arthur's agent and friend, Donald Dell, who was on that trip, was so impressed when Ilana lost a close three-setter to Chrissie Evert in the semifinals, and again when Ilana and Linky upset Chrissie and Virginia Wade in doubles, that he signed Ilana and Linky as clients and landed Ilana a contract with World TeamTennis. Ilana's father said he couldn't believe that overnight, his seventeen-year-old daughter was making more than he made as a salesman.

Ilana and Linky were happy they had each other as they traveled the tour together playing doubles, but when Linky decided to quit the circuit in 1977 to attend university in South Africa, it was the start of Ilana's ennui. By the time we shared dinner in Atlanta, Ilana felt that her plans to keep playing tennis had begun to unravel. She knew she didn't want to be a teaching pro, and she didn't want to live in South Africa, either (the dismantling of apartheid wouldn't begin for another sixteen years), so she kept playing tournaments with no real goal or direction. "I'm not sure what to do next," she said to me.

Ilana was upbeat and dryly funny throughout dinner, but it was obvious how unhappy she was. I also sensed that tennis had never been a great joy for her (she later admitted that she couldn't separate how she did in competition from the person she was; it affected her self-esteem). She felt pressure to keep playing and winning for her parents because they had invested so much in her. "When I win," she said, "the feeling is more relief, not joy. I don't ever remember not feeling pressure when I play."

I suggested that maybe Ilana could come to New York for a bit instead of returning right away to South Africa. "We could practice," I said, "and maybe you could buy some time to think about your next move."

Ilana thought that was a good idea, and we quickly resumed laughing and telling stories the rest of the evening. She was so much fun to be with, so grounded and calm and smart, that after I left I unexpectedly found myself thinking about her. Ilana had become a beautiful woman with dark brown eyes that can suddenly light up with laughter, and that wonderful accent of hers—I could listen to it all day. Most of all, I could tell that Ilana was a good and sensitive soul, very direct and very caring.

As it turned out, Ilana had felt a spark at that dinner too. I think it was a shock to both of us that our unspoken feelings for each other kept deepening once she got to New York, even though the topic of being gay went unmentioned between us and our relationship stayed platonic for weeks. I'd assumed Ilana was gay because she was always hanging around with one of the handful of lesbian players on the circuit. In fact, Ilana was so naive she had no idea her closeted friend was a lesbian. The woman would get a room with only one bed when her girlfriend was visiting, and Ilana would tell them, "Hey, why don't you take my room? It's got two beds." It's hilarious to Ilana now. When she ran into me on the road when I was traveling with Marilyn, Ilana thought nothing of that, either.

Ilana wasn't even sure she *might* be gay until we spent our first three or four weeks hanging out together. Martina was still my regular doubles partner then, but there was a tournament coming up in Sweden in November 1979 that she was planning to skip, and so I asked Ilana if she'd like to travel from New York to Stockholm with me. In Sweden, between matches, we ventured out into the dank weather to shop or sightsee a bit but spent a lot of time hanging out in our hotel, ordering room service. It was there that Ilana surprised me one day by telling me, "I think I'm falling in love with you." I told her, "I feel differently about you than anybody else." That night, we made love.

I didn't know it was Ilana's first time with a woman until she told me days afterward. It was another surprise—and one that scared me. I've never been someone who is into one-night stands or casual sex. The few times I tried it, it felt lousy to me. I need to be in love with my partner or sex is meaningless. When I'm with someone, my feeling is *You're precious, I'm precious, so let's both be kind and good to each other.* And I took pains to be that way with Ilana. I wanted to make sure our love was real, and not just an infatuation. (There's an old joke among lesbians about how quickly women get attached: you have one date with someone, and the U-Haul is pulling up in the driveway the next day.) I felt more determined to be careful when Ilana told me, "I feel great. I'm also petrified."

Admitting you're gay and telling someone "I love you" is not something done lightly. And so, as cautiously happy as we were, we also knew our lives were about to become more complicated. As our relationship continued, so did our determination to keep it a secret. We didn't tell a soul.

After Stockholm, Ilana and I traveled together for the rest of the winter season: Stuttgart, Brighton, Melbourne, Sydney. We'd play, practice, see a bit of each city. It was becoming clear to me that she was *the* one. From the start, we just seemed to fit and complement each other so beautifully. We both had the same values and devotion to family. She's focused on concrete outcomes, and I still usually take the thirty-thousand-foot view of things first. I gush emotion, and she often proceeds with more caution—or freezes me with a look that cracks me up.

One day recently, I was struggling to write something and Ilana provided me with the perfect line on her way out the door. I said, "Wait, wait—don't go! Come back. You know me better than I know myself."

"I'm running away as fast as I can," she joked, clicking the door shut behind her.

I doubt I was fooling many people on the circuit by not acknowledging that Ilana and I were lovers. Ilana was certain that her parents would be shattered if they knew. The only time I had tried to discuss my sexuality with my mother by then, she stood up before I could even start and said, "We don't talk about these kinds of things in our family." Then she left the room. After that, I just avoided the subject.

There were other reasons Ilana and I kept our relationship a secret: The corporate community wasn't ready for a gay spokesperson, and endorsement deals were a big key to my retirement strategy. I was still playing some tournaments, and the money was better than ever, but there were also plans in the works for some significant clothing endorsements for me, along with television commercials, more coaching, and speaking and broadcasting gigs. Things were looking promising.

Larry and I were still entangled in business, but less so than before. We were living apart, but Larry still didn't want to consent to a divorce. He told me he would always love me without conditions. He held out hope that someday I would come back.

How do you tell someone so dear and important to you that something ineffable is missing with him? We kept hitting the same impasse. Rather than pressure Larry and hurt him even more, I kept putting off the inevitable. I'm terrible at letting go, and I hoped he'd want a divorce too, in his own time. But it did frighten me now that I was with Ilana when Larry said something like "You don't want a divorce—it wouldn't be good for your image." It was an observation, but to me, it also seemed like a subtle warning. The irony was, Ilana admitted that she was initially "thrilled" that I was still married, if only on paper. "I want to hide—believe me, I'm *happy* to hide," she said.

MY SINGLES CAREER ENJOYED a bit of a renaissance after Ilana and I got together. Avon replaced Virginia Slims as the tour sponsor for a couple of years, a move that both sides came to regret before we reunited with Virginia Slims in 1983. At Detroit's Cobo Arena, I won the year-end championships in late February for the first time in six years. Ilana and I won the doubles. The momentum carried over to the next singles tournament I played, in Houston. Martina was No. 1 in the world by now and riding a twenty-eight-match winning streak when we met in the final. I beat her in straight sets in just fifty minutes. Again Ilana and I won the doubles.

A week later, I lost in the first round. That's the way it goes. As I got older I found I didn't recover from matches as quickly. I wasn't as mobile. It seemed to take more effort to get the same oomph on my shots. I found myself treasuring the moments when I still hit a great winner or ran down a ball. Rod Laver and I talked about it. He's five years older than me and he told me, "Billie, you'll find that when you're out hitting some days, you just want to hit one ball—one ball—that feels like it did in the old days."

Once in a while I could recapture my best tennis, but I spent a lot of time in 1980 battling more ailments. I'd be feeling fine and then my tennis elbow would flare up, or a knee, or my foot. The press was busy now talking about the "Old Lady's comeback." The truth was, it was becoming harder and harder for me to stay in shape, and it took me longer to get sharp again after each setback. Not that any of that dented my enthusiasm. I entered Roland-Garros for the first time in eight years. I lost in the quarters, but went on to Wimbledon with high hopes anyway.

On the days when I played as well as I had ten or fifteen years earlier, the feeling was sublime. At Wimbledon, I outlasted sixteen-year-old Pam Shriver in a three-hour match on Court 2, the so-called Graveyard of Champions, and then lost to Martina in a three-set match in the quarterfinals. Martina and I resumed playing doubles together, ending the temporary break that had opened the way for Ilana and me to team up over the winter.

Martina and I lost in the Wimbledon semifinals, but we won the 1980 U.S. Open, giving me my thirty-ninth—and last—Grand Slam title. It was also my last tournament with Martina as my partner. That winter, my body began rebelling again. I had surgery to unblock my chronically bad sinus, then had a nagging virus, then a strained arm muscle. In November, I underwent surgery again to repair residual damage in my knees. I still didn't want to retire, but then I heard secondhand that Martina had avoided telling me for months that she'd decided to play doubles in the 1981 season with Pam Shriver. That hurt, given the success we had had together.

Ilana and I were living together in my apartment on Sixty-Sixth Street in New York by now. I played World TeamTennis that spring and some Avon events, but I skipped playing Wimbledon for the first time in twenty years and accepted a job to call some matches there for NBC. I was basically semi-retired from tennis and that wasn't all bad, especially when an old problem came boomeranging back around.

For years I had been trying to get Marilyn out of my life, and then out of the house in Malibu. Our relationship as a steady couple had ended a little over a year after it began, and it was a mistake not to cut ties completely with her by 1975. She had now been in the Malibu house for nearly five years, and my business manager was paying all the bills for the property because he had tried, unsuccessfully, to extract even minimal rent from Marilyn. In 1978, I gave her notice that she needed to prepare to leave, setting off a chain of events that I feared could end very, very badly.

The whole thing was weighing on my mind when Ilana and I arrived in Florida to play the United Airlines tournament outside Orlando the last week of April 1981. We had only been there a day when I lost my opening singles match. To make the best of the unexpected time off, Ilana and I decided to make a forty-minute drive north and spend the afternoon at Disney World, a place she'd never been. There were no cell phones then. As we returned to our condo at the Grenelefe Golf & Tennis Resort, Ilana said, "Look . . . That's weird."

There were at least twenty or thirty pink message slips taped on the door. I knew it could only mean one thing. I turned to Ilana and said, "My life will never be the same."

Chapter 25

I T WAS SOMETIME in 1978 when a friend told me she had just
visited the Beverly Hills salon where Marilyn was working and
overheard her talking about some letters of mine. She was brag-
ging, "I could sell them for a lot of money." The story gave me a
queasy feeling that would resurface often in succeeding years. I still
feel it today, whenever I think of Marilyn and how badly it all ended.

In the days before emails and texts, hotel phone charges were
exorbitant and letters were how I stayed connected to people I
cared about. I wrote letters on airplanes, in coffee shops, during rain
delays, on hotel stationery in lonely rooms wherever my world travels took me. Shortly after my relationship with Marilyn began, she
asked me to write to her from the road and I was happy to do it. My
letters were expressive and affectionate, but, as I said, as time went
on my feelings toward her changed. I found myself writing to her to
keep her calm because I was afraid of what she might do. I sent her
dozens of letters, and she apparently kept them all.

The only reason a tabloid might want to buy those letters was
because I was famous, and they were evidence that, at one point
in my life, I had cheated on my husband with a woman. That was a
scandal, and scandals sell. Before "the Marilyn thing"—as everyone
around me came to call it—I always had faith in people, or at least
gave them the benefit of the doubt. For years after Marilyn, it was
hard for me to trust again.

My friend's story about Marilyn proved true. Marilyn began
making threats about the letters directly to me in the summer of
1978. The catalyst was when I told her that Larry and I were think-

ing about putting the Malibu house on the market. She waved a stack of the letters in my face when I was visiting and said, "These would make a good book!" I asked for them back. She refused. For the first time, I wondered if that was why she had encouraged me to write her in the first place. I was later told she kept the letters in a safety deposit box.

Marilyn was never the most consistent person, but by the time her threats started I had begun hearing from friends in Los Angeles that she had been in and out of substance abuse treatment. The house was supposedly robbed twice while she was living there, and among the things that went missing was a beautiful bracelet Elton had given me. "Well, you have insurance, right?" Marilyn said. Her nonchalance made me wonder whether the house was actually robbed or she had sold the jewelry. When I began talking to her about leaving the Malibu house, she was again drinking and taking drugs, which only made her more volatile.

Things got so bad that I avoided going to the house when I was in Los Angeles. When we did see each other there was always an argument. One time when I turned to leave, she screamed and pounded my chest with her fists until I had to grab her wrists to make her stop. Another day, she took a bottle of her pills and rattled it at me, threatening to take some. She told me she wanted me to divorce Larry so we could be together again. I said, "Marilyn, please—it's over between you and me. Can't you see?" She wouldn't accept it even though she dated other people after returning to L.A. Her behavior became so worrisome that I suggested that she see a psychologist I knew, and she did. After a couple of sessions, the therapist told me that the only way that Marilyn could get better and start living her own life was if I didn't help her anymore and disconnected completely. So I tried.

In the summer of 1979, about a year after I alerted Marilyn that she'd need to find someplace else to live, I asked my business manager, Jim Jorgensen, to inform Marilyn that we were selling the house. That didn't go over well, either. She told Jim, "Why would Billie Jean want to hurt me that way? I have never hurt Billie Jean. But I could hurt her and hurt her a lot." I had heard that kind of threat so often by then that I asked Jim to start negotiating with Marilyn to leave the house and return the letters. At one point I had Jim relay to Marilyn that she could live in the house until it was sold and she would get half of the net profits from the sale. Larry and I had paid $132,500 for the place, which was now valued at more than $500,000, so it was a generous offer. In return, I would get the letters back, she would leave me alone, and she would have no further claims against me.

"That would be fine," she said. For the first time, I felt a sliver of hope that we could put everything behind us, and Marilyn would get her life together. But Marilyn only became more desperate and self-destructive. She refused to allow prospective buyers into the house and took down the For Sale sign. At one point she claimed that she had some wealthy friends willing to buy the house for her. That never happened.

Jim had a lot of contact with Marilyn because he paid the bills for the house, and Marilyn phoned him so often she knew his number by heart. I assume that's why Marilyn gave Jim's number to the sheriff's deputies and ambulance crew that found her slumped in her car the night she drove off a cliff on Malibu Canyon Road in 1980. She avoided serious injury that time. But in October 1980, after a night of drinking, she threw herself off the high deck of the Malibu house, a fall of about thirty feet. She was found by police officers at five the next morning, badly injured, lying on the sand by the pilings. Again, she gave the first responders Jim's number. Marilyn had fractured her spine and she was hospitalized for a month. She spent the rest of her life walking with a cane or riding in a wheelchair.

Marilyn told Jim after both incidents that she had intended to kill herself. Jim wasn't sure if she meant it, but we eventually learned that Marilyn had left a suicide note before her plunge off the balcony. Four months later, in February 1981, Marilyn was taken by ambulance to the Malibu medical center to have her stomach pumped because of an alcohol overdose.

How do you deal with someone as troubled as she became? Marilyn had a few friends checking on her throughout. She had always told me that she had no family besides a stepbrother, and I didn't find out until December 1981 that that was untrue.

Larry was eventually aware of Marilyn's threats and self-inflicted damage. He understood, too, that she would never leave the house unless we reached some kind of financial settlement. The deed to the Malibu house was in both of our names, so we had to work it out together. In the spring of 1981, we raised our initial offer: If Marilyn would move out of the house and return my letters, Larry and I would agree to pay her $125,000 up front against half of the net profits from the sale, whenever it happened. My hope was that the cash advance could help fund Marilyn's move. At this point, a Los Angeles attorney named Joel Ladin called Jim and told him that Marilyn had retained him and she needed the money right away. Jim said we would advance a total of $25,000 and hold the remaining $100,000 in escrow until she returned the letters and moved out.

In early April, we sent two checks totaling $25,000 to Marilyn and Ladin, which they promptly cashed. Again, we thought we had an agreement. We waited for them to return the letters and give us Marilyn's moving date. We were still waiting during the last week of April 1981 when Jim phoned me and said, "Billie Jean, I've got some bad news. I just spoke to Marilyn's lawyer and he told me the deal is off."

Ladin was now saying that Marilyn claimed to have found more letters at the house and after he read them he decided they were worth much more than our agreement. Marilyn now wanted the full title to the house, and she wanted financial support for the rest of her life. I think I screamed when Jim told me her latest demands. The blood was pounding in my ears so hard I could barely hear the rest of what he said. As soon as I hung up, I called Larry.

"They're going to hurt us badly," I said. "She's blackmailing us, and it will never end."

It was time to get our own lawyer, so Pat Kingsley put me in touch with Dennis Wasser, a level-headed family attorney in Los Angeles who represented a lot of public figures. We hoped to continue negotiations with Marilyn's lawyer, but Ladin wasn't returning Dennis's phone calls. On April 28, 1981, Marilyn filed suit in Los Angeles County Superior Court to demand the house, half of my earnings during the seven years we were supposedly together, and lifetime support.

Her court filing was the reason all those message slips were on the door when Ilana and I returned to our condo in Florida. I had been outed. My worst nightmare had come true.

THE LEGAL ARGUMENT THAT Marilyn's side made was based on the famous "palimony" decision two years earlier against the actor Lee Marvin, which entitled his live-in girlfriend, Michelle Triola Marvin, to sue him for a portion of the money he had made when they were together, just as if they were married. The ruling had never before been applied to same-sex partners. There was a media feeding frenzy as soon as the court papers were filed. The press quickly came up with the new term "galimony" to describe Marilyn's demands. And I was right: My life never was the same.

Marilyn's betrayal was such an utter breach of privacy and trust, such a soul-destroying violation and trauma for me, I would never wish being outed on anybody. Nor would I ever out anybody else. I sometimes ask myself, *Would I ever have been ready to come out on my own?* I think so. But it should have been my choice. Nobody should have to come out unless they're ready.

The day that the news of Marilyn's lawsuit broke I went into shock. I felt scared, hurt, mortified, angry, sick, dazed, panicked, shamed, and exposed—and the feelings grew more acute as the days dragged on. I feared that Ilana was going to be dragged into this mess, and I was heartsick for Larry, for our families, for women's tennis. I worried how the fallout from the lawsuit might ruin so many years of hard work or feed into derogatory stereotypes about all women athletes.

As soon as Ilana and I got inside our Grenelefe condo we bolted the door and I started making phone calls. I couldn't reach Larry, who was on a flight, so I called Jim. I called Dennis Wasser. I called my agent, Bob Kain, the number-two guy at IMG, who handled all my television jobs and marketing deals. I spoke to Pat, who was based in Los Angeles, to start figuring out how to handle the media. Pat told me to send Ilana home to South Africa as soon as possible, so Ilana booked a flight. Looking back, I wasn't thinking clearly and should not have agreed to that. We should have stuck it out together, though Ilana was as terrified as I was.

I knew that I, too, needed to get out of Florida right away, before the press started pounding at my door. So we both started packing immediately. The safest place I could think of was my Manhattan apartment, where no journalists could get near me, where I could be quiet and think. Ilana and I chose the same night flight to New York, but then she would connect through JFK and travel on immediately to South Africa. I needed to warn my parents about what was coming, but I couldn't face them, so I asked Pat to call them as we were traveling.

By the time we landed in New York, Pat and Dennis Wasser had already released a press statement in order to make the morning newspaper deadlines. I was quoted saying, "The allegations contained in this lawsuit are untrue and unfounded. I am completely shocked and disappointed by the actions Ms. Barnett has taken." The statement identified Marilyn as "a woman who worked as my secretary in the early to mid '70's." It noted that she had emotional issues, including a suicide attempt.

When I read the statement, I was furious because it was released without my approval. A lawyer's instinct is to deny everything, then try to get the case dismissed. A PR expert will tell you to do the same thing. But this felt wrong. Yes, most of the allegations in the lawsuit were false. But the assertion that Marilyn and I had been lovers was correct. I had hated lying before I was outed, and I hated it even more afterward. Dennis and Pat told me it was too late to reel back the denial, but I disagreed.

I paced the floor of my apartment that first night, and again the next day and night, often bouncing a tennis ball on my racket, wearing out a path on the floor as I went. I spoke on the phone again with Pat and Dennis, trying to assess the damage and plan my next move. I wanted to tell the truth, to face the public and speak from my heart. I wanted to acknowledge having an affair with Marilyn and admit that it had been a mistake to cheat on Larry.

"If I don't do that," I argued, "we'll never be free of Marilyn and I'll never, ever feel peace again. This is blackmail. The story won't fade away, it will just keep coming out in bits and pieces, and I'll have to keep covering up with denials. It will never end. So why not answer all the questions now, and get it over with?"

Pat thought I was out of my mind. "Nobody's ever done this before," she said. Admitting to a lesbian affair would destroy my reputation. Dennis thought it was too risky from a legal standpoint. Bob worried that I would lose my endorsements just as I was planning to retire from playing. Our back-and-forth occasionally got heated. There was no crisis management primer on how to handle this. I told Pat and Dennis, "I've worked with these media people all of my life, since I've been young, and they've been fair to me. I want to tell the truth. I've always talked to them from my heart, and I'm not going to go hide now."

"Please don't do this—take my advice," Dennis said.

"I am not taking your advice," I shot back.

Larry was the only one willing to support whatever I decided. I didn't assume he would back me up, but he did.

"Are you sure?" I asked Larry. "It's going to hurt you, and my parents, and a lot of other people. It's going to hurt women's sports. It could ruin everything we've done."

"Don't worry about other people," Larry said. "For once in your life, Billie Jean, do exactly what you want to do for yourself."

I called Pat Kingsley back and said, "I want you to call a press conference."

WHEN I MAKE UP my mind, there is no persuading me to back down. As soon as Pat realized that, she shifted gears. She generously dedicated her entire office staff to my case and nothing else for several days. She had the most impressive Rolodex in the business, and she started flipping through it to set up the news conference for the next day. We decided it would take place at a hotel near the Los

Angeles airport. Then Pat lined up a series of interviews to get my side of the story out in different media, including exclusives with *The New York Times* and *People* magazine and a *20/20* sit-down with ABC's Barbara Walters.

Things were moving quickly. Larry hired Henry Holmes, a law school buddy of his, to join the legal team and represent him. Marilyn had also named Larry in the suit for "preventing" her from claiming her alleged rights to the house since Larry and I owned it together. Larry said he wanted a real pit bull to fight back and Henry, who would go on to represent clients like George Foreman and Chuck Norris, was already developing that kind of reputation in entertainment circles.

By the next day, Henry had filed an unlawful detainer suit against Marilyn to evict her from the house. Then he obtained an emergency injunction to prevent her or her attorney from selling any of my letters or revealing their contents.

While that was happening, I called friends, sponsors, and business associates to say that I would understand if they wanted to distance themselves from me. I was supposed to play doubles the following week in Tokyo with the fifteen-year-old prodigy Andrea Jaeger and one of my first calls was to her parents to say I'd step aside. They and Andrea were adamant that she still wanted to play with me. I called Jerry Diamond at the Women's Tennis Association to tell him I was going to admit the affair and to offer my resignation as WTA president. Even though he would have to bring it to a vote with the board, Jerry personally thought I should stay on and encouraged me to stay strong.

Larry flew to New York and we booked a flight to Los Angeles out of Newark instead of LaGuardia or Kennedy because I was paranoid about getting ambushed by photographers. We planned to arrive at the press conference together, and we used the time on the flight to prepare the statements we would make before taking questions. As the two of us headed west, Ilana was making her way alone to the other side of the world. I wasn't able to talk to her and I didn't know how she was doing. I was a nervous wreck.

My poor, bewildered parents met us at the hotel. We hugged one another and said, "I love you." There was no talk about Marilyn or the lawsuit, but I never doubted that my parents would stand up for me. They had been asked not to say anything to the press, but when a friendly reporter reached my father by phone, my dad said they backed me "100 percent."

"We wouldn't be much of a mother and father if we didn't, would we?"

The hotel conference room was packed when we walked in. There were so many cameras pointed at us I lost count. Larry and I took our seats together at a table behind a thicket of microphones while my parents sat against the wall, damp eyed and grim faced. I tried not to look in their direction. Larry introduced me as "the person I love dearly," adding, "I've known Billie Jean for nineteen years and I don't think that anything that transpires will affect our relationship."

When it was time for me to speak, I was scared to death, but I pushed forward. Larry kept his arm around the back of my chair and I squared my shoulders, concentrated on staying composed, leaned toward the microphones, and said in a steady voice, "I did have an affair with Marilyn Barnett. It has been over for quite some time . . ." I could hear a few gasps in the room, then nothing but the camera shutters clicking furiously as I continued: "I made a mistake, and I'll assume all responsibility for it." (To this day, my use of the word *mistake* offends some people. They thought I meant being gay was the "mistake." What I was referring to was betraying my marriage vows.) I thanked my parents for supporting me, and Larry, "my lover, my husband and my best friend . . . In some ways, I think we're closer today than we've ever been, and our marriage is stronger."

We were certainly close that day. Our united stand was real. But our marriage was a front disguising the life I was really leading and blurring even this supposed moment of truth. The charade was excruciating and again I let it play out for the same reasons I always did: for the sake of my family, for all the good things I had been part of building with Larry and everyone else, and now, for Ilana. But that's the trouble with secrets. One begets another, and another.

That press conference was the longest twenty minutes of my life.

I felt like a drowning swimmer grasping at anything that might keep me afloat. When I was done with my opening statement there was total silence. It felt like a year to me before the first reporter piped up. I felt ashamed to be having this forced public conversation about my sexuality. I assumed that the world still wasn't ready to accept me as a lesbian—and, more to the point, I was still not ready to accept it myself.

"I only hope the fans will have compassion and understanding," I said.

I was asked how I felt about having my private life exposed because I'm a public figure, and I answered, "It may not be fair but that's the way it is, and I've accepted it."

After I had taken the last question, Larry and I and my parents stood in a line with our arms around one another as a show of solidarity. Tellingly, all of us are looking off in different directions, alone in our own worlds of hurt as the cameras recorded the moment. Once on the elevator, it wasn't until I hugged my father that I realized he was shaking. I held on to him even tighter, hoping it would steady us both.

The deceptions only spread as Pat set up interview after interview. I don't know what psychological mechanism kept me going, but I kept lying and kept hating myself for it. I just wanted to be left alone.

Within days, Larry and I were on the cover of *People,* showing off my wedding band. We sat for a sympathetic Q&A with the former editor of *womenSports,* our friend Cheryl McCall. The story was headlined "Larry and Billie Jean King Work to Renew Their Marriage—and Put Her Affair Behind Them."

Bob Kain was so worried about my finances after I was outed that he called me three times a day until he talked me into writing a book. "You have to do it," he said. Bob hoped rushing it to press would help repair my image in addition to making me some money and perhaps salvaging some endorsement contracts. Frank Deford was willing to write it. But Frank began interviewing me just three weeks after I had been outed, and everything with Marilyn remained so raw and bitter I barely gave him any time. I came off in the book as confused, which was true. All I knew was that I had hurt or let down just about everybody I knew or loved, and I still didn't know how it would end. In all of my interviews after I was outed, I was so afraid of implicating others that I insisted that Marilyn was my first and only relationship with a woman, and that it had been over fairly quickly.

The containment strategy was yet another mind-bending part of the entire episode. Who turns being outed into a way to burrow deeper into the closet? But that's what I did. I had been on record as in favor of gay liberation since my *Playboy* interview six years earlier, and I openly supported Renée Richards and transgender rights. But now I again denied and equivocated about my own sexuality, which was probably the worst part of it all. It wasn't a personal reckoning as much as a whitewashing.

"I hate being called a homosexual because I don't feel that way—it really upsets me," I told *People*. "I particularly like working with children . . . Now I think [parents] are going to bag it and say, 'I don't want this creep around my kids' . . . If you have one gay experience, does that mean you're gay? If you have one heterosexual experience, does that mean you're straight? Life doesn't work quite so cut and dried."

It was a cop-out, of course. What kind of a message was I sending to others who were struggling with their sexuality? It's "just a phase"? That being called gay or lesbian is pejorative? Not good. I handled the crisis as best I could. And I've had to live with those decisions. If I let myself think back to that time, the trauma feels nearly as fresh today as it did then.

The insinuation that gays and lesbians are bad people or predatory sexual creatures was something I encountered in all of my interviews, including the one with Barbara Walters, which reached the biggest audience. Pat had volunteered her own living room in Los Angeles for the set, and Larry and I held hands and sat on a couch as Barbara asked her questions, which were tough and direct.

"You know, Billie Jean, it's now being said in various newspaper reports that in women's golf, women's tennis, homosexuality is rampant," Barbara said with a concerned look on her face. "It's also said that the younger players are often seduced by the older ones."

"I don't feel it's true at all," I said.

Questions like that were a nightmare. Tabloid reporters were indeed flooding the women's tour now, looking for evidence of "rampant" lesbianism. The *New York Post* printed a lurid story about "the scandal shaking women's tennis," and claimed that Tracy Austin's mother, Jeanne, was among those who had hired locker room "shower guards" to protect their daughters. Jeanne vehemently denied it. Chrissie Evert denounced the report. Pam Shriver, Andrea Jaeger, and other young players said they had to fend off reporters. *The National Enquirer* was offering bounties ranging from $5,000 for dirt on lesbians on tour to $25,000 for anyone who produced my letters to Marilyn. That appalled me. "If they [the media] want to bother me, fine, if they want to hurt me, or try to hurt me, fine," I told the *Los Angeles Times,* "but please, leave the others alone."

Nancy Lopez, the most popular golfer on the LPGA Tour, admitted that "a lot of people who are straight are scared" about being tarred by innuendo. And Nancy was married.

It meant the world to me that other players stood with me. Chrissie was among those who spoke out strongly on my behalf, writing an editorial for *Tennis* magazine titled "In Defense of Billie Jean." Rosie was on the phone all the time with me, offering support. Martina publicly decried "the gay witch hunt" that was going on. The WTA board voted ten to five to keep me as president rather than accept my resignation, and Jerry Diamond publicly brushed off the "sexual McCarthyism" that was swirling around us and said our tour would survive.

Gloria Steinem wrote me a touching letter that read, in part, "It breaks my heart to see you suffering or penalized in any way for living in a still unenlightened time, but please know your troubles have probably hastened a better understanding for everyone." I wasn't sure. I do believe that acknowledging my affair with Marilyn opened a lot of conversations.

Larry Kramer, the gay activist and author, always maintained that the most important thing LGBTQ+ people have ever done is come out, because it allows other people to see that we're relatable, real. I agree. Overnight, I had just become one of the first (perhaps only) lesbians that many people thought they knew. Maybe people who admired me or just knew my name realized it wasn't fair to keep labeling gays and lesbians as degenerates or psychiatric cases. We were their neighbors, teachers, friends, even sports heroes.

I told the press, "No matter what happens now, I'll still have my titles, my wins . . . I may lose my endorsements, but I still have me, my self-esteem. And I'll start over."

Our media blitz did ease the immediate crisis somewhat. Most of the coverage was on my side, if only because Marilyn had done a spiteful thing and I had "come clean." Larry was enormously supportive too, even when Barbara asked if he understood why I had the affair.

"Certainly—and I felt I contributed to it," Larry answered.

"How?"

"By not fulfilling her need to have me there," he continued. "I wanted to do my own thing. I was running seventeen tennis camps around the country, and starting World TeamTennis, and starting *womenSports* magazine. It was rather selfish."

The fact that Larry and I didn't immediately file for divorce after I was outed made our marriage even more curious to people than before. There was conjecture that Larry had to be gay, which he laughed off by saying, "It's not contagious. I didn't catch it." When I look back at that time today, some of the remarks he and I made in those moments of duress still stand as the most clarifying statements either of us has ever given about how we made sense of our relationship, and how we viewed what love is, come what may.

"You have to look at the personalities involved," Larry said. "Most people have some glimpse of Billie Jean as a high-charged, emotional person with a high level of personal contact. She's very compelling and draining. She has a need for total attention. I'm different. I don't . . . You resolve these [differences] in any relationship by either making certain tolerances or breaking up the relationship . . . I'm a very stubborn person. That reflects on my relationship with Billie Jean. There is a high degree of loyalty.

"Now, other people may not see it as loyalty, but I love Billie Jean. I've never stopped loving her, and that translates not into possession, but into trying to do whatever makes her the happiest. Most people look at love as an ability to possess people. I look at it as sharing with them, loving them, and wanting the best for them. I love Billie Jean and I'll always love Billie Jean. That doesn't mean that she might not be happier, because of her capacity and needs for attention, with some other person . . . That may be too philosophical or too detached for most people, but that's how I feel. It's not about owning her or possessing her time, necessarily."

"Larry and I have been through so much together," I said. "And that in itself can bind you."

Chapter 26

I N THE FIRST TWO MONTHS after Marilyn's suit was filed, I lost at least $500,000 in endorsements and marketing deals. In the long run, I lost millions. The ad agency for E. R. Squibb & Sons immediately stopped running a television commercial for Theragran-M vitamins that featured me and my mother. They made a point of publicly dropping me as their spokesperson. A virtually completed $500,000 deal to bring out a Billie Jean King clothing line under the Wimbledon brand was canceled abruptly. I also lost a $300,000 contract with Murjani Jeans, a $90,000 Japanese clothing contract, and $45,000 from Charleston Hosiery, whose chief executive called me a "slut" in a letter when he fired me. I received a lot of hate mail.

Within a year I was the only major tennis player in the world without a sportswear contract. I owned thirty-nine Grand Slam titles, and I was playing in clothing bought straight off the rack for the first time since I was a kid. Yonex, whose rackets I had been using, said they were behind me—they just didn't renew my contract when the time came. Nike said they were "impressed by my candor" and stood by me at first—then later proposed drastically reducing my fee; I walked away from them. My relationship with Nike founder Phil Knight was never repaired.

Larry was still trying to raise money to revive World TeamTennis, and we lost about $150,000 in sponsorship commitments after the Marilyn story broke. We were still able to come up with the capital for a limited summer season. All told, Larry suffered business losses of at least $400,000, plus he was incurring heavy legal fees.

Avon, the chief sponsor of the women's tour at more than $3 million a year, denied that it was pulling out. They were gone within a year.

I was deeply worried about how Randy's San Francisco Giants teammates would react to the news about me and Marilyn. Randy told me the day the story broke he was hunched down in his seat on the team bus after a game, avoiding eye contact because he didn't want to fight anybody who made a snide remark about his sister. It was Darrell Evans, a respected veteran on the team, who broke the ice first. "Tough day, huh, Moffitt?" Randy looked up at him and nodded. "Don't worry, man," Evans said, clapping Randy on the shoulder. Then Randy's other teammates came by one by one to slap him on the shoulder and tell him it would be okay, too.

I cried when Randy told me that.

The collateral damage caused by having to live a public life has always been hard for me. Though I knowingly signed up for it, not everyone around me did. Shielding them sometimes consumed me. Despite all my regrets, I'm not sorry about lying to protect Ilana, for example, by going out of my way to continue to shoot down rumors that we were a couple. I insisted to Neil Amdur of *The New York Times* that Ilana was a longtime family friend as well as a tennis partner, nothing more. "But if being around me is going to jeopardize Ilana," I said, "I don't want her around."

Poor Ilana. What could she be thinking if she was reading any of this in South Africa? After she spent nearly a month in exile, we were reunited at Hilton Head, where we had decided to practice to prepare for Roland-Garros. It was highly emotional. We had missed each other terribly and needed to be together. She told me that while we were apart she had no idea whether I still wanted to stay with her, and she was scared to death of being outed while back in Johannesburg. Homosexuality was still a crime in South Africa. Her parents had asked her about me when the news finally traveled there, and she told them, "I don't know anything about it."

We cautiously resumed our relationship, which essentially meant a return to doing what people in the closet do—never betraying a hint of affection in public, editing our every word, avoiding anything close to a lingering glance that might cause people to wonder. You submerge your true self. You make swaths of yourself invisible. Ilana told me never to mention her. We were both so scalded by what had just happened, we continued to behave that way for years.

Once Ilana and I arrived in Paris to play Roland-Garros, I was still so stressed about being outed, having her around and trying to avoid the assembled world press, that when I looked in the hotel mirror one morning I saw blotches all over my face. "Ilana! Did you see this?" I called out. Overnight I had developed vitiligo, an auto-immune disease of the skin that's sometimes caused by stress. The cells that produce pigment die off, leaving white patches. It was literally as if I'd seen a ghost.

My carefully laid plans for retirement were now up in smoke. I had lost most of my future income and I had more than half a million dollars in legal fees to pay. I was nearly thirty-eight years old, I had been playing tennis for twenty-five years, and I'd already had five knee operations, plus multiple foot, sinus, and heel surgeries. Once again, retirement would have to wait. I had to keep playing—or risk going broke.

I TRIED TO SOLDIER ON after I was outed but played only six tournament singles matches the rest of 1981. I lost five of them. A few weeks after Roland-Garros, I returned to Wimbledon. I had kept my promise to not enter as a player. NBC had kept its commitment to have me work as a color analyst, although once I arrived, the NBC executive producer Don Ohlmeyer told me some of the network executives were spooked by the Marilyn scandal, and they wanted to cut back my airtime to just a few of the women's matches. He convinced them to still let me be in the booth to call part of the men's final—"I want you to be the first woman broadcaster ever to do that," he said—and so I was there with Dick Enberg and Bud Collins for the start of the unforgettable Borg-McEnroe title match. Then NBC yanked me after the first set. I was deeply grateful that Don fought for me.

Early in that same Wimbledon fortnight, Martina had approached me for advice. She had given a long interview to Steve Goldstein, a New York *Daily News* reporter, after I was outed. She told him she was bisexual (which is how she identified then) but asked him not to print the story because she was finally close to getting her U.S. citizenship. Admitting homosexuality could be a disqualifier at the time.

Martina's attorneys were concerned enough about it to have her file for citizenship in the more liberal state of California rather than Texas, which was now her adopted home. In her private interview with the Immigration and Naturalization Service agent, which is conducted under oath, a question about her sexual preference did come up.

"Bisexual," Martina answered.

The agent moved on to the next question without looking up, to Martina's enormous relief.

It was an open secret by then that Martina had been with the writer Rita Mae Brown, whose best-selling memoir, *Rubyfruit Jungle,* established her as a leading voice for gay and lesbian rights in the 1970s. She and Martina had bought a house together in Charlottesville, Virginia, and lived openly as a couple until the spring of 1981, when Martina left Rita Mae and started training with the basketball star and coach Nancy Lieberman. Now, Martina was concerned that Nancy would be implicated as a lesbian.

When Martina and I met to talk, we sat by a window looking out at the courts. "This reporter is going to out me, Billie," Martina said. "What do you think I should do?"

"Well, if you're comfortable enough in your own skin, I think you should come out immediately on your own so you can control the message."

"Really?"

"It's up to you," I stressed, "but I'm telling you, from my experience, nothing is worse than having to react and play defense. You're doomed anyway. So 'fess up and get it done."

Martina was still deliberating what to do when her photo appeared on the front page of the *Daily News* on July 30, 1981, with a story about how she was worried that being bisexual would affect the women's tour. The next day, she confirmed that she was bisexual in *The Dallas Morning News,* but she insisted that Nancy was just a friend and "shouldn't have to suffer." Women's tennis had now had two stars outed in three months.

I made a World TeamTennis swing through California with mixed results. At a match near Oakland, a heckler was riding me so badly I finally wheeled and gave him the finger and barked at him, daring him to tell me his name. The press jumped on the story, and the photos of me losing it made the newspapers. At The Forum in Los Angeles, our next stop, the crowd of nearly three thousand spectators gave me a standing ovation when my name was announced, and I thought, *Maybe things might be okay someday after all.* Then we held a press conference to announce that World TeamTennis would be back the next year with twice as many teams, and that I was going to serve as commissioner—a first for women in any pro league. Some reporters used the opportunity to ask questions about the Marilyn case instead.

I was so upset and weary by then, I decided to go into hiding. I didn't enter the U.S. Open. I was in New York during the tournament, but I stayed away. I was apprehensive about going out in public. I was accustomed to people looking at me but now I thought they were judging me.

Just when it seemed like this was going to be my new normal, word came that I had been chosen as one of the twenty-five most influential women in the United States in a poll conducted by *World Almanac.* I finished the voting tied with the *Washington Post* publisher Katharine Graham, the woman who greenlighted the newspaper's landmark Watergate investigation. The honor meant a lot to me and was the most emphatic sign yet that maybe I wouldn't have to live as a pariah after all.

After some deliberation, I went to the Women's Sports Foundation's year-end awards gala a few weeks later. There had been some discussion at a board meeting about whether to disinvite me. Sure enough, heads turned when I walked in. I felt the same old familiar

Meeting President Nelson Mandela with Ilana in 2008 at his office in Houghton, Johannesburg, was a dream of a lifetime. Ilana helped make the unforgettable meeting happen. To me, Mandela taught and reinforced the great lessons in life, starting with forgiveness, resilience, and his unshakable belief that love transcends hate.

When President Obama presented me in 2009 with the Presidential Medal of Freedom, the highest civilian honor in the U.S., for being an "agent of change," I thought about everyone who helped me along the way.

I remember watching Queen Elizabeth II's coronation in 1953 at my friend Judy Wallick's house. Her family was the first in our neighborhood to have a TV. I would never have imagined that forty-seven years later I'd be in England and meet Her Majesty the Queen at Wimbledon.

The Donnelly Awards have provided scholarships to young players living with diabetes since 1998. The inspirations for the awards were my friends and WTT colleagues Diane Donnelly Stone and her sister, Tracey Donnelly Maltby. This photo is from the 2011 awards ceremony. Back row, left to right: Diane, her daughter Danielle, scholarship winner Elizabeth Profit, me, an unidentified Novo Nordisk representative, award winner Nicole Selvaggio, and Tracey. Front row, left to right: Diane and Tracey's children, Nick Stone, Christo Maltby, and Susanna Maltby.

Ilana and I instantly fell in love with taking cruises with family and friends. Here, a bunch of us are pictured on a Mediterranean trip that was also the last cruise we were able to take with our mothers, Ruth and Betty.

My brother, Randy, Ilana, and I are flanked by Randy's daughters and their families. Left to right: James and Alysha Gosse (holding son, Derek); and Miranda and her husband, Rusty Harrah, with their son, Cason (plaid shirt). Standing in front of me are their other children, Evan Harrah and Byron Gosse.

Former and current tennis players, including nearly every retired or active No. 1–ranked player since the Women's Tennis Association was founded, gathered at the WTA's fortieth-anniversary celebration at the All England Club on June 30, 2013.

Our friend Anne Guerrant had the idea to have a tennis round robin—what else?—as part of my seventieth-birthday festivities in Las Vegas in 2013. I love celebrating this way, because my birthdays always feel like a reunion.

Members of our wonderful World TeamTennis staff over the years gathered in Las Vegas to help me celebrate my seventieth birthday at Caesar's Palace. We're still one big extended family. Many of us have worked together for decades.

Every time we go on a cruise we play tennis at each stop where we disembark. Here we're shown on our 2014 trip to the Mexican Riviera to celebrate the marriage of Rosie Casals and Connie Spooner.

I love every chance to catch up with former player Ingrid Löfdahl Bentzer (red jacket) and her children Helene (far left) and Jake (far right). Ilana and I were thrilled when Ingrid asked us to be their godparents. In front are Annie and Max, Helene's children.

Our friend and business partner Mark Walter introduced Ilana and me to the crowd at Dodger Stadium after we became part of the Los Angeles Dodgers ownership group in September 2018. (One perk of ownership: I later exchanged this shirt for one that actually fit me. Ha!)

When Wimbledon started later than usual in 2018, Ilana and I were excited to be able to attend our first NYC Pride March and I was asked to be one of the grand marshals. We had a blast riding the parade route in a convertible, experiencing the vibrant sense of community, and waving back at the enthusiastic crowds that were celebrating the day.

Former New York mayor David Dinkins always told Ilana and me, "If you two ever get married, I'm your guy!" Until the writing of this book, David's wife, Joyce (shown here), and one of their aides were the only people who knew we quietly tied the knot at the Dinkinses' Upper East Side apartment on October 19, 2018. This photo was taken that day.

In November 2018, the Billie Jean King Leadership Initiative hosted a spectacular party for my seventy-fifth birthday that helped raise funds for my archive collection and its home, the New-York Historical Society. The unforgettable celebration featured live entertainment by numerous friends, including Emma Stone, Alan Cumming, Kate Clinton, Nona Hendryx, Cyndi Lauper, and Sarah Bareilles.

I've always loved meeting the adorable first-grade students of the Billie Jean King Namesake Classroom at the Girls Prep Lower East Side School in New York. This photo of our hug lineup was taken in 2019.

The people of Long Beach made me who I am. Now, my hope for the Billie Jean King Main Library, which opened with this ribbon-cutting ceremony in September 2019, is that our state-of-the-art facilities and programs will help more city residents chase their dreams. Flanking me that day was Councilmember Jeannine Pearce (white dress) and Long Beach Mayor Robert Garcia, at right.

Members of our current team at the Billie Jean King Leadership Initiative and Billie Jean King Enterprises gathered at the 2019 U.S. Open for a BJKLI event hosted by our advisory board member Christiane Amanpour, the groundbreaking newswoman whose global work I admired long before we became friends.

It's been inspiring to see subsequent generations of WTA players use the platform of tennis to fight for social justice. Here, Naomi Osaka of Japan walks out before her first-round match at the 2020 U.S. Open wearing a mask in honor of the late Breonna Taylor. Osaka went on to win the championship, and wore different names on her masks before each of her next six matches to highlight the violent deaths of six other Black Americans: Elijah McClain, Ahmaud Arbery, Trayvon Martin, George Floyd, Philando Castile, and Tamir Rice.

I'm a happy camper here because I'm wearing my beloved lavender dress that the designer Ted Tinling nicknamed my "Madame Superstar" outfit, and my blue suede shoes. I'm about to hit a serve at the 1974 U.S. Open at Forest Hills, where I defeated Evonne Goolagong in the final in one of the best matches I ever played.

My New York Apples teammates and I celebrate our 1977 World TeamTennis championship. Left to right: Linda Siegelman, Ray Ruffels, Virginia Wade, Fred Stolle, team owner Sol Berg, Sandy Mayer, me, and Lindsey Beaven.

I could finally exhale after I beat Bobby Riggs, 6–4, 6–3, 6–3, and tossed my racket into the air at the Houston Astrodome. An estimated 90 million people watched the match worldwide, 50 million of them in the U.S. I felt I had to win to protect and advance the hard-won progress women were making everywhere by then, not just in tennis.

sense of dread—until everyone put down their drinks and napkins, pushed back their chairs, and rose to give me a standing ovation. It still chokes me up to think about it. It meant so much because those people were my own.

By December, my anxiety level was through the roof again. The first lawsuit against Marilyn was going to trial, and I knew both she and I would have to testify.

Our lawyers tried to get cameras banned from the court-room during the trial, but judges had a habit of allowing them in celebrity-driven Los Angeles. From the moment Marilyn had filed her lawsuit, the case had been a public spectacle—a reality show before reality TV shows were common. Now this one would be acted out on live television.

Our unlawful detainer suit—a legal term for eviction—would be tried first, before Marilyn's galimony case began. Because it was a property dispute, it would be decided by a judge without a jury.

When the trial began on December 9, 1981, Larry and I had to wade through a small sea of reporters and gawkers just to get to the courthouse in downtown Los Angeles. Marilyn looked fragile and gaunt as she struggled to her seat. Her back and legs were in braces, and she used a cane to walk. In spite of all the pain she had caused me and so many other people in my life, I had to fight the urge to feel sorry for her.

For the trial, Henry Holmes represented Larry, and Dennis Was-ser represented me. We all sat together at the plaintiff's table while Dennis made a straightforward presentation of our case. I testi-fied that Larry and I bought and owned the house together. Larry produced the deed. We said we wanted to sell the property, Mari-lyn had no lease and was uncooperative, and we wanted to evict her. We noted that there was no evidence of the claim filed by Marilyn that I had bought the house for her, and no evidence that there was a verbal agreement between her and me to give her the house and take care of her financially. Larry was drawn into the mess because the house was community property. Since Larry's name was on the deed, she was going after his assets as well as mine.

Now Ladin presented Marilyn's case. When he called her as his first witness, I stared at the desk where I was seated. Privately, Larry and our lawyers had been telling me for weeks that Marilyn's case was untenable, motivated more by spite and a craving for publicity than any sound legal claims. But it felt like a nightmare all the same. Once you're in a courtroom, you never know.

Marilyn testified that she had given up "her career, her identity, her pride, and her home," to accompany me on tour in 1973. She said it was because I had promised "to take care of her financially." She alleged that I had also told her to "go out and buy herself a beach house" because I knew how much she loved the beach. She admitted that she had told people the house was hers, though it was not.

Her attorney asked why.

"Because in 1974 gay people were not accepted, and because of who Billie was at the time, I tried to protect her," she said. "Whatever the situation warranted is what I said to protect Billie."

"In essence you lied?"

"Yes, I did lie."

When Dennis rose to cross-examine Marilyn, he asked her if she remembered that what I actually told her was "If you like the beach, why don't you buy *yourself* a home on the beach?" She said she didn't. She conceded that she never asked to have her name put on the title of the Malibu house. Asked about sacrificing her career for me, she admitted that she had gone back to work in 1974 and I sent her new clients to try to help her.

Dennis asked her why she had kept all the letters I sent her.

"For sentimental reasons," Marilyn said.

To anyone who didn't know Marilyn's troubled backstory, she might've come across on the stand that day as reasonable, mild-mannered, even harmless or sympathetic. But everyone on our team knew that I had feared her dark side ever since she reacted so extremely to my first request for her to move out of the house, and then again as she kept up her outbursts and hurt herself.

I actually got to the point where I feared that Marilyn was capable of physical violence toward me, too, and I told people that. I had visions of her showing up at a World TeamTennis match or somewhere else one day with a handgun and shooting me. And that was before *The Miami News* wrote about Marilyn's family just as our trial began. Much of it was news to me. Marilyn's biological father, Melvin McRae, had been a career criminal who was in and out of jail. Her mother, Kathryn (Kay) McRae, divorced him and remarried a Hollywood press agent named Bev Barnett after Marilyn and her younger brother, Randall, were born. Bev died suddenly fourteen months after the wedding, and Marilyn's mother, Kay, died in 1969 under circumstances that Kay's sister, Irene Hensen, considered suspicious.

Hensen, who lived in Florida, told *The Miami News* that Kay was found dead in bed with a three-to-four-inch gash on her left temple. Hensen said that when she arrived in L.A. for the funeral she visited the scene of her sister's death and found dried blood everywhere, "on the walls, on the ceiling, on the carpet." Henson said Marilyn, then twenty-one, and her younger brother gave her different stories about exactly how Kay died. *The Miami News* reported that the Los Angeles Coroner's report attributed Kay's death to alcoholism, but Hensen repeatedly asked police for an investigation. She was denied.

The whole episode was still gnawing at Hensen twelve years later when she spoke to *The Miami News* after Marilyn's lawsuit became public. She also contacted our legal team, so Henry Holmes knew Hensen's claims when Marilyn approached him one day to chat outside the courthouse during a break. "I know you're on the other side," Marilyn told Henry, "but I hear you're a nice person." She knew that Henry had celebrity clients, the same as she did, and so they talked about that a bit. During another break in the proceedings shortly afterward, Marilyn was walking out with her attorney and she turned and said, "Henry! Look this way!" Henry saw something metal in her hand and dove to the floor. He thought she had a gun. When he looked up, Marilyn was pointing a small camera at him and said, "What? I just want to take your picture."

———

THE TRIAL LASTED three days, and Larry, Jim Jorgensen, and I were called back to the stand by Ladin and cross-examined extensively about every aspect of the Malibu house arrangements. During Marilyn's time on the stand, Henry asked her about her motives for including Larry in her suit.

"You did not like Mr. King, did you?"

"That is true," she said.

"You were jealous of Mr. King, correct?"

"Yes."

Anyone hoping for more salacious details about our affair beyond that was disappointed. The few times our sexual relationship was brought up in testimony, Judge Julius M. Title ruled it to be irrelevant. By December 11, 1981, the third day of the trial, the judge delivered his verdict: Marilyn had to move out of the Malibu house within thirty days. Judge Title ruled that Larry and I never intended to give Marilyn the house, and that Marilyn "did not have clean hands" when she came to court. The judge said Marilyn was using the secret stack of love letters as leverage over me by "threatening adverse publicity" unless she was paid her escalating series of demands. "If that isn't attempted extortion, it certainly comes close to it," Judge Title said.

The verdict was a complete victory for us. But there was no joy in winning the case, only relief. The damage was already done, and there was still the galimony suit left to fight. Thankfully, after Judge Title's decision, the other case unraveled as well. Nearly a year later, on November 19, 1982, another superior court judge dismissed the suit, ruling that Marilyn had no grounds to sue us. Dennis Wasser called me in Australia, where I was playing, to give me the news. It was a welcome thirty-ninth-birthday present, and a total relief to not have to go back to court.

About seven months after the galimony suit was dismissed, that Malibu house that caused so much grief was destroyed during a violent Pacific storm before Larry and I could sell it. We ended up selling the cleared lot instead. Marilyn dropped out of sight after the trial, and I never saw or heard from her again. I later found out that she moved into an apartment at the Beverly Hills home of a friend, and some of her wealthy clients helped her with expenses. She was eventually diagnosed with cancer, and the actors Jill St. John and her husband, Robert Wagner, paid her medical bills. After several surgeries, Marilyn apparently gave up hope. She tried to commit suicide again in 1997, and this time she succeeded. She was forty-nine. Jill and a few other friends scattered her ashes in the surf off Malibu.

Chapter 27

I NEVER DREAMED OF, nor wanted to, still be playing on
tour at the age of thirty-eight and thirty-nine, but there I was.
Ilana and I were playing doubles again together, and I even had
a mini renaissance in singles now and then. In Boston, I beat
nineteen-year-old Pam Shriver. At the 1982 Italian Open in May,
I saved six match points in the third set against Patricia Medrado
of Brazil to win. The crowd went crazy for me, chanting, *"Forza,
Guglielomo, dai, dai!"* I knew that *dai* means "Come on!" in Italian. Someone had to tell me *Guglielomo* means "Little Bill," a term
of endearment. How much did I love that? Then I won the singles
title in Birmingham, England, my last tune-up tournament before
Wimbledon.

Once back at the All England Club, I rallied after losing the first
set to upset nineteen-year-old Tracy Austin and advance out of the
Wimbledon quarterfinals for the first time in seven years. Arthur
Ashe, a developing friend, made a point later to tell me that the guys
in the men's locker room stopped to watch the match on TV and
applauded as I clawed my way back against Tracy, a two-time U.S.
Open champion by then and former world No. 1 who was nineteen
years my junior. Arthur said it was only the third time he'd ever seen
that locker room show of respect in his nineteen years of coming to
Wimbledon. It was so sweet of him to share that with me.

My 1982 run ended with a loss to Chrissie in the semis, but
I roared back to the Wimbledon semis again in 1983 at the age of
thirty-nine, making me the oldest woman to advance that far in

sixty-three years. Now that I was back to being the underdog I was again a crowd favorite at the All England Club.

At times like that, or when I was back out on the road elsewhere, I felt like an aging gunslinger in the Old West. The young players wanted a shot at me so they could say they had beaten Billie Jean King. I didn't blame them. Every older player has to put up with that, as well as the negative feedback from the media at post-match press conferences: *When are you going to retire . . . Is this it for you?* If you linger too long on those questions, doubt can overtake you. I needed the money, so I always responded with optimism no matter how I felt. As I told Bud Collins after I beat Pam in Boston, "I'm not going to believe the people who tell me I'm too old to play." But when I played that 1982 Wimbledon semifinal against Chrissie that I lost in three sets, I knew that to win I had to really believe, deep in the core of me, that I still had it. I realized I no longer had that conviction.

By early 1983, I was still competing in singles and doubles but running on little more than fumes, my fierce sense of survival and the energy of the crowds. In Boston in March, the fans chanted, *"Billie! Billie! Billie!"* before, during, and after I beat Kathy Jordan, the defending champ. It was wonderful, even a bit overwhelming, to be around long enough to feel such adoration and appreciation.

When I got to Wimbledon in 1983, I was just five months shy of forty. I was playing well until I ran into Andrea Jaeger, now a rosy-cheeked Chicago girl of eighteen. She had so much confidence, backed up by that same stinging two-fisted backhand she had when we played doubles together when she was fifteen.

It was Andrea's first match on Centre Court. As we turned the last corner to walk out, she confessed that she wasn't sure when to curtsy for the Royal Box, so I was giving her a quick lesson on how to count to three as we stopped and dipped in unison. I was pointing out other features of the stadium to her, the way you might give a guest a tour of your house. But once the match began, she didn't play like a newcomer. It was the most lopsided loss of my Wimbledon singles career, 6–1, 6–1.

As we made our way back to the locker room I felt sick with disappointment. We again had to pass below the Royal Box, and Andrea and I counted to three and bobbed in unison one more time, just as Karen Hantze and I had done on my first visit to Wimbledon in 1961. Then I looked back over my shoulder—something I never do—and took it all in one more time: the perfect symmetry of the place, the powder-blue sky above, the velvet green carpet of grass, and the beautiful round clock ticking away the minutes until the next champions were crowned on Centre Court. Wimbledon was still the home of my heart and I would be back, but never again as a singles player.

AFTER 850 TOUR SINGLES MATCHES, countless miles, and twenty-seven years of competitive tennis, I decided to stop playing in December 1983. I'll never know how much more I could've won if amassing titles was my obsession, but like a lot of us then, building the women's tour was my priority. My career ledger still read thirty-nine Grand Slam singles and doubles championships, including my record twenty titles at Wimbledon. From 1971 through 1975, I won seven of the ten Grand Slam singles tournaments I played, and I took six of those seven titles in straight sets. I ended with a major finals singles record of 12–6, and four of those six losses were to Margaret Court, the other best player of my generation. Overall, I won 125 singles titles, 36 women's doubles titles, and 3 WTT championships. I owned the year-end world No. 1 ranking seven of the ten years from 1966 through 1975. Any epitaph about me should also read this: I got to live my dreams. I've had an amazing life.

But to say I "retired" isn't right. I transitioned. The day after I quit, I continued my work as World TeamTennis commissioner. I started working for HBO as a commentator during the network's coverage of Wimbledon. One of my colleagues there was Arthur Ashe, and our friendship grew even more.

Now that I was done playing I still had one more major transition to make that I had been putting off much of my adult life.

World TeamTennis was based in Chicago when I became commissioner. Larry, our longtime business partner Bill Schoen, and I were co-owners of the Chicago Fyre franchise, which Ilana coached to the World TeamTennis title in 1983. I had my apartment near Lincoln Center in New York City, and at first, Ilana and I traveled between New York and Chicago as needed. We made Chicago our main residence three years later since World TeamTennis was our main business. Ilana, needing a U.S. base, had bought her own apartment in Chicago, which she shared with a South African friend. Keeping the league alive was a constant battle. I again started overeating and my weight soared. In addition to the daily operations, there were always sponsors to chase, commitments to keep, owners to please. One owner, with whom I usually got along great, was so angry when his team lost a player eligibility issue he phoned me and ranted for three hours. At one point, I put the phone down on the bed and picked it up now and then when I heard him pause to say, "Yes, I understand . . ." He just had to get it off his chest.

By the summer of 1987, Ilana had grown tired of the fact that I was still married to Larry. He and I had separate lives and separate finances, and our shared business interests were whittled down to relatively few enterprises. Ilana and I had played surrogate moms to Larry's nephew Shane between 1984 and 1986 when Shane was studying in New York. Shane lived with Ilana and me at our place near Lincoln Center, and it was a sweet time for all of us. But now Ilana told me I had to make a decision: Did I want to be with her, or stay married to Larry? She was right. It wasn't fair to her, or to Larry, who still clung to his married-for-life stance.

I finally filed for divorce.

When we signed the divorce papers in Henry Holmes's office, it was painful. I remember Larry fiddling with his wedding band, then taking it off and setting it on the table. And that was it. Twenty-two years, over. I found myself replaying parts of our life, and it was very sad. Yet I also had a new beginning with Ilana. For the first time, we had a cleared path, a clean break.

In the settlement, Larry and I split everything down the middle.

He got the Hawaii house and property; I knew how much he loved it. Some pain and bitterness lingered for a while. But we navigated the emotions over time and became friends again.

Larry eventually remarried, to Nancy Bolger, a wonderful woman who worked in publicity for the WTA/Virginia Slims tour. They've been together for three decades and raised two children, Sky and Katie King. Ilana and I are their godparents. Katie loves animals so much she got a degree in zoology. Sometimes Sky and I stay up late talking about ways we can fix the world, just like his dad and I used to do.

When I was coming out, few people talked about "families of origin" and "families of choice" like we do today. Ilana and I are blessed. Randy moved from Arizona back to Long Beach after our parents passed away, and his two daughters are both married—Alysha to James Gosse, and Miranda to Rusty Harrah. Their children are Byron and Derek Gosse and Evan and Cason Harrah. Ilana's sister, Merle, and her husband, Richard Blackman, live near us in New York and their adult children, Lara and Josh, have developed friendships with Katie and Sky King. We love them all like our own. We also do our best to stay in touch with family and friends scattered around the world and our extended family in South Africa. Ilana remained close to Christinah Seema, her family's housekeeper when she was a child, until Christinah's death in 2021, and she continues to be close to Christinah's family. Ilana has funded private school educations for Christinah's daughter, Dipuo, and her grandson, Neo. Ingrid Löfdahl-Bentzer's children, Jake and Helene, Melissa and Paul Keary's son, Cameron, and Janet Young Langford's kids, Anthony and Jennifer, are our godchildren as well.

We've shared great times and major life occasions with all of them. Openly acknowledging we're a couple has allowed Ilana and me to give and receive love in measures beyond anything we'd have otherwise known.

Chapter 28

I DIDN'T KNOW a great deal about being an activist when I started fighting for equality, but I picked up insights along the way that still govern my life. Marching in the streets is great—people feel good when they get to yell and scream and vent their frustrations and gather with like-minded people—but that's not enough. Once you organize, you have to mobilize. You have to say: How are we going to actually *get* the change we really want? What concrete things have we accomplished? How do we get people to join us? Because that's what a successful movement is.

You have to have a fire in your belly and put your ego on the shelf each day because it's not about you, it's about the change you're seeking and everyone that is in the fight with you. Everyone has a role to play; everyone wants to be heard. You're not going to get exactly what you want every time, so you have to learn to adapt and listen, recognize who has the power and cultivate allies, because those people in power—the same people you're fighting—are often the ones who are going to make your dreams come true.

Ilana always tells me I have an amazing ability to avoid taking things personally—"You just start over and over again with people," she says—and I think being able to forgive, forget, and keep moving has helped me throughout my life. It was that way with Jack Kramer and me, believe it or not. During the 1984 Olympics in Los Angeles, UCLA Chancellor Charles Young had seated Jack and me next to each other at a dinner party, not knowing about the many showdowns we had had. It turned out to be a terrific night. Jack and I made amends for some of the things we had said or done over the years and said how sorry we were that we had had to go through that. I told Jack how I had attended one of his pro tour events when I was twelve, and how deeply it affected me because I knew I was watching the best players in the world. I also liked the fact that he was a great businessman and promoter as well as a great champion. Jack told me, "I have a granddaughter now." He shared some stories that inferred he finally understood why women were fighting so hard for change. Jack and I had a great relationship after that.

The years that Arthur Ashe and I worked at HBO were another gift. For the better part of a decade, the two of us spent a lot of time together at Wimbledon, working as commentators for the network starting in 1984. Being thrown together gave us a chance to get to know each other. That didn't seem possible when I was pushing to help start the women's tennis tour and Arthur and the male players wanted little to do with us.

Arthur suffered from a congenital heart condition that ended his tennis career in 1979 after he suffered a heart attack at the age of thirty-six. He underwent two cardiac bypass surgeries by 1983, and was stunned when he was diagnosed with HIV/AIDS in September 1988 after experiencing sudden paralysis in his right arm. After extensive tests and exploratory brain surgery, doctors discovered that Arthur had toxoplasmosis, a parasitic disease that is commonly found in people infected with HIV. Scientists didn't start screening donated blood until 1985, which was too late for Arthur. His doctors guessed that he probably picked up HIV/AIDS from a transfusion during his second heart surgery.

Arthur and his wife, Jeanne, decided to keep his HIV-positive diagnosis confidential to protect their privacy and that of their daughter, Camera, then two. HIV and AIDS had emerged as an epidemic a few years earlier, mainly affecting gays, hemophiliacs, and intravenous drug users. The hysteria that an AIDS diagnosis could generate then could turn you into a pariah overnight. The public didn't know, for example, that Rock Hudson was gay until he was dying of AIDS, and three public figures I had met—Freddie Mercury, Halston, and Rudolf Nureyev—concealed that they had HIV/AIDS until the news appeared in their obituaries. It took a few years for the epidemic to spread to other populations and for science to unravel some of the disease's mysteries. By the time Earvin "Magic" Johnson of the Los Angeles Lakers became the first active sports superstar to reveal he was HIV positive in 1991, we had learned that the virus doesn't care if you're gay or straight—any kind of unprotected sex can transmit HIV.

A few of us at HBO learned from Seth Abraham, the president of HBO Sports, about Arthur's diagnosis soon after it had been made, but we swore ourselves to secrecy, not even telling Arthur that we knew. We all noticed times when Arthur was struggling. He sometimes had trouble writing with his weakened right arm. He lost weight. The "silent and generous conspiracy of silence" that protected him—Arthur's words for it later—began to fall apart when Doug Smith, a tennis writer for *USA Today* and a lifelong friend of Arthur's from Richmond, Virginia, visited Arthur with some devastating news for both of them. The newspaper was going to run a story reporting that Arthur had HIV/AIDS.

Arthur pleaded for privacy instead. When no such promise was forthcoming, he felt forced to call a press conference the next day in New York to tell the world the truth. Ilana and I had just flown from New York to Chicago that morning when someone at HBO called to tell me the news, and to ask if I could attend as a show of support. There wasn't enough time to fly back, so I called and reached Arthur just minutes before he walked out to a microphone to face the media.

"Arthur, I am so sorry you were outed like this," I said. "It's horrible when you have your privacy invaded."

I'll never forget the sadness in his voice as he answered, "Ah, Billie, they're such rats. I don't want to do this. I can't *believe* they're doing this to me." I listened to him and thought about the pain his family must be feeling as well. It sent me back to how raw and exposed I felt after Marilyn outed me.

Later that year, Arthur came to Wimbledon as always and we ate breakfast together every morning before going to the HBO studio. We talked about our sport, about race, and about how he had turned his research of the history of Black athletes into a three-volume set of books titled *Hard Road to Glory*. He told me about his recent trip to South Africa at the request of Nelson Mandela, who had finally been released from prison.

One day I asked him, "Arthur, what's been the most difficult thing for you?"

"Being a Black man," he said without hesitating.

Camera was five or six by then, old enough to understand what was happening. Arthur told me he was taking her to all the courts where he had played and telling her his stories. I hope she remembers how extraordinary her father was.

In the final months of Arthur's life, he and Jeanne put together a fund-raiser at the 1992 U.S. Open for the new Arthur Ashe Foundation for the Defeat of AIDS. (The event, which has since raised millions of dollars for the cause, is now called Arthur Ashe Kids' Day.) Arthur took time during the tournament to travel to Washington, D.C., to protest our government's treatment of Haitian refugees. He was also racing to finish his memoir.

Even after suffering another mild heart attack, Arthur was still making the rounds of every benefit and news show he could squeeze in to talk about athletes, education, apartheid, and AIDS. He made a speech on the floor of the United Nations on World AIDS Day on December 1, 1992. Two months after that, Arthur died of AIDS-related pneumonia. He was forty-nine.

It was my honor to be among the speakers at Arthur's memorial service in New York, which was attended by more than five thousand people despite a February snowstorm. I've thought about Arthur a lot since then, including during the summer of 2020, in the midst of the Black Lives Matter protests that were sweeping the country. It felt like sweet justice when the statues of Confederate heroes along Monument Avenue in Arthur's hometown of Richmond were taken down until only the statues of Arthur and Confederate General Robert E. Lee remained—and then Virginia Governor Ralph Northam ruled that the Lee statue must go, too, sparking a flurry of lawsuits to block its removal.

When Arthur's statue was originally placed on that boulevard in 1996, opponents argued that he didn't belong there amid the exist-

ing memorials of Confederate icons. Now look. Arthur may outlast
them all.

BY THE TIME Althea Gibson broke the color barrier for African
Americans at the tennis majors in the 1950s, the Black-run Amateur Tennis Association had been giving African Americans places
to play in segregated America since 1916. The ATA helped Althea
launch her tennis career and later championed Arthur.

I was so motivated by Althea's skill and example when I saw her
as a junior player I made sure that Larry and I were among those who
worked to make tennis an equal-opportunity sport, at first through
the Tennis for Everyone clinics we started in under-resourced neighborhoods in the late 1960s, and then in our other ventures. Gladys
Heldman always felt the same way about encouraging diversity.

At the start of the Virginia Slims tour, Gladys approached Dr.
Clyde C. Freeman, president of the ATA, to ask for his help. That's
how Bonnie Logan became the first African American player to
join our tour in 1971, and Ann Koger and Sylvia Hooks followed by
1973, continuing a lineage that stretched back to Althea and forward to other female players of color that came after them, such as
Kim Sands, Renée Blount, Leslie Allen, Andrea Buchanan, Katrina
Adams, Lori McNeil, Zina Garrison, Chanda Rubin, and, of course,
Venus and Serena Williams.

Like Althea and the Original 9, the first African American players on the Slims tour were underappreciated pioneers. Bonnie was
an amazing athlete who played five sports in college. She was also
one of the first African Americans to play tennis in South Africa
during apartheid. Ann competed with Bonnie on both the men's and
women's teams at Morgan State University and they won collegiate
titles. Sylvia had an academic scholarship to Central State University in Wilberforce, Ohio, another historically Black school, and
later got her master's degree at Stanford.

When Gladys and Dr. Freeman held a press conference with
Bonnie in New York in November 1972 to announce the collaboration between the ATA and the Slims tour, it was yet another case

of Gladys finding a like-minded ally to work with while rattling the cage of the USLTA in a wonderfully progressive way. The next day's *New York Times* story noted how our new working relationship put the USLTA "in a delicate position" because the USLTA had "little contact with the ATA despite similar objectives in junior development." The insinuation was clear: The USLTA wasn't doing all it could to serve the Black community.

I wish I could say it was always trouble-free for Bonnie, Ann, and Sylvia once they joined our tour. It wasn't. They all said they had some terrific experiences. Our crowds in Philadelphia were filled with ATA members who gave them a warm reception. In Houston, Ann recalls how the Black staff at our tournament site came out to take a peek at them because, she says, "They told us they had never seen Black women professional tennis players before, and we made them proud." But at our tour stop in Boca Raton, Florida, some staffers tried to direct Ann, Bonnie, and Sylvia to the club's service entrance even though they arrived wearing their tennis gear. "We're players—we don't work here!" they said. At our tournament site at the Jockey Club in Miami, they were dismayed to see Confederate flags flying from every other flagpole around the top rim of the grandstand. Ann secretly climbed up there one night and took one of the flags down. When she saw Peachy Kellmeyer later, Ann motioned to the remaining Confederate flags and said, "You know they lost. That's an insult to us, and every other American." Someone got the message. "The next day," Ann says, "all those Confederate flags were gone."

Tournament housing could be another issue. Many players still stayed with host families in private homes to save money, but Bonnie, Ann, and Sylvia dryly noted how available rooms disappeared when they showed up at the tournament desk. They heard every excuse imaginable—suddenly, a child was sick, or there was a death in the family. I happened to run into Sylvia at the Jockey Club right after she had been informed that there was no lodging available for them with any host families. "Can you please wait right here?" I asked her. I went to the tournament check-in desk and said, calm but as direct as I could be, "You know, there must be some mistake.

My friends here told me that you have no housing for them. And if that is true, I can assure you that I will not play in this tournament. And neither will anyone else. Understand? So, what are you going to do for them?"

They found Ann, Bonnie, and Sylvia rooms in a nice Holiday Inn.

"We were all trying to make it a better world," Sylvia says now of those pioneering days, "and the world wasn't always having it."

ARTHUR'S DEATH TOUCHED Ilana and me so personally we wanted to get more involved in the fight against AIDS. Just weeks after his funeral, Ilana and I flew to Los Angeles to attend Elton's first Oscar viewing party and fund-raiser for his AIDS foundation. Elton had started the effort after learning about Ryan White, an Indiana boy who was ostracized so badly after he was diagnosed with AIDS that he and his family eventually left their hometown of Kokomo to escape the personal attacks. One of the last straws was the day a bullet came flying through a window at the Whites' house.

Elton was deeply affected by knowing that he had been given a second chance at life despite his addictions while Ryan, a hemophiliac, was dying of AIDS because of a tainted blood transfusion. Elton had befriended Ryan, given the White family money to help them move, and was at Ryan's bedside when he passed away at the age of eighteen.

Elton and I had always talked about finding a way to put music and sports together in a program, and Ilana came up with the perfect idea. She mentioned to Elton that the twentieth anniversary of the Battle of the Sexes was approaching in September 1993, so why not use it to raise money for his AIDS foundation? That's how the annual Smash Hits all-star fund-raisers started. We've raised millions of dollars since.

The first event featured a private concert by Elton and dinner at the Beverly Wilshire hotel. The next day we had a World TeamTennis match at the Forum featuring Jimmy Connors, Vitas Gerulaitis, and Martina. But the biggest stir was made by Bobby Riggs, who showed up wearing a pink sweater and finally got me to play a rematch—this time, fifteen minutes of mixed doubles. We were happy to see each other again. In some ways, Bobby hadn't changed a bit. He told reporters that he and Martina would have beaten Elton and me had we played a full set. "I'd bet a thousand dollars on it!" Bobby crowed. He still had some nice shots for a seventy-five-year-old.

Over the years, Bobby and I went back and forth over the meaning of the Battle of the Sexes. I would always say, "It was about social change, Bobby. It wasn't about a hustle, don't you see? This was historical, what you and I did."

A day or two before Bobby died from cancer in 1995 at the age of seventy-seven, I called to check on him. Lornie Kuhle, who remained a devoted friend of Bobby's throughout his life, alerted Ilana and me that Bobby wasn't doing well. His voice was very weak, but one of the last things he said to me was, "We did make a difference, didn't we?"

I said, "I love you, Bobby." He said, "I love you."

I HIT MY FIFTIETH BIRTHDAY a month after Elton's first AIDS fund-raiser, and Charles Schulz surprised me by drawing the invitations. My parents and Randy and his wife, Pam, flew to New York for a surprise party in my honor. By then, Mom and Dad had moved from Long Beach to a place they built to fit their wishes in the forest above the town of Prescott, Arizona. Just down the hill was the Pine Cone Inn, where they could dance to swing music every Friday night. Mom took art classes at Yavapai College and spent her days painting. Dad had retired from the Long Beach fire department in 1977 after thirty-five years and worked for a while as a part-time scout for the Milwaukee Brewers baseball team.

I saw them as often as I could, which wasn't enough. Usually I went by myself. Ilana felt awkward when we visited them because it still went unacknowledged that we were a couple. If we did go together, we slept in separate bedrooms. My mother hadn't given up hope that I might wake up one morning and be straight. Sometimes she still asked, "Any new boyfriends, Sis?" Something had to give. I was fifty years old and still tiptoeing around my parents, trying not to upset my dad or disappoint my mom. All my life I wanted to be the "good girl." Then one day I realized that always trying to be the good girl was making my life unbearable.

Chapter 29

I GOT OUT of the car, stopped at a stone archway, and looked down at a seam in the concrete sidewalk. Across that line was the entrance to the Renfrew Center for Eating Disorders in Philadelphia. There was no missing the symbolism here. Ilana had dropped me off and kissed me goodbye and now I stood here all alone thinking, *If I cross this threshold, this is genuinely my moment of truth.* By the beginning of 1995, I had amassed all sorts of accomplishments and firsts. I'd been inducted into the International Tennis Hall of Fame. I'd invented myself not once, but twice—first as an athlete and activist, and again after Marilyn outed me. And yet, I knew that I had to face one more struggle, or I was finished.

I had recently turned fifty-one, I was at least forty pounds overweight, and I had hit bottom emotionally, physically, and spiritually. Ilana and I were still closeted to most people. After I stopped competing, I wasn't working out regularly and my weight occasionally hit 200 pounds. I became detached, almost remote, which isn't like me at all. I couldn't stop overeating, no matter how hard I tried. I felt depressed and disconnected from myself and the people I loved. It became difficult for me to function.

Some days I would gobble up ten candy bars and a quart of ice cream, but it would only momentarily satisfy me. Sometimes I'd allow myself all the chips or Snickers bars I wanted, then I'd go on an extreme diet to lose the weight. During one diet I drank nothing but powdered shakes that I mixed in a blender and lost something like fifty pounds. Then I'd binge and my weight would balloon again. I was tormented that I hadn't been able to live out my life or personal challenges the way I wanted. In my mind, I pictured myself standing in a circle of solid barriers and when I'd walk out from the center toward any place in that circle I would get stopped. It was as if I had no place to go, I couldn't get out. I felt my soul was imprisoned; a battle was going on inside me. I wasn't being truthful.

My therapist saw how desperate my behavior was, and suggested that it might be time for in-patient treatment. I called two clinical psychologist friends, Kay Loveland and Julie Anthony, and asked them to recommend a treatment center. Both independently suggested Renfrew. I believe taking their advice saved my life.

I was willing to stop everything and spend the recommended five weeks in residential treatment. In fact, I welcomed it, knowing that I had to put my workaholic drive aside for once and make my health my top priority. Ilana told me not to worry, she would take care of everything while I was away. The night before my admission, we drove from New York to Philadelphia and checked into a hotel on Rittenhouse Square. We ate dinner knowing that it would be our last meal together for a while. In the morning, Ilana and I were quiet as she drove me along the familiar leafy streets of Chestnut Hill where I had stayed when I was an amateur in the 1950s and '60s. That was also where I first started binging on Bassetts Ice Cream. Talk about coming full circle.

Renfrew was just a few miles away. The facility sits in a neighborhood of horse farms and old stone mansions. The residential center I checked into is part of a cluster of colonial-style buildings surrounded by pastures and forests. I felt nervous anticipation, but also a readiness to face whatever came next. Ilana has always been skeptical about psychotherapy, but she promised to do anything I needed to support me and help me work through things, including attending couples therapy.

Renfrew was homey and welcoming, but it was by no means a resort. The residents, as we were called, lived in comfortable but spare double rooms. The sheets were a plastic blend, a sobering concession to the fact that some residents were tempted to purge once alone. Most of the residents had roommates, but my treatment team decided I needed my own space so I could be alone with my thoughts and have some peace. But other than when I slept, I was rarely by myself during the next thirty-five days. Unless we were in individual therapy, residents had some sort of group meeting most of the day, from eight in the morning until lights out at 10 p.m. We were encouraged to keep a daily journal. We were served three meals a day in a communal dining room, along with snacks and desserts.

To my initial dismay, I was told I was not there to lose weight. The philosophy at Renfrew was not to create a make-believe space where you had none of the temptations or choices you faced in the outside world; the object was to help you understand and manage the emotions behind your eating disorder and to start normalizing your relationship with food. Neither sugar nor caffeine was banned, and smokers could light up outside. Everyone was given an individualized meal plan based on their needs. We were simply asked to pay attention to our eating, an approach that would be called "mindfulness" today.

A lot of hospitals at the time treated the symptoms of eating disorders without looking for the underlying emotional issues or conflicts that were causing the problem. Renfrew was different. It used an integrated approach to treat the whole person, from medical, nutritional, social, and psychological perspectives. They delved into my relationships in my life as possible sources of dysfunction, as well as paths to healing.

As soon as I checked in, I was placed on a team with other residents. Each team had its own group of therapists. The individual therapist assigned to me was named Lynn, and she was so insightful I still keep in touch with her. We met three times weekly during my stay at Renfrew. Between Lynn and group sessions with my peers, I found out how little I knew about eating disorders.

Eating disorders can affect people of "every age, sex, gender, race, ethnicity, and socioeconomic group," according to the National Eating Disorders Association website. You really can't generalize about who is at risk, but EDs tend to show up in adolescence, most often among girls. Some people, including me, mask our disease well into middle age. Renfrew's patients range in age from their teens to older adults. When I was there, most of my fellow residents were in either high school or college.

The most commonly treated types of ED are anorexia nervosa, bulimia, and binge-eating disorder. The definitions can be tricky, but NEDA describes anorexia nervosa as a disorder characterized by "weight loss (or lack of appropriate weight gain in growing children); difficulties maintaining an appropriate body weight for height, age, and stature; and, in many individuals, a distorted body image."

Bulimia nervosa is "binge eating and compensatory behaviors such as self-induced vomiting designed to undo or compensate for the effects of binge eating."

Binge-eating disorder, which is what I have, is now the most commonly diagnosed ED in the United States, but it wasn't recognized in the fourth edition of the *Diagnostic and Statistical Manual of Mental Disorders* (DSM-4) when I went in for treatment. Whatever didn't fit neatly into the other two categories was lumped into "Eating Disorder Not Otherwise Specified." That was my initial diagnosis.

The updated DSM-5 now recognizes binge eating as "a severe, life-threatening, and treatable eating disorder characterized by recurrent episodes of eating large quantities of food (often very quickly and to the point of discomfort); a feeling of a loss of control during the binge; experiencing shame, distress or guilt afterwards; and not regularly using unhealthy compensatory measures (e.g., purging) to counter the binge eating."

Elton has talked candidly about how he struggled with bulimia, and addictions to drugs, alcohol, and sex in the 1970s and '80s. I never knew; I only suspected. He cut me out of his life for five years after I asked him directly if he was using drugs—"Of course not!" he said, turning red. He only got back in touch, out of the blue, after he entered a treatment center near Chicago in early 1991. He called from there and asked Ilana and me to come see him. I had always told him no matter how tough life got, I would love him unconditionally. We were there the next morning.

I overate, too, but unlike Elton, I never threw up. Studies summarized on the NEDA website have shown that athletes are particularly prone to eating disorders because we are constantly monitoring our weight. Our need to control our bodies can become an obsession. I'm a perfectionist by nature, which is another risk factor. The Olympic gymnasts Cathy Rigby and Nadia Comaneci both nearly died from self-starvation. As I would soon find out, the great young tennis star Monica Seles was also suffering from a binge-eating disorder after she was stabbed by a deranged fan of Stephanie Graf in 1993, and her father died of cancer not long afterward.

Starting as a teenager, Ilana often struggled with food issues. Eventually she experienced large swings in her weight as she went on a series of diets starting in 1972, after she had gained twenty-five pounds on her first trip to Europe and the United Kingdom. She told me if she won she ate because she was happy, and if she lost she ate because she was depressed. What turned her around was training for, and completing, the 1981 New York City Marathon. Ilana says running changed her life because it was something that was totally self-driven and empowering. The outcome wasn't clouded for her by, say, a tennis opponent having a bad day or some other variable.

Through talking to Lynn and listening to others in group therapy, I started to understand that eating disorders are an unhealthy relationship with food that stems from what Renfrew calls a "dysfunctional relationship with the self." For me, having an ED is a daily fight, much like being an alcoholic. I know I'm in trouble when I start to get two voices going in my head. I wake up in the morning thinking I might want a quart of ice cream and start obsessing about it. One voice will say, *No. You need to take care of yourself and eat properly and exercise.* All the rational stuff. The other voice goes, *Forget it. I want it.* There can be this tug-of-war all day long, and it's exhausting. I have to pay attention because it's not really about the food or hunger—something emotional is going on.

One of the most pivotal questions Lynn asked me after we began working on my eating disorder was "What's in it for you to be overweight?" I had never thought about it before. "Relief," I said. "Comfort. Protection from being harassed, especially over my sexuality."

Just being asked to describe it brought up feelings I had suppressed for years. I tore through a lot of Kleenex, crying—and I'm not a crier. I realized the gut pain I so often felt was caused by emotions I tamped down. When I overate, it was about trying to numb the hurt. I learned that another of my issues is deflection. When a subject matter is painful or anxiety producing, it's hard for me to keep my mind from going off on tangents. Even in treatment at Renfrew, it was much easier for me to delve into the science of EDs—I was fascinated to learn that brain scans show how sugar activates the same neurological pathways as nicotine or cocaine—rather than focus on addressing my own food addiction. There were so many people in pain at Renfrew, my immediate impulse was to help them fix their problems, which is another thing I've been doing my whole life. When the staff at Renfrew saw me behaving that way, they stopped me and said I had to take care of myself first.

We were offered a range of therapy models—talk therapy, art and movement therapy, and psychodrama sessions where residents and staff acted out scenes from our childhoods to revisit and resolve past traumas. There was a lot of visualization involved, and I threw myself into that. I was shocked by the things that came up, and also what I couldn't remember. It was agonizing. In one exercise, we were told to visualize a safe space.

I couldn't find one.

WHEN I TRIED to figure out where the unsafe feelings first came from, it made me look back at a childhood spent coping with my fear of my father's unpredictable anger and my very capable mother's tendency to silence or subjugate herself. Both dynamics affected me. I was always on edge, ready for the switch to flip, trying to please everybody. So I grew up restless and hypervigilant. I compartmentalized. Then I had to hide my sexuality. Then I was constantly worrying about being exposed.

By my forties, I also developed the first serious health challenge of my life. I noticed one day that my heart was racing. When I lay on my left side it felt like my heart was flopping around in my chest. I was scared and smart enough to get it treated right away, and I was diagnosed with atrial fibrillation, or A-fib. My cardiologist told me the condition occurs when the upper heart chambers fire out of sync with the two lower chambers and cause arrythmia. If left untreated, it can lead to stroke, heart failure, and other complications. I'm lucky that I've been able to control it for the most part with medication. But there have been several occasions when doctors had to admit me to the hospital, sedate me, and use defibrillator paddles to shock my speeding heart back into place. I've had two cardiac ablations.

There were so many confusing and painful emotions that I tried to numb with food and denial. When Frank Deford and I were collaborating on the book that was rushed into print after I was outed, I wanted the title to be *Misfit* because I felt like I was always on the outside looking in, walled off from the rest of the world because of what I was hiding. I was still battling those thoughts a decade later when *Life* magazine included me on its 1990 list of "The 100 Most Important Americans of the 20th Century" along with Eleanor Roosevelt, Dr. Martin Luther King Jr., Albert Einstein, Bob Dylan, Jackie Robinson, and Muhammad Ali. It was a huge honor. But I kept asking myself, *If they think I'm so great, why am I so miserable? What's wrong?*

At Renfrew I learned that isolation is another symptom of an eating disorder. That's why the group therapy experience and participation of family members was considered so important. Ilana, true to her word, dropped her aversion to therapy, telling me early on, "I'll do anything that is going to help you get through this." My parents were not as easy to get onboard the treatment train. Convincing them to allow me to fly them to Philadelphia for family therapy was difficult. They couldn't understand why I needed therapy in the first place. They didn't want to discuss my sexuality or the possibility that I might have an eating disorder. They were in almost total denial, which made me think: *That's exactly where I was.*

We did get Mom and Dad on conference calls a couple times for sessions with the family therapist. When I begged and pleaded for them to come to Renfrew—I was starting to get upset about their refusal to buy in—they finally agreed to one weekend. They were unhappy about it. But it was crucial to my recovery.

I had to come out to them once and for all, to their faces, and tell them how miserable it made me when I couldn't be totally honest, especially with the people I loved most. I was weary of being so cautious and measured, dancing around the truth, cauterizing my feelings. Dealing with my sexuality has been the hardest, longest-lasting challenge of my life.

My parents joined us on a Friday night when residents, former residents, and their families all gathered in a large room for an open group meeting. We all introduced ourselves and some shared our stories about how our eating disorders had wrecked our health and relationships. I felt my dad stiffen in the chair next to me. At one point he leaned over and whispered, "Sis, you're not like these girls."

I said, "Dad, I am. I'm just like them."

My dad heard me, and he was terrific for the rest of the weekend even after we went through some extremely painful sessions as a family. Mom was a mess. She kept trying to take all the responsibility and saying, "Where did I go wrong?"

"Mom, you didn't—you were and are great," I assured her.

After a difficult afternoon on Saturday, my dad was walking down a hallway with me and said, "Be patient with your mother. She'll come around. She just takes longer." It was such a sweet moment, and the beginning of a profound change in us all.

In individual therapy, I was dumbstruck when Lynn uttered one of the most important things anyone has ever said to me: "Do you realize you've given all your power away to your parents? What does it feel like, always trying to take care of their feelings instead of your own? When are you going to take your power back?"

She was right. Realizing that was the turning point. I now knew what had to change.

I can see now how I was making accommodations for everyone, not just my parents, by concealing my true sexuality, even after I was outed. I was driven so far underground, some of the aftereffects took me decades to unwind and created one of the great paradoxes of my life. In tennis I was among those out front catching blowback and credit, shouldering enormous responsibility and blame in constantly shifting amounts. Whether it happened by circumstance or conscious choice is hardly the point. There were mountains to scale, setbacks to absorb, secrets I dared not utter. Some days—including that night I played Bobby—I felt as if nothing could stop me. Sometimes our achievements tore along at such a breakneck pace that to this day when people ask what I remember about the seventies, I answer, "I remember always being tired."

And yet, while people saw me joust fearlessly in public and even called me a militant, they had little idea how much I privately struggled for clarity, for honesty. I had my first committed lesbian relationship in my twenties, but I was fifty-one before I could finally look at my mother and father and say the words, "I am gay." It took Ilana's assertion of her place in my life to prod me to finally allow what I wanted to supplant my avoidance of divorcing Larry. Had it been gratitude, affection, duty, guilt, self-preservation, an aversion to more pain that caused the delay? Yes. It took my time at Renfrew to show me how my eating disorder was symptomatic of so many things. Social conditioning is a powerful, powerful thing.

So is love.

Chapter 30

———————

I THINK EVERYTHING we go through is a process of self-discovery, but tennis can accelerate what you learn because it engages all of your senses. As a singles player, you go it alone. You have to summon whatever it takes—energy, self-awareness, determination, ambition—to drive yourself to the finish. You have to have the sensitivity to take in everything and yet a certain obstinacy when it comes to ignoring your fears and advancing fatigue, calculating the risks and then going for broke sometimes anyway. You make decisions in nanoseconds, often under duress, and you can find out about yourself really quickly.

Sometimes I liked what I saw in me, and other times I didn't. Either way, one of the most important things I learned is that there are times when you think you cannot take another step, when you're sure you can't continue another minute, and then you find there's some reserve in your body, in your soul, that you didn't know you had. You go into a different gear—there are an indefinable number of them—that allows you to rise to the occasion. There's a place you go sometimes that you didn't realize you could go, and you win yourself a new beginning.

That was me, after Renfrew.

Ilana and I became more open in our lives. We stopped hiding from friends and acquaintances that we were a couple, then we expanded the circle from there. My parents finally accepted Ilana and me as partners, and we made a point to visit them together. (One of their favorite things was to have us take them shopping at Costco, and then grab hot dogs and Cokes for lunch and chat.) Now when I

phoned home, Mom ended our calls by saying, "Give Ilana our love."
It was just four little words. But they meant the world to me.

If interviewers asked about my sexuality now, I answered honestly. I didn't identify Ilana as my partner at first because she was the
chief executive officer and commissioner of World TeamTennis by
2001 and we were both wary of the corporate blowback that might
ensue if we were vocal about being an out couple. It wasn't until the
spring of 2006 when HBO aired *Billie Jean King: Portrait of a Pioneer*,
a documentary by the producer Margaret Grossi, the interviewer
and story adviser Mary Carillo, and the associate producer Helen
Russell, that Ilana discussed our relationship for the first time on
camera. That was when we came all the way out of the closet.

We stepped further into the open that summer after the USTA
president, Franklin Johnson, told me the board had voted unanimously to rename the entire Flushing Meadows complex, home of
the U.S. Open, the Billie Jean King National Tennis Center. The
first thing I thought was, *The USTA is not only going to name the place
after a woman—but after someone who led a revolt against them for open
tennis and equal opportunities?* Amazing.

The ceremony was held at Arthur Ashe Stadium, the tennis center's main stadium, and it brought me to tears. My father had passed
away only two and a half months earlier, at the age of eighty-eight.
Not having him there was so poignant, especially when I saw that
the USTA had flown out the color guard from the Long Beach fire
department in honor of my dad, including a captain who knew him
personally. It was hard to believe that somebody who always seemed
so much larger than life could be gone. But my mother and Ilana
were beside me that day, as were Randy's daughters, Alysha and
Miranda, and I thanked them during my remarks. It was the first
time I had acknowledged Ilana's real place in my life on a public
stage, not to mention on a live television broadcast that was being
beamed to 184 countries.

After twenty-seven years, I finally felt comfortable enough to
bring our love out into the open, on our terms. As we stood on the
floor of the stadium together, Diana Ross sang rousing renditions of
"Respect" and "Ain't No Mountain High Enough." Chrissie, Venus

Williams, Jimmy Connors, and John McEnroe made some heartfelt remarks about our shared connection over the years. By the time Mayor Michael Bloomberg led me to the podium for my speech, I admit I was a bit overwhelmed. My voice was a little soft as I started, and someone in the crowd shouted, "Louder!"

"Well, that's the first time anybody's said that to me," I said with a laugh.

I emphasized in my speech that this honor wasn't about me. It symbolized what can happen in life when you believe. The national tennis center is on forty-six and a half acres of public-park land. I was a public-park kid who came along when tennis wasn't as hospitable to someone like me. Now that I had my name on the place, I wanted to invite everybody to come out and play: people of all genders and colors, the LGBTQ+ community, people with disabilities. No one has to be on the outside looking in, not in tennis or anywhere else.

"*Mi casa es su casa,*" I said that night. "My house is your house! This is *our* house."

FIVE YEARS AFTER Ilana and I stepped out completely, the NBA executive Rick Welts came forward in 2011 as the first openly gay male executive in North American sports. He's since been voted into the NBA Hall of Fame for his front office work. The following year, our friend Sally Ride, the first female astronaut America sent into space, was dying of cancer and she and her life partner, Tam O'Shaughnessy, decided to publicly reveal they were a couple for the first time—though not until Sally's obituary. Two years after that, in 2014, Apple's Tim Cook came out as the first openly gay CEO of a Fortune 500 company. Tim wrote about it in a first-person article for *Bloomberg,* and acknowledged that he was worried about the reaction outside Apple because "the world is still not friendly to gay or trans people in many countries but also within our country."

Feeling safe enough to come out is a crucial consideration that I always emphasize. Not everyone lives and works in a place where diversity is tolerated. What I've found is that if you can achieve a comfort level or push through whatever else is inhibiting you, your worst fears may not come true. If you don't give people a chance, they never have the opportunity to surprise you—often in the most wonderful ways.

Telling the truth has had a transformative effect on my life and relationships and happiness. When Barack Obama and Hillary Clinton each ran for president, I no longer worried about my sexuality being a liability. Ilana and I were seen as assets and were invited to work as surrogates for both candidates through three campaigns. If I was traveling for business, I would call the campaign staff in whatever place I was and say, "Put me to work. What can I do to help while I'm here?" In 2020, Ilana and I also worked for the Joe Biden–Kamala Harris presidential ticket and supported efforts to get out the vote. The night they won the election, we sent a text to Hillary thanking her for her landmark run for the White House, which helped crack open the door that Kamala kicked down.

When Donald Trump was president, many of the things we fought for in the 1960s and '70s were relitigated and remain under attack. We suddenly had a president who bragged about sexual assault and penalized anyone he sees as Other. As his four-year stay went on, his behavior became even more divisive and objectionable, culminating with the January 2021 attack on the U.S. Capitol building. I'll never forget seeing a sign at the 2017 Women's March that read "I can't believe we still have to protest this stuff." I get the frustration. I sometimes feel it myself.

But if you're in the business of change, you have to be prepared to play the long game. Even now, in my late seventies as I write, I've never felt comfortable enough to stop pushing. Diversity, equity, and inclusion (DE&I) are the animating principles behind all the work that Ilana and I do in business, in politics, in the LGBTQ+ rights arena, and in the other social justice causes we support.

The recurring question we ask ourselves whenever we consider any undertaking is *When this is done, will we have helped make the world a better place?* If the answer is no, then we move on to other possibilities. I often joke with Ilana that we want to make lots and lots of money before I'm out of here so we can give it all away. The way we define success is doing well *and* doing good.

I've always said that it helps women in business to know sports because men have created both cultures, and having that knowledge helps you navigate your path and pick up vital cues and subtleties. Sports teach you how to assert yourself and create sustained bonds even in competitive environments; you learn how to weather setbacks and conflict, handle pressure, and push through to get the outcome you want, whether it's with teammates or by yourself. Those are vital skills in business. To me, it's not surprising that research by EY (Ernst & Young's global organization) and espnW has shown that 94 percent of women at the C-suite level say they played sports, and more than half competed at the university level. UBS, a company we work with, has data that shows that women-led companies are outperforming corporations led by men. Women often have to be more resourceful to survive and advance.

Ed Woolard, the former CEO of DuPont and one of our most important business mentors and dear friends, has helped me refine some pointers that we could pass along to audiences of all ages about what makes people successful, happy human beings. We came up with three components for inner and outer success:

1. Be a problem solver and an innovator, and realize that once you identify a problem, it's important to be part of the solution.
2. Never stop learning, and never stop learning how to learn.
3. Relationships are everything.

WHILE MUCH IS understandably made of the early part of my life and career, what too often goes overlooked is that Ilana and I have been together for forty years and the story of our time together has never been fully told or understood. Granted, part of that was our doing. But when I look at our personal life together and what we've accomplished as businesswomen and social activists, it's significant.

Stylistically and temperamentally, we're very different, but those differences complement each other. I bring emotion, energy, and vision; Ilana is an ideas person, too, but she's more results oriented, and excels at selling concepts and finding ways to finish the job, close the deal. She tempers my runaway enthusiasm, and she says I raise her ability to be more open-minded, more forgiving. We're partners in every sense of the word. Our values align seamlessly. I don't think Ilana gets enough recognition for her pivotal role and leadership in everything we do, let alone what she's accomplished independently.

By the time I turned seventy in 2013, we began thinking seriously about my legacy. What could I leave behind that would be enduring and meaningful for future generations? One answer came in 2014, when Ilana and I worked with Paul Keary, Kim Davis, Michael Coakley, and Therese O'Higgins at the strategic advisory firm Teneo to start the Billie Jean King Leadership Initiative, our non-profit undertaking to promote equality and inclusion and advocate for pay equality.

Studies have shown that creativity and productivity increase in businesses where workplace diversity and inclusion are supported, and that improves the bottom line for employers and employees alike. People are better on the job when they can be themselves. But how do you get employers onboard who may be lagging?

We decided to start working with large corporations that set trends in workplace practices at the C-suite level, knowing that CEOs can do things overnight if they want to, and corporations can help move governments and change legislation.

One example is Marc Benioff, the founder of Salesforce, a cloud-based software company. Ilana and I met Marc in April 2015 at the White House when we were attending the Equal Pay Day event, which is meant to raise awareness about the gender pay gap. In 2019, an American woman had to work for sixteen months to earn what a white American man made in twelve months, if both of them worked full-time. Overall, women in the U.S. make only about 82 percent of what men do, and the gap is far worse for African American and Latinx women, who earn 62 percent and 55 percent, respectively. President Obama made the Lilly Ledbetter Fair Pay

Act of 2009 the first bill he signed after taking office; this important piece of legislation widened the time frame and conditions under which an employee can sue their employer for discrimination. But we still need to do more. Many people don't realize that women and minorities fall behind from the timing of their very first promotion, and then it's hard to catch up, according to the 2019 Women in the Workplace study, one of the most comprehensive examinations to date of the experiences of working women and men.

Marc is a very unusual CEO who has become one of the BJKLI's greatest allies. He's a delightful, brilliant man who has always had a social conscience and designed a model of corporate giving that is replicated all over the world. But Marc was surprised after two of his executive vice presidents, Cindy Robbins and Leyla Seka, urged him to do an internal audit of their seventeen thousand employees, and the data showed what the two women expected: In many cases, he was paying women in his company less than men who had similar jobs. Over the next two years, Marc spent nearly $9 million to correct the compensation gaps that existed by gender *and* race *and* ethnicity across the company. When *60 Minutes* interviewed him about it, Marc admitted that he had been in denial that the inequities existed at first, and so are many of his fellow CEOs.

"I've had CEOs call me and say, 'This is not true, this is not real' and I'll say to them, 'This *is* true. Look at the numbers,'" Marc told *60 Minutes*. "CEOs, with one button on a computer, can pay every man and every woman equally. We have the data. We know what everyone makes. There's no excuse."

At the BJKLI, we've partnered with Starbucks, which announced in 2018 that it had reached its goal to provide 100 percent pay equity for employees of all genders and races performing similar work across the U.S. We've worked with Deloitte, the professional services network, to get the facts out about workplace diversity and promote practical solutions for how to foster it.

The BJKLI is still a young organization, but we've produced some insightful research on Millennials, who will make up 75 percent of the global workforce by 2025. They have made it clear that they don't want to work in a place that isn't inclusive, and they will leave such jobs for more diverse workplaces. I've seen members of older generations roll their eyes when they talk about this group of younger workers, claiming that they are self-absorbed and irresponsible. I don't see them that way. Our research shows that Millennials and Gen Z are the two greatest generations for inclusion. I think they are going to help solve problems. They aren't so hung up on people's looks and customs. They don't buy into the traditional boundaries of gender and race. They're deeply interested in collaboration and connection. They've grown up using social media and technology, and they're adept at building community. They think and work a lot on how they want to present themselves to the world, and quite often, they have an entrepreneurial streak—even if it's only focused on building their online followings. They have big ideas, and they don't shrink from the public square. They're comfortable with the idea of being influencers, even disrupters. And the technology we have now makes it easier to do all of that than ever before.

Technology has revolutionized the speed and logistics of activism. A message can go viral even if you don't have huge resources to fight your battles. Ideas can carry you. Sometimes a cell phone is all it takes. I use Twitter and Instagram as daily consciousness-raising tools. I told Kristi Gaylord, my social media person, "If you said I have a half-million followers, I'd say, 'Don't talk to me about it till I get a million!'" Then we broke up laughing. She knows I'm only half-joking.

Illuminating the challenges and paths to achieving equality is important because power and influence are still mostly held by white men. I've spent my whole life watching men stick up for each other and help each other. I've seen men—even men who otherwise have little in common *except* that they're men—actively organize with each other to shut women out. Women don't bond or organize that way.

Women also have to fight people's tendencies to tell us when we do lead or succeed, "Thanks for what you do for women." We never limit male leaders by telling them, "Thanks for what you do for men." This double standard has to stop. Any time women are discounted as if we're only representing half the population, it also consigns us to less of the marketplace, fewer opportunities, less money, less influence, and so on. We are never going to fulfill our potential until people realize that when women lead, we lead for everyone. When I fight for equality, I fight for everyone. If I see guys getting a raw deal, I fight to lift them too.

Every year, the BJKLI hosts a powerful symposium where we bring together thought leaders, CEOs, academics, community leaders, and artists to share in an open forum about what's working and where there is room for change. Our 2016 symposium was specifically focused on, and organized, for men because too often, especially in relation to women's conferences, men are removed from the conversation or effort. I couldn't have achieved what I have without the support of male allies. One of the things the BJKLI stresses is that equity is not a women's issue, an LGBTQ+ issue, or a minority issue—it's everyone's responsibility. None of us is as strong as all of us are together.

I genuinely believe that some men don't know how much they create obstacles for achieving diversity. When you're the dominant group, others are often invisible to you. People in subdominant or marginalized groups—people of color, the disabled, women, the LGBTQ+ community—don't have that luxury. We *have* to learn to navigate the dominant group's world to survive, let alone thrive. Our welfare depends on it.

SPORTS CONSISTENTLY REMINDS US how talent comes from all places, and how much we can achieve together, especially when we accept each other without prejudice and recognize that our differences make this a richer world. Tennis and sports remain a big part of what Ilana and I do, even though we sold our majority stake in World TeamTennis in 2017 and Ilana stepped down as commissioner.

I will never stop believing that our co-ed team format, if adopted wholesale, would lift the popularity of pro tennis and college tennis closer to the other team sports we compete against. After three decades, Ilana and I were simply ready to hand over the day-to-day operations of World TeamTennis, but we retained ownership of the Philadelphia Freedoms. Our interest in fostering diversity and inclusion at all levels of sports remains unchanged. We want to see management suites and coaching ranks reflect the diversity we've long seen on the playing field and in the rest of society.

To that end, in 2017, Ilana and I formed Billie Jean King Enterprises with a team of longtime trusted colleagues and strong leaders, Merle Blackman, Marjorie Gantman, Therese O'Higgins, Barbara Perry, Diane (Donnelly) Stone, and Nancy Falconer. The business is dedicated to creating strategic marketing partnerships, consulting on diversity and inclusion, and managing all aspects of my brand and legacy for the future. The company works in concert with the BJKLI to create meaningful and impactful change, efforts we plan to continue to grow.

Ilana and I also continue to encourage investment in women's sports. We're driven to help other women's sports progress to the level of women's pro tennis. When we had a chance in 2020 to join the ownership group of Angel City FC, the first National Women's Soccer League team that will be owned and run almost entirely by women, we took it.

The founders and original investors of the expansion team, which will be based in Los Angeles and begin play in 2022, include more than a dozen former members of the U.S. women's national soccer team; an array of women from the tech, finance, and entertainment industries; and some notable women of color, including Serena Williams, Candace Parker, and Eva Longoria. Alexis Ohanian, Serena's husband, was the lead founding investor. In previous years, I had consulted at times with Julie Foudy and other leaders of the U.S. women's national team as they fought the U.S. Soccer Federation for more equitable treatment, and again when the players were working to start their own professional league so they could make a living between World Cups and playing in the Olympics.

Ilana and I have also supported projects such as the XS Tennis and Education Foundation in Chicago, a program founded by the former player Kamau Murray for kids from under-resourced neighborhoods to learn tennis as a way to get ahead in life. One hundred percent of the attendees have landed college scholarships. It was through working with Kamau that we came to know two of Chicago's leading philanthropists, Mark and Kimbra Walter. Mark is CEO of the investment firm Guggenheim Partners and an owner and the chairman of the Los Angeles Dodgers, whose ownership group includes Magic Johnson. Mark and Ilana got to know each other better at the U.S. Open. At one of the subsequent fund-raisers for XS, our conversation with Mark turned toward the sports teams the Guggenheim group owns, and Mark asked if Ilana and I would be interested in becoming part owners of the WNBA's Los Angeles Sparks.

I said, "Why not the Dodgers as well?"

Mark looked at me and said, "Why not the Dodgers?"

That's how Ilana and I came into the Dodgers ownership group in 2018. Mark is committed to diversity, and Ilana and I certainly qualify. The Pride Night that we hosted at Dodger Stadium in 2019 drew 54,307 fans, making it the team's best-attended regular season home game in seven years. Some nights when Ilana and I sit in the box seats taking in a game, I wish my parents could be there beside me. Dad and Mom would have had a good laugh the night the Dodgers held a Billie Jean King bobblehead-doll giveaway in 2019 and I threw out the first pitch like I was a kid back on 36th Street. I thought about Dad a lot, too, when Ilana and I were in Arlington, Texas, in November 2020, watching the Dodgers clinch their first World Series title in thirty-two years. The last few games were so tense we were hanging on every pitch. I thought a lot about Randy, who I always hoped would win a World Series ring. The Dodgers were the first major pro team he and I supported after Dad passed his deep love of baseball along to us.

MUCH LIKE MY WORRIES about whether my business opportunities would ever rebound after I was outed, my fear of being ostracized from working with young people did not come true. I've always seen coaching and business mentoring as forms of leadership, and both

pursuits became even bigger passions of mine once I stopped playing and had more time. I have never forgotten how life-changing my
teachers, coaches, and the support of the Long Beach community
were for me. It's rewarding to help people experience some of the
same joys you've known.

Few people knew I had just come from in-patient treatment at
Renfrew when I was captain of the 1995 U.S. Fed Cup team seven
weeks later against Italy, one of nine times I served as the team's
coach and manager. The first stint was a prelude to my work as the
U.S. coach at the 1996 Atlanta Summer Olympics, and again at the
2000 Sydney Games. I love the Olympics because they've always
given women athletes and people of color a place to aspire to, even
when other avenues were closed. Tennis had been absent from the
Games from 1928 to 1988, and I never thought I'd get to experience
being an Olympian. Walking out for my first opening ceremony in
Atlanta, and then watching Muhammad Ali, dressed all in white,
stride out as the surprise choice to light the Olympic flame in the
stadium cauldron, is seared in my mind.

The Atlanta Olympics were also important because they became
known as the Gender Equity Games. The world got to see the first
generation of women and girls who had grown up benefiting from
Title IX. Women now had more training, coaching, financial support, and opportunities to play sports, and the results were astonishing: The U.S. women swept the team gold medals in basketball,
softball, gymnastics, and soccer, and we took the tennis gold medals
in women's singles (Lindsay Davenport) and doubles (Mary Joe Fernandez and Gigi Fernandez).

Across the board, our women athletes emphatically showed what
we always said could happen when we have emotional investment,
money, belief, and enthusiasm behind us. It created a wave. The
WNBA began play the following year, and the U.S. soccer team's
victory in Atlanta set the stage for the sensational 1999 Women's
World Cup in the United States. The American World Cup organizers had been warned they'd never fill the football stadiums they
chose—sound familiar?—but the 1999 tournament was a huge success that shattered attendance records.

Women's ice hockey got a boost from the Olympics as well, after its inclusion in the Nagano Winter Games in 1998. Ilana and I have also worked closely with members of the U.S. and Canadian national women's teams when they formed their first-ever players' association in 2019. We organized and helped fund the Chicago stop of their Dream Gap tour in the fall of 2019 to showcase their ability. Ilana has continued to help them with the details of starting their own professional league, and we've both participated in their exploratory talks with the National Hockey League.

One of the consistent messages I've stressed to the women in both hockey and soccer is the imperative to create jobs and opportunities for people beyond the dozen or two dozen slots on each national team. It's crucial to lift girls and women at all levels of the sport.

Coaching, like business mentoring, is a rewarding way to impact lives. Sometimes just a single conversation can flip a switch for someone. When I coached Lindsay Davenport in the 1995 Fed Cup, I seemed to surprise her one day by asking her, "Have you ever thought of becoming No. 1?" Shyly, she said, "No." Lindsay is close to six feet three, and early in her career she got a lot of negative feedback that she was too heavy and slow to be a champion. I told her, "The critics never talk about your positives. So I'm going to tell you: You're the best striker of the ball, men or women. You hate to lose. You care deeply, you're really smart, you have a good serve and some of the best hands in the game. That's why you can be No. 1 in the world." Once Lindsay worked hard to get in top condition, she went on to win three Grand Slam singles titles and spent ninety-eight weeks as the top-ranked player in the world. If I contributed even a tiny bit, I'm thrilled.

Of course, things in coaching don't always go as planned. I still laugh about the time I invited Jennifer Capriati to play for our Fed Cup team, in part on Lindsay's recommendation. When we got to the competition, Jennifer was spraying balls all over the court, which was shocking because it was so unlike her. "What's going on?" I said to Lindsay, who paused a beat, looked back at me uncertainly, and stammered, "Well . . . um, Jennifer didn't want to tell you this, but . . . um, she forgot her contact lenses." Through gritted teeth I said, "Lindsay? We. Could. Have. Sent. For. Them. Haven't you guys ever heard of FedEx?"

One of my earliest but best coaching experiences was working with Martina for six years, starting in 1989 with the fifteen months she spent chasing her record ninth Wimbledon singles title. Martina had started to doubt herself when the German teenager Stefanie Graf swept the majors in 1988 and supplanted her at No. 1. The following April, eighteen-year-old Gabriela Sabatini beat Martina in the semis at the Bausch & Lomb Championships on Amelia Island, Florida, and more doubt crept in.

I began to work part-time with Martina and her full-time coach, Craig Kardon, who had first suggested I assist them. I had agreed to watch some videotape of Martina's matches when I ran into them at Hilton Head, and right away I told them about an error she was making: once at the net, Martina was committing too soon to cover one part of the court or another, and her opponents were waiting to see where she went, and then passing her in the open court. "Stand your ground," I told her. "You're quick enough. When they strike the ball, *then* you go to the ball." She and Craig started calling me "the Jolt" because they felt whenever I showed up at practice I drove everyone to work harder. Sometimes they'd play Elton's song "The Bitch Is Back" over the sound system to tease me.

The transformation in Martina's game didn't happen overnight. She lost to Graf at Wimbledon and the U.S. Open finals in 1989. That fall, she experienced another trough of self-doubt: "I don't know if I'm good enough anymore," she said, bursting into tears one day at a practice in Chicago. We navigated that too. Martina was thirty-two when we began working together, the same age I was when I won my last major singles title. Having played tournament tennis to the age of forty, I knew that for a player that age the biggest obstacle to winning may well be psychological, not physical. So I asked Martina to drill back down to the time when her love for tennis was sweet and uncomplicated and just beginning.

"Use all your senses," I urged her. "What's the first thing that comes to mind?"

"Oh, I loved going to our town club, I loved being with my grandmother, I just couldn't get enough," Martina said. She mentioned the smell of the red clay, the *plunk-plunk-plunk* of the balls she hit against the backboard at her little club in Revnice.

"Do you think you could bring back some of that excitement and passion now?"

"I can try," she said. Then she repeated that she wasn't sure she was good enough to dominate anymore. She asked me what I thought.

"I think your 90 percent is better than just about everybody else's 100 percent," I said, and I meant it. "The first thing I want you to do in the morning, and the last thing before you go to sleep at night, is write out, 'I won Wimbledon in 1990.' Can you do that?"

She said she would. I also suggested that she was suffering from burnout and should skip Roland-Garros that year and funnel all her energy into preparing for Wimbledon, which she did. She went to Antigua for her first extended vacation in sixteen years and came back laughing about finally having a suntan on her stomach. For weeks before Wimbledon, Craig kept drilling her on sharpening her strokes. We also made her rehearse match point over and over. She's such an unbelievable learner and gifted athlete I felt we always had to keep challenging her or she'd get bored. Great champions love to be challenged.

Martina had always had a lot of joy when she played, and all we did was help her reconnect with it. She did win her record ninth Wimbledon singles title that year, then rejoiced by climbing from the court through the stands to her supporters in her player's box because she couldn't wait to give all of us a hug.

I WAS EXCITED to take on another responsibility in September 2020 when the International Tennis Federation announced that the Fed Cup would be renamed the Billie Jean King Cup. My hope going forward is that the year-long tournament, which started as a sixteen-team, one-week event in my day and had grown to 116 participating nations by 2020, will be even more appreciated as the World Cup of our sport.

Representing my country has always been an important calling for me, and I've tried to convey to today's players my genuine enthusiasm and reasons for participating in the event. As the U.S. team's captain, I had the joy of initiating Venus and Serena Williams to Fed Cup and Olympic play and coaching them both over the years. Venus was seven and Serena was six when I first met them and their parents, Richard and Oracene, at a free World TeamTennis and Domino's Pizza–sponsored clinic in April 1988 in Long Beach. I watched them hit a few balls that day, just as I did with all the other kids. The Williams sisters stood out.

I saw the girls again when Rosie and I partnered with them in an exhibition doubles match in Hilton Head in 1992 and 1993, and I attended Venus's pro debut at the 1994 Bank of the West Classic in Oakland. Even then, as a fourteen-year-old, she reminded me of Althea because of her long legs and reach and quiet carriage on court. In time, Venus would hold the women's record for the fastest serve ever (129 miles per hour) for a while, in addition to seizing the No. 1 ranking and seven major singles titles. As for Serena, by the spring of 2022, she remained one major title away from matching Margaret Court's career record of twenty-four Grand Slam singles titles.

Both sisters have matured into accomplished businesswomen with diverse interests in entertainment, clothing, design, team ownership, and activism. They excel at connecting with other influencers and getting their messages out, especially on social media. Their popularity drove the U.S. Open's decision in 2001 to move the women's singles final to prime-time—we had come a long way from being shunted to the backlot courts—and it was a huge occasion when the Williams sisters played each other in the first one. Two Black players had never opposed each other in a Grand Slam singles final anywhere until then, and Venus won that showdown.

Venus was also instrumental in pushing Wimbledon and Roland-Garros to finally offer equal pay—first by speaking to the Grand Slam board in 2005, and then by writing an editorial for *The Times of London* the following year, winning support from British prime minister Tony Blair. In one of the most moving parts of her remarks to the board, Venus said, "When your eyes are closed, you can't really tell who's next to you, who's a man and who's a woman. Think about your daughters, your wives, your sisters. How would you like them to be treated? All of our hearts beat the same."

Wimbledon became the next-to-last major to level men's and women's prize money, which they announced in February 2007, a month before Roland-Garros did the same. (Because Roland-Garros is played a month earlier, Wimbledon was the last major to actually pay out equal prize money, and it was fitting when Venus won that year. I was sitting in the Royal Box cheering her on.) So many of us were proud that she and Larry Scott, then chairman and CEO of the WTA, finished the equal pay fight at the majors that my generation started.

I'm also gratified that we can say a tennis player has been the highest-paid female athlete in the world every year since *Forbes* started tracking the data in 1990. In 2019, women tennis players comprised the entire Top Ten, with Naomi Osaka of Japan passing Serena for the first time at the top. From those $1 contracts the Original 9 signed with Gladys, look what we've achieved.

The Williams sisters epitomize the cultural force a modern female athlete can be, and they've inspired a next generation of players who look like them and want to play like them. Women's tennis is a power game and a global sport more than ever. Naomi Osaka and Coco Gauff's fathers both followed Richard Williams's blueprint for developing his daughters into top players, right down to taking their girls to some of the same places and coaches in Florida where the Williamses trained. In that way, the baton gets passed, again and again. By the summer of 2020, Naomi and Coco also showed a strong interest in taking stands for social justice. They independently spoke up during the protests in the U.S. about the police killing of an unarmed man, George Floyd, and other Blacks such as Breonna Taylor. On her way to winning the U.S. Open, Naomi, the daughter of a Japanese mother and Haitian father, wore a different face mask every day that she played, each bearing the name of a Black victim of racial injustice or police brutality. Asked what statement she was trying to make, she told reporters the message others took away "is more the question. . . . I feel like I'm a vessel at this point, in order to spread awareness."

THE FED CUP WAS ALREADY the world's largest annual international team competition in women's sports before it was renamed after me, but there are still many countries where women encounter huge obstacles to compete at all, let alone advance to the international level. Ilana and I recently gave Lilitha Ndungane, a talented young Black player in Johannesburg, a scholarship to study at St. Mary's, where South Africa's Federation Cup captain worked as head coach.

In 2018, Ilana read that the International Tennis Federation had struck a twenty-five-year, $3 billion deal to sell the Davis Cup's commercial rights to a Spanish investment group named Kosmos. The Davis Cup's 119-year-old competition format has been revamped so the final stages will now be concentrated into a week-long event featuring eighteen nations in one place, competing for $18 million in annual prize money. The Kosmos chief executive Javier Alonso said that without the controversial changes, "I don't think Davis Cup would have survived." As the ITF well knew, the Fed Cup was facing similar challenges. During the 2018 U.S. Open, Ilana met with the ITF president, David Haggerty, who assured her that he and the ITF wanted to attract more money for the women's competition and adopt a format change as well.

Renaming the competition the Billie Jean King Cup and having me serve as a global ambassador for the rebranded event was the concept that the ITF's leadership eventually agreed on. The fact that tennis already had the Hopman Cup, Davis Cup, and Laver Cup named after men, but no international competition named after a woman, was something the ITF wanted to address. I had played in the very first competition and supported the Fed Cup over the years, winning a record eleven titles as a player and captain. And of course, as I've said, I love the team format.

Thanks to the efforts of everyone involved, more significant sponsorships have already materialized, and the first Billie Jean King Cup planned to offer $12 million in prize money to the twelve national teams that make the final round in 2021—the same pro-rata amount that the eighteen men's teams in that year's Davis Cup final will earn. We closed the gender pay gap for the first time, and our total prize money ranks as the world's largest purse for an annual women's team competition.

Chapter 31

I N THE LATE FALL of 2008, I was staying with my mom in Prescott when the phone rang early one morning. Ilana was visiting family in South Africa, and her voice was happy and excited. "Billie! Can you get on the next plane to Jo'burg?" she said. "Nelson Mandela has time to meet you!"

Mandela had been a hero of mine since the late 1960s, when I first learned about his actions to fight apartheid that led to his imprisonment. He had just turned ninety, was in frail health, and rarely accepted visitors. By then, Ilana and I had been working for two or three years with Mandela's staff, hoping to meet him. I packed my bags and left as soon as I could.

During the day and a half it took me to fly from Phoenix to London to South Africa, I had a lot of time to think about Mandela. After he was released from prison in 1990 he published an autobiography, *Long Walk to Freedom,* which I devoured. The book followed Mandela's life from his rural childhood through his twenty-seven-year prison stay to his election as the first Black president of South Africa in 1994. I marveled at his resilience and resolve, his exquisite wisdom and grace. He wasn't bitter or vengeful. Instead of punishing his former white enemies when he came to power, Mandela offered them a role as partners in the rebuilding of South Africa. He started Truth and Reconciliation Commission hearings, hoping that they would facilitate a national catharsis.

"No one is born hating another person because of the color of his skin, or his background, or his religion," Mandela wrote. "People must learn to hate, and if they can learn to hate, they can be taught to love."

Mandela embodied everything I love most. Kindness. Generosity. Freedom. Equality. Forgiveness. The belief in transcendence and redemption. I just wanted to be in his presence for a moment, absorb some of his wisdom, and thank him because of the ways he had changed the world.

Ilana picked me up at the airport and whisked me the next morning to an 11 o'clock meeting at the Nelson Mandela Foundation office in the Houghton neighborhood. The streets looked familiar. As we pulled up to the gate I realized this was the same area where I had stayed with a host family in 1966, the first year I played in the South African Championships and inadvertently earned their Black housekeeper a dressing down. Now, seeing people of all colors inside Mandela's compound was a reminder of the breathtaking progress that had been made. These people were executives and stakeholders in the new South Africa that Mandela had always stood for.

Mandela was sitting in a comfortable leather chair behind his desk in an office lined with books and framed photographs. He was wearing one of his trademark batik shirts designed in rich golds and browns. When he stood to greet us I was surprised by how tall he was. It added to his presence. I could see that Ilana was battling her emotions as much as I was. "I can't breathe," she whispered.

We settled in for a short conversation. Mandela's memory was crystal clear about the conditions under which he lived at Robben Island prison. He talked about how difficult it was being there, but he said he could find humanity in everyone, even the guards. Mandela and a couple of his fellow political prisoners slowly broke down the barriers by talking with their white jailers. Some guards ended up making their daily life a little less onerous.

When it was time to go, we didn't dare ask for a photo, but Mandela's private secretary, Zelda la Grange, offered to snap one on Ilana's phone. I'm forever grateful she did. As we walked out of the building into the noonday sun, I was still under Mandela's spell. That hadn't changed by the time Ilana and I journeyed back to

South Africa a couple of years later and made a point to stop in Cape Town for a few days. On clear days you can see the outline of Robben Island across a stretch of the Atlantic Ocean north of the city. Ilana and I had to take a ferry to get to the bleak prison, which is now a national museum.

Our guide was himself a freed Robben Island prisoner, and he showed us the crude eight-by-seven-foot cell where Mandela spent so much of his adult life. The cell had no heat, air conditioning, running water, or toilet, just a container in the corner. It had no proper bed, just an inch-thick straw mat placed under a thin felt pad with a couple of coarse wool blankets to fend off the cold. Mandela was facing a life sentence when he arrived there and was forced to do hard labor in a quarry. I cannot imagine the courage or stamina it took to endure that kind of suffering. Later, as we were walking around the prison grounds, I saw faded white lines painted on a green section of the concrete exercise yard and asked our guide, "Is that a tennis court?"

The guide explained that Mandela had persuaded the warden to allow the prisoners to make a homemade court to get some exercise. Mandela wrote in his autobiography that a net was set up a few days after they put down their painted court "and suddenly we had our own Wimbledon in our front yard." What the warden didn't know was that the prisoners would sometimes pass messages to the outside world by inserting them inside tennis balls that they pretended to hit over the wall by mistake.

I felt a new and even deeper connection to Mandela after I knew those stories. He never let anything stop him.

As I walked around Robben Island, I also recalled watching the day Mandela was released in 1990 from a different prison and the celebration scenes as he walked out. I still marvel at how he reimagined the country in ways people had doubted were possible. For me, nothing has compared to meeting the man himself and walking in some of the same places he tread.

IN JULY 2009, President Obama organized a White House round-table discussion to celebrate the thirty-seventh anniversary of Title IX. I was invited to be on a panel of speakers, along with Arne Duncan, the secretary of education at the time. Duncan emphasized that Title IX is about leveling the playing field in every area of education, from sports activities to science and technology.

After the program, Valerie Jarrett, chair of the president's Council on Women and Girls, invited me to have lunch with her and two others in the White House mess in the basement of the West Wing. All through lunch, I was a little distracted by how they seemed to be looking at me and then at each other with faint smiles on their faces. After our meal, I asked to meet the kitchen staff, which I always try to do if possible, and I was asking the chef, cooks, and dishwashers what it was like to work in the White House when Valerie poked her head in to tell me the president wanted to see me.

I thought she was talking about the president of one of the organizations who had been on the Title IX program with us. "Okay, I'll be right there," I said, turning back to the kitchen staff.

"Billie?" Valerie persisted, "the president *of the United States* would like to meet you."

What! Me? Now?

We literally had to run through the West Wing to reach the Oval Office before the window of opportunity closed. I was still a little breathless when Valerie walked me through the door and there was President Obama, standing in front of his desk. He was warm and relaxed as he shook my hand and greeted me with that silky voice of his. I was so shy I didn't sit in one of the striped hardback chairs next to his where the photographer could take our picture together. I plunked down on a pale yellow couch across from him instead.

After some small talk that included revisiting the Riggs match, Obama smiled and said, "You know, I watched you practice at Punahou."

I knew the place well. It's a private high school in Honolulu where I had sometimes held tennis clinics when Larry and I had our place in Hawaii.

"That was you?" I said. Obama nodded. He had attended Punahou from 1971 to 1979, and I clearly remember seeing a young Black boy standing with a white boy behind the fence, watching me hit. The Black boy stood out because almost all the other faces at Punahou were white or Asian. I think he came back more than once, but he never said anything to me.

"Why didn't you ask me to hit with you?" I said.

"Oh, I would have never done that," he answered. Later, I learned the rest of the story. He had joined the tennis program at Punahou, but a bigoted coach ruined the sport for him. The president wrote about it in his first memoir, *Dreams from My Father,* describing a white tennis pro "who told me during a tournament that I shouldn't touch the schedule of matches pinned to the bulletin board because my color might rub off."

About a week later, I found out why our introduction had been arranged. I received a phone call from Valerie telling me that I had been selected for the Presidential Medal of Freedom, America's highest civilian honor. It had never been awarded to a woman athlete. (The great University of Tennessee women's basketball coach Pat Summitt was selected three years later.)

The 2009 recipients were chosen by Obama because we were all "agents of change." The day of the ceremony, August 12, 2009, is hard to forget for a lot of reasons. When I arrived at the visitors' gate to the White House with Tip Nunn, my dear friend and long-time publicist, the guard wouldn't let us through even when I told him why I was there and that we had only an hour before the ceremony began. The guard, who was maybe thirty years old, looked at me blankly and said, "Sorry, ma'am. Your name's not on the list."

The temperature was in the high 80s, one of those dreadfully humid midsummer Washington days. As Tip tried to phone someone for help because I was in danger of missing my pre-ceremony commitments, Sidney Poitier arrived. The guard wouldn't let him in, either. Then Stephen Hawking, the brilliant theoretical physicist, approached in his customized wheelchair, accompanied by his attendant. They were also made to wait. By the time Archbishop

Desmond Tutu glided past us and breezed through the gate with his entourage, I was wilting in the heat.

At last, a very apologetic intern appeared and guided us to the reception in the East Room, where I got to chat with the other honorees. Former Supreme Court Justice Sandra Day O'Connor was standing next to Muhammad Yunus, who had won the Nobel Prize for his pioneering work with microloans. Rev. Joseph Lowery, the civil rights icon who founded the Southern Christian Leadership Conference, stood across the room not far from Dr. Joseph Medicine Crow, the last living Plains Indian war chief and the author of books on Native American history and culture. Stuart Milk, the nephew of the late gay activist Harvey Milk, was there to accept the honor on behalf of his slain uncle.

President Obama opened the ceremony by introducing each of us. When he got to me, the president emphasized that I had been chosen for my work for equal opportunity and human rights, not just my Grand Slam tennis titles.

"We honor what she calls 'all the off-the-court stuff,'" the president said, citing what I had done to "make the future brighter for all LGBT Americans" and "to broaden the reach of the game, to change how women athletes and women everywhere view themselves, and to give everyone, regardless of gender or sexual orientation—including my two daughters—a chance to compete both on the court and in life."

What a thrill to hear a U.S. president say "LGBT."

When President Obama draped the blue-and-white ribbon around my neck I lifted the medal and kissed it. I'd requested that the name engraved on the back read "Billie Jean Moffitt King." I was again thinking of my patriotic father, who didn't live long enough to see this day. I was also thinking about my mom, who after years of angst had come to accept me for who I am. She was now beaming at me from the audience as she sat with Ilana and eight other family members, including my mother-in-law, Ruth, whose letter asking me to catch up with Ilana two decades earlier had changed all of our lives in ways we never could have foreseen.

I HAD A FEW more encounters with Barack and Michelle Obama during their eight-year stay in the White House. They were so kind and easygoing and always made Ilana and me feel welcome.

President Obama's staff contacted me in 2014 as the Winter Olympics in Sochi approached. The Russians had poured many billions of dollars into building up the Black Sea resort town to host the Winter Games. But human rights groups had grown increasingly alarmed over Vladimir Putin's authoritarian government and his crackdown against dissent and freedom of expression, particularly in the LGBTQ+ community. The summer before the Games, Putin signed a federal law banning "propaganda of non-traditional sexual relations" and the police started arresting gay rights activists. Mobs often beat up protesters.

The Sochi Games presented both a crisis and an opportunity for the international sports community and for the Obama administration. Rather than boycott the Olympics and punish innocent athletes, the president, first lady, and Vice President Joe Biden decided to stay home to signal the United States' disapproval of Russia's human rights violations. To make an even stronger statement, Obama decided to send a five-person delegation to represent the U.S. in Sochi that consisted of three openly gay athletes—the Olympic skating champion Brian Boitano, the Olympic ice hockey player Caitlin Cahow, and me. I thought it was brave of Brian to publicly come out as gay two days after he was named to our Sochi delegation. When the president asked me to go to Sochi, I immediately said yes. Ilana and I have traveled in the Middle East and Asia where homosexuality is illegal, and we are always a little on edge doing so. You never know what might happen whether you're an ordinary tourist or an honored guest.

President Obama's decision to send us provoked enough discussion that the writers at *Saturday Night Live* noticed. They highlighted our mission in a skit that featured Kate McKinnon appearing as me on "Weekend Update." I almost fell off the couch laughing when I saw her burst into the camera frame next to host Seth Myers wearing a short brown wig, wire-rimmed glasses, and a Sochi T-shirt, preening and waving her arms like she had just won Wimbledon.

"Billie Jean King! You seem excited to be going to Sochi!" Seth said.

"I couldn't be more excited, Seth!" she boomed. "I'm President Obama's big gay middle finger, and this bird's about to get flipped. BJK's about to double down, and Putin's going to find himself in the epicenter of a gay tornado! I'm gonna drive my Subaru Outback into Red Square doing donuts and blasting Melissa Etheridge."

"You seem very confident."

"That's right, Seth. There is no demographic in this world that gives less of a flip than seventy-year-old lesbians!"

"Be careful. There could be trouble."

"Trouble? I'm *from* trouble," she boasted.

It was hilarious.

As much as I desired to travel to Sochi, my mother's health had been failing by the time the president asked me to make the trip. As the start date of the Olympics grew closer, there was no way I was going to leave her side, so I canceled. Mom was ninety-one, and dementia had taken most of her memory, but I believe she knew I was there as she left this world. Mildred Rose (Betty) Jerman Moffitt died on February 7, 2014, the same day as the opening ceremony.

What a sweet soul my mother was. Mom always yearned to travel more but she refused to leave Dad at home. Once she was alone after sixty-five years of marriage, I asked her what she'd like to do, and one of my great pleasures in life was being able to fulfill her wishes. We saw some of her favorite entertainers live. Mom was thrilled when we met Tony Bennett at his eightieth birthday party and surprised again when Diana Krall confided to her backstage, "You're the first one I'm telling this—I'm going to have twins!" Ilana and I brought Mom on cruises to places in the Mediterranean, to Greece, to Alaska. Those were such special times.

Ilana's mother, Ruth, would pass away just two months later, leaving another great void in our lives. No matter how old you are when a parent dies, it's like losing an anchor that kept you safely moored. I had a heavy heart as I took care of my mom's affairs. I visited with family and friends. By the time I was done with all my obligations, there was still enough time left in the sixteen-day Olympics for me to spend a few days there and attend the closing ceremony. I'm so glad I did.

From what I had been reading to prepare for Sochi, the repression that characterized the old Soviet Bloc system had morphed into something lawless and even more sinister in Russia. I read reports of the murder of a gay man in Volgograd in 2013. I read about a spike in hate crimes against LGBTQ+ people. Thugs were using dating apps to lure unsuspecting gay men to locations where they would be beaten and much worse.

I read news accounts about how artistic expression was being squelched in the weeks before Sochi and protesters were being shadowed and arrested. When other nations and athletes criticized the crackdowns, Putin declared that gays attending the Olympics should feel "at ease"—but he couldn't resist adding, with a whiff of contempt, "so long as they leave the children in peace." The mayor of Sochi declared that there "were no gay people in this city," which was, of course, ridiculous.

I planned to try to meet as many Russians as I could in my short time there. I had long ago learned that just because a nation's government officials are bigots doesn't mean that all its citizens are the same. When I landed in Sochi, I and others were whisked off in a bulletproof van. The vehicle was so heavy we nearly got stuck on one of the mountain roads that wound its way up to the bobsled track. There were security people around me everywhere I went, and I was feeling sad, jet-lagged, and a little on edge when I arrived at our hotel and gave a brief press conference about an hour later. I told reporters I supported the calls for sexual orientation to be added to the Olympic Charter's anti-discrimination policy. I voiced my concern for LGBTQ+ people who were facing prejudice and violence in Russia.

As I spoke, I was aware of a thin teenage boy with light brown hair listening intently to what I was saying. Just as my handlers were trying to move me along to the next stop, the pale young man mustered the courage to step forward, trailed by a Canadian documentary crew that tipped me off that they had been interviewing him. I stopped in my tracks.

"Hi, I'm Vladislav, I'm gay, and I am born in Sochi," he said in a rush of heavily accented English. "Every day I endure bullying, violence, fear. I'm seventeen years old, and everybody in school knows about my sexuality."

He had a narrow face and frightened eyes. His whole body was shaking. I asked if I could hold his hands in mine, and when I took them, they kept quivering. I looked at him and said, "If we could do one thing for you—if *I* could—what would that be? What can I do to help you?"

"I don't know who can help me in Russia, I think I need to go away from Russia—I'm afraid to stay," he told me.

I turned to someone from the State Department and one of the staffers from the American Embassy who was part of our contingent and said, "What can we do for him?" As someone wrote down Vlad's contact details, I turned to him and we hugged and I promised I would be in touch.

I couldn't get that boy out of my mind the remaining two days of the trip.

Vlad was being bullied by his classmates, who had outed him after hacking his Facebook account. He was being persecuted by his schoolteachers, one of whom had walked past Vlad in the school hallway a few days before we met and whispered in his ear, "You will end up badly, homo." He felt in danger for good reason. I found out that Vlad's full name was Vladimir Slavskii, and the only reason he wasn't in jail for being a gay activist was probably because, at seventeen, he was still underage. He described how he was spat on, hit, stoned, doused with bottles of urine, and nearly raped by thugs hiding in the bushes. His attackers had begun to undress, but he was able to escape. He knew another man who was tortured and managed to flee to Lithuania just before police arrived to arrest him. "It's awful, it's horrible, and police don't want to help me," Vlad said. "They say I need to hide my sexuality."

After I asked our government staffers in Sochi to help Vlad get a visa to the United States, I followed up with calls to the State Department. The Canadian director and activist Noam Gonick, whose moving documentary that included Vlad was called *To Russia with Love,* also remained deeply involved in helping Vlad. Vlad was able to get an expedited visa through the Unaccompanied Refugee Minors program that's run by the U.S. State Department's Office of Refugee Resettlement.

Gonick's extraordinary film provided a searing look at the impact of Russia's anti-gay laws in the days leading up to the Sochi Games, and some of it had to be shot in secret. Several times, Noam and his film crew were nearly arrested.

I called Dan Bridges, then the athletic director at my alma mater, Cal State L.A. I asked him how Vlad might be able to remain in the U.S. once here. Dan was accustomed to dealing with international students and he told me Cal State L.A. could sponsor a student visa for Vlad so he could stay after he applied for asylum. Things were really coming together. Now he had a place to go. I said I would pay for Vlad's travel, tuition, and room and board to go to Cal State L.A., which Vlad did.

When Vlad landed in New York that June, Ilana and I spent time with him before he traveled on to Los Angeles. He still seemed so wan and nervous, but we were greatly relieved that he was out of Russia. He said he was worried he would be arrested when he got to the Sochi airport, then at customs, then right up to the moment they closed the cabin door and his plane took off. He told us life had become so much worse for LGBTQ+ people in Russia once outside scrutiny faded after the Games. There had been more government crackdowns. He was grateful to be alive.

That same week in New York, Vlad went to the West Village to see his first Pride march and Noam captured that on film too. Vlad couldn't stop smiling. "Oh my God, it *is* possible . . . There is free people! There is happy people!" Vlad says in the film, his mouth slightly open in wonder. After going to school for a while at Cal State L.A., Vlad fell in love with the man he would marry. He moved to

Pennsylvania and continued his studies. He is applying for American citizenship. When asked before his last semester if he's happy he left Russia, Vlad laughed and said, "*Infinitely* happy."

My mother's life ended just as a new one for someone else I know had begun.

Chapter 32

TODAY WHEN I see LGBTQ+ teens who think it's unremarkable to openly be who they are, I'm thrilled. Sometimes I'm so happy I laugh out loud. I love how they self-identify and have appropriated the word *queer* so it's no longer a slur. I smiled when the U.S. National Team ice hockey captain Meghan Duggan appeared at the Women's Sports Foundation gala a couple of years ago and spoke about her pregnancy and her wife without a whiff of self-consciousness. It's gratifying because it means we've succeeded in making the world better for the next generations. But I always try to make sure people know history, because the more you know about history, the more you know about yourself and, most importantly, it helps you shape the future.

Who would've guessed, for example, that forty-four years after the King-Riggs match, a Hollywood film about it would give me another international platform to talk about equality and sexual identity? But when the Academy Award winner Danny Boyle, the director of *Trainspotting* and *Slumdog Millionaire,* approached Ilana and me with his business partner, Christian Colson, about doing a Battle of the Sexes movie with their team, it felt right.

Other people had suggested the idea over the years, but Danny had the funding in place. The script was going to be handled by *Slumdog Millionaire* screenwriter Simon Beaufoy, who also wrote *The Full Monty,* a hilarious movie with great heart. Danny wanted the wife-and-husband team of Valerie Faris and Jonathan Dayton to codirect the film. Their previous credits included the blockbuster *Little Miss Sunshine.* Emma Stone, the actress they chose to play me, had won the Oscar for her performance in *La La Land* by the time they started production, and Steve Carrell was an inspired choice to play Bobby Riggs. A subplot of the film dealt with my relationship with Marilyn Barnett. Though the filmmakers took some dramatic license—it was entertainment, not a documentary—I think the movie sent an empowering message.

Emma and I didn't talk a great deal before filming because she had her own process of preparing for the role. Afterward, we became great friends. Emma was going on twenty-nine when we met, the same age I was when I played Bobby, and she's a deep person. She said a question that I had texted her along the way—"Emma, what will your legacy be?"—stuck with her. Before portraying me, she had some awareness of how hard we had fought for equal rights and opportunities when I was her age. But she said once she did extended research, and then as she began to try to inhabit the role, something changed in her. She said the work of putting on ten to fifteen pounds of muscle changed her self-belief; she was stronger than she knew. She said she found the courage to trust her voice in her own life, and once the film was finished, she began to use that voice more.

The sexual abuse charges against the Hollywood studio chief Harvey Weinstein hit the news during our promotional tour for the film, sparking a torrent of anguished stories from women around the world who suddenly felt freer to share their own abuse experiences—many of them on social media, under the hashtag #MeToo.

Emma joined more than three hundred entertainment industry workers in forming a new group called TIME'S UP, which was announced on New Year's Day 2018 in collaboration with the Alianza Nacional de Campesinas. That's a group of more than 700,000 female farmworkers that had published an open letter in *Time* magazine describing the workplace abuse they face and expressing solidarity with victims everywhere. TIME'S UP laid out an ambitious agenda to promote equality and confront systemic abuse and discrimination in blue-collar workplaces nationwide, not just in Hollywood. A legal defense fund administered by the National Women's Law Center was also established and raised $22 million in the first year alone. By 2020, the fund had helped more than four thousand people.

In one of the joint interviews we did, Emma related our tennis fight for equal pay to her personal experiences in Hollywood. She told *Out* magazine she needed her male costars to take a pay cut so she could have parity with them. "That's something that's also not discussed, necessarily—that our getting equal pay is going to require people to selflessly say, 'That's what's fair.'"

Then she highlighted the positive domino effect that follows when someone takes a principled stand. "If my male costar, who has a higher [salary] quote than me but believes we are equal, takes a pay cut so that I can match him, that changes my quote in the future and changes my *life*," Emma said. "This is Billie Jean's feminism, and I love it . . . It's not about, 'Women are this and men are that.' It is, 'We are all the same, we are all equal. We all deserve the same respect and rights.'"

Emma said she realized she couldn't truly understand being a sports hero, "but I do know what it's like to struggle and to be afraid and to be a public person, to feel like you can't share all of yourself, to be afraid of saying the wrong thing or not furthering goodness in the world." Referring to the impact of the Riggs match, Emma told another interviewer, "And to think, it all started with a young girl who had vulnerabilities and fears, and yet the courage to speak out. She taught me that you don't have to be perfect to be great, and that you can push through your fears and still have a voice.

"I think that's a great story to share with the world right now."

THE RELENTLESS ATTEMPTS in the Trump years to eliminate hard-won protections for U.S. citizens and immigrants exceeded anything I've seen in America since police were using fire hoses and attack dogs on civil rights demonstrators in the 1960s. I never imagined I'd see a day when an American president would separate immigrant families and cage their children at our Mexican border, or callously allow tear gas and rubber bullets to be fired at peaceful protesters so he could walk from the White House to Lafayette

Square for a photo op, and then hold up a Bible—upside down—in front of a landmark church. I never expected storefronts across the country to be boarded up in advance of an American election or a sitting president to exhort his supporters to march on our Capitol building, as Trump did, the day Congress met to certify his loss. It's all a reminder that progress is often so painstakingly slow to achieve, democracy is fragile, and it can be undone so quickly if we're not vigilant. We can't relax. We still have work to do in every area.

And so, as much as I lament the deep need for the Black Lives Matter movement—which was started in 2013 by Alicia Garza, Patrisse Cullors, and Opal Tometi in response to the acquittal of Trayvon Martin's killer, George Zimmerman—I was encouraged by the enormous momentum the effort to combat systemic racism had gained by the summer of 2020. The massive public protests and responses to the police killings of George Floyd and Breonna Taylor, and the shotgun murder of jogger Ahmaud Arbery by a retired cop and his son, could not be ignored at any level of society, politics, or government. Even before Jacob Blake was severely injured by a Kenosha, Wisconsin, officer who shot him seven times in the back as he walked to his car, we finally reached a critical mass where people in this country—and the world over—rose up and said, *Enough*.

The pain was hard to bear, but what encouraged me most were the spontaneous outpourings of compassion, the new legislation that was introduced, and the reassessment of the lens through which we've told history. For so many years all we've been taught is white history. The sight of protesters of all colors engaging in numbers we hadn't seen since the 1960s was, to me, a reaffirmation of the good values that I believe truly define America as a country. When I looked at those crowds, the other thing I saw was voters. Voters who were tired of seeing so many ideals profaned and so many people hurting.

By the time the bitterly contested 2020 elections arrived in November, I was among those who believed our democracy was in danger. A record 158.4 million Americans voted in that presidential election. After four incredibly tense days, people poured into the streets to celebrate the moment the networks declared Joe Biden and

Kamala Harris the winners by about seven million votes, and many of them were crying with joy and relief. But, as feared, President Trump refused to concede the election for the next two months, culminating with his rally speech just outside the White House that preceded the violent storming of the Capitol building. The results were horrific—five people died, including a police officer. And yet, what the disturbing chain of events ultimately affirmed was that our democracy still works. Trump and his supporters did not win any of the sixty-plus lawsuits they filed contesting the vote; judge after judge ruled that there was no proof of widespread fraud. Members of the House of Representatives and the Senate were shaken by the Capitol riot, but they returned to work in their ransacked chambers that same evening and stayed till 4 a.m. to finish certifying Biden and Harris as the winners. The pace of those two weeks was dizzying: We went from the Capitol insurrection on Wednesday, January 6, to Trump's impeachment (for the second time) the following Wednesday to Biden and Harris's inauguration the Wednesday after that, under unprecedented security that included twenty-five thousand National Guard troops.

I thought President Biden struck the perfect tone in his inaugural address when he emphasized unity. "I know the forces that divide us are deep and they are real, but I also know they are not new," he said. "Our 'better angels' have always prevailed . . . And we can do so now." Harris also stressed their intent to heal the country, and eloquently captured the emotion and import of becoming the first woman—and person of color—to ascend to the vice presidency. "I may be the first," Harris said, "but I will not be the last." Twenty-two-year-old Amanda Gorman, our national youth poet laureate, delivered a stirring reading of her sensational inaugural poem, "The Hill We Climb," calling us "a nation that isn't broken, but simply unfinished . . . There is always light, if only we're brave enough to see it. If only we're brave enough to be it."

Harris is the daughter of an Indian American mother and a Jamaican American father, and she knows that she stands on the shoulders of pioneers and social justice advocates who came before her. Biden acknowledged that his election turned on the support of Black Americans, starting with his campaign-saving victory in the South Carolina primary that pivoted when James Clyburn, the state's Democratic congressman, endorsed him.

As Ilana and I watched Harris give her victory speech, I thought back to a night three years earlier when we met her backstage at a Human Rights Campaign dinner in Washington, D.C., and we discussed if she intended to run for president. I thought, too, of pioneering women who preceded her: Eleanor Roosevelt, Shirley Chisholm, Barbara Jordan, Ann Richards, Geraldine Ferraro, Dolores Huerta, Madeline Albright, Maxine Waters, Hillary Clinton, Sandra Day O'Connor, Ruth Bader Ginsburg, Sonia Sotomayor, and Elena Kagan. Harris's ascent validated all the work and fighting to get women this far. We knew we could be it. Now we see it.

THERE WAS SOMETHING starkly different about the 2020 Black Lives Matter protests when compared to the civil rights actions of the 1960s. I had the same feeling watching the first Women's March on Washington in January 2017, the day after Donald Trump's inauguration. More than a million people participated in Washington alone that day, another 5 million Americans hit the streets in other women's marches across the country, and a few million more marched around the world—all to protest policies and statements that targeted people of color, women, immigrants, LGBTQ+ people, the poor, the sick, and the physically challenged. They were taking a stand for the most vulnerable among us.

These movements were visibly made up of far more diverse coalitions than I've ever seen come together in the U.S. No matter which cause it was—Black Lives Matter, #MeToo, TIME'S UP, get-out-the-vote efforts, or combating violence against Asian Americans—we saw women and men, people of all colors, ages, ethnicities, religions, and sexual orientations marching side by side in recognition of our shared humanity. Even majority-white communities where few Blacks live were taking to the streets and lying on the ground for eight minutes and forty-six seconds to show their disgust for how George Floyd died, and proclaim their solidarity with the Black Lives Matter movement. For the first time in my life, I thought we are getting close to unlocking how to make equality happen, because the effort *has* to be inclusive. It has to be achieved together. Otherwise it won't work. As President John F. Kennedy once put it, "Freedom is indivisible, and when one man is enslaved, all are not free."

The Zulu tribe in South Africa has a term that beautifully expresses a similar thought: *Sawubona*. It's a common greeting that literally means, "I see you, you are important to me, and I value you." It's meant to encourage each individual to see and respect people as they are, and to pay attention to their virtues and needs, sorrows and desires. When someone says *Sawubona* to you, a typical response is *Shikoba*—I exist for you. I value you too.

When people in the social justice world talk about "intersectionality," our indivisibility is basically what they mean. We're all part of one system. You can't discuss equal opportunity or racism without acknowledging the core causes that contribute to people being left behind. You can't achieve women's liberation without addressing racism, sexism, reproductive rights, and gross disparities in wages and wealth distribution.

You can't separate how the Arctic Circle is warming from what industrialized nations are doing to contribute to it. Today's generation seems to know that more than previous generations did. The Swedish teenager Greta Thunberg has gained worldwide renown for speaking truth to power about the quality of the world we'll be leaving her generation if we don't ramp up our efforts to stem climate change.

In my lifetime, gun violence has become a human rights crisis in the United States that has awakened a new movement and inspired another crop of young leaders. Some of them were survivors of the shooting on February 14, 2018, by a gunman at Marjory Stoneman Douglas High School in Parkland, Florida. The gunman killed seventeen students and staff members and injured seventeen more. The tragedy was just another in the wave of massacres in the U.S. that we tend to recognize in shorthand by the names of the places where they happen rather than the names of the victims: Columbine. Virginia Tech. Sandy Hook. Las Vegas. The Pulse nightclub in Orlando. Parkland. Squirrel Hill. In almost every case, politicians send their thoughts and prayers, and then don't do enough.

The Stoneman Douglas students refused to accept that. A group of them organized the March for Our Lives, one of the biggest youth-led protests since the Vietnam era. With help from large and small donors, and logistical assistance from seasoned advocacy groups, the student leaders David Hogg, Emma González, Cameron Kasky, Alex Wind, Alfonso Calderon, Sarah Chadwick, Jaclyn Corin, and Delaney Tarr were able to mobilize an estimated 800,000 people to march on Washington less than a month after the killings at their school. Hundreds of other March for Our Lives events took place across the country. When Hogg was later asked by *Teen Vogue* what he says when people remark that the Stoneman Douglas students got so much attention because they were predominantly white, he didn't blink. He said, "I agree with them."

The students recognized that they came from a privileged community where gunfire rarely erupts, so for the Washington march they had reached out in impressive fashion to include students from neighborhoods in Chicago and Washington, D.C., where gun violence is a devastating, everyday event. They've continued to do more coalition building with other youth groups. It is another assertion of how we're all connected.

In all, there were about two dozen speakers at that first March for Our Lives in Washington, all of them students and young activists. The young were leading the old. Children were saying they were sick of seeing other children shot.

One of the most moving moments was provided by Emma González, then eighteen. She had been working at a table for the school's gay-straight alliance the day of the killings, handing out valentines in the high school courtyard. She lost a close friend in the gunfire and had to hide with other students in the school gymnasium for two hours until police let them out.

When Emma took the podium in Washington, she read the names of all the victims to underscore that each was a human being, not a statistic. Then she stood in silence for a long while, and the hundreds of thousands of demonstrators looking on grew completely quiet themselves. Finally she said, "Since the time that I came out here, it has been six minutes and twenty seconds. The shooter has ceased shooting, and will soon abandon his rifle, blend in with the students as they escape, and walk free for an hour before arrest.

"Fight for your lives before it's someone else's job."

Wow.

Her call to action was only nine words, yet it captured everything.

WHILE EMMA WAS addressing the March for Our Lives crowd on the Washington Mall that day, Ilana and I had joined an estimated 175,000 marchers for the same cause in New York City. The staging area was on Central Park West, not far from where John Lennon was shot by a deranged fan.

The following year, I made a point to seek out Emma when we were both invited guests at the Pride March in New York City. The event is held on the last Sunday in June to commemorate the anniversary of the Stonewall riots that launched the gay rights movement. Ilana and I had never been to the march before because it always conflicted with Wimbledon. But in 2018, Wimbledon started later than usual, so I was able to accept an invitation to be one of the parade's grand marshals.

Emma hadn't been born when Hillary Clinton stood up at the Fourth United Nations Conference on Women in Beijing in 1995 and declared, "Human rights are women's rights, and women's rights are human rights." But as we spoke, it was clear to me that Emma, like many of her generation, gets it. She and other student leaders from across the country kept pushing for more cultural change with their Vote for Our Lives effort in the months before the 2020 election, an expansion on their March for Our Lives theme. Young people backed the Biden-Harris ticket and Stacey Abrams's efforts to help register voters in Georgia for two runoffs that decided control of the U.S. Senate through 2022. They continue to lobby state and national legislators for tighter gun control laws. They see the fight for equality and the fight against gun violence as all one thing. "The best way to get things done is to appeal to both sides and listen," Emma told *Yahoo News*. "What we've really been focused on is inclusion and trying to really combine these communities spread around the United States. We've been trying to get everyone on the same page, to figure out what everybody's asking for, and see if we can, as a giant movement, ask together."

All of these movements—#NeverAgain, Black Lives Matter, TIME'S UP, #MeToo—are really about equality for every human being. As a gay woman, I know what the alternative is, and it's no way to live. That's why I've always said I don't care where you come from, what religion, what color, what gender or sexuality you claim, everyone deserves to have the best that life has to offer. That's why I've made working for equity my life's calling.

After saying goodbye to Emma, Ilana and I climbed into an open convertible for the Pride parade down Seventh Avenue. As we moved along the route, it looked like a happiness factory had exploded and released all the joy in the world into the streets of New York. There were balloons and flags and costumes, singing and dancing. I smiled and waved to the cheering crowds lining the sidewalks and people waved back. It was so meaningful to experience that sense of community.

I believe that the global fight for LGBTQ+ rights will be as important as any civil rights issue we're facing in the twenty-first century. And it's important that America helps lead the way. In June 2020, the Supreme Court rejected the Trump administration's attempts to roll back LGBTQ+ rights and ruled that transgender people are indeed protected in the workplace. Though that particular ruling focused on employment discrimination, legal scholars told *The New York Times* the decision could force expanded civil rights protections in education, health care, housing, and other areas of daily life. Once again, an opponent advanced us by trying to undermine us.

President Obama's stance on gay issues evolved over time, but I always trusted that he would do the right thing. He did away with the awful "don't ask, don't tell" policy in the military. He instructed the Justice Department to stop enforcing the hateful Defense of

Marriage Act. He interpreted the Civil Rights Act as protecting LGBTQ+ persons from discrimination. In 2012, he announced his full support of same-sex marriage and declared it a civil right three years before the U.S. Supreme Court ruled in *Obergefell v. Hodges* that the right of same-sex couples to marry was protected under the Constitution.

As the marriage laws changed, more and more of our friends were having weddings. Ilana and I were on a cruise with Rosie and Connie Spooner just after they married in a beautiful ceremony in 2014 after being a couple for thirty-six years. Plenty of tears were flowing that day. Elton had run to the altar with David Furnish soon after same-sex marriage was legalized in the U.K., and he started nudging Ilana and me to consider it. He even offered to sing at our wedding if we'd take the plunge. John McEnroe saw me at Elton's Smash Hit fund-raiser in Las Vegas and needled me: "C'mon, Billie Jean! Why not get married? Wrap it up and put a bow on it already!"

For me, it wasn't that simple, and it had nothing to do with any reservations about Ilana, who is the love of my life. My hesitation didn't have anything to do with finances and property, either. That's all been taken care of between us. My problem was that marriage still evoked conflicted feelings for me. Besides, Ilana and I already considered ourselves partners for life. We had worn each other's rings for years. Why change anything?

But in the fall of 2018, Ilana and I called our good friend David Dinkins, the former mayor of New York City, and told him we were ready to take him up on an offer he'd been making to us for years: "If you ever get married, I'm your guy!" After much discussion, Ilana and I had developed our own reasons for wanting to be married. We recognized that so many people had worked so hard to get the laws changed to give us the choice. Emotionally, we had arrived at a place where it became important to us to formalize our love for each other. As I said to Ilana as we were discussing it, "Years from now, I never want anyone to question how much I was committed to you."

That's how we secretly came to tie the knot at the mayor's apartment on the Upper East Side of New York on October 19, 2018. We didn't register at Bloomingdale's. Nobody threw rice or smashed wedding cake in the other's face. One of the brides wore jeans and a lovely red scarf and the other had on a black shirt, a comfortable warm-up suit, and pearls—ha!—a personal touch of glamour that Ilana still teases me about.

The only people who knew about our marriage until the writing of this book were the folks who processed our marriage license at city hall, David and his wife, Joyce, and an aide of theirs who acted as witnesses for the ceremony at the Dinkinses' apartment. (David's death in November 2020, at the age of ninety-three, came less than two months after Joyce passed away. She was eighty-nine.)

David loved to marry people and asked us to allow him to choose the vows. They were perfect: short, sweet, heartfelt. We said "I promise" instead of the traditional refrain, "I do." Ilana and I had taken off our rings beforehand, and now we took turns slipping them back on each other's finger. I loved that part. David popped open a bottle of champagne when we were done, and although Ilana and I are teetotalers, on that day we had a few sips.

"So much of our life has been public, keeping this private was something special that we could hold on to, just for us," Ilana later told a friend. "We didn't need the world to know. It was just about Billie and me and how we felt. There was something so nice about that, for both of us."

IN THE FALL OF 2019, I traveled to my hometown of Long Beach with a film crew and returned to many of the places that were touchstones in my life: my childhood home in Wrigley Heights; Houghton Park, where I met my dear coach Clyde Walker six decades earlier; the church where I asked Rev. Richards to baptize me and daydreamed about finding my mission in life; Charles Evan Hughes, my junior high school, and Los Cerritos, the elementary school where I used to race across the schoolyard and love the feeling of the wind in my hair.

The city had decided to name its new, state-of-the-art library after me and held a ceremony to dedicate the elegant 93,500-square-foot building. The Billie Jean King Main Library sits in the heart of Long Beach's downtown civic center and was built as part of the area's $520 million revitalization project that was championed by Long Beach's visionary mayor, Robert Garcia. In addition to stacks of books, the library offers cutting-edge technology, computers, veterans' programs, job search services, meeting space, children's programs, and a "maker's space" that includes art and 3-D printing studios—scads of things to help the community navigate the twenty-first century. I always say that Long Beach made me, and now I hope our library will be a place where people find needed support to create the future they want.

When I dropped by Los Cerritos on that trip, the fifth graders I visited with didn't know I was coming. They were reading a book for young readers by Brad Metzler and the illustrator Christopher Eliopoulos called *I Am Billie Jean King,* which is part of the Ordinary People Change the World series. The students' assignment that day was to come to class prepared to say what they wanted to be when they grew up, using the last line of the book—"I am Billie Jean King and I champion equality"—as an example. As I walked in, the teacher was calling on them and they were saying how they wanted to make a difference in the world:

"I want to protect the environment."

"I want to be an activist against gun violence."

"I want to be an anesthesiologist—"

"Whoa, that's a really important job, anesthesiologist—get it right," I joked. Heads turned. Eyes widened. The looks on their faces were priceless.

For the next thirty minutes or so, we talked. Those kids' enthusiasm and innocence took me back to when I was their age and no dream seemed too big to me, either. I told them, "This is a pivotal three years that can catapult you into high school and college and the rest of your life. Enjoy this time. Pay attention to your teachers. And girls, boys, everyone—I want you to think of each other. Not by race, gender—none of that. Stick up for each other, not just yourselves. Keep doing the right thing. Not if it's popular—if it's *right.* Be kind and good to each other."

Los Cerritos is a diverse school, and when I took the students' questions, race and gender came up a lot. I told them how I was once a child in their shoes, wondering what my place in the world would be, and I found my calling when I went to a tennis tournament and noticed everyone was white. "That day, I promised myself I was going to work for equality for the rest of my life because I wanted everyone to be included. Because every single one of you matters. You count. I don't care what other people tell you—you matter and you count. Don't let others define you. You define yourself. You decide in your heart and mind."

We resumed calling on the other children who hadn't had a chance to declare their dreams—"I want to be a video game designer . . . I want to be a cardiovascular surgeon," came the replies. The kids were impressive. As we neared the end, one boy raised his hand and volunteered, "I want to say that my parents support gay and lesbian rights. And I want to be an anti-bullying activist."

"Have you been bullied?" I asked him.

"No, but I know friends who have," he said. "I have two dads, and sometimes that's treated like a bad thing. But they taught me that love is love, no matter who you love. And that I shouldn't listen to bad things."

"It's about being yourself, right? Believing in yourself," I told him. "It used to be very shame based but listen to yourself. You know who you are. This is your journey. *You* get to decide."

Epilogue

I 'M IN SUCH A HAPPY PLACE emotionally now. I wish I could have had this well-being when I was in my twenties, my thirties, and my forties. The journey has been so rewarding, even if sometimes a struggle. It's just fascinating, life. I've told people if I die right now I'd be really ticked off because I'm not finished. Time is running out for real, and I've always had a sense of urgency. I wish I had nine lives.

When you read about history, you think it's gone by very fast, but when you live it, it's very slow. Progress is slow. Sometimes we have what seem like overnight revolutions, but these usually represent sudden tipping points after a long period of struggle. The road to success is filled with obstacles, the ebb and flow of measurable victories and setbacks; that's the nature of the change game. Winning is a process. It's important to stay in the moment for each battle as it's happening. Be clear about your goals. You must decide for yourself, *What would define winning?* And if you can come to see even failure as feedback, the information will help you plan your next step.

Sometimes I ask people to imagine themselves at the end of their life. I say, *When you look at yourself in the mirror, when you're older and wrinkled like I am, how will you want to remember yourself? How will you want others to remember you? What will you want to say that you stood for, and did with your life?* I think it's important to think about these things in a daily, intentional way. Each of us can be an influencer, whether it's by running for office or operating in a space as intimate as our own home.

The time in my life leading up to the Original 9's breakaway, the founding of the Women's Tennis Association, and the Battle of the Sexes was particularly tumultuous. Even though we had fears, we still forged ahead. You never know whether you're going to touch the hearts and minds of people unless you put yourself out there. You often hear people say that life is a marathon. Rather, I think life is a series of sprints—you get to start over and over and over again, always adapting to the long and winding road in front of you.

I'd give anything to be born again now. God, it would be great. When I look around at what's still left to be done it makes me feel the way I did when I was twelve. Life goes so fast. I keep prodding the people I work with, "You know, in a few years I'll be eighty. So what are we *doing*?"

I've got my health and energy now, and I'm not done fighting yet.

I've always been a dreamer, and I continue to imagine what I'd like the world to look like. Although the country took a turn toward intolerance during Donald Trump's presidency, I know a more tolerant, open, compassionate America is out there, because I've seen it.

I've marched and worked for a time when our legislatures from city hall to the state houses, the corridors of Congress to the White House, are occupied by more women and we finally have a woman president. Even if I don't see it happen, I know it's coming.

I'm frequently asked what advice I'd give to children today, and I often talk about how girls are taught to be perfect, boys are taught to be brave, and both approaches are wrong. No one is brave all the time and none of us is perfect. Girls rarely think they are good enough, boys are too often discouraged from being vulnerable, and we've got to stop it. Each of us can be anything we want to be.

When I talk to LGBTQ+ youth who are still grappling with their gender and sexual identities, I tell them they are going to make it. But the most important thing is that first they've got to feel safe and have allies. I didn't come out completely and wasn't comfortable in my own skin until I was fifty-one. I wish I could have done it sooner. To the parents of an LGBTQ+ child, I say they really are important to their child, and if nothing else, if only this, just tell them you love them.

You only need one person in the world who loves you unconditionally and you can make it. Every child only needs one. Just hearing *I love you and I accept you* can make so much else go away. It can work magic in a person's life.

Once I began living truthfully I felt like I could breathe again. I no longer have to lie or hide. I can be my authentic self, and I can say this with pride: It's been a lovely, sometimes lonely, often soul-shaking, ultimately gratifying ride. It's been full of sparks and recrimination. But I came through it.

I am free.

Acknowledgments

I am fortunate to have a supportive family that gave me the space to be who I am, the confidence to lead, and the love to keep me moving forward. Ilana Kloss, my partner of more than four decades, is my love and my rock in life, my partner in business, and my true soulmate. My parents, Bill and Betty Moffitt, gave me love, support, discipline, and faith; in doing so, they gave me the foundation that allowed me to be me. My brother, Randy Moffitt, truly understands me and makes me laugh. R.J. is the very best brother I could ever have. Our bond is unbreakable. Ilana and I are blessed to have a large immediate and extended family, each of whom is an important and valued part of our lives. I send my heartfelt thanks to them, and to our friends and family from Ilana's South African homeland who have opened their homes and their hearts to us over the years.

Writing a book like this is a labor of love. I am forever grateful to those who helped us get started right and finish strong. I have trusted them with my life story. Johnette Howard brought her rich writing talents, journalistic sense, and valuable perspective on her life and mine to this project and I am grateful to her for seeing this endeavor through to the end. Maryanne Vollers is a beautiful writer who framed our story in the beginning and is very much a big part of this book. Jonathan Segal, my exceptional editor at Knopf, provided much-needed direction, expertise, and support to make sure that this story is told right and is something readers will enjoy. Thank you to Jonathan and to everyone involved at Knopf. My literary agent, David Black, gave us indispensable advice and surehanded guidance and care throughout this project. Helen Russell, my decades-long friend and dedicated researcher, put in countless hours and added valuable perspective to the text and photographs in this book. The peerless Donn Gobbie helped to ensure that the key moments of the birth of women's professional tennis were accurate by sharing his seminal academic research with us.

Success is best measured by the character of those around you, and Ilana and I have been very blessed to have an extended family of friends who enrich our lives and push us to be the best we can be. Larry King played an enormous role in my life and career and remains a dear and generous friend whose recollections helped greatly in the telling of this story. Ilana and I send boundless gratitude and love to Merle and Richard Blackman, who are family first but have also been a constant source of support and counsel for us in life, finance, and business matters since the early 1990s. My cousin, Donna Lee Chavez, was an extraordinary help in piecing together significant parts of our family history. Ilana and I have enjoyed traveling and cruising to far-flung places for the past twenty-five years with our close-knit, fun-loving core group of Rosie Casals, Connie Spooner, Victoria Salinas Wright, and J.R. Wright. To them and our family of friends all over the world, Ilana and I say thank you. We cherish the times we share, the memories we have made, and the future we have together.

Without the love and support of the people of Long Beach when I was a child and the backing they gave me later in life, I may never have had this journey. Everyone comes from somewhere, but I know I am so fortunate to have the people of Long Beach in my corner. Susan Williams Catherwood introduced me to tennis and changed my life. Jerry Cromwell and I spent our formative years practicing together to make our tennis dreams come true. Clyde Walker first showed me how to be a champion and my other coaches and teachers gave me the confidence to go for it. Without Long Beach, especially the Long Beach Tennis Patrons and the Long Beach Century Club, who knows where my journey would have gone. My deepest gratitude also goes out to all the Long Beach citizens and officials involved in the Billie Jean King Main Library, the breathtaking new facility the city opened in 2019.

One of the best parts of having a long career in tennis is being part of a team. I had some of the best team experiences, especially early in my career. To Rosie, Owen Davidson, Carole Caldwell Graebner, Karen Hantze Susman, Barbara Browning, Kathy Chabot, and Pam Davis, and all of my doubles partners and teammates, thank you for making tennis fun for me. Most people think tennis is an individual sport, but I see it as a community of lifelong friends. Sincerest thanks to the host families who opened their homes to young players like me over the years and helped make our tennis travels possible, especially Barbara and Jack Clark. Nowhere in my life is the phrase "Relationships are everything" more important and meaningful than the connection I share with my tennis family. We could never have changed our sport without the courage of Gladys Heldman and the Original 9: Rosie, Valerie Ziegenfuss, Kristy Pigeon, Judy Tegart Dalton, Kerry Melville Reid, Peaches Bartkowicz, Nancy Richey, and Julie Heldman. Women's tennis would have never achieved success as a business enterprise without the support of Joseph Cullman 3rd, Ellen Merlo, and our other allies at the Virginia Slims brand. They gave us everything we needed to be stars and to change our sport. It was an honor to stand with all of them and write our own history.

In 1973, with our sport still divided into two women's pro tours, more than sixty players heeded a call to gather at the Gloucester Hotel in London and form the Women's Tennis Association to advocate for our interests as a group. I thank those women who set us on our historic course, and the exceptional executive directors, CEOs, trustees, and presidents I was privileged to work with at the WTA. Thank you to the incomparable Peachy Kellmeyer for your lifetime of service, wisdom, and incalculable contributions to the WTA and all of women's sports. Thank you to Chrissie Evert and Martina Navratilova for taking our game to new heights and making so many personal sacrifices, including missing some majors, for the betterment of our tour and World TeamTennis. Today our legacy and the WTA lives on alongside the other major stakeholders in the sport—the Association of Tennis Professionals, the International Tennis Federation (ITF), and the four major tournaments, the Australian Open, Roland-Garros, Wimbledon, and the U.S. Open.

Special thanks to everyone at the USTA, which has been at the forefront of equality since 1973, and had a huge impact on my life. We'd have never succeeded without the tournament owners, promoters, staffers, and volunteers around the world who believed in women's tennis and ensured we had places to play. Thank you to the International Tennis Hall of Fame for preserving our history and ensuring our stories continue to be told.

The Women's Sports Foundation was started in 1974 with a vision to protect and grow women's sports and Title IX. Thanks to the committed people who have worked and contributed to the foundation over the years, our dream is very much alive today and positioned well for tomorrow.

For more than four decades World TeamTennis was one of the biggest parts of my life and a concrete example of my vision for a world in which everyone's contributions are valued equally, regardless of our differences or gender. The Philadelphia Freedoms, my first WTT home, holds a special place in my heart because of my long association with the city and team as a player, coach, and owner. Thanks to all of you past and present, from the professional ranks to the WTT Junior Nationals to the community level, for keeping the ball in play.

The Cal State L.A. community will forever be part of my life and legacy. They championed me and have celebrated me and are forever committed to the growth of students and student athletes.

Over the years I have been blessed to work with some of the greatest writers, broadcasters, photographers, producers, editors, and network executives in the world. My best years in broadcasting were spent working with Seth Abraham, Ross Greenburg, Rick Bernstein, and the crew at HBO Sports, which was at the forefront of chronicling women's sports. Thank you to Christiane Amanpour and Robin Roberts, two groundbreaking newswomen whose extraordinary work and push for diversity, fairness, and inclusion earned my deepest respect long before I was fortunate enough to count them as friends.

I have been fortunate over the years to have an "A Team" of agents, attorneys, doctors, and healthcare professionals working on my behalf. These people are the best in the business, and I appreciate all you do and all you have done for me. So many people have believed in our game, invested in our vision, and helped us make a difference in the lives of others. You have given me the opportunity, access, and an open invitation to be part of your team. For that I am forever grateful.

My personal team is led by the friends and colleagues that keep Team BJK, Billie Jean King Enterprises, and the Billie Jean King Leadership Initiative running and moving forward. Thank you Marjorie Gantman, Therese O'Higgins, Barbara Perry, Kristi Gaylord, and Nancy Falconer. Tip Nunn has been by my side for more than thirty years as my superb publicist, loyal friend, organizer extraordinaire, and sounding board. Thank you to Dianne Donnelly, my dear friend and assistant whom I've known for more than three decades. Diane and her sister, Tracy Donnelly Maltby, were the inspiration for the Donnelly Awards, which since 1998 have provided scholarships to young players living with diabetes. All of you are there for us 365 days a year, 24/7, and Ilana and I greatly appreciate you and everything you do. You feel like family.

The New-York Historical Society has been the home of my personal archives since 2016, and I could not have partnered with a better place or group of people. Thank you to everyone at the N-YHS and to members of our BJKLI advisory board who have devoted themselves to helping us chart a course for future generations, particularly when it comes to advancing diversity, equity, and inclusion.

Ilana and I were privileged to be part of the founding board of the Elton John AIDS Foundation and we remain proud of the millions of dollars that have been raised through our WTT Smash Hits events to help organizations that fight AIDS and HIV.

As Ilana and I look to our immediate future, I am thankful for the Los Angeles Dodgers, the Los Angeles Sparks, the Angel City FC, the Philadelphia Freedoms, the global Billie Jean King Cup, and all of the people who work so hard to continue to build these legacies.

This book was completed during the COVID-19 pandemic. Thank you to those who have been on the front lines and risked so much to save so many. Your extraordinary sacrifice and dedication will never be forgotten.

It is no exaggeration to say that nearly everything important in my life has flowed from my involvement in tennis. The pure joy I felt when I first began hitting the ball at age eleven is the same joy I experience hitting the ball today. It's a love that will never be extinguished. When I came of age, the entire world—not just sports—was a far different place. It's amazing what can happen when we refuse to accept limits and set out to summon our best selves by pursuing what we dream about, and love.

You never do anything alone, and that is especially true for me in recognizing, acknowledging, and thanking all of those who have graced my life journey, and everyone who contributed or agreed to be interviewed for this book. Space doesn't permit me to mention everyone by name, but please know that without you, this life of mine would be incomplete, and would feel far less rich. You have played a major role in my happiness, my success, and my achievements.

We are not done yet.

Appendix I

Billie Jean (Moffitt) King

Born:	November 22, 1943, Long Beach, California.
Height:	5'5"
Weight:	140 pounds
Playing style:	Righthanded, one–handed backhand.
Education:	California State University, Los Angeles
Status:	Turned pro 1968.
Career Singles Titles:	126 (42 amateur, 84 professional, including 9 National Tennis League events)
Career Finals:	166
Won–lost:	126–40
International Tennis Hall of Fame Induction:	1987
Career earnings:	$2,012,193*
Top Ranking:	Year–End World No. 1 in 1966, 1967, 1968, 1971[†], 1972, 1973, 1974[†]

* NOTE: There are no reliable comprehensive records that capture King's total prize money, especially between 1968 and 1970, the early years of pro tennis. During those years, King played some tour events and Grand Slam majors, but was also one of the first four women who competed on George MacCall's National Tennis League tour, a barnstorming pro troupe that had its own schedule of events. The Women's Tennis Association lists King's career earnings as $1,966,487, but that total is incomplete and understated.

† Source information: There was no consensus world ranking authority for women's tennis until the WTA rankings began in 1975. Before that, leading media outlets compiled their own world rankings list. King was the consensus World No. 1 in 1966, 1967, 1968, and 1972, according to World Tennis magazine, Lance Tingay of the London Daily Telegraph and Boston sports writer Bud Collins. Only Collins ranked King No. 1 in 1971 (the year King skipped two majors to play the first all–women's pro tour she helped created) and again in 1974. Evonne Goolagong topped the World Tennis and Tingay rankings in 1971 and Chris Evert was their world No. 1 in 1974.

I. Grand Slams

Singles Finals: 18 (12 titles)

OUTCOME	YEAR	CHAMPIONSHIP	OPPONENT	SCORE
Finalist	1963	Wimbledon	Margaret Smith	3–6, 4–6
Finalist	1965	U.S. Championships	Margaret Smith	6–8, 5–7
Winner	1966	Wimbledon	Maria Bueno	6–3, 3–6,6–1
Winner	1967	Wimbledon	Ann (Haydon) Jones	6–3, 6–4
Winner	1967	U.S. Championships	Ann Jones	11–9, 6–4
Winner	1968	Australian Championships	Margaret (Smith) Court	6–1, 6–2

Open Era (8 titles)

OUTCOME	YEAR	CHAMPIONSHIP	OPPONENT	SCORE
Winner	1968	Wimbledon	Judy Tegart	9–7, 7–5
Finalist	1968	U.S. Open	Virginia Wade	4–6, 4–6
Finalist	1969	Australian Open	Margaret Court	4–6, 1–6
Finalist	1969	Wimbledon	Ann Jones	6–3, 3–6, 2–6
Finalist	1970	Wimbledon	Margaret Court	12–14, 9–11
Winner	1971	U.S. Open	Rosemary Casals	6–4, 7–6
Winner	1972	Roland-Garros	Evonne Goolagong	6–3, 6–3
Winner	1972	Wimbledon	Evonne Goolagong	6–3, 6–3
Winner	1972	U.S. Open	Kerry Melville	6–3, 7–5
Winner	1973	Wimbledon	Chris Evert	6–0, 7–5
Winner	1974	U.S. Open	Evonne Goolagong	3–6, 6–3, 7–5
Winner	1975	Wimbledon	Evonne Goolagong Cawley	6–0, 6–1

GRAND SLAM TOURNAMENT SINGLES TIMELINE[*]

	1959	'60	'61	'62	'63	'64	'65
AUSTRALIAN OPEN	A	A	A	A	A	A	SF
ROLAND-GARROS	A	A	A	A	A	A	A
WIMBLEDON	A	A	2R	Q	F	SF	SF
US OPEN	1R	3R	2R	1R	4R	Q	F

	'66	'67	'68	'69	'70	'71	'72
AUSTRALIAN OPEN	A	A	W	F	A	A	A
ROLAND-GARROS	A	Q	SF	Q	Q	A	W
WIMBLEDON	W	W	W	F	F	SF	W
US OPEN	2R	W	F	Q	A	W	W

	'73	'74	'75	'76	'77	'78	'79
AUSTRALIAN OPEN	A	A	A	A	A/A	A	A
ROLAND-GARROS	A	A	A	A	A	A	A
WIMBLEDON	W	Q	W	A	Q	Q	Q
US OPEN	3R	W	A	A	Q	A	SF

	'80	'81	'82	'83	'84	W–L
AUSTRALIAN OPEN	A	A	Q	2R	A	16–4
ROLAND-GARROS	Q	A	3R	A	A	21–6
WIMBLEDON	Q	A	SF	SF	A	95–15
US OPEN	A	A	1R	A	A	58–14

* Key: (W) Won; (A) absent; (F) finalist; (SF) semifinalist; (Q) quarterfinalist; (#R) rounds 4, 3, 2, 1; (RR) round robin; W–L (Won–Lost)

Grand Slam Doubles Finals: 29 (16 titles)

OUTCOME	YEAR	CHAMPIONSHIP	PARTNER	OPPONENT	SCORE
Winner	1961	Wimbledon	Karen Hantze	Jan Lehane Margaret Smith	6–3, 6–4
Winner	1962	Wimbledon	Karen Hantze Susman	Sandra Reynolds Renee Schuurman	5–7, 6–3, 7–5
Finalist	1962	U.S. Championships	Karen Hantze Susman	Maria Bueno Darlene Hard	6–4, 3–6, 2–6
Finalist	1964	Wimbledon	Karen Hantze Susman	Margaret Smith Lesley Turner	5–7, 2–6
Winner	1964	U.S. Championships	Karen Hantze Susman	Margaret Smith Lesley Turner	3–6, 6–2, 6–4
Finalist	1965	Australian Championships	Lesley Turner	Margaret Smith Lesley Turner	6–1, 2–6, 3–6
Winner	1965	Wimbledon	Maria Bueno	Françoise Dürr Janine Lieffrig	6–2, 7–5
Finalist	1965	U.S. Championships	Karen Hantze Susman	Carole Caldwell Graebner Nancy Richey	4–6, 4–6
Finalist	1966	U.S. Championships	Rosemary Casals	Maria Bueno Nancy Richey	3–6, 4–6
Winner	1967	Wimbledon	Rosemary Casals	Maria Bueno Nancy Richey	9–11, 6–4, 6–2
Winner	1967	U.S. Championships	Rosemary Casals	Mary Ann Eisel Donna Floyd Fales	4–6, 6–3, 6–4

Open Era (18 Finals, 10 Titles)

OUTCOME	YEAR	CHAMPIONSHIP	PARTNER	OPPONENT	SCORE
Finalist	1968	Roland-Garros	Rosemary Casals	Françoise Dürr Ann (Haydon) Jones	5–7, 6–4, 4–6
Winner	1968	Wimbledon	Rosemary Casals	Françoise Dürr Ann Jones	3–6, 6–4, 7–5
Finalist	1968	U.S. Open	Rosemary Casals	Maria Bueno Margaret Court	6–4, 7–9, 6–8
Finalist	1969	Australian Open	Rosemary Casals	Margaret Court Judy Tegart	4–6, 4–6
Finalist	1970	Roland-Garros	Rosemary Casals	Françoise Dürr Gail Sherriff Chanfreau	1–6, 6–3, 3–6
Winner	1970	Wimbledon	Rosemary Casals	Françoise Dürr Virginia Wade	6–2, 6–3
Winner	1971	Wimbledon	Rosemary Casals	Margaret Court Evonne Goolagong	6–3, 6–2

OUTCOME	YEAR	CHAMPIONSHIP	PARTNER	OPPONENT	SCORE
Winner	1972	Roland-Garros	Betty Stöve	Winnie Shaw Nell Truman	6–1, 6–2
Winner	1972	Wimbledon	Betty Stöve	Françoise Dürr Judy Tegart Dalton	6–2, 4–6, 6–3
Winner	1973	Wimbledon	Rosemary Casals	Françoise Dürr Betty Stöve	6–1, 4–6, 7–5
Finalist	1973	U.S. Open	Rosemary Casals	Margaret Court Virginia Wade	6–3, 3–6, 5–7
Winner	1974	U.S. Open	Rosemary Casals	Françoise Dürr Betty Stöve	7–6, 6–7, 6–4
Finalist	1975	U.S. Open	Rosemary Casals	Margaret Court Virginia Wade	5–7, 6–2, 5–7
Finalist	1976	Wimbledon	Betty Stöve	Chris Evert Martina Navratilova	1–6, 6–3, 5–7
Winner	1978	U.S. Open	Martina Navratilova	Kerry Melville Reid Wendy Turnbull	7–6, 6–4
Winner	1979	Wimbledon	Martina Navratilova	Betty Stöve Wendy Turnbull	5–7, 6–3, 6–2
Finalist	1979	U.S. Open	Martina Navratilova	Betty Stöve Wendy Turnbull	5–7, 3–6
Winner	1980	U.S. Open	Martina Navratilova	Pam Shriver Betty Stöve	7–6, 7–5

Grand Slam Mixed Doubles finals: 18 (11 titles)

OUTCOME	YEAR	CHAMPIONSHIP	PARTNER	OPPONENTS	SCORE
Finalist	1966	Wimbledon	Dennis Ralston	Margaret Smith Ken Fletcher	6–4, 3–6, 3–6
Winner	1967	Roland-Garros	Owen Davidson	Ann (Haydon) Jones Ion Tiriac	6–3, 6–1
Winner	1967	Wimbledon	Owen Davidson	Maria Bueno Ken Fletcher	7–5, 6–2
Winner	1967	U.S. Championships	Owen Davidson	Rosemary Casals Stan Smith	6–3, 6–2
Winner	1968	Australian Championships	Dick Crealy	Margaret (Smith) Court Allan Stone	walkover

Open Era (7 Titles)

OUTCOME	YEAR	CHAMPIONSHIP	PARTNER	OPPONENT	SCORE
Finalist	1968	Roland-Garros	Owen Davidson	Françoise Dürr Jean–Claude Barclay	1–6, 4–6
Winner	1970	Roland-Garros	Bob Hewitt	Françoise Dürr Jean–Claude Barclay	3–6, 6–4, 6–2
Winner	1971	Wimbledon	Owen Davidson	Margaret Court Marty Reissen	3–6, 6–2, 15–13
Winner	1971	U.S. Open	Owen Davidson	Betty Stöve Robert Maud	6–3, 7–5
Winner	1973	Wimbledon	Owen Davidson	Janet Newberry Raul Ramirez	6–3, 6–2
Winner	1973	U.S. Open	Owen Davidson	Margaret Court Marty Reissen	6–3, 3–6, 7–6
Winner	1974	Wimbledon	Owen Davidson	Lesley Charles Mark Farrell	6–3, 9–7
Finalist	1975	U.S. Open	Fred Stolle	Rosemary Casals Dick Stockton	3–6, 6–7
Winner	1976	U.S. Open	Phil Dent	Betty Stöve Frew McMillan	3–6, 6–2, 7–5
Finalist	1977	U.S. Open	Vitas Gerulaitis	Betty Stöve Frew McMillan	2–6, 6–3, 3–6
Finalist	1978	Wimbledon	Ray Ruffels	Betty Stöve Frew McMillan	2–6, 2–6
Finalist	1978	U.S. Open	Ray Ruffels	Betty Stöve Frew McMillan	3–6, 6–7
Finalist	1983	Wimbledon	Steve Denton	Wendy Turnbull John Lloyd	7–6 (5), 6–7 (5), 5–7

II. Career Singles[*]

Finals

Titles: 125 (42 amateur, 83 professional)
Finals: 167[†]

NO.	RESULT	WEEK OF	TOURNAMENT NAME AND LOCATION	SURFACE	OPPONENT	SCORE
1.	F	May 14, 1961	Southern California Championships, Los Angeles, U.S.	Hard	Karen Hantze	4–6, 1–6
2.	W	July 24, 1961	Pennsylvania Lawn Tennis Championships, Haverford, Pa, U.S.	Grass	Justina Bricka	6–3, 6–4
3.	W	July 31, 1961	Philadelphia & District Women's Grass Court Championships, Pennsylvania, U.S.	Grass	Edda Buding	6–3, 6–4
4.	W	April 9, 1962	Pasadena Metropolitan Tournament, Pasadena, California, U.S.	Hard	Carole Caldwell	6–3, 3–6, 9–7
5.	F	May 13, 1962	Southern California Championships, Los Angeles, U.S.	Hard	Karen Hantze Susman	3–6, 4–6
6.	W	April 1, 1963	Pasadena Metropolitan Tournament, Pasadena, California, U.S.	Hard	Patricia Cody	6–2, 6–2
7.	W	May 6, 1963	Southern California Championships, Los Angeles, U.S.	Hard	Darlene Hard	6–4, 6–3
8.	F	June 24, 1963	Wimbledon, London, England	Grass	Margaret Smith (Court)	3–6, 4–6
9.	W	July 8, 1963	Irish Championships, Dublin	Grass	Carole Caldwell	6–4, 6–3
10.	F	September 22, 1963	Pacific Southwest Championships, Los Angeles, U.S.	Hard	Darlene Hard	3–6, 3–6

* Key: F (finalist), W (Winner)
† Note: Total includes King's 8–5 record in National Tennis League title matches, which are listed in separate table below.)

NO.	RESULT	WEEK OF	TOURNAMENT NAME AND LOCATION	SURFACE	OPPONENT	SCORE
11.	F	January 12, 1964	Dallas Indoor Invitational, Dallas, Texas, U.S.	Indoor	Nancy Richey	2–6, 5–7
12.	F	May 10, 1964	Southern California Championships, Los Angeles, US	Hard	Carole Caldwell	5–7, 6–3. 1–6
13.	W	July 27, 1964	Eastern Grass Court Championships, South Orange, New Jersey, U.S.	Grass	Nancy Richey	7–5, 3–6, 8–6
14.	F	August 3, 1964	Piping Rock Invitational, Locust Valley, New York, U.S.	Grass	Nancy Richey	3–6, 6–1, 4–6
15.	W	August 10, 1964	Essex County Club Invitational, Manchester–by–the–Sea, Massachusetts, U.S.	Grass	Karen Hantze Susman	6–4, 4–6, 11–9
16.	F	October 4, 1964	Pacific Southwest Championships, Los Angeles, California, U.S.	Hard	Maria Bueno	6–3, 3–6, 2–6
17.	F	November 29, 1964	New South Wales Championships, Sydney, Australia	Grass	Margaret Smith	4–6, 3–6
18.	F	April 19, 1965	Ojai Valley Tennis Tournament, Women's Open Invitational, Ojai, California.	Hard	Kathleen Harter	6–1, 4–6, 6–2
19.	W	May 3, 1965	Southern California Championships, Los Angeles, U.S.	Hard	Kathleen Harter	6–3, 6–1
20.	W	May 17, 1965	California State Championships, Portola Valley, U.S.	Hard	Rosemary Casals	6–2, 8–6
21.	W	July 19, 1965	Pennsylvania Lawn Tennis Championships, Haverford, Pa., U.S.	Grass	Carole Caldwell Graebner	6–1, 6–2
22.	W	July 26, 1965	Eastern Grass Court Championships, South Orange, New Jersey, U.S.	Grass	Jane Albert	7–5, 6–3

NO.	RESULT	WEEK OF	TOURNAMENT NAME AND LOCATION	SURFACE	OPPONENT	SCORE
23.	W	August 15, 1965	Essex County Club Invitational, Manchester–by–the–Sea, Massachusetts, U.S.	Grass	Carol Hanks Aucamp	6–2, 10–8
24.	F	September 12, 1965	U.S. Championships, Forest Hills, New York, U.S.	Grass	Margaret Smith	6–8, 5–7
25.	W	February 14, 1966	U.S. Indoor Championships, Chestnut Hill, Massachusetts, U.S.	Indoor	Mary-Ann Eisel	6–0, 6–2
26.	W	March 14, 1966	Thunderbird Invitational Tennis Tournament, Phoenix, Arizona, U.S.	Hard	Mary-Ann Eisel	6–3, 6–2
27.	W	March 28, 1966	South African Tennis Championships, Johannesburg	Hard	Margaret (Smith) Court	6–3, 6–2
28.	W	April 18, 1966	Ojai Valley Tennis Tournament, Women's Open Invitational Ojai, California	Hard	Rosemary Casals	6–2, 6–4
29.	W	May 2, 1966	Southern California Championships, Los Angeles, U.S.	Hard	Tory Ann Fretz	6–3, 10–8
30.	W	May 16, 1966	U.S. Hard Court Championships, La Jolla, California, U.S.	Hard	Patti Hogan	7–5, 6–0
31.	W	May 23, 1966	Tulsa Invitational Tennis Championship, Tulsa, Oklahoma, U.S.	Clay	Carol Hanks Aucamp	6–0, 6–1
32.	W	May 30, 1966	North of England Championships, Manchester, United Kingdom	Grass	Winnie Shaw	6–2, 6–1
33.	W	June 20, 1966	Wimbledon, London, England*	Grass	Maria Bueno	6–3, 3–6, 6–1
34.	W	August 8, 1966	Piping Rock Invitational, Locust Valley, New York, U.S.	Grass	Karen Krantzcke	6–2, 6–0

* This victory was King's first major ("Grand Slam") singles title

NO.	RESULT	WEEK OF	TOURNAMENT NAME AND LOCATION	SURFACE	OPPONENT	SCORE
35.	F	February 13, 1967	New England Women's Indoors, Salem, Massachusetts	Indoor	Mary-Ann Eisel	4–6, 7–5, 9–11
36.	W	February 13, 1967	U.S. Indoor Championships, Winchester, Massachusetts, U.S.	Indoor	Trudy Groenman	6–1, 6–0
37.	W	February 27, 1967	Pacific Coast Indoor Tennis Championships, San Rafael, California, U.S.	Indoor	Patti Hogan	6–3, 8–6
38.	W	March 20, 1967	South African Tennis Championships, Johannesburg	Hard	Maria Bueno	7–5, 5–7, 6–2
39.	W	May 1, 1967	California State Championships, Portola Valley, U.S.	Hard	Rosemary Casals	6–1, 6–3
40.	W	May 8, 1967	Charlotte Invitation Tennis Tournament, Charlotte, North Carolina, U.S.	Clay	Peaches Bartkowicz	6–1, 6–2
41.	W	June 26, 1967	Wimbledon, London, England	Grass	Ann (Haydon) Jones	6–3, 6–4
42.	W	July 31, 1967	Eastern Grass Court Championships, South Orange, New Jersey, U.S.	Grass	Kathleen Harter	4–6, 6–2, 6–3
43.	W	August 14, 1967	Essex County Club Invitational, Manchester–by–the–Sea, Massachusetts, U.S.	Grass	Kerry Melville	8–6, 6–1
44.	W	August 28, 1967	U.S. Championships, New York, NY, U.S.	Grass	Ann Jones	11–9, 6–4
45.	W	September 18, 1967	Pacific Southwest Championships, Los Angeles, U.S.	Hard	Rosemary Casals	6–0, 6–4
46.	W	October 30, 1967	Championships of South America, Buenos Aires, Argentina	Clay	Rosemary Casals	6–3, 3–6, 6–2
47.	W	November 27, 1967	Victorian Championships, Melbourne, Australia	Grass	Lesley Turner	6–3, 3–6, 7–5

NO.	RESULT	WEEK OF	TOURNAMENT NAME AND LOCATION	SURFACE	OPPONENT	SCORE
48.	F	December 17, 1967	South Australian Championships, Adelaide, Australia	Grass	Judy Tegart	6–4, 1–6, 4–6
49.	W	January 1, 1968	Western Australia Championships, Perth	Grass	Margaret Court	6–2, 6–4
50.	W	January 8, 1968	Tasmanian Championships, Hobart, Australia	Grass	Judy Tegart	6–2, 6–4
51.	W	January 15, 1968	Australian Championships, Melbourne, Australia	Grass	Margaret Court	6–1, 6–2
52.	W	February 12, 1968	New England Women's Invitational Indoor Tennis Championships, Salem, Massachusetts, U.S.	Indoor	Mary-Ann Eisel	6–3, 6–4
53.	W	February 19, 1968	U.S. Indoor Championships, Winchester, Massachusetts, U.S.	Indoor	Rosemary Casals	6–3, 9–7
54.	F	March 25, 1968	Madison Square Garden Challenge Trophy, New York, NY*	Indoor	Nancy Richey	6–4, 5–7, 0–6

Open Era

NO.	RESULT	WEEK OF	TOURNAMENT NAME AND LOCATION	SURFACE	OPPONENT	SCORE
55.	W	June 24, 1968	Wimbledon, London, England	Grass	Judy Tegart	9–7, 7–5
56.	F	July 25, 1968	Tennis for Everyone Pro Invitational, Oakland, California, U.S.	Indoor	Rosemary Casals	8–10, 6–2, 0–6
57.	F	September 9, 1968	U.S. Open, New York, New York, U.S.	Grass	Virginia Wade	4–6, 2–6
58.	F	January 27, 1969	Australian Open, Melbourne, Australia	Grass	Margaret Court	4–6, 1–6
59.	W	March 31, 1969	South African Open, Johannesburg	Hard	Nancy Richey	6–3, 6–4
60.	W	April 14, 1969	Natal Open, Durban, South Africa	Hard	Annette Van Zyl	6–4, 6–1

* This was King's last tournament as an amateur. She and three other women—Rosie Casals, Ann Haydon Jones, and Françoise Durr—joined George MacCall's National Tennis League in 1968, a barnstorming pro tour that lasted two years.

NO.	RESULT	WEEK OF	TOURNAMENT NAME AND LOCATION	SURFACE	OPPONENT	SCORE
61.	F	June 14, 1969	West of England Open, Bristol, England	Grass	Margaret Court	3–6, 3–6
62.	F	July 5, 1969	Wimbledon, London, England	Grass	Ann Jones	6–3, 3–6, 2–6
63.	W	July 11, 1969	Irish Open, Dublin, Ireland	Grass	Virginia Wade	6–2, 6–2
64.	W	September 22, 1969	Pacific Southwest Open, Los Angeles, U.S.	Hard	Ann Jones	6–2, 6–3
65.	F	October 12, 1969	Howard Hughes Open, Las Vegas, Nevada, U.S.	Hard	Nancy Richey	6–2, 4–6, 1–6
66.	F	November 23, 1969	British Covered Court Open, London, England	Indoor	Ann Jones	11–9, 2–6, 7–9
67.	W	November 24, 1969	Stockholm Indoor Open, Stockholm, Sweden	Indoor	Julie Heldman	9–7, 6–2
68.	F	February 8, 1970	International Tennis Players Association Open, Philadelphia, U.S.	Indoor	Margaret Court	3–6, 6–8 (12–14)
69.	F	February 15, 1970	Maureen Connolly Brinker Memorial, Dallas, U.S.	Indoor	Margaret Court	6–1, 3–6, 9–11
70.	W	March 7, 1970	Honolulu Professional Tennis Classic, Honolulu, Hawaii	Indoor	Rosemary Casals	6–4, 6–4
71.	W	March 16, 1970	Dunlop International, Sydney, Australia	Grass	Margaret Court	6–2, 4–6, 6–3
72.	F	April 3, 1970	South African Open, Johannesburg, South Africa	Hard	Margaret Court	4–6, 6–1, 3–6
73.	W	April 6, 1970	Natal Open, Durban, South Africa	Hard	Margaret Court	6–4, 2–6, 6–2
74.	W	April 20, 1970	Italian Open, Rome, Italy	Clay	Julie Heldman	6–1, 6–3
75.	F	July 4, 1970	Wimbledon, London, England	Grass	Margaret Court	12–14, 9–11

NO.	RESULT	WEEK OF	TOURNAMENT NAME AND LOCATION	SURFACE	OPPONENT	SCORE
76.	W	November 2, 1970	Virginia Slims Invitational, Richmond, Virginia, U.S.	Indoor	Nancy Richey	6–3, 6–3
77.	W	November 16, 1970	Embassy Indoor Tennis Championships, Wembley Arena, London	Indoor	Ann Jones	8–6, 3–6, 6–1
78.	W	January 4, 1971	British Motor Cars Pro– Tennis Championships, San Francisco, U.S. *	Indoor	Rosemary Casals	6–3, 6–4
79.	W	January 11, 1971	Billie Jean King Invitational (Virginia Slims), Long Beach, California, U.S.	Indoor	Rosemary Casals	6–1, 6–2
80.	W	January 18, 1971	Virginia Slims Invitational, Milwaukee, Wisconsin, U.S.	Indoor	Rosemary Casals	6–3, 6–2
81.	W	January 25, 1971	Virginia Slims Invitational, Oklahoma City, Oklahoma, U.S.	Indoor	Rosemary Casals	1–6, 7–6, 6–4
82.	W	February 2, 1971	Virginia Slims Invitational, Sewanee and Chattanooga, Tennessee, U.S.	Indoor	Ann Jones	6–4, 6–1
83.	W	February 23, 1971	U.S. Indoor Championships (Virginia Slims Nationals), Winchester, Mass	Indoor	Rosemary Casals	4–6, 6–2, 6–3
84.	W	March 15, 1971	Kmart Invitational (Virginia Slims), Rochester and Troy, Michigan, U.S.	Indoor	Rosemary Casals	3–6, 6–1, 6–2
85.	W	April 19, 1971	Virginia Slims Invitational, San Diego, California, U.S.	Indoor	Rosemary Casals	4–6, 7–5, 6–1
86.	W	May 17, 1971	German Open, Hamburg, West Germany	Clay	Helga Niessen Masthoff	6–3, 6–2

* King and her fellow members of the Original 9—Rosie Casals, Nancy Richey, Julie Heldman, Valerie Ziegenfuss, Kristy Pigeon, Peaches Bartkowicz, Judy Dalton and Kerry Melville—were the founding players of the first all–women's pro tennis tour, which began its first full season in 1971 at the British Motor Cars event. World Tennis publisher Gladys Heldman established and ran the breakaway tour from its start in Houston in 1970 and landed the circuit sponsorship from Virginia Slims, and others.

NO.	RESULT	WEEK OF	TOURNAMENT NAME AND LOCATION	SURFACE	OPPONENT	SCORE
87.	W	July 12, 1971	Rothmans North of England Tennis Championships, Hoylake	Grass	Rosemary Casals	6–3, 6–3
88.	W	July 19, 1971	Austrian Open, Kitzbühel, Austria	Clay	Laura Rossouw	6–2, 4–6, 7–5
89.	W	August 2, 1971	Virginia Slims International, Houston, Texas, U.S.	Indoor	Kerry Melville	6–4, 4–6, 6–1
90.	W	August 9, 1971	U.S. Clay Court Championships, Indianapolis, Indiana, U.S.	Clay	Linda Tuero	6–4, 7–5
91.	W	August 30, 1971	U.S. Open, New York, New York, U.S.	Grass	Rosemary Casals	6–4, 7–6(2)
92.	W	September 13, 1971	Virginia Slims Invitational, Louisville, Kentucky, U.S.	Indoor	Rosemary Casals	6–1, 4–6, 6–3
93.	W	September 27, 1971	Virginia Slims Thunderbird Invitational, Phoenix, Arizona, U.S*	Hard	Rosemary Casals	7–5, 6–1
94.	W	October 25, 1971	Embassy Indoor Championships (British Indoors), Wembley Arena, London	Indoor	Françoise Dürr	6–1, 5–7, 7–5
95.	W	January 10, 1972	British Motor Cars Pro–Tennis Championships (Virginia Slims), San Francisco, U.S.	Indoor	Kerry Melville	7–6, 7–6
96.	W	March 20, 1972	Virginia Slims of Richmond, Richmond, Virginia, U.S.	Clay (indoor)	Nancy Richey	6–3, 6–4
97.	W	April 17, 1972	Virginia Slims Conquistadores, Tucson, Arizona, U.S.	Hard	Françoise Dürr	6–0, 6–3
98.	W	May 1, 1972	Virginia Slims of Indianapolis, Indianapolis, Indiana, U.S.	Indoor	Nancy Richey	6–3, 6–3

* King at this 1971 tournament became the first woman pro athlete in any sport to win $100,000 USD in a calendar year. She repeated the feat in 1972.

NO.	RESULT	WEEK OF	TOURNAMENT NAME AND LOCATION	SURFACE	OPPONENT	SCORE
99.	W	May 22, 1972	Roland-Garros, Paris, France*	Clay	Evonne Goolagong	6–3, 6–3
100.	W	June 5, 1972	John Player Round Robin, Nottingham, England	Grass	Virginia Wade Rosemary Casals Evonne Goolagong	6–7, 6–3, 6–4 6–7, 6–4, 7–5†
101.	W	June 12, 1972	W.D. & H.O. Wills Open, Bristol, England	Grass	Kerry Melville	6–3, 6–2
102.	W	June 26, 1972	Wimbledon, London, England	Grass	Evonne Goolagong	6–3, 6–3
103.	F	August 14, 1972	Virginia Slims, South Denver H.S. Stadium, Denver, Colorado	Hard	Nancy Richey Gunter	6–1, 4–6, 4–6
104.	W	August 28, 1972	U.S. Open, New York, New York, U.S.	Grass	Kerry Melville	6–3, 7–5
105.	W	September 11, 1972	Four Roses Premium Tennis Classic, Charlotte, North Carolina, U.S.	Clay	Margaret Court	6–2, 6–2
106.	F	September 18, 1972	Golden Gate Pacific Coast Tennis Classic, San Francisco, California, U.S.	Hard	Margaret Court	4–6, 1–6
107.	W	September 25, 1972	Virginia Slims Thunderbird, Phoenix, Arizona, U.S.	Hard	Margaret Court	7–6, 6–3
108.	W	February 19, 1973	Virginia Slims of Indianapolis, Indianapolis, Indiana, U.S.	Indoor	Rosemary Casals	5–7, 6–2, 6–4
109.	F	March 5, 1973	Virginia Slims of Chicago, Chicago, Illinois, U.S.	Indoor	Margaret Court	2–6, 6–4, 4–6
110.	F	April 9, 1973	Virginia Slims of Boston, Boston, Massachusetts, U.S.	Indoor	Margaret Court	2–6, 4–6

* King's win at Roland-Garros in 1972 gave her a career sweep of all four Grand Slam singles titles.
† Unfinished (rain)

NO.	RESULT	WEEK OF	TOURNAMENT NAME AND LOCATION	SURFACE	OPPONENT	SCORE
111.	W	May 7, 1973	Toray Sillok, Tokyo, Japan	Indoor	Nancy Richey	7–6, 5–7, 6–3
112.	W	June 4, 1973	Gulf Coast Professional Women's Tennis Tournament, Mobile, Alabama	Hard	Françoise Dürr	6–3, 7–5
113.	W	June 11, 1973	John Player Tournament, Nottingham, England	Grass	Virginia Wade	8–6, 6–4
114.	W	June 25, 1973	Wimbledon, London, England	Grass	Chris Evert	6–0, 7–5
115.	W	July 30, 1973	Virginia Slims of Denver, Denver, Colorado, U.S.	Hard	Betty Stöve	6–4, 6–2
116.	F	August 6, 1973	Commerce Union Bank Classic, Nashville, Tennessee, U.S.	Clay	Margaret Court	3–6, 6–4, 2–6
117.	W	October 1, 1973	Faberge Thunderbird Classic (Virginia Slims), Phoenix, Arizona, U.S.	Hard	Nancy Richey	6–1, 6–3
118.	W	October 22, 1973	Hawaii Women's Pro Tennis Tournament by Virginia Slims, Honolulu, Hawaii	Hard	Helen Gourlay	6–1, 6–1
119.	W	November 19, 1973	Gunze Classic, Tokyo, Japan	Indoor	Nancy Richey	6–4, 6–4
120.	F	November 23, 1973	Lady Baltimore, Baltimore, Maryland, U.S.	Indoor	Rosemary Casals	6–3, 6–7, 4–6
121.	W	January 14, 1974	Virginia Slims of San Francisco, San Francisco, California, U.S.	Indoor	Chris Evert	7–6, 6–2
122.	F	January 24, 1974	Virginia Slims of Mission Viejo, Mission Viejo, California, U.S.	Hard	Chris Evert	3–6, 1–6
123.	W	January 28, 1974	Virginia Slims of Washington, D.C., U.S.	Indoor	Kerry Melville	6–0, 6–2
124.	W	February 18, 1974	Virginia Slims of Detroit, Michigan, U.S.	Indoor	Rosemary Casals	6–1, 6–1
125.	W	March 18, 1974	Akron Tennis Open (Virginia Slims), Ohio, U.S.	Indoor	Nancy Richey	6–3, 7–5

NO.	RESULT	WEEK OF	TOURNAMENT NAME AND LOCATION	SURFACE	OPPONENT	SCORE
126.	W	March 25, 1974	U.S. Indoor Championships (Virginia Slims), Felt Forum, New York, N.Y.	Indoor	Chris Evert	6–3, 3–6, 6–2
127.	F	April 22, 1974	Virginia Slims of Philadelphia	Indoor	Olga Morozova	6–7, 1–6
128.	W	August 26, 1974	U.S. Open, New York, New York, U.S.	Grass	Evonne Goolagong	3–6, 6–3, 7–5
129.	F	January 6, 1975	Virginia Slims of San Francisco, San Francisco, California, U.S.	Indoor	Chris Evert	1–6, 1–6
130.	W	January 13, 1975	Virginia Slims of Sarasota, Sarasota, Florida, U.S.	Indoor	Chris Evert	6–2, 6–3
131.	W	April 19, 1975	L'Eggs World Series, Austin, Texas, U.S.	Hard	Chris Evert	6–4, 3–6, 7–6
132.	W	June 16, 1975	Eastbourne, England	Grass	Virginia Wade	7–5, 6–4, 6–4
133.	W	June 23, 1975	Wimbledon, London, England	Grass	Evonne Goolagong Cawley	6–0, 6–1
134.	W	March 20, 1977	Lionel Cup, San Antonio, Texas, U.S.	Hard/Indoor	Mary Hamm	6–3, 3–6, 6–3
135.	F	March 28, 1977	Family Circle Cup, Hilton Head, South Carolina, U.S.	Clay	Chris Evert	0–6– 1–6
136.	W	April 11, 1977	Lionel Cup, Port Washington, New York, U.S.	Indoor	Caroline Stoll	6–1, 6–1
137.	W	October 10, 1977	Thunderbird Classic, Phoenix, Arizona, U.S.	Hard	Wendy Turnbull	1–6, 6–1, 6–0
138.	W	October 17, 1977	Colgate Brazil Open, São Paulo, Brazil	Indoor	Betty Stöve	6–1, 6–4
139.	W	October 24, 1977	Borinquen Classic, San Juan, Puerto Rico	Hard	Janet Newberry	6–1, 6–3

NO	RESULT	WEEK OF	TOURNAMENT NAME AND LOCATION	SURFACE	OPPONENT	SCORE
140.	F	November 1, 1977	Colgate Series Championship, Rancho Mirage, California, U.S.	Hard	Chris Evert	2–6, 2–6
141.	W	November 21, 1977	Gunze World Tennis Tournament, Kobe and Tokyo, Japan	Indoor	Martina Navratilova	7–5, 5–7, 6–1
142.	W	December 5, 1977	Bremar Cup, London	Indoor	Virginia Wade	6–3, 6–1
143.	F	January 16, 1978	Virginia Slims of Houston, Houston, Texas, U.S.	Indoor	Martina Navratilova	6–1, 2–6, 2–6
144.	F	February 27, 1978	Virginia Slims of Kansas City, Kansas City, Missouri, U.S.	Indoor	Martina Navratilova	5–7, 6–2, 3–6
145.	F	March 26, 1978	Virginia Slims of Philadelphia, Philadelphia, Pennsylvania, U.S.	Indoor	Chris Evert	0–6, 4–6
146.	W	September 10, 1979	Toray Sillook, Tokyo, Japan	Indoor	Evonne Goolagong Cawley	6–4, 7–5
147.	W	October 29, 1979	Stockholm Open, Sweden	Indoor	Betty Stöve	6–3, 6–7, 7–5
148.	W	February 18, 1980	Avon Championships of Detroit, Michigan, U.S.	Indoor	Evonne Goolagong Cawley	6–3, 6–0
149.	W	February 25, 1980	Avon Championships of Houston, Texas, U.S.	Indoor	Martina Navratilova	6–1, 6–3
150.	W	September 8, 1980	Toray Sillook, Tokyo	Indoor	Terry Holladay	7–5, 6–4
151.	W	June 7, 1982	Edgbaston Cup, Birmingham, England	Grass	Rosalyn Fairbank	6–2, 6–1
152.	F	January 17, 1983	Central Trust Tennis Championships, Cincinnati, Ohio, U.S.	Indoor	Hana Mandlikova	4–6, 3–6
153.	W	May 30, 1983	Kentish Times Festival, Beckenham, United Kingdom	Grass	Barbara Potter	6–4, 6–3
154.	W	June 6, 1983	Edgbaston Cup, Birmingham, England	Grass	Alycia Moulton	6–0, 7–5

National Tennis League Finals

Billie Jean King, Rosie Casals, Ann Jones and Françoise Dürr turned pro in April of 1968 to comprise the women's division of the National Tennis League tour. Before the tour folded in March 1970, a handful of other women players—including Althea Gibson—made occasional appearances at NTL events.

FINALS: 13 (8 Wins)

NO.	RESULT	DATE	EVENT	SURFACE	OPPONENT	SCORE
1.	W	April 14, 1968	National Tennis League Professional Tour, Cannes, France	Indoor	Rosemary Casals	10–6
2.	F	April 21, 1968	National Tennis League Professional Tour, Pau, France	Indoor	Ann Jones	4–6, 6–3, 4–6
3.	W	April 19, 1968	National Tennis League Professional Tour, Paris, France	Indoor	Ann Jones	9–7, 6–4
4.	W	May 6, 1968	Wembley National Tennis League Professional Tour, London, England	Indoor	Ann Jones	4–6, 9–7, 7–5
5.	F	May 18, 1968	Madison Square Garden Pro Tournament, New York, NY, U.S..	Indoor	Ann Jones	4–6, 4–6
6.	W	July 19, 1968	National Tennis League Professional Tour, Los Angeles, California	Indoor	Ann Jones	12–10, 6–3
7.	W	August 10, 1968	National Tennis League Professional Tour, Binghamton, NY, U.S.	Clay	Rosemary Casals	10–8, 6–2
8.	F	August 18, 1968	Colonial Pro Invitational, Fort Worth, Texas, U.S.	Clay	Ann Jones	1–6, 2–6
9.	W	March 3, 1969	International Pro Tennis Invitational, Los Angeles, Calif., U.S.	Indoor	Ann Jones	17–15, 6–3

NO.	RESULT	DATE	EVENT	SURFACE	OPPONENT	SCORE
10.	F	August 3, 1969	St. Louis Professional Tournament, St. Louis, Missouri, U.S.	Outdoor	Rosemary Casals	6–4, 6–2
11.	W	August 10, 1969	Masters Tennis Tournament, Binghamton, New York, U.S.	Clay	Ann Jones	10–8, 3–6, 6–4
12.	F	August 24, 1969	National Tennis League Professional Tour, Baltimore, U.S.	Grass	Rosemary Casals	3–6, 1–6
13.	W	October 5, 1969	Midland Racquet Club Invitational, Midland, Texas, U.S.	Hard	Rosemary Casals	6–3, 6–3

Appendix II

Billie Jean (Moffitt) King International Team Play

Billie Jean King represented the United States in international team competition as a player or captain starting with the Wightman Cup in 1961 and ending at the 2000 Olympic Summer Games, a span of thirty-nine years. The Federation Cup—now the largest annual women's sporting event in the world with more than 110 participating nations—was renamed the Billie Jean King Cup in 2020 by the International Tennis Federation.

Federation Cup

AS PLAYER

Years played	9 (1963–67, 1976–79)
Ties played:	36
Singles win–loss:	26–3
Doubles win–loss:	26–1
Total win–loss:	52–4
Titles won:	7 (1963, 1966–67, 1976–79)

AS CAPTAIN

Years captained:	9 (1965*, 1976*, 1995–96, 1998–2003)
Titles won:	4 (1976*, 1996, 1999–2000)
Ties captained:	27
Ties won–loss record:	22–5

* served as player–captain

APPENDIX II

Year-by-Year Results

AS PLAYER

Fed Cup 1963—The Queen's Club, London, Great Britain (wood, indoors)

First round: USA d. Italy 3–0

R1 HARD, Darlene d. PERICOLI, Lea, 6–4, 2–6, 6–2
R2 MOFFITT, Billie Jean d. LAZZARINO, Sylvana\, 6–8, 6–1, 6–2
R3 CALDWELL, Carole/HARD, Darlene d. LAZZARINO, Sylvana/PERICOLI, Lea, 6–4, 6–1

Quarterfinal: USA d. Netherlands 3–0

R1 HARD, Darlene d. DE JONG, Eva, 6–2, 6–2
R2 MOFFITT, Billie Jean d. RIDDERHOF, Jenny, 6–2, 6–2
R3 CALDWELL, Carole/MOFFITT, Billie Jean d. DE JONG, Eva/RIDDERHOF, Jenny, 6–0, 6–3

Semifinal: USA d. Great Britain 3–0

R1 HARD, Darlene d. JONES, Ann, 6–2, 6–4
R2 MOFFITT, Billie Jean d. TRUMAN, Christine, 6–3, 3–6, 6–4
R3 CALDWELL, Carole/HARD, Darlene d. JONES, Ann/TRUMAN, Christine, 2–6, 9–7 6–3

Final: USA d. Australia 2–1

R1 HARD, Darlene l. SMITH, Margaret, 3–6, 0–6
R2 MOFFITT, Billie Jean d. TURNER, Lesley, 5–7, 6–0, 6–3
R3 HARD, Darlene/MOFFITT, Billie Jean d. SMITH, Margaret/TURNER, Lesley, 6–3, 11–13, 6–3

Fed Cup 1964—Germantown Cricket Club, Philadelphia, PA, USA (grass, outdoor)

Second round: USA d. Ireland 3–0

R1 MOFFITT, Billie Jean d. HOULIHAN, Geraldine, 6–2, 6–2
R2 RICHEY, Nancy d. O'NEILL, Eleanor, 6–3, 6–2
R3 MOFFITT, Billie Jean/SUSMAN, Karen d. HOULIHAN, Geraldine/O'NEILL, Eleanor, 6–1, 6–2

Quarterfinal: USA d. Argentina 3–0

R1 MOFFITT, Billie Jean, d. BAYLON, Norma, 12–10, 9–7
R2 RICHEY, Nancy d. BOCIO, Ana–Maria, 6–3 6–2
R3 MOFFITT, Billie Jean/SUSMAN, Karen d. BAYLON, Norma/BOCIO, Ana–Maria, 6–4, 6–1

Semifinal: USA d. Great Britain 3–0

R1 MOFFITT, Billie Jean, d. JONES, Ann, 6–4, 6–3
R2 RICHEY, Nancy, d. CATT, Deidre, 6–4, 6–3
R3 MOFFITT, Billie Jean/SUSMAN, Karen d. CATT, Deidre/JONES, Ann, 6–1 6–3

Final: Australia d. USA 2–1

R1   MOFFITT, Billie Jean, l. SMITH, Margaret, 2–6, 3–6
R2   RICHEY, Nancy l. TURNER, Lesley, 5–7 1–6
R3   MOFFITT, Billie Jean/SUSMAN, Karen d. SMITH, Margaret/TURNER,
      Lesley, 4–6, 7–5, 6–1

Fed Cup 1965: Kooyong Club, Melbourne, Australia (grass, outdoor)

Quarterfinal: USA d. Italy 3–0

R1   MOFFITT, Billie Jean d. PERICOLI, Lea, 6–3, 6–1
R2   GRAEBNER, Carole d. GORDIGIANI, Francesca, 6–1, 6–0
R3   GRAEBNER, Carole/MOFFITT, Billie Jean d. GORDIGIANI,
      Francesca/PERICOLI, Lea, 6–0, 6–2

Semifinal: USA d. Great Britain 3–0

R1   GRAEBNER, Carole d. TRUMAN, Christine, 6–3, 6–2
R2   MOFFITT, Billie Jean d. JONES, Ann, 6–2, 6–4
R3   GRAEBNER, Carole/MOFFITT, Billie Jean d. JONES, Ann/TRUMAN,
      Christine, 4–6 8–6 6–4

Final: Australia d. USA 2–1

R1   GRAEBNER, Carole (USA) l. TURNER, Lesley, 3–6, 6–2, 3–6
R2   MOFFITT, Billie Jean (USA) l. SMITH, Margaret, 4–6, 6–8
R3   GRAEBNER, Carole/MOFFITT, Billie Jean d. SMITH,
      Margaret/TEGART, Judy, 7–5, 4–6, 6–4

Fed Cup 1966: Turin Press Sporting Club, Turin, Italy (clay, outdoor)

Second round: USA d. Sweden 3–0

R1   KING, Billie Jean d. SANDBERG, Christina, 6–2, 6–3
R2   HELDMAN, Julie d. LUNDQUIST, Eva, 6–4, 6–0
R3   GRAEBNER, Carole/KING, Billie Jean d. LOFDAHL,
      Ingrid/LUNDQUIST, Eva, 6–3, 6–1

Quarterfinal: USA d. France 2–1

R1   HELDMAN, Julie d. LIEFFRIG, Janine, 6–0 6–4
R2   KING, Billie Jean d. DURR, Francoise, 5–7 6–2 6–3
R3   GRAEBNER, Carole/KING, Billie Jean l. DURR, Francoise/LIEFFRIG,
      Janine, 2–6, 6–2, 3–6

Semifinal: USA d. Great Britain 2–1

R1   HELDMAN, Julie d. SHAW, Winnie, 6–4, 5–7, 6–3
R2   KING, Billie Jean l. JONES, Ann, 1–6, 4–6
R3   GRAEBNER, Carole/KING, Billie Jean d. JONES, Ann/STARKIE, Elizabeth,
      4–6, 6–3, 6–0

Final: USA d. West Germany 3–0

R1   HELDMAN, Julie d. NIESSEN, Helga, 4–6, 7–5, 6–1
R2   KING, Billie Jean d. BUDING, Edda, 6–3, 3–6, 6–1

R3 GRAEBNER, Carole/KING, Billie Jean d. BUDING, Edda/HOSL,
Helga 6–4, 6–2

Fed Cup 1967: Blau–Weiss T.C., Berlin, West Germany (clay, outdoor)

Second round: USA d. Rhodesia 3–0

R1 KING, Billie Jean d. WALKDEN, Patricia, 6–3, 2–6, 6–3
R2 CASALS, Rosie d. MORRIS, Fiona, 6–3, 6–4
R3 CASALS, Rosie/KING, Billie Jean d. MORRIS, Fiona/WALKDEN, Patricia,
6–3, 6–0

Quarterfinal: USA d. South Africa 3–0

R1 CASALS, Rosie d. SWAN, Glenda, 6–1, 6–4
R2 KING, Billie Jean d. VAN ZYL, Annette, 6–2, 6–4
R3 CASALS, Rosie/KING, Billie Jean d. SWAN, Glenda/VAN ZYL, Annette,
7–5, 6–4

Semifinal: USA d. West Germany 3–0

R1 CASALS, Rosie d. HOSL, Helga, 6–2, 7–5
R2 KING, Billie Jean d. NIESSEN, Helga, 6–1, 7–5
R3 CASALS, Rosie/KING, Billie Jean d. BUDING, Edda/HOSL, Helga,
6–4, 2–6, 8–6

Final: USA d. Great Britain 2–0

R1 CASALS, Rosie d. WADE, Virginia 9–7, 8–6
R2 KING, Billie Jean d. JONES, Ann, 6–3, 6–4
R3 CASALS, Rosie/KING, Billie Jean U JONES, Ann/WADE, Virginia, 6–8, 9–7 *

Fed Cup 1976: Spectrum Stadium, Philadelphia, PA, USA (carpet, indoor)

First round: USA d. Israel 3–0

R1 CASALS, Rosie d. ZUBARY, Hagit, 6–1, 6–0
R2 KING, Billie Jean d. PELED, Paulina, 6–1 6–0
R3 CASALS, Rosie/KING, Billie Jean d. PELED, Paulina/ZUBARY, Hagit,
6–3 6–1

Second round: USA d. Yugoslavia 3–0

R1 CASALS, Rosie d. ALAVANTIC, Dora, 6–1, 6–1
R2 KING, Billie Jean d. JAUSOVEC, Mima 6–0, 7–6
R3 CASALS, Rosie/KING, Billie Jean d. ALAVANTIC, Dora/JAUSOVEC, Mima,
6–0, 6–0

Quarterfinals: USA d. Switzerland 3–0

R1 CASALS, Rosie d. SIMMEN, Monica, 6–1, 6–1
R2 KING, Billie Jean d. DELHEES, Petra, 6–2, 6–1
R3 CASALS, Rosie/KING, Billie Jean d. EICHENBERGER, Susi/SIMMEN,
Monica, 6–0, 6–1

* Match not finished

Semifinals: USA d. Netherlands 3–0

R1 CASALS, Rosie d. VESSIES, Elly, 6–1, 6–2
R2 KING, Billie Jean d. STOVE, Betty, 6–2, 6–3
R3 CASALS, Rosie/KING, Billie Jean d. STOVE, Betty/ZWAAN, Tine, 6–1, 6–4

Final: USA d. Australia 2–1

R1 CASALS, Rosie l. REID, Kerry, 6–1, 3–6, 5–7
R2 KING, Billie Jean d. CAWLEY, Evonne, 7–6(4), 6–4
R3 CASALS, Rosie/KING, Billie Jean d. CAWLEY, Evonne/REID, Kerry, 7–5, 6–3

Fed Cup 1977: Devonshire Park, Eastbourne, Great Britain (grass, outdoor)

First round: USA d. Austria 3–0

R1 EVERT, Chris d. BERNEGGER, Sabine, 6–0, 6–0
R2 KING, Billie Jean d. WIMMER, Helena, 6–2, 6–2
R3 CASALS, Rosie/EVERT, Chris d. BERNEGGER, Sabine/WIMMER, Helena, 6–0, 6–1

Second round: USA d. Switzerland 3–0

R1 EVERT, Chris d. RUEGG, Anne–Marie, 6–3, 6–0
R2 KING, Billie Jean d. JOLISSAINT, Christiane, 6–0, 6–3
R3 CASALS, Rosie/EVERT, Chris d. DELHEES, Petra/SIMMEN, Monica, 6–0 7–5

Quarterfinal: USA d. France 3–0

R1 KING, Billie Jean d. THIBAULT, Frederique 6–0 6–0
R2 EVERT, Chris d. DURR, Francoise 6–1 6–3
R3 CASALS, Rosie/EVERT, Chris d. DURR, Francoise/BENEDETTI, Gail, 6–3, 7–5

Semifinal: USA d. South Africa 3–0

R1 KING, Billie Jean d. STEVENS, Greer, 6–2, 6–0
R2 EVERT, Chris d. CUYPERS, Brigette, 6–1, 6–1
R3 CASALS, Rosie/EVERT, Chris d. BOSHOFF, Linky/KLOSS, Ilana, 6–0, 3–6, 9–7

Final: USA d. Australia 2–1

R1 KING, Billie Jean d. FROMHOLTZ, Dianne, 6–1, 2–6, 6–2
R2 EVERT, Chris d. REID, Kerry 7–5, 6–3
R3 CASALS, Rosie/EVERT, Chris l. REID, Kerry/TURNBULL, Wendy, 3–6, 3–6

Fed Cup 1978: Kooyong Club, Melbourne, Australia (grass, outdoor)

First round: USA d. Korea, Republic 3–0

R1 AUSTIN, Tracy d. CHOI, Kyeong-Mi, 6–0, 6–0
R2 EVERT, Chris d. HAN, Yoon-Ja, 6–1, 6–0
R3 EVERT, Chris/KING, Billie Jean d. CHA, Eun-Jeong/CHOI, Kyeong-Mi, 6–1 6–0

Second round: USA d. New Zealand 3–0

R1   AUSTIN, Tracy d. PERRY, Brenda, 6–1, 6–2
R2   EVERT, Chris d. CHALONER, Judy, 6–1, 6–1
R3   EVERT, Chris/KING, Billie Jean d. CHALONER, Judy/NEWTON, Chris, 6–1, 6–1

Quarterfinal: USA d. France 3–0

R1   AUSTIN, Tracy d. THIBAULT, Frederique, 6–4, 6–3
R2   EVERT, Chris d. SIMON, Brigitte, 6–2, 6–2
R3   EVERT, Chris/KING, Billie Jean d. DURR, Francoise/BENEDETTI, Gail, 5–7, 6–3, 6–2

Semifinal: USA d. Great Britain 3–0

R1   AUSTIN, Tracy d. TYLER, Michelle, 6–1, 6–1
R2   EVERT, Chris d. WADE, Virginia, 6–2, 6–4
R3   CASALS, Rosie/KING, Billie Jean d. BARKER, Sue/HOBBS, Anne, 1–6, 6–3, 6–4

Final: USA d. Australia 2–1

R1   AUSTIN, Tracy l. REID, Kerry, 3–6, 3–6
R2   EVERT, Chris d. TURNBULL, Wendy, 3–6, 6–1, 6–1
R3   EVERT, Chris/KING, Billie Jean d. REID, Kerry/TURNBULL, Wendy, 4–6, 6–1, 6–4

Fed Cup 1979: RSHE Club Campo, Madrid, Spain (clay, outdoor)

First round: USA d. Philippines w/o

Second round: USA d. West Germany 3–0

R1   AUSTIN, Tracy d. RIEDEL, Iris, 6–1, 6–3
R2   EVERT–LLOYD, Chris d. HANIKA, Sylvia, 6–4, 6–2
R3   CASALS, Rosie/EVERT–LLOYD, Chris d. EBBINGHAUS, Katja/HANIKA, Sylvia, 6–1, 6–4

Quarterfinal: USA d. France 3–0

R1   AUSTIN, Tracy d. THIBAULT, Frederique, 6–4, 6–0
R2   EVERT–LLOYD, Chris d. SIMON, Brigitte, 6–0, 6–0
R3   CASALS, Rosie/EVERT–LLOYD, Chris d. DURR, Francoise/THIBAULT, Frederique, 6–1, 6–4

Semifinal: USA d. USSR 2–0

R1   AUSTIN, Tracy d. CHMYREVA, Natasha, 6–0, 6–1
R2   EVERT–LLOYD, Chris d. MOROZOVA, Olga, 6–4, 8–6
R3   CASALS, Rosie/KING, Billie Jean U. MOROZOVA, Olga/ZAITSEVA, Olga, 9–8, unf*

* Match not finished

Final: USA d. Australia 3–0

R1 AUSTIN, Tracy d. REID, Kerry, 6–3, 6–0

R2 EVERT–LLOYD, Chris d. FROMHOLTZ, Dianne, 2–6, 6–3, 8–6

R3 CASALS, Rosie/KING, Billie Jean d. REID, Kerry/TURNBULL, Wendy, 3–6, 6–3, 8–6

AS CAPTAIN

Fed Cup 1995

World Group first round: USA d. Austria 5–0 at Turnberry Isle Club, Aventura, FL, USA (hard, outdoor)

R1 FRAZIER, Amy d. WIESNER, Judith, 3–6, 6–4, 6–3

R2 FERNANDEZ, Mary Joe d. SCHETT, Barbara, 6–2, 6–4

R3 FERNANDEZ, Mary Joe d. WIESNER, Judith, 6–3, 2–6, 6–3

R4 FRAZIER, Amy d. SCHETT, Barbara, 6–3, 5–7, 6–3

R5 FERNANDEZ, Gigi/NAVRATILOVA, Martina d. SCHETT, Barbara/SCHWARZ, Petra, 6–2, 6–1

World Group semifinals: USA d. FRA 3–2 at Trask Coliseum, Wilmington, NC, USA (carpet, indoor)

R1 FERNANDEZ, Mary Joe l. PIERCE, Mary 6–7(1), 3–6

R2 DAVENPORT, Lindsay d. HALARD, Julie, 7–6(0), 7–5

R3 DAVENPORT, Lindsay d. PIERCE, Mary, 6–3, 4–6, 6–0

R4 FERNANDEZ, Mary Joe l. HALARD, Julie, 6–1 5–7 1–6

R5 DAVENPORT, Lindsay/FERNANDEZ, Gigi d. HALARD, Julie/TAUZIAT, Nathalie, 6–1, 7–6(2)

Final: Spain d. USA 3–2 at Valencia T.C., Valencia, Spain (clay, outdoor)

R1 RUBIN, Chanda l. MARTINEZ, Conchita, 5–7, 6–7(3)

R2 FERNANDEZ, Mary Joe l. SANCHEZ VICARIO, Arantxa, 3–6, 2–6

R3 FERNANDEZ, Mary Joe l. MARTINEZ, Conchita, 3–6, 4–6

R4 RUBIN, Chanda d. SANCHEZ VICARIO, Arantxa , 1–6, 6–4, 6–4

R5 DAVENPORT, Lindsay/FERNANDEZ, Gigi d. RUANO PASCUAL, Virginia/SANCHEZ LORENZO, Maria, 6–3, 7–6(3)

Fed Cup 1996

World Group first round: USA d. Austria 3–2 at Hellbrunn Stadium, Salzburg, Austria (clay, outdoor)

R1 FERNANDEZ, Mary Joe d. WIESNER, Judith, 6–3, 7–6(5)

R2 CAPRIATI, Jennifer l. PAULUS, Barbara, 2–6, 4–6

R3 FERNANDEZ, Mary Joe d. PAULUS, Barbara, 6–3, 7–6(4)

R4 CAPRIATI, Jennifer l. WIESNER, Judith, 1–6, 1–6

R5 FERNANDEZ, Gigi/FERNANDEZ, Mary Joe d. SCHWARZ, Petra/WIESNER, Judith, 6–0, 6–4

World Group semifinals: USA d. Japan 5–0 at Rainbow Hall, Nagoya, Japan (carpet, indoor)

R1   DAVENPORT, Lindsay d. DATE, Kimiko, 6–2, 6–1
R2   SELES, Monica d. SUGIYAMA, Ai, 6–2, 6–2
R3   SELES, Monica d. DATE, Kimiko, 6–0, 6–2
R4   DAVENPORT, Lindsay d. SUGIYAMA, Ai, 7–6(8), 7–5
R5   DAVENPORT, Lindsay/WILD, Linda d. NAGATSUKA, Kyoko/SUGIYAMA, Ai, 6–2, 6–1

Final: USA d. Spain 5–0 at Convention Centre, Atlantic City, USA (carpet, indoor)

R1   SELES, Monica d. MARTINEZ, Conchita, 6–2, 6–4
R2   DAVENPORT, Lindsay d. SANCHEZ VICARIO, Arantxa, 7–5, 6–1
R3   SELES, Monica d. SANCHEZ VICARIO, Arantxa, 3–6, 6–3, 6–1
R4   DAVENPORT, Lindsay d. LEON GARCIA, Gala, 7–5 6–2
R5   FERNANDEZ, Mary Joe/WILD, Linda d. LEON GARCIA, Gala/RUANO PASCUAL, Virginia, 6–1, 6–4

Fed Cup 1998

World Group first round: USA d. Netherlands 5–0 at East Beach T.C., Kiawah Island, SC, USA (clay, outdoor)

R1   DAVENPORT, Lindsay d. HOPMANS, Amanda, 6–4, 6–1
R2   SELES, Monica d. OREMANS, Miriam, 6–1, 6–2
R3   DAVENPORT, Lindsay d. OREMANS, Miriam, 6–1, 6–2
R4   SELES, Monica d. HOPMANS, Amanda, 6–1, 6–2
R5   FERNANDEZ, Mary Joe/RAYMOND, Lisa d. BOLLEGRAF, Manon/VIS, Caroline, 6–1, ret.

World Group semifinals: Spain d. USA 3–2 at Campo Villa T.C., Madrid, Spain (clay, outdoor)

R1   RAYMOND, Lisa l. SANCHEZ VICARIO, Arantxa, 7–6(4), 3–6, 0–6
R2   SELES, Monica d. MARTINEZ, Conchita, 6–3, 3–6, 6–1
R3   SELES, Monica d. SANCHEZ VICARIO, Arantxa, 6–4, 6–0
R4   RAYMOND, Lisa l. MARTINEZ, Conchita, 6–7(1), 4–6
R5   FERNANDEZ, Mary Joe/RAYMOND, Lisa l. MARTINEZ, Conchita/SANCHEZ VICARIO, Arantxa, 4–6, 7–6(5), 9–11

Fed Cup 1999

World Group first round: USA d. Croatia 5–0 at Raleigh Racquet Club, Raleigh, NC, USA (clay, outdoor)

R1   RUBIN, Chanda d. MAJOLI, Iva, 7–6(5), 4–6 ,10–8
R2   SELES, Monica d. TALAJA, Silvija, 6–3, 6–1
R3   SELES, Monica d. MAJOLI, Iva, 6–0, 6–3
R4   RUBIN, Chanda d. TALAJA, Silvija, 6–3, 6–4
R5   RUBIN, Chanda/SELES, Monica d. MAJOLI, Iva/TALAJA, Silvija, 6–3, 6–2

World Group semifinals: USA d. Italy 4–1 at Ancona Tennis Association, Ancona, Italy (clay, outdoor)

R1 WILLIAMS, Venus d. GRANDE, Rita, 6–2, 6–3
R2 SELES, Monica l. FARINA, Silvia, 4–6, 6–4, 4–6
R3 WILLIAMS, Venus d. FARINA, Silvia, 6–1, 6–1
R4 WILLIAMS, Serena d. GRANDE, Rita, 6–1 6–1
R5 WILLIAMS, Serena/WILLIAMS, Venus d. GARBIN, Tathiana/SERRA ZANETTI, Adrianna, 6–2, 6–2

Final: USA d. Russia 4–1 at Taube Tennis Stadium, Stanford, CA, USA (hard, outdoor)

R1 WILLIAMS, Venus d. LIKHOVTSEVA, Elena, 6–3, 6–4
R2 DAVENPORT, Lindsay d. DEMENTIEVA, Elena, 6–4, 6–0
R3 DAVENPORT, Lindsay d. LIKHOVTSEVA, Elena, 6–4, 6–4
R4 WILLIAMS, Venus l. DEMENTIEVA, Elena, 6–1, 3–6, 6–7(5)
R5 WILLIAMS, Serena/WILLIAMS, Venus d. DEMENTIEVA, Elena/MAKAROVA, Elena, 6–2, 6–1

Fed Cup 2000: Final Four in Las Vegas, NV, USA (carpet, indoor)

Semifinals: USA d. Belgium 2–1

R1 SELES, Monica d. HENIN, Justine, 7–6(1), 6–2
R2 DAVENPORT, Lindsay d. CLIJSTERS, Kim 7–6(4), 4–6, 6–3
R3 CAPRIATI, Jennifer/RAYMOND, Lisa l. CALLENS, Els/VAN ROOST, Dominique, 3–6, 5–7

Final: USA d. Spain 5–0

R1 SELES, Monica d. MARTINEZ, Conchita, 6–2, 6–3
R2 DAVENPORT, Lindsay d. SANCHEZ VICARIO, Arantxa, 6–2, 1–6, 6–3
R3 DAVENPORT, Lindsay d. MARTINEZ, Conchita, 6–1, 6–2
R4 CAPRIATI, Jennifer d. SANCHEZ VICARIO, Arantxa, 6–1, 1–0, ret.
R5 CAPRIATI, Jennifer/RAYMOND, Lisa d. RUANO PASCUAL, Virginia/SERNA, Magui, 4–6, 6–4, 6–2

Fed Cup 2002

World Group first round: Austria d. USA 3–2 at Olde Providence Racquet Club, Charlotte, NC, USA (clay, outdoor)

R1 SELES, Monica l. SCHWARTZ, Barbara, 6–7(7), 2–6
R2 CAPRIATI, Jennifer l. FAUTH, Evelyn, w/o
R3 SHAUGHNESSY, Meghann l. SCHWARTZ, Barbara, 6–4, 6–7(7), 7–9
R4 SELES, Monica d. FAUTH, Evelyn, 6–3, 6–3
R5 RAYMOND, Lisa/SELES, Monica, d. FAUTH, Evelyn MARUSKA, Marion, 6–1, 7–6(4)

World Group play–offs: USA d. Israel at Cooper Tennis Complex, Springfield, MO, USA (hard, outdoor)

R1 DAVENPORT, Lindsay d. SMASHNOVA, Anna, 6–3, 6–3
R2 SELES, Monica d. OBZILER, Tzipi, 6–4 6–2
R3 SELES, Monica d. SMASHNOVA, Anna, 6–4, 6–0

R4 DAVENPORT, Lindsay d. OBZILER, Tzipi, 2–6, 6–1, 7–6(1)
R5 RAYMOND, Lisa/SHAUGHNESSY, Meghann d. OBZILER,
Tzipi/ROSEN, Hila, 6–3, 6–0

Fed Cup 2003

World Group first round: USA d. Czech Republic 5–0 at The Paul E. Tsongas Arena, Lowell, USA (hard, indoor)

R1 WILLIAMS, Venus d. BEDANOVA, Daja, 6–1, 6–0
R2 WILLIAMS, Serena d. BENESOVA, Iveta, 7–5, 6–1
R3 WILLIAMS, Serena d. KOUKALOVA, Klara, 6–2, 6–2
R4 WILLIAMS, Venus d. BENESOVA, Iveta, 6–3, 6–2
R5 WILLIAMS, Serena/WILLIAMS, Venus d. BEDANOVA,
Daja/BIRNEROVA, Eva, 6–0, 6–1

World Group quarterfinals: USA d. Italy 5–0 at William H.G. Fitzgerald Tennis Centre, Washington D.C., USA (hard, outdoor)

R1 SHAUGHNESSY, Meghann d. SCHIAVONE, Francesca, 6–3, 6–4
R2 RUBIN, Chanda d. GRANDE, Rita, 6–3, 6–3
R3 RUBIN, Chanda d. SCHIAVONE, Francesca, 5–7, 6–4, 6–0
R4 SHAUGHNESSY, Meghann d. GRANDE, Rita, 6–3, 7–5
R5 RAYMOND, Lisa/STEVENSON, Alexandra d. GARBIN,
Tathiana/SERRA ZANETTI, Antonella, 6–1, 6–2

World Group semifinals: USA d. Belgium 4–1 at Olympic Stadium, Moscow, Russia (Final Four) (carpet, indoor)

R1 RAYMOND, Lisa d. CALLENS, Els, 6–2, 6–1
R2 SHAUGHNESSY, Meghann d. FLIPKENS, Kirsten, 6–7(4), 7–6(8), 9–7
R3 SHAUGHNESSY, Meghann l. CALLENS, Els, 3–6, 6–7(5)
R4 RAYMOND, Lisa d. CLIJSTERS, Elke, 6–2, 6–1
R5 NAVRATILOVA, Martina/RAYMOND, Lisa d. CLIJSTERS,
Elke/MAES, Caroline, 6–1, 6–4

Final: France d. USA 4–1 at Olympic Stadium, Moscow, Russia (Final Four) (carpet, indoor)

R1 RAYMOND, Lisa l. MAURESMO, Amelie, 4–6, 3–6
R2 SHAUGHNESSY, Meghann l. PIERCE, Mary, 3–6, 6–3, 6–8
R3 SHAUGHNESSY, Meghann l. MAURESMO, Amelie, 2–6, 1–6
R4 STEVENSON, Alexandra l. LOIT, Emilie, 4–6, 2–6
R5 NAVRATILOVA, Martina/RAYMOND, Lisa d. COHEN–ALORO,
Stephanie/LOIT, Emilie, 6–4, 6–0

Wightman Cup

The Wightman Cup was an annual team competition for women between teams from the United States and Great Britain. It began in 1923 and was discontinued in 1989.

Years Played: 8 (1961–1967, 1970)
Wightman Cup Team Titles Won: 8 (1961–1967, 1970)

U.S. Olympic Team Coach
1996 Summer Games, Atlanta, Georgia

MEDAL RESULTS

Lindsay Davenport, Gold, Women's Singles
Gigi Fernandez and Mary Joe Fernandez, Gold, Women's Doubles

TEAM USA ROSTER

Lindsay Davenport
Mary Joe Fernandez
Monica Seles
Chanda Rubin
Gigi Fernandez

2000 Olympic Summer Games, Sydney, Australia

MEDAL RESULTS

Venus Williams, Gold, Women's Singles
Monica Seles, Bronze, Women's Singles
Venus Williams and Serena Williams, Gold, Women's Doubles.

TEAM USA ROSTER

Venus Williams
Serena Williams
Monica Seles
Lindsay Davenport (injured)

Appendix III

World TeamTennis

If you've ever seen a World TeamTennis match, you have seen my life philosophy in action: men and women competing together, on a team, and all genders making equal contributions to the result.

—BILLIE JEAN KING

World TeamTennis, which was conceived and launched by Billie Jean King, her former husband Larry King, Dennis Murphy, and a team of investors in 1974, stands out among professional sports leagues for its emphasis on gender equity. The Philadelphia Freedoms made King the first player chosen in the inaugural World TeamTennis draft in 1974, and she also served as the team's coach. King played 10 WTT seasons and was a member of three title-winning teams—the New York Sets (1976), New York Apples (1977), and Chicago Fyre (1983). She was the first woman to run a pro league when she became WTT commissioner in 1981. Ilana Kloss succeed King as commissioner in February 2001.

Almost every major champion of the Open era has participated in World TeamTennis since it began play, including Venus and Serena Williams, Chris Evert, Martina Navratilova, Rod Laver, John McEnroe, Jimmy Connors, Bjorn Borg, Tracy Austin, Evonne Goolagong Cawley, Roy Emerson, Ken Rosewall, Fred Stolle, Vitas Gerulaitis, Andre Agassi, Pete Sampras, Stefanie Graf, Andy Roddick, Lindsay Davenport, Kim Clijsters, Justine Henin, Bob and Mike Bryan, Martina Hingis, Maria Sharapova, Sloane Stephens, and Naomi Osaka. The league has also offered the WTT Junior Nationals and WTT community tennis leagues to help develop the game at the grass roots level.

The WTT pro league has featured numerous firsts and innovations (see below), many of which have been implemented by the four Grand Slam tournaments, the Women's Tennis Association and men's Association of Tennis Professionals tours.

FORMAT AND SCORING

- Each World TeamTennis match consists of five sets–women's singles, men's singles, women's doubles, men's doubles and mixed doubles, making WTT the first pro league where women and men received equal playing time and can make an equal contribution to team scoring.

- Streamlined scoring: Sets consist of five games (not six) with no-ad scoring and a nine-point tiebreak played when a set is tied 4–all. Let serves are played. The first player to four points wins the game.

- On-court coaching permitted.

- The home team coach determines the order of sets (singles, doubles and mixed doubles).

- Player substitutions are allowed, and limited to one player, per event, per gender at the conclusion of any point. A player who is substituted out cannot return to the match in that same set.

- Instant replay technology was introduced with the Coach's Challenge (2005).

- WTT was among the first sports leagues to use an all–electronic line–calling system, and then the first league to make season–long use of new Hawk–Eye technology which makes live line calls on every point.

- Coach's timeouts during match play were added in 2012. Coaches and a team's entire roster of players may enter the court area during these breaks.

- Introduced 25-second service clock (2015).

- Introduced on-player microphones, a first for pro tennis competitions (2017).

- Every set matters: WTT's Extended Play feature gives the trailing team a chance to come from behind in sudden death if it wins the fifth set.

FAN EXPERIENCE

- WTT encourages fan participation. WTT crowds are encouraged to be vocal and may enter/exit the stadium during play without having to wait for a changeover.

- WTT started the practice of players hitting balls (often autographed) to fans in the stands after their matches as keepsakes.

- Fans keep match balls hit out of play.

- Teams host kids clinics each night before matches and children age sixteen and under can come on the court after every WTT match and get player autographs.

- Music played between points and sets, and at halftime.

- Players have their names on the back of their shirts.

- WTT has given away more than 300,000 junior tennis racquets between 2010 and 2020 alone through clinics, WTT matches, and other youth activities.

- Matches played on distinctive, branded multicolored courts.

Billie Jean King

WTT Year-by-Year Team Results

1974 Philadelphia Freedoms

Regular season record:

 1st Place, Eastern Division (39–5)

Playoffs:

 Round 1: Philadelphia def. Cleveland Nets, 49–44

 Semifinals: Philadelphia def. Pittsburgh Triangles, 52–45

 Championship Round: Denver Racquets def. Philadelphia, 55–45

Philadelphia roster:

 Julie Anthony, Brian Fairlie, Tory Fretz, Billie Jean King, Kathy Kukyendall, Buster Mottram, Fred Stolle. Coach: Billie Jean King.

1975 New York Sets

Regular season:

 2nd place, Eastern Division (34–10)

Playoffs:

 First round, Boston Lobsters def. New York Sets, 25–24.

New York Sets roster:

 Mona Schallau, Billie Jean King, Sandy Mayer, Betsy Nagelsen, Charlie Owens, Fred Stolle, Virginia Wade.

1976 New York Sets (League Champions)

Regular season:

 1st Place, Eastern Division (33–10)

Playoffs:

 Semifinals (Best of Three), New York def. Pittsburgh, 25–26, 29–21, 28–26; San Francisco Golden Gaters def. Phoenix, 32–16, 24–18

 Championship Round (Best of Five): New York def. San Francisco, 3–0. (Match scores: 31–23, 29–21 OT, 31–13)

New York roster:

 Lindsey Beaven, Phil Dent, Billie Jean King, Sandy Mayer, Linda Siegelman, Fred Stolle, Virginia Wade. Coach: Fred Stolle.

1977 New York Apples (League Champions)*

Regular season record:

 2nd Place, Eastern Division, (33–11)

Playoffs:

 First round: New York def. Indiana Loves, 89–63

 Semifinals, New York def. Boston Lobsters, 58–41, Phoenix def. San Diego, 83–74.

 Championship Round: New York def. Phoenix, 55–39.

New York roster:

 Lindsey Beaven, Billie Jean King, Sandy Mayer, Ray Ruffels, Linda Siegelman, Fred Stolle, Virginia Wade.

* Scores listed are cumulative team totals for each playoff series.

1978 New York Apples

Regular season record:
    2nd Place, Eastern Division, (22–22)
Playoffs:
    Round 1 (best of three), New York def. Anaheim 2–0 (29–16, 27–20)
    Semifinals (best of three), Los Angeles def. New York 2–0 (28–20, 26–16)
New York Roster:
    Mary Carillo, Vitas Gerulaitis, Billie Jean King, Julie Anthony, Ray Ruffels, JoAnne Russell, Fred Stolle

1981 Oakland Breakers

Regular season record:
    3rd Place, (5–7)
Playoffs:
    (None) Los Angeles Strings declared champion of the four-team WTT, based on league-leading 9–3 record
Oakland Breakers roster:
    John Austin, Fritz Buehning, Phil Dent, Billie Jean King, Ann Kiyomura, Ilana Kloss, Bernie Mitton, Peter Rennert.

1982 Los Angeles Strings

Regular season record:
    3rd Place (9–5)
Los Angeles Strings roster:
    Vijay Amritraj, Billie Jean King, Trey Waltke, Ilana Kloss. Coach: Vijay Amritraj

1983 Chicago Fyre (League Champions)

Regular season:
    1st place, 12–1
Playoffs:
    Championship Round: Chicago Fyre def. Los Angeles Strings, 26–20.
Chicago Fyre roster:
    Billie Jean King, Lloyd Bourne, Sharon Walsh, Trey Waltke, Coach: Ilana Kloss.

1984 Chicago Fire

Playoffs:
    The league held a one-week season, single-elimination tournament played entirely at The Forum in Los Angeles.
Semifinals: Long Beach Breakers def. Chicago Fire 29–19 (OT), San Diego Buds def. Los Angeles Strings, 26–24.
    Championship round: San Diego Buds d. Long Beach Breakers 30–13
Chicago Fire roster:
    Billie Jean King, Ben Testerman, Sharon Walsh, Trey Waltke

Index

Billie Jean holding brother, Randy: The Billie Jean King Collection, New-York Historical Society

Moffitt family front yard: The Billie Jean King Collection, New-York Historical Society

Billie Jean with neighborhood friends: The Billie Jean King Collection, New-York Historical Society

Billie Jean with softball team: The Billie Jean King Collection, New-York Historical Society

Susan Williams, Jerry Cromwell, Allan Robbins, and Billie Jean: The Billie Jean King Collection, New-York Historical Society

Jerry Cromwell, coach Clyde Walker, and Billie Jean: The Billie Jean King Collection, New-York Historical Society

Perry T. Jones and Billie Jean: The Billie Jean King Collection, New-York Historical Society

Uncle Art, Aunt Gladys, Bill Moffitt: Courtesy Donna Lee Chavez

Kehoe Family: Courtesy R.J. Moffitt

Althea Gibson and Alice Marble: © Bettmann / Getty Images

Wightman Cup team: The Billie Jean King Collection, New-York Historical Society, Edmund Gilchrist, Jr.

Karen Hantze and Billie Jean win doubles at Wimbledon: © AELTC / Michael Cole

Billie Jean, Carole Caldwell, and Darlene Hard win first Fed Cup: © TopFoto

Mervyn Rose: © Bert Hardy / Picture Post / Hulton Archive / Getty Images

Billie Jean and Sen. Robert F. Kennedy: Edward Fernberger, International Tennis Hall of Fame

Billie Jean and Larry on their wedding day: The Billie Jean King Collection, New-York Historical Society

Billie Jean and Frank Brennan: © Richard Meek / The LIFE Picture Collection via Getty Images

Althea Gibson, Arthur Ashe, and Billie Jean: Edward Fernberger, International Tennis Hall of Fame

Billie Jean, 1966 Wimbledon ladies singles championship: Keystone Press / Alamy

Ann Jones, Françoise Dürr, Rosie Casals, Billie Jean, and Roy Emerson sign as professionals: © Bettmann / Getty Images

Original 9: Houston Post Photographs, Houston Public Library, HMRC

Billie Jean and Chrissie Evert: © AP

Virginia Slims players in Richmond, VA: Courtesy International Tennis Hall of Fame

Billie Jean earns $100,000: © AP

Virginia Wade, Evonne Goolagong, Ted Tinling, Rosie Casals, and Billie Jean: © Michael Webb / Keystone / Hulton Archive / Getty Images

Billie Jean, Joe Cullman 3rd, and Gladys Heldman: Courtesy International Tennis Hall of Fame

Billie Jean sitting with the press: © Focus on Sport / Getty Images

Billie Jean and Gloria Steinem: © Ann Phillips

Randy pitching with the San Francisco Giants: © S.F. Giants

Billie Jean with Sen. Birch Bayh: Courtesy of Barack Obama Presidential Library

Ted Tinling with Bonnie Logan, Sylvia Hooks, and Ann Koger: Edward Fernberger, International Tennis Hall of Fame

Bob Hope, Billie Jean, and Tony Randall: © Bob & Dolores Hope Foundation

Billie Jean, Lany Kaligis, and Ilana Kloss at the founding of the WTA: © Monte Fresco / Mirrorpix

Billie Jean, Billy Talbert, and Owen Davidson: © AELTC / Michael Cole

Bobby Riggs and Billie Jean: © Ann Limongello / Walt Disney Television via Getty Images

Billie Jean on litter at Battle of the Sexes match: © AP

Billie Jean hitting stretch backhand: © George Kalinsky / Bettmann / Getty Images

Billie Jean testifying at U.S. Senate: © Bettmann / Getty Images

Billie Jean and Muhammad Ali: © Michael Leshnov

Larry King and Billie Jean with *womenSports* magazine: © Bettmann / Getty Images

Billie Jean with children at a Philadelphia Freedoms clinic: Nancy Moran © Billie Jean King Enterprises Inc.

Elton John with Billie Jean and Bernie Taupin: Photograph by Sam Emerson. ©HST Global Limited, Courtesy of Rocket Entertainment

Elton John with Billie Jean: © Terry O'Neill / Iconic Images

Billie Jean on stage with Elton John at Dodger Stadium: © Terry O'Neill / Iconic Images

Ilana Kloss, Elton John, Billie Jean, and David Furnish: Courtesy Ilana Kloss

Billie Jean, Jerry Diamond, Ann Jones negotiate at the AELTC: © Daily Express / Archive Photos / Getty Images

The Kloss family: MEDIA 24 / GALLO IMAGES

Linky Boshoff and Ilana Kloss play Billie Jean and Rosie Casals: © Adam C. Balch

President Ford, Billie Jean, and Arthur Ashe in the Oval Office: Ricardo Thomas / The Gerald R. Ford Presidential Library

Billie Jean stretch forehand: © Ellen Griesedieck

Bella Abzug, Billie Jean, Gloria Steinem, and Mary Anne Krupsak: © AP

Renée Richards and Billie Jean playing doubles: Larry Morris / The New York Times / Redux

Martina Navratilova and Billie Jean, Wimbledon 1979: © AELTC / Michael Cole

Lucy: © Billie Jean King Enterprises, Inc.

Larry King, Billie Jean, Betty Moffitt, and Bill Moffitt: © Julian Wasser

Peanuts comic strip: © 1986 Peanuts Worldwide LLC

Billie Jean, Martina Navratilova, Mary Carillo: © Globe Photos

Billie Jean and Venus Williams: Jerry Lenander © Billie Jean King Enterprises, Inc.

Billie Jean and Serena Williams: Jerry Lenander © Billie Jean King Enterprises, Inc.

Serena Williams, Billie Jean, Venus Williams, 2001 U.S. Open: © Howard Earl Simmons / NY Daily News Archive via Getty Images

2000 USA women's tennis team, Sydney Olympics: © Stephen Wake

Kloss family with Billie Jean, Provincetown, MA: © Helen R. Russell

Dignitaries at the renaming of the USTA Billie Jean King National Tennis Center: Municipal Archives, City of New York. Mayor Michael Bloomberg Photograph Collection

Image of court with U.S. flag at the renaming of the USTA Billie Jean King National Tennis Center: © Jamie Squire / Getty Images

Billie Jean with Sen. Hillary Clinton: © AP, Jason DeCrow

Ilana, President Mandela, and Billie Jean: Zelda la Grange © Ilana Kloss

Billie Jean presented Medal of Freedom by President Obama: © Chip Somodevilla / Getty Images

Billie Jean meeting Her Majesty the Queen of England: © AP, Oli Scarff

Donnelly Awards: © Susan Mullane / camerawork USA

Cruise with Ruth Kloss and Betty Moffitt: Courtesy Rosie Casals

Moffitt family: © Susan Mullane / camerawork USA

WTA fortieth anniversary: © Clive Brunskill / Getty Images

Tennis outing at Billie Jean's seventieth birthday: © Fred Mullane / camerawork USA

WTT staff at Billie Jean's seventieth birthday: © Susan Mullane / camerawork USA

Tennis tournament on cruise: © Ilana Kloss

Ingrid Löfdahl-Bentzer with family and Billie Jean: © Art Seitz

Ilana, Billie Jean, Mark Walter at Dodger Stadium: © Los Angeles Dodgers LLC

Ilana and Billie Jean at NYC Pride: © Robin Platzer / Twin Images / SIPA USA

Ilana, Joyce Dinkins, Mayor David Dinkins, and Billie Jean: © Ilana Kloss

Billie Jean's celebration of her seventy-fifth birthday: Jennifer Pottheiser © Billie Jean King Leadership Initiative

Billie Jean with her first-grade namesake class: © Marjorie A. Gantman

The opening of the Billie Jean King Main Library: © Stephen Carr

BJKLI event at the U.S. Open: Jason Markowitz © Billie Jean King Leadership Initiative

Naomi Osaka wearing Breonna Taylor mask at the U.S. Open: © AP, Frank Franklin

Billie Jean serving at 1974 U.S. Open: © Melchior DiGiacomo / Sports Illustrated via Getty Images

1977 World TeamTennis champions: © Cheryl Traendly

Billie Jean defeating Bobby Riggs: Russ Adams Productions, Courtesy International Tennis Hall of Fame